MORPHING AEROSPACE VEHICLES AND STRUCTURES

Aerospace Series List

Sense and Avoid in UAS: Research and Applications
Angelov
April 2012

Morphing Aerospace Vehicles and Structures
Valasek
March 2012

Gas Turbine Propulsion Systems
MacIsaac and Langton
July 2011

Basic Helicopter Aerodynamics, Third Edition
Seddon and Newman
June 2011

Advanced Control of Aircraft, Rockets and Spacecraft
Tewari
July 2011

Cooperative Path Planning of Unmanned Aerial Vehicles
Tsourdos et al.
November 2010

Principles of Flight for Pilots
Swatton
October 2010

Air Travel and Health: A Systems Perspective
Seabridge et al.
September 2010

Design and Analysis of Composite Structures: With applications to
Aerospace Structures
Kassapoglou
September 2010

Unmanned Aircraft Systems: UAVS Design, Development and Deployment
Austin
April 2010

Introduction to Antenna Placement and Installations
Macnamara
April 2010

Principles of Flight Simulation
Allerton
October 2009

Aircraft Fuel Systems
Langton et al.
May 2009

The Global Airline Industry
Belobaba
April 2009

Computational Modelling and Simulation of Aircraft and the Environment:
Volume 1 – Platform Kinematics and Synthetic Environment
Diston
April 2009

Handbook of Space Technology
Ley, Wittmann and Hallmann
April 2009

Aircraft Performance Theory and Practice for Pilots
Swatton
August 2008

Surrogate Modelling in Engineering Design: A Practical Guide
Forrester, Sobester and Keane
August 2008

Aircraft Systems, Third Edition
Moir and Seabridge
March 2008

Introduction to Aircraft Aeroelasticity And Loads
Wright and Cooper
December 2007

Stability and Control of Aircraft Systems
Langton
September 2006

Military Avionics Systems
Moir and Seabridge
February 2006

Design and Development of Aircraft Systems
Moir and Seabridge
June 2004

Aircraft Loading and Structural Layout
Howe
May 2004

Aircraft Display Systems
Jukes
December 2003

Civil Avionics Systems
Moir and Seabridge
December 2002

MORPHING AEROSPACE VEHICLES AND STRUCTURES

Edited by

John Valasek
Aerospace Engineering Department
Texas A&M University
USA

A John Wiley & Sons, Ltd., Publication

This edition first published 2012
© 2012, John Wiley & Sons, Ltd

Registered office
John Wiley & Sons Ltd, The Atrium, Southern Gate, Chichester, West Sussex, PO19 8SQ, United Kingdom

For details of our global editorial offices, for customer services and for information about how to apply for permission to reuse the copyright material in this book please see our website at www.wiley.com.

Library of Congress Cataloging-in-Publication Data

Morphing aerospace vehicles and structures / edited by John Valasek.
       p. cm. – (AIAA progress series)
    Includes bibliographical references and index.
    ISBN 978-0-470-97286-1 (cloth) – ISBN 978-1-60086-903-7
  1. Aerospace engineering.   2. Wing-warping (Aerodynamics)   3. Airplanes–Design and construction.
4. Airplanes–Wings–Design and construction.   I. Valasek, John.   II. American Institute of Aeronautics and Astronautics.
    TL565.M67 2012
    629.1′2–dc23

                                                                                                    2011045495

A catalogue record for this book is available from the British Library.

ISBN: 978-0-470-97286-1

Typeset in 10/12pt Times by Aptara Inc., New Delhi, India
Printed and bound in Singapore by Markono Print Media Pte Ltd

Contents

List of Contributors

Gregg Abate, Air Force Research Laboratory, Eglin AFB, Florida, USA

Anna C. Carruthers, Department of Zoology, Oxford University, UK

Animesh Chakravarthy, Department of Mechanical and Aerospace Engineering, University of Florida, Gainesville, Florida, USA

Suman Chakravorty, Aerospace Engineering Department, Texas A&M University, College Station, Texas, USA

Ephrahim Garcia, Sibley School of Mechanical and Aerospace Engineering, Cornell University, Ithaca, New York, USA

Daniel T. Grant, Department of Mechanical and Aerospace Engineering, University of Florida, Gainesville, Florida, USA

Jared Grauer, Aerospace Engineering Department, University of Maryland and National Institute of Aerospace, USA

Darren J. Hartl, Aerospace Engineering Department, Texas A&M University, College Station, Texas, USA

James Hubbard Jr, Aerospace Engineering Department, University of Maryland and National Institute of Aerospace, USA

Tatjana Y. Hubel, Royal Veterinary College, UK

Kenton Kirkpatrick, Aerospace Engineering Department, Texas A&M University, College Station, Texas, USA

Mrinal Kumar, Department of Mechanical and Aerospace Engineering, University of Florida, Gainesville, Florida, USA

Dimitris C. Lagoudas, Aerospace Engineering Department, Texas A&M University, College Station, Texas, USA

Amanda Lampton, Systems Technology Inc., Hawthorne, California, USA

Rick Lind, Department of Mechanical and Aerospace Engineering, University of Florida, Gainesville, Florida, USA

Borna Obradovic, Aerospace Engineering Department, University of Texas – Arlington, Arlington, Texas, USA

Justin R. Schick, Aerospace Engineering Department, Texas A&M University, College Station, Texas, USA

Wei Shyy, Department of Mechanical Engineering, The Hong Kong University of Science and Technology, PRC

Stephen Sorley, Department of Mechanical and Aerospace Engineering, University of Florida, Gainesville, Florida, USA

Kamesh Subbarao, Aerospace Engineering Department, University of Texas – Arlington, Arlington, Texas, USA

Graham K. Taylor, Department of Zoology, Oxford University, UK

John Valasek, Aerospace Engineering Department, Texas A&M University, College Station, Texas, USA

Simon M. Walker, Department of Zoology, Oxford University, UK

Adam M. Wickenheiser, Department of Mechanical and Aerospace Engineering, George Washington University, Washington, DC

Foreword

Morphing systems are reconfigurable systems whose features include geometric shape change, but also can include color, aural or electromagnetic changes. Morphing aircraft with retractable landing gear, flaps and slats and variable sweep wings are not unusual today, but they were futuristic 70 or 80 years ago. Who has not marveled to see the morphing wing of a commercial jet robotically change shape as it deploys spoilers and flaps when landing? On the other hand, the missions for these aircraft are conventional. This book looks at morphing systems with an eye to the future in which missions will be challenging and today's solutions simply will not work.

I first came across the term "morphology" in 1971 while reading the final draft of Professor Holt Ashley's textbook *Engineering Analysis of Flight Vehicles*. His first chapter is entitled "Morphology of the Airplane." Holt was my research adviser at Stanford in the late 1960s and, more importantly a distinguished educator, researcher, engineer and master of the written English language. When I suggested that he change "morphology" to something like "shape," he replied: "But morphology is such a wonderful word! So descriptive!" And so it is.

My four-year stint as a DARPA program manager included development of game-changing morphing aircraft for a specific military mission. The DARPA program was very successful and we showed that: (1) morphing shape change is not expensive, compared to the system benefits it provides; and (2) morphing concepts succeed when the airplane mission involves design conflicts requiring the choice of either building a large wing/engine combination or a smaller mechanized wing with smaller engines and fuel requirements. Sometimes, no other approach other than morphing worked.

Future aircraft missions will require aircraft shape and feature changes that, in turn, require new component technologies, from engines to wing mechanisms to smart materials, as well as expanded analysis techniques. This book provides valuable information to begin this journey into the future. It begins with bio-inspiration. The Russian engineer Genrich Altshuller observed that "In nature there are lots of hidden patents." Chapter 8 on perching aircraft suggests a unique use for integrated morphing technologies, while Chapter 9 on smart materials and control of morphing devices provides a window on the challenging problems of system integration.

Oliver Wendell Holmes once wrote: "A man's mind stretched by a new idea can never go back to its original dimensions." This book provides an opportunity for mind expansion. I encourage you to read it, absorb the ideas and contribute to the morphing aircraft future.

Terry A. Weisshaar
Professor Emeritus
Purdue University
West Lafayette, Indiana
USA

Series Preface

The field of aerospace is wide ranging and multi-disciplinary, covering a large variety of products, disciplines and domains, not merely in engineering but in many related supporting activities. These combine to enable the aerospace industry to produce exciting and technologically advanced vehicles. The wealth of knowledge and experience that has been gained by expert practitioners in the various aerospace fields needs to be passed onto others working in the industry, including those just entering from University.

The *Aerospace Series* aims to be a practical and topical series of books aimed at engineering professionals, operators, users and allied professions such as commercial and legal executives in the aerospace industry. The range of topics is intended to be wide ranging, covering design and development, manufacture, operation and support of aircraft as well as topics such as infrastructure operations and developments in research and technology. The intention is to provide a source of relevant information that will be of interest and benefit to all those people working in aerospace.

There has been much interest world-wide in the development of morphing air-vehicles to improve performance, and possibly change mission requirements in-flight, by enabling the air-vehicle to adjust its external shape and structural/aerodynamic/control characteristics to adapt to the changing flight environment. Many different concepts have been proposed, with a few being demonstrated on a range of different prototype flying vehicles.

This book, *Morphing Aerospace Vehicles and Structures*, is the first textbook to provide an overview of the current status of morphing air-vehicles, and to provide guidance as to likely future directions in this exciting technology. Starting with the bio-inspired geometric changes of insects, birds and bats that are the motivation for many morphing concepts, the book then describes issues relating to the flight control and dynamics of morphing air-vehicles, and also the application of smart materials and hierarchical control for morphing. It is a welcome addition to the Wiley Aerospace Series.

Peter Belobaba, Jonathan Cooper, Roy Langton and Allan Seabridge

Acknowledgments

Several individuals and organizations have made special and significant contributions to this book, and I wish to recognize their efforts. My wife Stephanie has encouraged me to write a book for many years. This book would not have been realized without her tireless support and steadfast encouragement, all while she pursued her graduate studies. My graduate and undergraduate research students who contributed to this book have been a joy to work with, and a constant source of inspiration. Teachers can learn from their students, and indeed I have and continue to do so. I am grateful to many of my faculty colleagues in various departments at Texas A&M University who have shared their valuable insights and provided suggestions on the research. Special thanks are bestowed upon Dr. Sharon M. Swartz of Brown University, for graciously providing a specialized review and critique of Chapter 2.

This book was begun during my Faculty Development Leave, and I am indebted to my Department Heads in the Aerospace Engineering Department at Texas A&M University during and since that time: Dr. Helen L. Reed, Dr. Walter E. Haisler, and Dr. Dimitris C. Lagoudas. They not only encouraged me to pursue it, but also provided me with the full opportunity and means to do so.

While all of the authors in this book have obtained funding for their portion of the work from various sponsors, two sponsors in particular have provided exceptional support overall. The U.S. Air Force Office of Scientific Research provided support under contract FA9550-08-1-0038, with technical monitors Dr. Scott Wells, Dr. William M. McEneaney, and Dr. Fariba Fahroo. The National Aeronautics and Space Administration was instrumental in providing early support through the Texas Institute of Intelligent Bio-Nano Materials and Structures for Aerospace Vehicles (TiiMS). The technical monitor was Dr. Tom Gates. This generous support is gratefully acknowledged.

The wonderful staff at John Wiley & Sons Ltd., Chichester, have been instrumental and contributed a great deal to this endeavor. They have also been only a pleasure to work with. Commissioning Editors David Palmer and Debbie Cox conceived the original idea for the book, approached me with it and patiently encouraged me to pursue it, and then championed it to the publisher. Project Editors Claire Bailey and Liz Wingett skillfully managed both the author and the manuscript to completion. Project Editor of Engineering Technology Nicky Skinner was a warm and generous colleague whom I enjoyed getting to know and work with, who tragically passed on during the final stages. She is greatly missed by me and all who knew her, and her memory is embossed in the final product.

Finally, I would like to thank all of the authors who contributed chapters and their expertise. I am blessed to have you as colleagues and collaborators, and pleased to call you friends.

John Valasek
College Station, Texas, USA
July 2011

1

Introduction

John Valasek

Texas A&M University, USA

> *A flying machine is impossible, in spite of the testimony of the birds*
> —John Le Conte, well-known naturalist, "The Problem of the Flying
> Machine," Popular Science Monthly, November 1888, p. 69.

1.1   Introduction

Current interest in morphing vehicles has been fueled by advances in smart technologies such as materials, sensors, actuators, their associated support hardware and microelectronics. These advances have led to a series of breakthroughs in a wide variety of disciplines that, when fully realized for aircraft applications, have the potential to produce large improvements in aircraft safety, affordability, and environmental compatibility. The road to these advances and applications is paved with the efforts of pioneers going back several centuries. This chapter seeks to succinctly map out this road by highlighting the contributions of these pioneers and showing the historical connections between bio-inspiration and aeronautical engineering. A second objective is to demonstrate that the field of morphing has now come nearly full circle over the past 100 plus years. Birds inspired the pioneer aviators, who sought solutions to aerodynamic and control problems of flight. But a smooth and continuous shape-changing capability like that of birds was beyond the technologies of the day, so the concept of variable geometry using conventional hinges and pivots evolved and was used for many years. With new results in bio-inspiration and recent advances in aerodynamics, controls, structures, and materials, researchers are finally converging upon the set of tools and technologies needed to realize the original dream of aircraft which are capable of smooth and continuous shape-changing. The focus and scope of this chapter are intentionally limited to concepts and aircraft that are accessible through the unclassified, open literature.

Morphing Aerospace Vehicles and Structures, First Edition. Edited by John Valasek.
© 2012 John Wiley & Sons, Ltd. Published 2012 by John Wiley & Sons, Ltd.

Figure 1.1   Lilienthal Glider circa 1880s showing bird influence. Reproduced by permission of Archives Otto-Lilienthal Museum

1.2   The Early Years: Bio-Inspiration

Otto Lilienthal was a nineteenth-century Prussian aviator who had a lifelong fascination with bird flight which led him into a professional career as a designer. He appeared on the aviation scene in 1891 by designing, building, and flying a series of gliders. Between 1891 and 1896 he completed nearly 2,000 flights in 16 different types of gliders, an example of which is shown in Figure 1.1. The wings of these gliders were described as resembling "the outstretched pinions of a soaring bird." The bird species which captivated him most were storks, and the extent to which birds influenced Lilienthal is evidenced by two of the many books which he wrote on aviation: *Our Teachers in Soaring Flight* in 1897, and *Birdflight as the Basis for Aviation: A Contribution toward a System of Aviation* in 1889 (Lilienthal 1889). His observations on bird twist and camber distributions were influential in the development of his air-pressure tables and airfoil data. Interestingly, Lilienthal also made attempts at powered flight but chose to only study wings with orntithopteric wingtips. His insistence on the use of flapping wing tips in preference to a conventional propeller is an indication of the extent to which he was captivated by bird flight (Crouch 1989). Several early pioneers recognized the value in morphing as a control effect. Edson Fessenden Gallaudet, Professor of Physics at Yale, applied the concept of wing warping to a kite in 1898. While not entirely successful, this kite nonetheless embodied the basic structural concepts which would appear in aircraft designs much later (Crouch 1989). Independently, Orville and Wilbur Wright, correctly deduced that wing warping could provide lateral control. Wilbur remarked to Octave Chanute in 1900 that "My observation of the flight of buzzards leads me to believe that they regain their lateral balance, when partly overturned by a gust of wind, by a torsion of the tips of the wings. If the rear edge of the right wing tip is twisted upward and the left downward, the bird becomes an animated windmill and instantly begins to turn, a line from its head to its tail being the axis" (Wright 1900). This observation led to the design of the 1902 Wright Glider, which incorporated wing warping for lateral (roll) control (Figure 1.2). The warping was accomplished by wires attached to the pilot's belt, which were controlled by his shifting body position. Although this craft was flown by the Wrights as both a kite and a glider, it was during flights of the latter type that the need for a directional (yaw) control was first realized, and then solved with the creation of the rudder.

Figure 1.2 1902 Wright Glider featuring lateral and directional control by warping. Reproduced by permission of United States Air Force Historical Research Agency

Correctly recognizing that achieving harmony of control would greatly improve the control and usefulness of an aircraft, in October 1902 the Wrights developed an interconnection between warping of the wing and warping of the vertical tail. Thus the concept of what would later become the aileron-to-rudder interconnect or ARI was born. With the problems of longitudinal control, lateral control, directional control, and control harmony solved, the 1902 Wright Glider became essentially the world's first successful airplane (Crouch 1989). These developments paved the way for the success of the powered 1903 Wright Flyer a year later.

The Etrich Taube ("dove" in German) series of designs have probably been the ultimate expression of bio-inspiration to aircraft design. In fact, except for the omission of flapping wings, the Taube designs are essentially bio-mimetic, i.e. directly mimicking a biological system (Figure 1.3). The Etrich Luft-Limousine / VII was somewhat unique for an airplane of

Figure 1.3 Etrich Luft-Limousine / VII four-seater passenger airplane of 1912

Figure 1.4 Rumpler Taube on the front page of the *New York Times Mid-Week Pictorial*, January 1st, 1917

its time since it employed multi-material construction. This consisted of an aluminum sheet covering from the nose to just behind the wings, with wood used everywhere else. The fuselage structure used wooden rings and channel-section longitudinal members and the windows were celluloid and wire gauze. The initial Taube designs were created by Igo Etrich in Austria in 1909. The original inspiration for the unique wing planform on Taube designs was not a bird wing, but the Zanonia macrocarpa seed, which falls from trees in a slow spin induced by a single wing. This was not successful, yet the influence of birds on later adaptations of this wing design can clearly be seen (Figure 1.4). Like the Wright designs, the Taube designs employed wing and horizontal tail warping via wires and external posts, although the vertical tail surfaces were hinged. Despite contemporary aircraft designs which featured vertical tails of a size and proportion that would be recognizable in modern designs, the Taube designs mimicked birds so much that the dorsal and ventral fins comprising the vertical tail surfaces were very small. Ultimately, the very small vertical tail surfaces became a distinguishing characteristic of the Taube designs.

The Wright and Taube designs demonstrated that warping controls can be effective on aircraft with thin and flexible wings. But the invention of the now conventional hinged controls, such as ailerons and rudders, was essential for later aircraft with more rigid structures and metallic materials. Thus the problem of materials and structures has been a central consideration to morphing aircraft from the outset. By the onset of the First World War in 1914 and in the years afterward, virtually all high performance aircraft used conventional hinged control surfaces instead of warping. With the advent of aircraft with relatively rigid metallic structures in the 1930s, the path to morphing clearly lay in changing the geometry of the aircraft via complex arrangements of conventional hinges, pivots, and rails rather than warping.

1.3 The Middle Years: Variable Geometry

During the inter-war years in France, Ivan Makhonine conceived the idea of a telescoping wing aircraft. The aim was to improve cruise performance by reducing the induced drag, or the drag due to the creation of lift. This was to be accomplished by reducing span loading which is the ratio of aircraft weight to wing span. As shown in Figure 1.5, the mechanism

Figure 1.5 The Makhonine MAK-101 telescoping wing airplane of 1933: wing tip extended (top) and retracted (bottom)

Figure 1.6   Sir Barnes Neville Wallis with a model of the Swallow, wings at low sweep

works like a stiletto knife, except that the wing can also be retracted automatically since it was pneumatically powered with a standby manual system. The fixed landing gear MAK-10 was first flown in 1931, followed by the retractable landing gear MAK-101 in 1933. The MAK-101 was flown many times over the next several years until it was destroyed in its hangar during a USAAF bombing raid late in the Second World War. Makhonine continued his research into the telescoping wing concept post-war, culminating in the last aircraft in the series, the MAK-123 which first flew in 1947. The MAK-123 was a four-seat passenger aircraft that flew well and was reported to have adequate handling qualities, but was damaged in a forced landing and never flew again.

British aircraft designer Sir Barnes Neville Wallis, well known as the inventor of the geodesic structural design concept used in the Vickers Wellington medium bomber, also investigated novel variable geometry configurations. Although he did not invent the swing-wing concept, Wallis devoted much effort to making what he called the "wing-controlled aerodyne" practical as a means of achieving supersonic flight. His two main goals were to use variable geometry as a solution to handling the center of gravity changes during flight, and to achieve laminar flow over the wing body. His Wild Goose design of the 1940s was a military mission supersonic concept with a slender laminar flow body and swing-wings. Several sub-scale models of the Wild Goose were successfully flown in the late 1940s and early 1950s. A full-scale piloted version of the Wild Goose was planned but later cancelled in 1952. The Swallow was a longer-range derivative of the Wild Goose, designed in the 1950s. Many sub-scale models were produced (Figure 1.6) and flown, and the results were so promising that full-scale versions were planned. However, these were not to be implemented due to the British defense funding climate of the late 1950s. Nevertheless, the Swallow was influential as a military concept

Figure 1.7 An illustration of the Swallow by Barnes Wallis

aircraft (Figure 1.7) and inspired various design features which later appeared in U.S. aircraft such as the General Dynamics F-111 Aardvark. During this same period in the USA, variable geometry research sponsored by NASA paved the way for experimental transonic designs such as the Bell X-5 (Figure 1.8). The X-5 was the first full-scale aircraft to be flown which was capable of sweeping its wings in flight. The wing sweep angles could be set in flight to 20, 45, and 60 degrees and were tested at subsonic and transonic speeds. With the wings fully extended, the low-speed performance was improved for take-off and landing, and with the wings swept back, the high speed performance was improved and drag was reduced. Results of this research directly influenced the design of the General Dynamics F-111 Aardvark and the Grumman F-14 Tomcat, both of which went into large-scale production. It is interesting

Figure 1.8 Bell X-5 showing variable sweep wing positions. Reproduced by permission of National Aeronautics and Space Administration

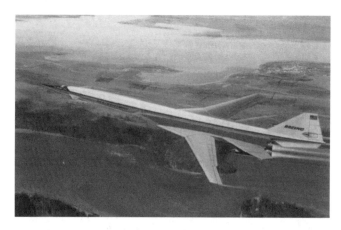

Figure 1.9 Boeing 2707 Supersonic Transport notional configuration with variable sweep wing

to note that the variable geometry concept eventually found its way into the commercial air transport sector as well. It was seriously considered for various conceptual designs, including the Boeing 2707 Supersonic Transport of the 1960s (Figure 1.9). Even though the B2707 never progressed beyond the full-scale mock-up stage, a large variable geometry supersonic aircraft appeared a decade later in the form of the Rockwell International B-1A bomber. NASA later conducted a research program with an aircraft that combined *both* variable geometry and shape changing similar to the traditional wing warping of the early pioneers. The AFTI F-111 Mission Adaptive Wing (MAW), shown in Figure 1.10, was intended to minimize penalties for off-design flight conditions through a combination of smooth-skin variable camber and variable wing sweep angle. As opposed to the hinged flaps with discontinuous surfaces and exposed mechanisms of conventional aircraft, the variable camber surfaces of the MAW feature smooth flexible upper surfaces and fully enclosed lower surfaces that can be actuated in flight to provide the desired wing camber. This flight research program was highly successful and served as a vital stepping stone toward the realization of a fully morphing aircraft.

With all of the successes of the variable geometry approach, it is not surprising that bio-inspiration was largely overlooked or simply not considered promising enough during this

Figure 1.10 NASA AFTI F-111 Mission Adaptive Wing. Reproduced by permission of National Aeronautics and Space Administration

period. John Harris opined in 1989 the feelings of some that "(Yet) birds are terrible models for human flight, and a too slavish attention to their example – often unconscious – has often impeded the development of aircraft. An airplane is not a bird, and designers throughout the history of aircraft development have had a hard time fully realizing this (Harris 1989)." In spite of this, a dramatic change in the way morphing aircraft were viewed was about to take place.

1.4 The Later Years: A Return to Bio-Inspiration

Recent discoveries in bird flight mechanics and new insights for bio-inspiration led many researchers to reconsider birds as models for morphing aircraft. Two significant and ambitious research programs that were to have far-reaching and productive effects on morphing aircraft appeared nearly simultaneously around 2000. The NASA Morphing Aircraft Project was a large and highly coordinated program conducted from 1994–2004 (Wlezien et al. 1998). It was a wide-ranging, large scope program that was specifically targeted at high pay-off applications that would enable efficient, multi-point adaptability aircraft and spacecraft. In the context of the project, the word "morphing" was defined as "efficient, multi-point adaptability" and could include macro, micro, structural and/or fluidic approaches. This program enabled and sponsored research across a broad range of technologies that included biotechnology, nanotechnology, biomaterials, adaptive structures, micro-flow control, biomimetic concepts, optimization, and controls. At its height this program supported between 80 to 100 researchers. The focal point for all technologies in this program was the notional NASA morphing unmanned air vehicle shown in Figure 1.11. This aircraft brought together most of the earlier morphing concepts, including bio-inspiration, warping, shape-changing, variable geometry, structures, materials, controls, and aerodynamics. Most importantly, it sought to address the contribution of propulsion in a fully integrated fashion. This notional aircraft continues to serve as useful concept and model for morphing research.

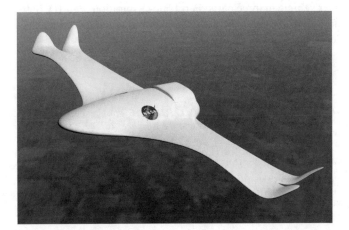

Figure 1.11 NASA morphing unmanned air vehicle concept. Reproduced by permission of National Aeronautics and Space Administration

The DARPA Morphing Aircraft Structures (MAS) Program dates back to 2002 and continued until 2007. The Defense Technology Directive stated that:

> Morphing is a capability to provide superior and/or new vehicle system performance while in flight by tailoring the vehicle's state to adapt to the external operational environment and multi-variable mission roles. In the context of this DTO, morphing aircraft are multi-role aircraft that change their external shape substantially to adapt to a changing mission environment during flight
> — (Anonymous 2006)

The DARPA Morphing Aircraft Structures Program responded to this DTO with objectives defined as the design and fabrication of effective combinations of integrated wing skins, actuators and mechanisms, structures, and flight controls to achieve the anticipated diverse, conflicting aircraft mission capabilities via wing shape change. For a notional aircraft, the DARPA/MAS program used a so-called Hunter-Killer unmanned aircraft concept that combined reconnaissance aircraft features of aircraft like the General Atomics Predator or Northrop Grumman Global Hawk, with the attack features of a fast attack aircraft such as the General Dynamics F-16. Studies indicated that morphing wings would enable multi-functional Hunter-Killer mission features such as: (1) responsiveness – time-critical ability to respond to unpredictable crisis situations; (2) agility – the ability to change system roles on demand; and (3) persistence – the ability to dominate large operational areas for long time periods. The DARPA/MAS program generated many useful results and insights, and culminated in the flight test of a small demonstrator.

1.5   Conclusion

This chapter has related the main historical research and development path of the morphing air vehicle, along the way highlighting key ideas and connections between bio-inspiration and aeronautical engineering. Over the course of these developments, it is clear that ideas which were once old are new again. The following chapters in this book tell the contemporary story of the morphing air vehicle in three parts: Part I Bio-inspiration, Part II Control and Dynamics, and Part III Smart Materials and Structures. The volume concludes with a discussion of current and future challenges, and a look at the way forward.

References

Anonymous (2006) *Defense Technology Objectives, DTO 71, DDR&E*. Washington, DC: U.S. Department of Defense.
Crouch, TD (1989) *A Dream of Wings, Americans and the Airplane, 1875–1905*. Washington, DC: Smithsonian Institution Press.
Harris, JS (1989) An airplane is not a bird. *American Heritage of Invention and Technology*, Fall: 18–22.
Lilienthal, O (1889) *Der Vogelflug als Grundlage der Fliegekunst*. Berlin: R. Gärtners Verlagsbuchhandlung.
Wlezien, RW, Horner, GC, McGowan, AR, Padula, A, Scott, MA, Silcox, RJ and Simpson, JO (1998) The aircraft morphing program. In *AIAA/ASME/ASCE/AHS/ASC Structures, Structural Dynamics & Materials Conference*, number AIAA-98-1927, Long Beach, CA, 20–23 April 1998, pp. 176–187.
Wright, W (1900) Wilbur Wright to Octave Chanute. *Papers*, 13 May.

Part I
Bio-Inspiration

2

Wing Morphing in Insects, Birds and Bats: Mechanism and Function

Graham K. Taylor[1], Anna C. Carruthers[1], Tatjana Y. Hubel[2], and Simon M. Walker[1]

[1]*Department of Zoology, Oxford University, UK*
[2]*Royal Veterinary College, UK*

2.1 Introduction

The great majority of wings are morphing designs with continuously variable planform, camber, or twist: such are the wings of insects, birds, and bats. Indeed, morphing wings may be said to be the norm at the length scales associated with flying animals, while the rigid wing designs that have been favored by engineers are typical only at the largest length scales. It is worth noting in this context that the membranous wings of the largest extinct pterosaurs are currently estimated to have had spans of approximately 10m (Witton and Naish 2008)—comparable to a light aircraft—so it is clear that Nature's morphing wing designs are workable across a wide range of length scales of current interest to engineers. Just as birds helped inspire the warping wing design of the Wright Flyer, Nature now offers a rich seam of inspiration for a new generation of morphing wing designs across a range of scales of interest to engineers.

In this chapter, we consider wing morphing in its broadest sense as any functional change in wing shape occurring during the course of flight. In flying animals, this encompasses those changes in wing shape that are associated with maneuver control, and those that are associated with the wingbeat cycle. We describe the extent of our current knowledge of such changes in wing shape for the three different groups of extant animals that are capable of powered flight: insects, birds, and bats. Although there are numerous other kinds of animal that are capable of controlled gliding flight, it is in these three groups that selection for flight performance has been most intense. We do not discuss in any detail the wings of the extinct pterosaurs, not least because so many aspects of their flight remain contentious. Even so, it will become apparent in the course of this chapter that our understanding of wing morphing in the three

Morphing Aerospace Vehicles and Structures, First Edition. Edited by John Valasek.
© 2012 John Wiley & Sons, Ltd. Published 2012 by John Wiley & Sons, Ltd.

extant groups remains quite limited. This is a reflection of the high dimensional complexity of the problem, as it is only really within the last few years that photogrammetric techniques have been extensively applied to measure the position of multiple points on the surface of the wings of insects (Walker *et al.* 2009a,b, 2010; but see Zarnack 1972), birds (Carruthers *et al.* 2010), and bats (Riskin *et al.* 2010). Indeed, at the time of writing, detailed three-dimensional surface reconstructions of a deforming wing are available only for insects.

Much more is known about the structural and mechanical basis of wing morphing in animals, and we begin each of the sections on insects, birds, and bats by describing in some detail the functional anatomy of the wings. This is an informative exercise, because the wing designs of these three groups encompass different levels of complexity and control. In insects, the wings are passive flexible structures, actuated at the root by muscles which apply forces either through various lever arrangements or through wholesale deformation of the thorax. In birds, the lifting surface is composed of numerous passive flexible elements, the feathers, attached to a muscularized skeleton that is capable of performing a wide range of different motions. In bats, the wings comprise an elastic, muscularized membrane that is stretched across a skeleton that is itself mostly actuated by muscles within the thorax. These represent three very different ways of building a morphing wing, albeit that the skeletal structures of the forelimbs of birds and bats are similar in the sense that they represent modifications of a common underlying form inherited from one distant reptilian ancestor.

Whereas a morphing wing based upon an insect-like design is an immediate possibility given existing materials, active materials with the properties needed to build a truly bat-like wing are unavailable at present. Hence, although bats' wings arguably come closer to most of our preconceptions of morphing wing designs than either birds or insects, and although insects' wings are in principle nothing more—or less—than smart structures, it would be a mistake to overlook insects when considering how to develop a morphing wing design at the scale of a micro-air vehicle (MAV). Birds represent something of a halfway house between these two extremes, and may well be the best source of immediate inspiration for vehicles on the scale of typical unmanned air vehicles (UAVs). Overall, our understanding of wing morphing in flying animals is too limited for us to be able to paint more than a broad-brush picture of what a bio-inspired morphing wing design might look like. Nevertheless, if this is sufficient to inspire the kind of detailed research that will be necessary to make such a design a reality, then we will have succeeded in one of our aims in writing this chapter.

2.2   Insects

Insects are the most diverse order of animals on Earth, with over one million described species and upwards of another five million species probably still to be described (Dudley 2000). Although many factors have contributed to their success as a group, flight is undoubtedly a key feature. With the possible exception of hummingbirds, neither bats nor birds come close to insects in terms of low speed maneuverability. Their range of body shapes and sizes is also unparalleled among their flying vertebrate counterparts. For example, insect wingspans cover four orders of magnitude, from tiny parasitic mymarid wasps (0.0002 m span), to the giant atlas moth *Attacus atlas* (span up to 0.3 m). Some extinct relatives of modern dragonflies even had wingspans up to 0.7 m, so an insect-like wing design is clearly workable in principle at the scale of operational MAVs.

Many of the largest insects, such as locusts (Orthoptera), dragonflies (Odonata), and butterflies (Lepidoptera) are able to glide, but all flying insects are specialized for flapping flight. Because there is no scope for making a very small wing sufficiently lightweight to be flapped and sufficiently rigid to resist aeroelastic deformation, it is unsurprising that insect wings have evolved to be highly deformable structures. Such deformations have been captured qualitatively using high-speed photography or film many times (e.g. Baker and Cooter 1979; Brackenbury 1991, 1994a,b; Nachtigall 1966; Wootton 1993), leading to much research into their mechanics (e.g. Ellington 1984; Ennos 1988a,b, 1989; Wootton 1981, 1995). However, only recently, with the advent of modern high-speed digital video cameras, has it become possible to make detailed quantitative measurements of these deformations in free-flight (Walker *et al.* 2009a,b, 2010). Consequently, we have only just begun to scratch at the surface of understanding the functional, aerodynamic significance of wing deformation in insect flight (Young *et al.* 2009).

In the next section, we outline the structure and mechanism of insect wings, with a view to providing the background needed to understand the mechanics of wing deformation in insects. Much more is known about the kinematics and functions of wing morphing in insects than in either birds or bats, so we describe the extent of our current knowledge at rather greater length than for either of the other two groups.

2.2.1 Wing Structure and Mechanism

2.2.1.1 Wing Skeleton and Membrane

Insect wings are surprisingly complex and varied in shape and structure, but all are passive structures comprising thin areas of membrane supported by thickened structural members called veins (Wootton 1981, 1992). Primitively, winged insects have two pairs of wings, but in many insects, one pair of wings has been modified to serve a function other than aerodynamic force production. Beetles (Coleoptera), earwigs (Dermaptera), cockroaches (Blattodea), and some bugs (Heteroptera) have hardened forewings, which are used to protect the more fragile hindwings when the insects are at rest. In flies (Diptera), the hindwings have been reduced to form the halteres, i.e. small gyroscopic sensors that play an important role in flight stabilization and control. However, among those wings whose primary function is still aerodynamic force production, there has been a general evolutionary trend towards a reduction of the number of supporting veins, and hence a relative increase in the area of membrane.

The wing veins are hollow fluid-filled structures, through which run the nerves innervating the numerous mechanosensors and chemosensors that are to be found on the wings. The diameter and cross-section of the veins vary greatly among different points on the wing, in such a way as to cope with the different external forces. For example, the hindwing of a desert locust *Schistocerca gregaria* contains some veins that are crimped to increase longitudinal flexibility, others that are V-shaped to reduce dorso-ventral bending, and still others that have thick walls and high sections to reduce torsion (Wootton *et al.* 2000). The veins and membranes alike are made from cuticle. This is a complex, composite, hierarchically structured metamaterial composed of highly crystalline chitin nanofibres embedded in a matrix of protein, polyphenols, and water, with small amounts of lipid (Vincent and Wegst 2004). Chitin itself is a polysaccharide akin to cellulose, but with an even greater degree of hydrogen bonding providing both stiffness and chemical stability. Numerous different protein types are contained within the cuticle, among which one known as resilin is of particular interest, owing to its exceptional elastic efficiency. Differences in the ratios of these components, and the inclusion of others (e.g. metal ions, calcium carbonate), allow insect cuticle to have a huge range of material properties suited to its many different roles.

Figures 2.1 and 2.2 show the wings of two morphologically-distinct and distantly-related species: the desert locust *Schistocerca gregaria* and the hoverfly *Eristalis tenax*. The main lines of flexion are marked as white dashed lines. The locust forewing is a relatively stiff structure, which has a high degree of positive camber inherent in its design, owing to the arrangement of its three main panels (Figure 2.1). The hindwing, in contrast, is a deployable structure that consists of just two distinct regions: a relatively stiff panel at the front, and a fan-like region behind that is supported by a number of radiating veins (Figure 2.1). Like the locust forewing, the hoverfly wing contains two main lines of flexion (Figure 2.2), but it is a much more flexible structure, which twists substantially at certain stages of the wing stroke. It also has a large flap-like structure near the wing root, called the alula, which we discuss further below. The leading edge of the hoverfly wing also contains a thickened, pigmented region, called the pterostigma (Figure 2.2). Similar structures are found in many insects, including dragonflies (Odonata), bees and wasps (Hymenoptera), and lacewings (Neuroptera). The pterostigma brings the chordwise centre of mass of the wing forward, which reduces torsional flutter (Norberg 1972).

The leading edges of the locust and hoverfly wings are made of thick supporting veins, with multiple cross-linkages to increase rigidity. In contrast, the trailing edges of both species end

Figure 2.1 Morphology of the fore- and hindwings of a desert locust *Schistocerca gregaria*. The black spots on the hindwing have been marked artificially for tracking. The forewing is a relatively stiff structure, comprising three panels separated by two lines of flexion (dashed white). The panels are angled so as to produce a positively cambered section. The hindwing is a deployable structure comprising a relatively stiff forward panel, which is separated from a fan-like region behind by a flexion line (dashed white). The fan-like region is able to fold radially against the body. Reproduced from Walker *et al.* (2009b)

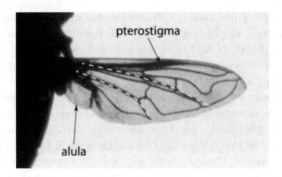

Figure 2.2   Morphology of the wing of a hoverfly *Eristalis tenax*. The wing has greatly reduced venation in comparison with the locust forewing shown in Figure 2.1, with two main lines of flexion (dashed white). The alula is a large flap-like structure near the wing root, which is able to be deployed at right angles to the rest of the wing. The pterostigma is the thickened, pigmented region near the leading edge of the wing, which is known in some insects to reduce torsional flutter by changing the mass distribution of the wing. Reproduced from Walker *et al.* (2009b)

in a thin membrane, with no supporting vein. This is important to allow the wing to deform correctly during flight, in much the same way as the sail on a boat has a stiff mast to provide a strong leading edge, but a flexible trailing edge so that it can be trimmed correctly depending upon its angle of attack. This kind of arrangement is vulnerable to damage, and unlike the feathers of birds (which can be replaced), or the wing membrane of bats (which can heal), any damage to insect wings is permanent. It is important, therefore, that the membranes and veins are reasonably resistant to external forces and impacts, so insect wings are generally designed to deform when contact is made with an external object. Specific fold lines for such deformations exist in some species, such as the wing tips of some Diptera (Wootton 1992). In other species, such as locusts, tearing of the membrane is checked by the cellular structure of the membrane that results from the presence of many cross veins.

2.2.1.2   Flight Musculature

Unlike the wings of birds and bats, insect wings are passive structures, with no intrinsic muscles. Any active changes to their shape must therefore be driven from the wing root by the muscles within the thorax. In most insects, each wing is actuated by five muscles or sets of muscles, but surprisingly, perhaps, only one set of these is attached directly to the wings in the majority of insects. With the notable exception of dragonflies (Odonata), most insects use their direct flight muscles only for fine control of the wingbeat. All of the more capable flying insects power their flight stroke through muscles which do not attach directly to the wing bases, so the stroke is driven through cyclical deformation of the thorax. This can be thought of as a flexible monocoque, flapping the wings as first-order levers over lateral fulcra (Wootton 2009). This makes for an exceptionally complex system, because there are few if any fixed points anywhere in the structure, and the action of a particular muscle will therefore depend upon the state of deformation of the thorax.

Cyclical deformation of the thorax is driven by the antagonistic action of longitudinal and dorsoventral muscles. The former compress the thorax from front to back, causing the dorsal surface of the thorax to bow upwards, and making the wings flip down; the latter compress the thorax from top to bottom, causing the wings to flip up. The use of indirect flight muscles to power the stroke allows larger attachment points for the muscles and requires less neurological complexity as all wings can be controlled simultaneously. This in turn permits faster contractions and therefore higher wingbeat frequencies (up to 100 Hz) than are possible using direct flight muscles for the power stroke. A further refinement of the indirect flight muscles is found in many more advanced insects, such as flies (Diptera), which use asynchronous flight muscles. These muscles only require a single nerve impulse to contract multiple times, which allows the thorax to act as a resonating structure, vibrating at a specific frequency determined by the precise arrangement of the muscles. Asynchronous flight muscles permit far higher wingbeat frequencies (up to 1000 Hz) as the muscle contraction rate is not limited by the rate at which nervous impulses can be sent (Wootton 1992).

It will come as no surprise, in light of this complexity, that we know rather little about the muscular basis of wing deformation in insects. Although it is possible to make inferences about the functions of the various flight muscles, their effects are so influenced by their interactions with other muscles and with the deformation of the thorax that there is little to be gained from going into further mechanistic detail here. Instead, we focus the remainder of this section upon what is known about the kinematics and function of wing morphing in insects, without regard to the driving system.

2.2.2   Gross Wing Morphing

2.2.2.1   Variable Planform

The membrane cuticle of insect wings is flexible, but relatively inextensible, so gross changes to wing planform can only be made by bending, twisting, or folding the wings. Additionally, in insects such as butterflies and moths (Lepidoptera), in which the two wing pairs may overlap a little during flight, the effective wing area and planform can be controlled by adjusting the overlap between the two wings, somewhat analogous to a conventional swing-wing aircraft. This may be of importance in the transition from flapping to gliding flight: for example, the scarlet mormon butterfly *Papilio rumanzovia* unlinks its forewing and hindwing pairs when gliding, presumably to increase the effective area of its wings, and to allow air to pass between them in a slot-like arrangement (Betts and Wootton 1988). Folding up of the wings in flight is only apparent in those insects which fold their hindwings beneath their forewings in a radial fashion when at rest. It therefore seems likely that such partial folding of the wings in flight is a case of evolutionary opportunism: of making the best use of a feature whose original function is stowage, rather than a specific adaptation for flight.

In birds and bats, the wings are often pulled in during the upstroke to reduce their effective area. This helps to minimize any negative loads that are experienced on the upstroke. Locusts (Orthoptera) achieve a similar effect by radially folding the hindwing into the body: the posterior part of the hindwing resembles an oriental hand-fan (Figure 2.1), and is pressed into the body during the upstroke as the wings are swept backward. This causes the innermost sections of the fan to fold into the body, and the outermost sections to corrugate, resulting in as much as a 30% decrease in projected area, as compared to the downstroke (Walker *et al.*

2009a). At rest, the same mechanism permits the hindwing fan to be folded completely so that it can be stowed beneath the forewing. Other functional aspects of the locust hindwing fan are discussed further below, but it is worth highlighting that more is understood about the radial folding of the locust hindwing fan than about any other example of wing morphing in nature. Detailed mechanical and kinematic measurements (Walker *et al.* 2009a,b; Wootton *et al.* 2000; Young *et al.* 2009), a finite element model (Herbert *et al.* 2000), numerical flow simulations (Young *et al.* 2009), and empirical flow measurements (Bomphrey *et al.* 2006; Young *et al.* 2009) are all available for this one system, yielding unparalleled insight into the mechanism and function of this canonical example of wing morphing in insect flight.

A quite different mechanism of transverse wing folding is found in cockroaches (Blattodea), beetles (Coleoptera) and earwigs (Dermaptera), in which the hindwings may be several times longer than the hardened forewings, and therefore have to undergo complex folding so that they can be tucked away fully (Haas *et al.* 2000; Haas and Wootton 1996). Stowage requirements are an important motivation for wanting to equip MAVs with morphing wings, so the specific mechanisms that permit a membranous wing to be tucked away when not in use may therefore be of particular interest in this respect. What is remarkable here is that the folding mechanisms are such that the wings do not collapse when they are subjected to the aerodynamic loadings that are associated with flapping flight. The various mechanisms that are involved each have only one degree of freedom, consisting of four adjoining panels constrained to rotate hingewise about four fold-lines converging at a single point (Haas and Wootton 1996). This is illustrated schematically in Figure 2.3. The wings might in some cases be held open actively or by aerodynamic or inertial forces (Haas and Wootton 1996), but storage of elastic potential energy by resilin in the wing membrane can also prevent unlocking of the wings in flight as part of an intrinsically bistable mechanism (Haas *et al.* 2000).

2.2.2.2   Variable Camber

The key benefit of camber in conventional airfoils is to improve aerodynamic performance. However, in insect wings, camber has another important role, which is to provide structural stability: a thin wing is resistant to forces directed upward if it is positively cambered, and is also resistant, though to a lesser extent, to forces directed down. Locust wings have strong positive camber on the downstroke (Figure 2.4), which helps the wing to resist inertial and aerodynamics forces that might otherwise buckle the wing. Camber is pronounced and less important on the upstroke, when the wings are feathered and sustain negative loads. Early in the downstroke, the positive camber of the hindwing results principally from the incidence of the forward panel relative to the hindwing fan, with a similar effect seen in the three panels of the forewing (Figure 2.1). Later in the downstroke, the positive camber of the hindwing is increased by an 'umbrella effect' operating in the hindwing fan.

The umbrella effect arises because the curvature of the trailing edge induces compressive forces in the radial veins of the hindwing fan when the trailing edge is placed under tension by the forward sweep of the hindwing (Wootton 1995; Wootton *et al.* 2000, 2003). This compression leads to Euler buckling of the radial veins (Wootton 1995), and is the principal source of the positive camber on the hindwing from mid to late downstroke. The hindwing fan is also slightly cambered during the early downstroke, prior to the action of the umbrella effect, and this presumably reflects pre-cambering of the radial veins, especially the shorter

(a)

(b)

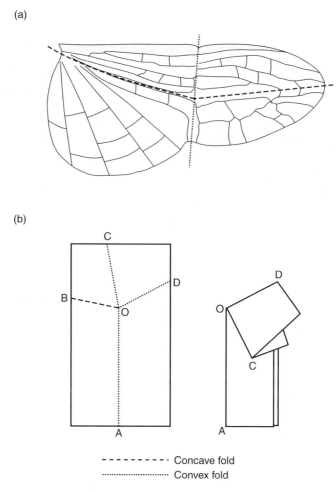

- - - - - - - - - Concave fold

·························· Convex fold

Figure 2.3 (a) Drawing of the wing of a cockroach (Blattodea), showing the four convergent fold lines (dashed). This is a simplified drawing: the actual pattern of venation is much more complex, with many smaller veins. (b) Schematic of the associated folding mechanism. Redrawn after Haas and Wootton (1996).

inner ones (Wootton *et al.* 2000). Young *et al.* (2009) used a three-dimensional numerical flow simulation based on detailed locust wing kinematics to demonstrate that the presence of camber on the fore- and hindwings resulted in a 12% increase in lift power economy compared to wings where the camber had been removed. This is because the presence of strong camber on the wings is important to the maintenance of attached flow, which seems to be a defining feature of locust flight, although not perhaps of the flight of many other insects.

In contrast to locusts, which have only limited scope to alter the angle of attack of their wings, hoverflies can flip their wings over at the end of each half-stroke so that useful lift can be produced on both the downstroke and upstroke (Figure 2.5). Hoverfly wings are extremely compliant, and make use of this compliance to produce camber automatically. The rotational

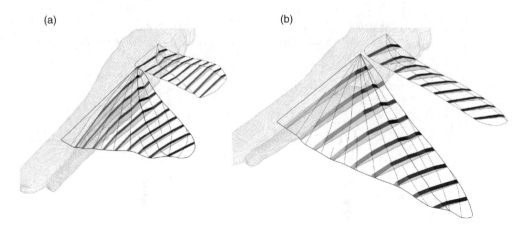

Figure 2.4 Wing camber of a desert locust *Schistocerca gregaria*. (a) early downstroke; (b) late down-stroke. The chordwise strips illustrating the camber of each section are shaded according to their local angle of incidence. Redrawn after Walker *et al.* (2009a)

axis of the wing lies in front of both the center of mass and center of aerodynamic pressure, so hoverfly wings tend to undergo torsion as a result of both inertial and aerodynamic forces. This leads to the automatic production of camber, which as in the locust is the result of a radiating vein structure (Ennos 1988a), enhanced in the case of the hoverfly by the curvature of the two main radiating veins (Figure 2.2). Hoverflies are thereby able to produce the appropriate direction of camber on both the upstroke and the downstroke (Figure 2.5; Walker *et al.* 2010), which improves both their structural stability and their aerodynamic performance (Du and Sun 2008, 2010; Vanella *et al.* 2009).

The automatic generation of camber in hoverflies and in locust hindwings is attributable to their radiating vein structure (Ennos 1988a; Wootton *et al.* 2000). However, a quite different mechanism of camber generation is used by some other insects, such as dragonflies (Odonata). This hinges upon an angular, and strongly three-dimensional complex of veins near the base of the wings (Wootton *et al.* 1998). An upwards force applied to the underside of the wing outboard of this complex levers the trailing edge down, thereby cambering the wing and

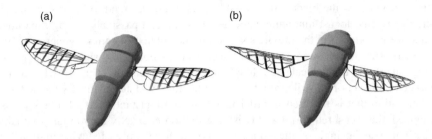

Figure 2.5 Wing camber of a hoverfly *Eristalis tenax*. (a) mid-downstroke; (b) mid-upstroke. The chordwise strips illustrating the camber of each section are shaded according to their local angle of incidence. Redrawn after Walker *et al.* (2010)

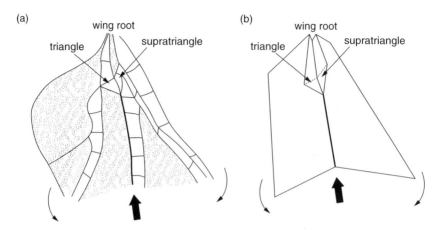

Figure 2.6 (a) Drawing of the basal triangle-supratriangle complex of a dragonfly. (b) Schematic of the associated mechanism of wing flexion and camber generation. Application of an upwards force outboard of the basal complex causes the leading and trailing edges of the wing to flex downward, thereby generating positive camber. Redrawn after Wootton *et al.* (1998)

increasing its angle of incidence (Figure 2.6). This mechanism holds down the trailing edge under the positive loading experienced during the downstroke in flight, thereby improving the wing's camber and angle of attack automatically. Interestingly, the same mechanism appears to have evolved separately on more than one occasion, with an analogous structure formed by a different set of veins in some extinct relatives of modern dragonflies Wootton *et al.* (1998).

2.2.2.3   Variable Twist

As is true of any wing that rotates about a fixed point, an insect's wing is expected to display a linearly increasing velocity gradient from root to tip. In forward flight, this leads to an approximately linear variation in the angle of the locally incident flow. Airplane propellors with fixed blades are therefore twisted so as to maintain an optimum angle of attack at all sections for a given airspeed. The hindwing of a locust operates more like a variable pitch propeller, but whereas the blades of a variable pitch propeller tend to be driven electrically or hydraulically, the locust hindwing achieves the same end passively through the umbrella effect that we introduced in the previous section in the context of camber generation (Walker *et al.* 2009a). The overall strength of this effect depends upon the local chord length of the hindwing fan relative to the local chord length of the panel ahead of it (Figure 2.1), so given an appropriate relative chord distribution, the umbrella effect will automatically create the linear twist distribution that is required in order to maintain a constant angle of attack across the wing. Indeed, the measured chord and twist distribution is exactly appropriate to counteract the linearly increasing angle of attack that would occur for an untwisted wing in root-flapping motion (Figure 2.7; Walker *et al.* 2009a).

The functional consequences of this automatic wing-twisting mechanism in locusts have been explored numerically by comparing the flow for a flat-plate model of the fore- and

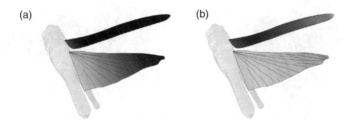

Figure 2.7 (a) angle of incidence; (b) aerodynamic angle of attack of the wings of a desert locust *Schistocerca gregaria*. Spanwise variation in angle of incidence and angle of attack is shown by the intensity of the shading of the wing, where darker shading corresponds to a lower angle. During the downstroke, the hindwing adopts an approximately linear twist distribution, which is visible in the steady gradation in shading of the hindwing in (a). This twist results in an approximately constant aerodynamic angle of attack along the hindwing, which is visible in the constant shading of the hindwing in (b). Redrawn after Walker *et al.* (2009a)

hindwings with that for a model with the measured spanwise twist distribution (Young *et al.* 2009). The model with the correctly varying spanwise twist resulted in a 53% increase in lift power economy over the flat plate model. As was also the case for automatic camber generation (see above), this improvement in lift power economy results because the twisting of the wings aids in the maintenance of attached flows, which leads in turn to more efficient flight, albeit with lower aerodynamic force coefficients (Young *et al.* 2009). Any change to the stiffness of the radial veins, the chord distribution, or the wing kinematics would be expected to cause a change in the angle of attack distribution, so this maintenance of near-constant angle of attack across the hindwing of a locust implies exquisite evolutionary optimization of its structural, morphological, and kinematic parameters. We emphasize that this is a dynamic mechanism of wing morphing, which adapts the wing continuously so as to optimize its aerodynamic function.

Hoverfly wings also display prominent spanwise twist throughout the upstroke and downstroke, but do so most noticeably at stroke reversal when a torsional wave passes along the wings (Figure 2.8). If the twisting of the wings were driven directly by muscles applying torsion at the wing root, then the change in angle of attack would be expected to proceed from root to tip at stroke reversal. In fact, the opposite happens, with the torsional wave running instead from tip to root (Figure 2.8). This is because the rotational axis of the wing lies close to the leading edge and ahead of the wing's center of mass (Ennos 1988b), which means that the velocity of the trailing edge lags behind the velocity of the leading edge at stroke reversal. The lag of the trailing edge increases from tip to root as a result of the wing's increasing chord, and the torsional wave therefore passes from tip to root along the wing (Ennos 1988b). Over-rotation of the wing at stroke reversal leads to a recoil effect in which the angle of incidence decreases slightly after stroke reversal (Walker *et al.* 2010). Bos *et al.* (2008) used a two-dimensional numerical flow simulation to show that this recoil can improve the lift-to-drag ratio of a flapping wing by up to 15%. This is because the effective angle of attack is lowered by the recoil effect at the start of the downstroke, such that the leading edge vortex which sits over the wing at the start of the downstroke generates less drag, but a similar amount of lift.

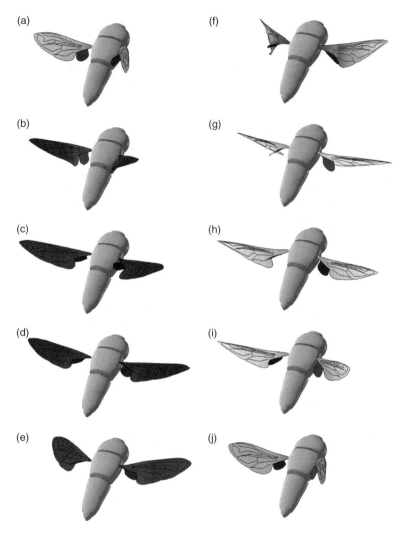

Figure 2.8 Angle of incidence of the wings of a hoverfly *Eristalis tenax* at ten stages of a single wingbeat, beginning with the downstroke. Spanwise variation in angle of incidence is shown by the intensity of the shading of the wing, where darker shading corresponds to a lower angle. The wing is twisted throughout the wingbeat, but is most noticeably twisted just after the lower point of stroke reversal (f), when a torsional wave passes along the wing from tip to root. Note the deflection of the alula during the upstroke. Redrawn after Walker *et al.* (2010)

2.2.2.4 Deflection of Accessory Surfaces

The received wisdom has long been that insects do not make use of accessory control devices like the flaps and slats of aircraft. Nevertheless, there is a prominent flap at the base of the wings of most higher flies, called the alula, which accounts for up to 10% of the wing surface in hoverflies. The alula has received almost no attention in the biomechanics literature, typically being noted only as an anatomical feature (but see Weis-Fogh 1973). The alula normally lies flat with respect to the wing in flight, but Walker *et al.* (2009b, 2010) noted that it was flipped upwards by approximately 90° relative to the morphological dorsal surface of the wing during some wingbeats in the hoverfly *Eristalis tenax* (Figure 2.8). Alula flipping is significantly related to body accelerations, and also to changes in wing kinematics, notably stroke amplitude, so it seems possible that the alula plays some role in flight control (Walker *et al.*, 2011). Numerical flow simulations of hoverflies reveal that the local aerodynamic loading in the vicinity of the alula is minimal during hovering (Du and Sun 2010), so an aerodynamic function analogous to that of an aircraft's flap is unlikely in hovering, although this cannot be ruled out in fast forward flight, when the flow velocity will be greater at the wing root.

2.3   Birds

Birds are the most speciose group of terrestrial vertebrates, with around 10000 living species. The adult body masses of extant flying birds span four orders of magnitude, ranging from 0.002 kg in the bee hummingbird *Mellisuga helenae* to at least 16 kg in the Kori bustard *Ardeotis kori*. Among other extant giants, the wandering albatross *Diomedea exulans* and andean condor *Vultur gryphus* have wingspans in excess of 3 m, while the extinct condor-like bird *Argentavis magnificens* might well have had a wingspan twice this size, although it was probably too large to have been capable of continuous flapping flight (Chatterjee *et al.* 2007).

The flight of birds has fascinated scientists for centuries, and inspired the Wright brothers' wing-warping control system, which was a central innovation enabling them to undertake the first manned, powered, controlled flights at Kitty Hawk. From observing the ease with which birds fly in their natural environment, one might be forgiven for thinking that wing morphing was a simple problem. It is not, of course, and although significant advances have been made towards quantifying how birds' wings deform in flight, our knowledge remains sparse in comparison with that which is known about insects. The picture is further complicated by the fact that birds have not two morphing wings, but three, with the horizontal tail changing shape in a manner that is closely coupled to changes in the wings themselves. In the next section, we outline the structure and mechanism of bird wings and tails, with a view to providing the background needed to understand how and why they morph in flight.

2.3.1   Wing Structure and Mechanism

2.3.1.1   Wing Skeleton

The bones of a bird's wing are essentially the same as those of a human upper limb, although two of the digits have been lost altogether and many of the remaining hand bones have become fused (Figure 2.9). The humerus (i.e. upper arm bone) connects the radius and ulna (i.e. lower arm bones) to the shoulder girdle. The wrist joint forms part of the wing leading edge, but between the wrist and shoulder runs a tendon supporting a triangular area of feathered membrane that forms the curved leading edge of the armwing. The thumb digit is greatly reduced, but retains some freedom of movement and supports a group of feathers known

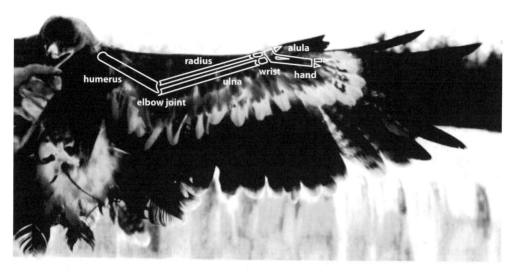

Figure 2.9 Schematic of the relative arrangement of the ten wing bones of a bird. The geometry of the bones is intended to be indicative, and should not be taken literally. Schematic after Videler (2005)

as the alula. The two remaining digits are greatly reduced, and the hand bones are partially fused, greatly restricting the potential number of degrees of freedom of movement in the handwing. In total, there are ten separate skeletal elements in each wing (Videler 2005), which is approximately half the number present in the wing of a bat, giving correspondingly lower dimensional complexity. This reduction in complexity is due also to the detailed arrangement of the bones and their soft tissue connections. For example, extension or flexion of the arm section of the wing automatically causes extension or flexion of the hand section, by virtue of the parallel sliding arrangement of the radius and ulna (Videler 2005). The same arrangement also means that the wrist has limited freedom of movement when the wing is outstretched.

2.3.1.2 Wing Feathers

The lifting surface of a bird's wing is formed by feathers, which arise from follicles within the skin, and which in the case of the flight feathers are attached by ligaments to the wing bones. This arrangement means that the flight feathers are spread automatically as the arm is outstretched, as is easy to see by manipulating a fresh, dead specimen. The flight feathers are large feathers that are responsible for the majority of lift and thrust production during flapping flight. The primary feathers connect to the bones of the hand and together form the handwing, which is the portion of wing outboard of the wrist. The secondary feathers connect to the ulna, and form the outer portion of the armwing, between the elbow and wrist. A varying number of tertial feathers may be connected to the humerus, and contribute to maintaining a blended wing-body effect in species with elongated wings. The alula feathers attach to the thumb remnant, and are folded flush against the upper surface of the wing leading edge when not deployed. The remainder of the wing contour is formed by the covert feathers, which provide all of the upper surface contour and most of the lower surface contour over the thick forward sections of the wing and body. They are highly flexible structures, and their slight roughness may serve to generate turbulence even when they lie flush to the wing surface. The covert feathers also extend across the body of the bird, and are important in producing the blended wing body effect that characterizes birds.

Feathers are lightweight, self-supporting structures, composed of a particular kind of keratin protein. They are complex hierarchical structures, comprising a hollow and relatively stiff central shaft, from which branch a series of parallel barbs on either side of the shaft. These barbs in turn branch to from barbules, which are tightly interlocked in the flight feathers via tiny hooks called barbicels. It is these hooks which are ultimately responsible for providing the integrity of the flattened vanes of the flight feathers. Typically, the inner vane of a flight feather is much broader than its outer vane, which stabilizes the feather against rotation about its shaft by ensuring that the center of aerodynamic pressure of each feather lies behind its shaft. All feathers display some degree of porosity, and this does not appear to be significantly greater for the coverts than for the primaries and secondaries (Müller and Patone 1998). The transmissivity of the inner vane is typically much lower than that of the outer vane, however, which is presumably important in keeping adjacent overlapping feathers pressed together in flight (Müller and Patone 1998). Hence, despite the porosity of the flight feathers, it is unlikely that an overlapping row of feathers would allow much air to pass through under normal flight conditions. On the contrary, porosity may be important in preventing leakage through the wing by helping to press the feathers together.

The lifting surface of each wing is composed of numerous separate feather elements, but the wing design of birds means that the degree of relative movement that is possible between the feathers and the skeleton is tightly restricted. The main flight feathers of the wings attach to the bone at the wrist joint and the tips of the wings (Stettenheim 1972). Similarly, on the leading edge of the wing, skin attaches to the bone at the wrist joint and the tips of the wings (Stettenheim 1972), which will help to keep the leading edge covert feathers in their intended position on either the upper or lower surface.

2.3.1.3   Wing Musculature

Bird wings contain some 45 muscles (Videler 2005), many of which are subdivided into different parts or have more than one insertion point upon the skeleton. Despite this complexity, the wingbeat is essentially powered by a single muscle on each half stroke. The active parts of both of these muscles are located well beneath the shoulder joint, and whereas the pectoralis muscle pulls the wings downward via a tendon attaching to the underside of the humerus, the supracoracoideus pulls the wing upward via a tendon that runs through a pulley-like arrangement to the top of the humerus. Both muscles also play an important role in wing rotation, and numerous smaller muscles are used alongside the two major muscles, especially during the transitions between downstroke and upstroke. The details of this arrangement are complex, and not yet fully understood, but it is worth recalling that there are four times fewer skeletal elements in the wings than there are muscles, so there is likely to be quite some redundancy within the system, notwithstanding that every muscle needs an antagonist. Indeed, because gravitational, aerodynamic, and elastic forces can all in principle act as muscle antagonists, it is not even necessary that the muscles themselves be arranged in antagonistic pairs or groupings, which would add further to the degree of possible redundancy.

2.3.1.4 Tail Feathers and Musculature

The tail of a bird comprises anything up to 24 flight feathers, radially arranged so as to form a fan-like structure behind the body. To a first approximation, the tail may be modeled as having three degrees of freedom: spread angle, elevation angle, and twist angle. In essence, it is shaped rather like a delta wing of variable sweep, although it remains contentious whether this is actually how it functions aerodynamically. The morphology of the tail feathers varies greatly between species, and is often subject to selection for display as well as for flight. The central pair of feathers is usually highly convex and roughly symmetrical when viewed from above, whereas the outer tail feathers are usually flatter, or even concave, and are highly asymmetrical when viewed from above. The transition between the tail and body is smoothed by the presence of tail covert feathers, so that the tail blends smoothly into the body. Six pairs of muscles are involved in the stabilization and control of tail posture, and although we know a little of their firing patterns during different flight maneuvers (Gatesy and Dial 1993), the biomechanics of tail function are far from fully understood.

2.3.2 Gross Wing Morphing

2.3.2.1 Variable Planform

One of the striking features of bird wings and tails is their ability to morph between different planforms in a fraction of a second. Changes in wing area are possible because the degree of overlap between adjacent flight feathers changes automatically as the bird flexes or spreads its wings and tail. This is used to good effect in soaring flight, during which birds continuously vary wing and tail area to effect changes in glide speed and glide angle. For example, a Harris' hawk *Parabuteo unicinctus* gliding in a tilted wind tunnel was found to reduce its wing area two-fold with increasing airspeed, so as to match its forward speed and sink rate to the flow conditions in the tunnel (Tucker and Heine 1990). Furthermore, at low flight speeds, spreading of the wings was accompanied by spreading of the tail, which presumably served both to maintain pitch equilibrium and to reduce wing loading (Tucker 1992).

Birds accomplish changes in wing span and area by flexing their wings, and when the wings are highly flexed, they automatically adopt a characteristic M-shaped planform. This is apparent in Figure 2.10, which shows the final stages of a perching sequence in a steppe eagle *Aquila nipalensis* (Carruthers *et al.* 2007). Perching in this species involves a highly stereotyped sequence of changes in wing shape, beginning with a shallow glide with wings outstretched. As the bird nears the perch, the wings are flexed into an M-shaped planform, which causes a dramatic reduction in area and brings the center of pressure forward, thereby initiating a rapid pitch-up maneuver. The wings are fully outstretched again at the end of the pitch-up maneuver, but are now held at such a high angle of attack that the wing enters deep stall, thereby producing the very high drag forces that are required for aerodynamic braking (Carruthers *et al.* 2007). This is an extremely fast movement, executed in a mere 0.2s, and is probably the clearest example found to date of how wing morphing can be used to control highly unsteady flight maneuvers.

Figure 2.10   A stereotyped sequence of changes in wing planform characterizes perching in this steppe eagle *Aquila nipalensis*. As the bird nears the perch, the wings are flexed into an M-shaped planform, which causes a dramatic reduction in area and brings the center of pressure forward, thereby initiating a rapid pitch-up maneuver. The timings in the top left of each frame indicate that this pattern of wing morphing is executed in just 0.2s. Redrawn after Carruthers *et al.* (2007)

2.3.2.2   Variable Camber

Very little is known about the camber of birds' wings in flight, and measurements made on museum specimens are notoriously unreliable (Withers 1981). Stereophotogrammetry has been used to reconstruct the shape of the upper wing surface of a house sparrow *Passer domesticus* during flapping flight in a small wind tunnel (Bilo 1971, 1972), while later work succeeded in measuring complete wing profiles on a common starling *Sturnus vulgaris* gliding in a wind tunnel (Brill *et al.* 1989). More recently, multi-station photogrammetry has been used to reconstruct the upper and lower surface of the wing of a steppe eagle *Aquila nipalensis* during perching (Carruthers *et al.* 2010). The thin trailing portion of the wing formed by the secondary feathers flexes during flight, giving rise to reflex camber under positive aerodynamic loading. The degree of reflex camber presumably varies dynamically in flight, but we have no quantitative information upon this at present.

2.3.2.3   Variable Twist and Spanwise Bending

The twisting of birds' wings is famous for having been a source of inspiration for the warping wing of the Wright Flyer. In fact, the manner in which the wing of a bird twists is much more complicated than this, as in birds the variable twist of the wings is closely related to their variable sweep. For example, in fast gliding flight, birds typically use a combination of backwards sweep and washout (i.e. lower angle of incidence towards the tips). This makes functional sense, because a combination of backwards sweep and washout can provide balance in a pitch-stable airframe (Thomas and Taylor 2001). However, the picture is complicated by the fact that the wing tip feathers of the handwing are separated in many species, so that the aerodynamic angle of attack of the individual feather elements can be very different from the angle of attack of the overall mean chord (Figure 2.11).

Spanwise bending of the wing tip feathers is almost certainly important in enhancing flight efficiency in birds. Indeed, the up-curved wing tip feathers of birds are said to have inspired the NASA research in the early 1970s that eventually led to the widespread use of winglets in modern aircraft (although the concept of using endplates to reduce induced drag can be traced back to an 1897 patent by Frederick W. Lanchester). In any case, the wing tip feathers of soaring birds differ in two important ways from the winglets of aircraft: first, they are slotted in structure, and second, they bend upwards only under large positive aerodynamic loading. The fact that the wing tip feathers only curve upwards under aerodynamic loading is important, because it means that the wing tip feathers are adaptive in their response to the forces experienced by the wing. The wing tip feathers of birds may therefore be worthy of further exploration in the context of current efforts to develop morphing winglets, or "morphlets," by the two largest manufacturers of civilian airliners.

2.3.3   Local Feather Deflections

Birds are unique among flying animals in that they display an array of local changes in wing shape due to deflections of the feathers. The best known example of this is the alula, which is widely thought to operate as a high-lift device, on the basis that it is clearly adapted to some aerodynamic function, and only comes into operation when it is deflected away from the

Figure 2.11   As is the case in many soaring species, the wing tip feathers of this steppe eagle *Aquila nipalensis* are separated. Because each feather is able to rotate about its central shaft, this means that the angle of attack of the individual feather elements may be quite different from the angle of attack of the overall mean chord. This greatly complicates interpretation of the rapid changes in wing twist that occur during maneuvers. Note the deflection of the alula at the leading edge of the wing, immediately outboard of the wrist joint

leading edge during high angle of attack maneuvers (e.g. Figure 2.11). Opinions differ as to whether the alula operates as a leading-edge slot or slat (Alvarez *et al.* 2001; Meseguer *et al.* 2005; Nachtigall and Kempf 1971; Stinton 2001), or as a vortex generator or strake (Carruthers *et al.* 2007; Videler *et al.* 2005; Videler 2004). These are not mutually exclusive possibilities, and it may well be that the alula functions as a slot/slat when the wing is extended to high aspect ratio, but functions as a vortex generator/strake when the wing is flexed to form a low aspect ratio M-wing planform.

Because the alula joint is muscularized, the alula has usually been assumed to operate as an active control device. Nevertheless, its potential for passive deflection has been noted on several occasions in wind tunnel studies on the wings of freshly-killed birds (Brown 1963; Graham 1930; Nachtigall and Kempf 1971), and deflection of the alula has also been observed to be initiated passively in a free-flying steppe eagle *Aquila nipalensis* (Carruthers *et al.* 2007). Deflection of the alula is initiated with a peeling motion at the feather tips, which must be a passive aeroelastic response, because the feathers are only muscularized at the base. Subsequent forward protraction of the alula is presumably driven muscularly, but it is possible that the muscle action is stimulated reflexively by the passive peeling of the alula, in which case the alula would deploy automatically at high angles of attack.

It is possible that other groups of feathers besides the alula play an aerodynamic role in modifying the flow at the leading edge. In particular, the covert feathers which form the surface of the rounded leading edge of the armwing deflect forwards *en masse* at high angles of attack (Azuma 1992; Blick 1976; Carruthers *et al.* 2007; Hertel 1963). These feathers are deflected during take-off, landing, flapping flight, and in some kinds of gust response, and can be seen deploying during the perching maneuver in Figure 2.10 (F–H). The feathers deflect from the tip rather than the root, implying that their deflection is a passive response to reversed flow at the leading edge. The coherent deflection of the leading edge covert feathers makes them superficially reminiscent of certain kinds of leading edge flap that are used on many conventional aircraft during take-off and landing. However, the leading edge covert feathers of birds are discrete elements, which makes the flap able to deploy either in part or in full. It is uncertain whether the leading edge flap plays any functional role, not least because it is unclear whether it deploys at a low enough angle of attack to serve any useful purpose. However, once deployed, the leading edge flap could in principle act either as a high-lift device (Carruthers *et al.* 2007) or as a turbulator (Jones *et al.* 2008).

The leading edge covert feathers are not the only covert feathers that deploy during flight as a consequence of reversed flow. The covert feathers that form the upper surface of the armwing have also been observed to deploy coherently in flight, and it has been suggested that they may serve as turbulence generators, owing to their apparent similarity to vortex generators used on aircraft (Blick 1976). However, a series of experimental measurements, numerical flow simulations, and flight tests, with movable upper surface flaps have shown that these can enhance lift at high angles of attack by blocking the reverse flow that otherwise forms between the trailing edge and the suction peak on the aerofoil (Schatz *et al.* 2004). This serves to delay flow separation, and it is possible that the upperwing covert feathers of birds function similarly, but with the ability to deploy locally in response to the local flow conditions.

2.4 Bats

There are approximately 1200 different species of bat, exhibiting great variation in flight morphology and ecology. Adult body mass spans three orders of magnitude, ranging from 0.002 kg in the bumblebee bat *Craseonycteris thonglongyai* to 1.2 kg in the golden-capped fruit bat *Acerodon jubatus*. The largest wingspan apparently occurs in the large flying fox *Pteropus vampyrus*, with a wingspan of up to 1.8 m. Bats are the only mammals capable of powered flight, and their proper scientific name, Chiroptera (lit. hand-wing), characterizes the key to this: a wing comprising an elastic muscularized membrane that is stretched between the elongated digits of the hand, the hindlimbs, and the body wall (Figure 2.12). This arrangement gives the potential for high-order control of wing deformation: simply counting the number of joints, there are > 20 degrees of freedom of motion in each wing, even before any account is taken of the rotational complexity of each joint, or of the elastic degrees of freedom of the wing bones and membrane.

Despite the obvious potential for high dimensional complexity, the number of independently-controllable degrees of freedom is likely to be constrained by the interconnectedness of the different wing components. For example, a recent study of the lesser dog-faced fruit bat *Cynopterus brachyotis* found that the 20 measured joint angles clustered into three distinct groups, within which the motion of the different joints was closely similar (Riskin *et al.* 2008). The first group corresponded to coupled spreading and flexing of the fingers, the second to coupled pitching of the wrist and bending of the elbow, and the third to coupled movements of

Figure 2.12   The wing of a bat comprises an elastic muscularized membrane that is stretched between the elongated digits of the hand, the hindlimbs, and the body wall. Photograph of a lesser dog-faced fruit bat *Cynopterus brachyotis* by N. Hristov and T. Hubel

the shoulder and hindlimbs. It is not yet clear whether these groups represent true functional units, but a large proportion of the motion occurring in a typical wingbeat can be modeled through the motion of these three joint assemblages. Hence, even this most complex of Nature's morphing wing designs may in principle be simplified so as to yield useful insight.

In the next section, we outline the structure and mechanism of bat wings, with a view to providing the background needed to understand the mechanics of wing morphing in bats. Rather little is known about the kinematic details of wing morphing in bats, but we describe the extent of our current knowledge further below.

2.4.1   Wing Structure and Mechanism

2.4.1.1   Wing Skeleton

The bones of a bat's wing are essentially the same as those of a human upper limb (Figure 2.12). The humerus (i.e. upper arm bone) connects a strong and elongated radius and partially-fused and reduced ulna (i.e. lower arm bones) to the shoulder girdle. The thumb is located close to the wrist, and although it varies in size across species, it is always comparatively short, with a claw at the end. The remaining four digits support the outer part of the wing membrane, and each digit comprises a highly elongated metacarpal (i.e. hand bone) and two to three phalanges (i.e. finger bones). The second digit is the shortest of the four fingers, and forms the outer part of the wing leading edge in conjunction with the outermost portion of the third digit (Norberg 1969).

The wings of bats have to resist extensive load changes over the course of a wingbeat cycle, and like birds, they have modified their bones in order to sustain the substantial forces associated with powered flight. Strain measurements made upon a grey-headed flying fox *Pteropus poliocephalus* in forward flight indicate strains up to 2×10^{-3} on the radius and humerus, with maximum bending experienced at mid-downstroke, and close to the lower stroke reversal point (Swartz *et al.* 1992). As with any mechanical element, the strength and stiffness of a bone depend upon its structural and material properties, and the shape and mineral content of the bones therefore vary dramatically across the different skeletal elements in order to accommodate the specific loads to which they are subjected. These changes in structural and material properties reflect the varying demands along the wing span, with high torsional and shear stresses over the inner part of the wing, and large bending forces over the outer part.

Unlike the bones of other mammals, which experience mainly bending loads, bat wing bones have to cope with an unusual amount of torsion. The arm bones of bats are therefore round and thin-walled, which allows them to resist torsional and bending moments alike. They are also made of a comparatively high-density bone material, which correlates with strength and stiffness, making even these long and delicate-looking bones strong and relatively heavy (Dumont 2010). In contrast, the finger bones are flattened, and show a dramatical decrease in mineralization towards the tip, increasing their ability to accommodate high bending forces and also leading to greater flexibility. The sparse mineralization of the finger bones also plays an important part in weight reduction of the outer part of the wing: considering that the greatest speeds and displacements are reached at the wing tip, a decrease in weight in this area leads to smaller inertial forces, resulting in energetic savings and higher maneuverability.

2.4.1.2   Wing Membrane

The lifting surface of a bat's wing is formed by a thin, elastic, muscularized membrane (Figure 2.12). The two largest areas of wing membrane are the handwing membrane, which runs from the second digit of the hand across the third, fourth, and fifth digits; and the armwing membrane, which runs from the fifth digit to the hindlimbs and body wall. The leading edge of the armwing is formed by a triangular portion of membrane between the wrist and shoulder joints. The leading edge of the handwing is formed by the flattened bones of the second and third digits, and by a small triangular portion of wing membrane in the vicinity of the thumb (Figure 2.12). In addition, many bats also have an area of membrane between their hindlimbs. This tail membrane is used in the control of flight maneuvers, but one of its main functions is to assist in feeding: insectivorous bats catch their prey by scooping it with their tail membrane, which serves as a catching device, essentially replacing the hands, which have been co-opted for locomotion. Indeed, due to their great flight abilities and flexible skeletal structure, bats can actually bend over in mid-flight, transfer the the insect into their mouth, and eat it immediately. To withstand such high demands, the tail membrane has evolved to be especially robust, and is supported by a long cartilaginous extension from each ankle.

The wing membrane itself is very thin and compliant, but is surprisingly robust. In the event of damage, it is one of the fastest-healing of all vertebrate tissues. The wing membrane is composed of two thin layers of external epidermis enclosing an internal layer of dermis. The dermis contains blood vessels, muscles, and a network of elastic fibers composed mainly of collagen and elastin fiber bundles. The fiber and muscle network gives the membrane highly anisotropic properties: maximum stiffness and strength are achieved parallel to the wing skeleton, while maximum elasticity is achieved parallel to the wing trailing edge (Swartz *et al.* 1996). Two types of muscle bundle are found in the membrane: larger muscle bundles originate on the wing skeleton and extend into the membrane, serving to brace the wing by anchoring it tightly to the bone; smaller muscle bundles emanate from, and end within, the membrane itself, probably serving to adjust local membrane stiffness or to tension the membrane. The underlying structural network of muscles and fibers correlates directly with the mechanical properties of the wing, and, like the bones whose mineralization changes along the wing span, the composition of the membrane varies between different wing areas to match their respective stresses and strains. It also varies among different species, with greater strength in large, load-carrying species (Swartz *et al.* 1996).

2.4.1.3   Flight Musculature

The flight musculature of bats is complicated: whereas the wingbeat of a bird is essentially powered by a single muscle on each half stroke, the wingbeat of bats is powered by the action of many different muscles on each half stroke. This difference reflects the much greater freedom of movement that exists within the shoulder girdle of bats as compared to birds, and gives bats greater potential for controlling the root-flapping motion of their wings at source. Relative to other mammals, bats have reduced or lost certain of the muscles located in the outermost portions of the forelimb. Nevertheless, the ability of bats to control their wing deformation still rests with the muscles controlling their joints, and with the muscle fibers embedded within the wing membrane, which are thought ultimately to provide fine control of membrane camber and tension.

2.4.2   Gross Wing Morphing

2.4.2.1   Variable Planform

Wing planform can change dramatically during maneuvering, and also varies cyclically over the course of every wingbeat cycle. This is attributable not only to the complexity of the musculoskeletal system, but also to aeroelastic deformation of the membrane. Detailed kinematic analyses are available for only a very few species, but these already show considerable differences between species. Some bats, such as the insectivorous Brazilian free-tailed bat *Tadarida brasiliensis* or the Cave Myotis *Myotis velifer* keep their wings almost fully extended throughout the wingbeat, with very little difference in span between the upstroke and downstroke. They merely flex their wrist backwards slightly during the upstroke, and show little change in planform through the wingbeat cycle. The complete opposite is true of the larger fruit bats. Species such as the lesser dog-faced fruit bat *Cynopterus brachyotis* show impressive deformations of their wings over the course of the wingbeat cycle. They decrease their wing span significantly during the upstroke by curling their wings in towards the body at the end of the downstroke, sometimes so extensively that the tips of their wings collide (Hubel *et al.* 2010). Qualitatively similar changes in span through the stroke cycle have also been observed

Figure 2.13   Bat wings adopt highly-cambered profiles in flight: this image was taken near the middle of the downstroke during forward flight. Note the strong positive camber of the armwing. Photograph of a Brazilian free-tailed bat *Tadarida brasiliensis*, by N. Hristov and T. Hubel.

in the nectar-feeding Pallas' long-tongued bat *Glossophaga soricina*, in which the wing span at mid-upstroke is between 60% and 70% of the wing span at mid-downstroke, depending upon flight speed (Wolf *et al.* 2010). These changes in span appear to depend principally upon changes in configuration of the inner, rather than outer, portion of the wing.

2.4.2.2   Variable Camber

Bat wings certainly adopt highly cambered profiles in flight (Figure 2.13), but we have relatively little quantitative knowledge of the camber of bat wings, or of how that camber changes over the course of a wingbeat. What is clear is that the membrane is a highly compliant surface, which will react quickly to the applied aerodynamic and inertial forces. Wind tunnel studies on artificial wings have shown that wings with compliant surfaces reach higher maximum lift coefficients, have steeper lift slopes, and stall at higher angles of attack than comparable rigid wings (Song *et al.* 2008). Recent measurements on a range of different-sized flying foxes showed no correlation between body size and wing camber, but did show a decrease in camber with increasing flight speed (Riskin *et al.* 2010). Cambers of around 10% of wing chord were measured at mid-downstroke. These results are consistent with camber measurements from the armwing of Pallas' long-tongued bat *Glossophaga soricina*, in which the mean camber decreases with increasing flight speed, reaching approximately 10% of wing chord at high flight speeds (Wolf *et al.* 2010). The camber of the armwing at mid-upstroke is roughly twice that at mid-downstroke at low flight speeds, approaching values as high as 25% of wing chord at the lowest flight speeds. These exceedingly high values of wing camber are probably associated with nose-up twisting of the handwing during the upstroke, which has the effect of depressing the trailing part of the armwing membrane relative to the portion of membrane between the arm bones and the wing leading edge.

2.4.2.3   Spanwise Bending and Torsion

Our knowledge of the bending and torsion that bat wings undergo during a wingbeat cycle is very limited, although the wing is certainly highly twisted during the wingbeat (Figure 2.13).

At low flight speeds, it is common for the handwing to invert completely during twisting at the start of the upstroke (Lindhe Norberg and Winter 2006; Riskin *et al.* 2008; Wolf *et al.* 2010). This is assumed to enhance thrust production, but the associated twist distribution has never been quantified.

2.5 Conclusion

It will be clear from the above that we still have much to learn about wing morphing in insects, birds, and bats. Nevertheless, it is already possible to draw a few general conclusions. It is striking that none of the three ways of building a morphing wing that we have described above closely resembles the prevailing concept of a morphing wing in aerospace engineering. Current morphing wing concepts tend to be predicated upon the use of materials with shape memory properties. However, this is not how natural selection has structured shape-changing wings. Instead, insects, birds, and bats achieve their wing morphing capability by using flexible lifting surfaces, actuated by moveable structural elements, attached to muscles that are largely or entirely extrinsic to the wings. This general arrangement resembles more closely the cable-driven warping of fabric-covered wings in the Wright Flyer, or even the swing-wing design of some military aircraft, than it does a morphing wing design based on the use of shape-memory alloys. We make no value judgement about the relative merits of the various ways of engineering a morphing wing, but think this is an important point to note.

It is also noteworthy that the evolutionary trend in all three groups of flying animals has been towards a reduction in the dimensional complexity of the wings. Insects have achieved this by reducing the number of structural veins in the wings; birds by fusing or losing wing bones; and bats by reducing the number of muscles within the wing. Hence, although an animal's wings may be able to change shape in a complex manner, the total number of independently-controlled degrees of freedom may not be that high. This makes sense from a control perspective, and is closely related to the fact that many changes in wing shape in flying animals are achieved as passive, automatic responses to loading. In insects, the wings are built as smart structures so as to adopt useful twist and camber distributions in flight; in birds, the feathers function as highly-distributed, automatically-moveable flaps; in bats the anisotropic properties of the wing membrane cause it to adopt appropriate camber when the wing is loaded.

It follows that a truly bio-inspired morphing wing design would have the look of complexity about it, but would be built upon relatively simple underlying principles. It would be actuated primarily from its base, via moveable structural elements with limited freedom of motion. No smart or active materials would be needed to build such a wing, because the structure itself would be smart. Above all, the wing would be built to conform to loading rather than to resist it. Realizing a wing design of this sort is clearly a difficult problem, but it seems to us that the materials and fabrication techniques that would be required to build such a wing are available already. The difficulty lies rather in the design process, and it is quite possible that this is so complex a problem that it demands an evolutionary solution.

Acknowledgements

The authors thank Sharon Swartz for providing helpful comments on this chapter.

References

Alvarez, J., Meseguer, J. and Pérez, A. (2001). On the role of the alula in the steady flight of birds. *Ardeola* **48**, 161–173.

Azuma, A. (1992). *The Biokinetics of Flying and Swimming*. New York: Springer-Verlag.

Baker, P. S. and Cooter, R. J. (1979). The natural flight of the migratory locust, *Locusta migratoria* L. I. Wing movements. *J. Comp. Physiol. A* **131**, 79–89.

Betts, C. R. and Wootton, R. J. (1988). Wing shape and flight behaviour in butterflies (Lepidoptera: Papilionidae and Hesperioidea): a preliminary analysis. *J. Exp. Biol.* **271**, 288.

Bilo, D. (1971). Flugbiophysik von Kleinvögeln. I. Kinematik und Aerodynamik des Flügelschlages beim Haussperling (*Passer domesticus* L.). *Z. Vergl. Physiol.* **71**, 382–454.

Bilo, D. (1972). Flugbiophysik von Kleinvögeln. II. Kinematik und Aerodynamik des Flügelaufschlages beim Haussperling (*Passer domesticus* L.). *Z. Vergl. Physiol.* **76**, 426–437.

Blick, E. F. (1976). The aerodynamics of birds. *AIAA Stud. J.* **Summer 1976**, 4–9.

Bomphrey, R. J., Taylor, G. K., Lawson, N. J. and Thomas, A. L. R. (2006). Digital particle image velocimetry measurements of the downwash distribution of a desert locust *Schistocerca gregaria*. *J. R. Soc. Interface* **3**, 311–317.

Bos, F. M., Lentink, D., Van Oudheusden, B. W. and Bijl, H. (2008). Influence of wing kinematics on aerodynamic performance in hovering insect flight. *J. Fluid Mech.* **594**, 341–368.

Brackenbury, J. (1991). Wing kinematics during natural leaping in the mantids *Mantis religiosa* and *Iris oratoria*. *J. Zool., Lond.* **223**, 341–356.

Brackenbury, J. (1994a). Hymenopteran wing kinematics - a qualitative study. *J. Zool., Lond* **233**, 523–540.

Brackenbury, J. (1994b). Wing folding and free-flight kinematics in Coleoptera (Insecta) - a comparative study. *J. Zool., Lond.* **232**, 253–283.

Brill, C., Mayer-Kunz, D. P. and Nachtigall, W. (1989). Wing profile data of a free-gliding bird. *Naturwiss.* **76**, 39–40.

Brown, R. H. J. (1963). The flight of birds. *Biol. Rev.* **38**, 460–489.

Carruthers, A. C., Thomas, A. L. R. and Taylor, G. K. (2007). Automatic aeroelastic devices in the wings of a steppe eagle *Aquila nipalensis*. *J. Exp. Biol.* **210**, 4136–4139.

Carruthers, A. C., Walker, S. M., Thomas, A. L. R. and Taylor, G. K. (2010). Aerodynamics of aerofoil sections measured on a free-flying bird. *Proc. IME G, J. Aero. Eng.* **224**, 855–864.

Chatterjee, S., Templin, R. J. and Campbell, K. E. (2007). The aerodynamics of *Argentavis*, the world's largest flying bird from the Miocene of Argentina. *PNAS* **24**, 12398–12403.

Du, G. and Sun, M. (2008). Effects of unsteady deformation of flapping wing on its aerodynamic forces. *Appl. Math. Mech.* **29**, 731–743.

Du, G. and Sun, M. (2010). Effects of wing deformation on aerodynamic forces in hovering hoverflies. *J. Exp. Biol.* **213**, 2273–2283.

Dumont, E. R. (2010). Bone density and the lightweight skeletons of birds. *Proc. R. Soc. Lond. B* **277**, 2193–2198.

Ellington, C. P. (1984). The aerodynamics of hovering insect flight. IV. Aerodynamic mechanisms. *Phil. Trans. R. Soc. Lond. B* **305**, 79–&.

Ennos, A. R. (1988a). The importance of torsion in the design of insect wings. *J. Exp. Biol.* **140**, 137–160.

Ennos, A. R. (1988b). The inertial cause of wing rotation in Diptera. *J. Exp. Biol.* **140**, 161–169.

Ennos, A. R. (1989). Inertial and aerodynamic torques on the wings of Diptera in flight. *J. Exp. Biol.* **142**, 87–95.

Gatesy, S. M. and Dial, K. P. (1993). Tail muscle activity patterns in walking and flying pigeons (*Columba livia*). *J. Exp. Biol.* **176**, 47–77.

Graham, R. R. (1930). Safety devices in the wings of birds. *Brit. Birds* **24**, 2–65.

Haas, F., Gorb, S. and Wootton, R. J. (2000). Elastic joints in dermapteran hind wings: materials and wing folding. *Arth. Struct. Dev.* **29**, 137–146.

Haas, F. and Wootton, R. J. (1996). Two basic mechanisms in insect wing folding. *Proc. R. Soc. Lond. B* **263**, 1651–1658.

Herbert, R. C., Young, P. G., Smith, C. W., Wootton, R. J. and Evans, K. E. (2000). The hind wing of a desert locust (*Schistocerca gregaria* Forskål) III. A finite element analysis of a deployable structure. *J. Exp. Biol.* **203**, 3003–3012.

Hertel, H. (1963). *Structure, form, movement*. Otto Krausskopf-Verlag: Mainz, Germany.

Hubel, T. Y., Riskin, D. K., Swartz, S. M. and Breuer, K. S. (2010). Wake structure and wing kinematics: the flight of the lesser dog-faced fruit bat, *Cynopterus brachyotis*. *J. Exp. Biol.* **213**, 3427–3440.

Jones, A. R., Bakhtian, N. M. and Babinsky, H. (2008). Low Reynolds number aerodynamics of leading-edge flaps. *J. Aircraft* **45**, 342–345.

Lindhe Norberg, U. M. and Winter, Y. (2006). Wing beat kinematics of a nectar-feeding bat, *Glossophaga soricina*, flying at different flight speeds and Strouhal numbers. *J. Exp. Biol.* **209**, 3887–3897.

Meseguer, J., Franchini, S., Perez-Grande, I. and Sanz, I. L. (2005). On the aerodynamics of leading-edge high-lift devices of avian wings. *Proc. Inst. Mech. Eng. G.* **219**, 63–68.

Müller, W. and Patone, G. (1998). Air transmissivity of feathers. *J. Exp. Biol.* **201**, 2591–2599.

Nachtigall, W. (1966). Die Kinematik der Schlagflügelbewegungen von Dipteren. Methodische und analytische Grundlagen zur Biophysik des Insektenflugs. *Z. Vergl. Physiol.* **52**, 155–211.

Nachtigall, W. and Kempf, B. (1971). Vergleichende untersuchungen zur flugbiologischen funktion des Daumenfittichs (Alula spuria) bei vögeln. *Z. Vergl. Physiol.* **71**, 326–341.

Norberg, R. A. (1972). The pterostigma of insect wings as an inertial regulator of wing pitch. *J. Comp. Physiol.* **81**, 13–26.

Norberg, U. M. (1969). An arrangement giving a stiff leading edge to the hand wing in bats. *J. Mamm.* **50**, 766–770.

Riskin, D. K., Iriarte-Díaz, J., Middleton, K. M., Breuer, K. S. and Swartz, S. M. (2010). The effect of body size on the wing movements of pteropodid bats, with insights into thrust and lift production. *J. Exp. Biol.* **213**, 4110–4122.

Riskin, D. K., Willis, D. J., Iriarte-Díaz, J., Hedrick, T. L., Kostandov, M., Chen, J., Laidlaw, D. H., Breuer, K. S. and Swartz, S. M. (2008). Quantifying the complexity of bat wing kinematics. *J. Theor. Biol.* **254**, 604–615.

Schatz, M., Knacke, T. and Thiele, F. (2004). Separation control by self-activated movable flaps. In: *42nd AIAA Aerospace Sciences Meeting & Exhibit*, AIAA-2004-1243. Reno, NV, USA.

Song, A., Tian, X., Israeli, E., Galvao, R., Bishop, K., Swartz, S. and Breuer, K. (2008). Aeromechanics of membrane wings with implications for animal flight. *AIAA J.* **46**, 2096–2106.

Stettenheim, P. (1972). The integument of birds. *Avian Biol.* **2**, 2–63.

Stinton, D. (2001). *The design of the aeroplane*. Blackwell: Oxford, 2nd edn.

Swartz, S. M., Bennett, M. B. and Carrier, D. R. (1992). Wing bone stresses in free flying bats and the evolution of skeletal design for flight. *Nature* **359**, 726–729.

Swartz, S. M., Groves, M. S., Kim, H. D. and Walsh, W. R. (1996). Mechanical properties of bat wing membrane skin. *J. Zool. Lond.* **239**, 357–378.

Thomas, A. L. R. and Taylor, G. K. (2001). Animal flight dynamics I. Stability in gliding flight. *J. Theor. Biol.* **212**, 399–424.

Tucker, V. A. (1992). Pitching equilibrium, wing span and tail span in a gliding Harris' hawk, *Parabuteo unicinctus*. *J. Exp. Biol.* **165**, 13–42.

Tucker, V. A. and Heine, C. (1990). Aerodynamics of gliding flight in a Harris' hawk, *Parabuteo unicinctus*. *J. Exp. Biol.* **149**, 486–492.

Vanella, M., Fitzgerald, T., Preidikman, S., Balaras, E. and Balachandran, B. (2009). Influence of flexibility on the aerodynamic performance of a hovering wing. *J. Exp. Biol.* **212**, 95–105.

Videler, J. J. (2005). *Avian flight*. Oxford University Press: Oxford.

Videler, J. J., Stamhuis, E. J. and Povel, G. D. E. (2004). Leading-edge vortex lifts swifts. *Science* **306**, 1960–1962.

Vincent, J. F. V. and Wegst, U. G. K. (2004). Design and mechanical properties of insect cuticle. *Arth. Struct. Dev.* **33**, 187–199.

Walker, S. M., Thomas, A. L. R. and Taylor, G. K. (2009a). Deformable wing kinematics in the desert locust: how and why do camber, twist and topography vary through the stroke? *J. R. Soc. Interface* **6**, 735–747.

Walker, S. M., Thomas, A. L. R. and Taylor, G. K. (2009b). Photogrammetric reconstruction of high-resolution surface topographies and deformable wing kinematics of tethered locusts and free-flying hoverflies. *J. R. Soc. Interface* **6**, 351–366.

Walker, S. M., Thomas, A. L. R. and Taylor, G. K. (2010). Deformable wing kinematics in free-flying hoverflies. *J. R. Soc. Interface* **7**, 131–142.

Walker, S. M., Thomas, A. L. R. and Taylor, G. K. (2011). Operation of the alula as an indicator of gear change in hoverflies, *J. Roy. Soc. Interface*. Published online before print November 9, 2011. doi: 10.1098/rsif.2011.0617

Weis-Fogh, T. (1973). Quick estimates of flight fitness in hoverfing animals, including novel mechanisms for lift production. *J. Exp. Biol.* **59**, 169–230.

Withers, P. C. (1981). An aerodynamic analysis of bird wings as fixed aerofoils. *J. Exp. Biol.* **90**, 155–162.

Witton, M. P. and Naish, D. (2008). A reappraisal of azhdarchid pterosaur functional morphology and paleoecology. *Plos One* **3**.

Wolf, M., C., J. L., von Busse, R., Winter, Y. and Hedenström, A. (2010). Kinematics of flight and the relationship to the vortex wake of a Pallas' long tongued bat (*Glossophaga soricina*). *J. Exp. Biol.* **213**, 2142–2153.

Wootton, R. J. (1981). Support and deformability in insect wings. *J. Zool., Lond.* **193**, 459–470.

Wootton, R. J. (1992). Functional morphology of insect wings. *Ann. Rev. Entomol.* **37**, 113–140.

Wootton, R. J. (1993). Leading edge section and asymmetric twisting in the wings of flying butterflies (Insecta, Papilionoidea). *J. Exp. Biol.* **180**, 117–119.

Wootton, R. J. (1995). Geometry and mechanics of insect hindwing fans: a modeling approach. *Proc. R. Soc. Lond. B* **262**, 181–187.

Wootton, R. J. (2009). Springy shells, pliant plates and minimal motors: Abstracting the insect thorax to drive a micro-air vehicle. In: *Flying insects and robots* (eds. Floreano, D., Zufferey, J.-C., Srinivasan, M. V. and Ellington, C. P.), pp. 207–217. Springer-Verlag: Berlin.

Wootton, R. J., Evans, K. E., Herbert, R. and Smith, C. W. (2000). The hind wing of a desert locust (*Schistocerca gregaria* Forskål) I. Functional morhpology and mode of operation. *J. Exp. Biol.* **203**, 2945–2955.

Wootton, R. J., Herbert, R. C., Young, P. G. and Evans, K. E. (2003). Approaches to the structural modelling of insect wings. *Phil. Trans. R. Soc. Lond. B* **358**, 1577–1587.

Wootton, R. J., Kukalová-Peck, J., Newman, D. J. S. and Muzón, J. (1998). Smart engineering in the mid-Carboniferous: how well could Palaeozoic dragonflies fly? *Science* **282**, 753–761.

Young, J., Walker, S. M., Bomphrey, R. J., Taylor, G. K. and Thomas, A. L. R. (2009). Details of insect wing design and deformation enhance aerodynamic function and flight efficiency. *Science* **325**, 1549–1552.

Zarnack, W. (1972). Flugbiophysik der Wanderheuschrecke (*Locusta migratoria* L.) I. Die Bewegungen der Vorderflügel. *J. Comp. Physiol.* **78**, 394–398.

3

Bio-Inspiration of Morphing for Micro Air Vehicles

Gregg Abate[1] and Wei Shyy[2]

[1] *Air Force Research Laboratory, Eglin AFB, Florida, USA*
[2] *Department of Mechanical Engineering, The Hong Kong University of Science and Technology, PRC*

3.1 Micro Air Vehicles

Micro air vehicles, or MAVs, are a relatively new class of flight vehicles made possible in the past 15 years by the ever-increasing advances in the micro-electronics industry coupled with continuing research in conventional aero-sciences. MAVs are a class of vehicles where the largest dimension is on the order of centimeters. The challenge for MAVs was set out by McMichael of the Defense Advanced Research Projects Agency (DARPA) in the mid-1990s (McMichael and Francis 1997). The challenge was to build and fly a MAV whose largest dimension was no greater than 15 centimeters. The issues associated with the fixed and flapping wing MAV aerodynamics are reviewed by Shyy *et al.* (1999). This challenge was met by both rigid wing platform exemplified by Aerovironment's Black Widow MAV (Grasmeyer and Keennon 2001), and flexible wing platform originated by researchers from the University of Florida (Ifju *et al.* 2002), and began a flurry of activity in this class of flight vehicle for the past 10 or more years.

MAVs are characterized by small vehicle size (O 10 cm or smaller), low flight speed (O 10 m/s), and low Reynolds number (O 1000–100,000), resulting in challenges not well addressed in the traditional aerospace literature. Aside from the typical hobbyist's interest in building and flying very small-scale vehicles, the utilitarian need to develop MAVs is the desire for increased situational awareness (especially in urban environments), remote sensing capability, "over the hill" reconnaissance, precision payload delivery, and aid in rescue missions. MAVs can provide a user with the "bird's eye" perspective for situational awareness that has never before been encountered.

The development of the MAVs began the focus on miniaturization of aerospace flight vehicles to smaller and smaller sizes never before considered for practical purposes. The

Morphing Aerospace Vehicles and Structures, First Edition. Edited by John Valasek.
© 2012 John Wiley & Sons, Ltd. Published 2012 by John Wiley & Sons, Ltd.

AeroVironment BATMAV (http://www.avinc.com/glossary/batmav) or the ARA Nighthawk (http://www.ara.com/robotics/Nighthawk.html) are militarized versions of MAVs that have been designed to satisfy the strict requirements for military procurement. However, numerous civil applications exist as well. As the ability to design, build, and fly MAVs began to improve, new applications for MAVs began to emerge. With the ever-evolving capability of the micro-electronics industry, driven in large part by smart phones and other personal electronic devices, useful payloads for MAVs began to be developed which include imagery, acoustic, and chemical sensors. In many ways, security forces, both civil and military, simply need a way to get the latest smart phone to a remote location and MAVs are the perfect size for such a concept. Other advances in micro-electronics, composite materials, and micro-electro-mechanical devices (MEMs) have opened up a wide realm of capability for MAVs.

Figures 3.1–3.3 depict examples of MAVs that have been developed in recent years. MAVs can be considered a sub-class of uninhabited air vehicles (UAVs). UAVs have been developed in recent years by leveraging traditional aerospace science technologies. However, the scientific and engineering disciplines that are well understood and employed in larger UAV development do not scale linearly or proportionally with decreased size. For instance, a MAV that is 50% the size of a larger UAV will have a mass that is ∼88% and moments of inertia that are ∼97% smaller than that of the full-sized UAV if everything were scaled down exactly the same. The resulting air loading for MAVs is much smaller than that of a larger UAV which leads to very lightweight MAV designs. Such concepts are much more susceptible to disturbances, such as gusts, to which larger UAVs are immune.

One great advantage of MAVs is that their small size results in very light structural loadings. As a result, morphing becomes much more practical at this scale. The challenge, however, is still the design of actuated surfaces with minimal weight penalty. Traditional morphing of aerospace vehicles includes deployment of flaps or slats and, to a lesser extent, wing sweep. However, because MAVs are in the exact size and flight regime of natural flyers, Nature has shown a much more varied approach to morphing that includes full wing articulation where

Figure 3.1   Example of a modern-day micro air vehicle. Courtesy of Prof. Sergey Shkarayev, University of Arizona

Figure 3.2 Example of a modern-day micro air vehicle. Courtesy of Prof. Peter Ifju, University of Florida

wing sweep, dihedral, size, and span are varied as well as the wing being made of passive deformable structures.

3.2 MAV Design Concepts

Imagine, if you will, a small flying air vehicle the size of a bird (e.g. a cardinal or pigeon) that can perform flight maneuvers comparable to the bird. Such a vehicle could provide imagery or other sensory data and communicate that data to a remote ground station. Emergency services could use such a vehicle to get imagery and other information in circumstances where human investigation is not possible or safe, such as response to natural disasters. Police and other peace-keeping forces could use these vehicles to gather intelligence information about nefarious activities. The small size of the vehicle would allow them to fly closer to the ground and to penetrate areas previously inaccessible by larger unmanned vehicles to gather information about covert activities. Such are the design concepts for the micro air vehicle.

MAVs are envisioned to get below the present-day capability of unmanned air systems and fly "below the rooftops" as depicted in Figure 3.4. If you have ever been in a city, you have no doubt been amazed at the ability of birds (noticeably pigeons) to deftly maneuver about in

Figure 3.3 Example of a modern-day micro air vehicle. Courtesy of AeroVironment, Inc.

Figure 3.4   Biologically inspired micro air vehicle flying "below the rooftops"

the complex environs of the city. While many MAVs exist and fly at this scale, the ability of MAVs to maneuver and achieve agility as seen in nature still remains elusive.

Now imagine a similarly capable vehicle the size of a large insect (e.g. a locust or dragonfly). Here this vehicle can access many smaller regions especially indoor applications such as buildings or caves, as depicted in Figure 3.5. Such a vehicle would have the ability to hover and transition to forward flight and would be sufficiently small to maneuver in very tight quarters. How many times have you heard the expression "I wish I could be a fly on the wall" when referring to eavesdropping. That is exactly the concept behind the "nano air vehicle" or NAV. The nano air vehicle, another design challenge put forward by DARPA in 2005 (http://www.darpa.mil/dso/thrusts/materials/multfunmat/nav/index.htm), is designed to push the design space for flight vehicles even smaller. A gross oversimplification is that MAVs are

Figure 3.5   Flapping wing MAV concept

Figure 3.6   Rotary wing nano air vehicle concept. Courtesy of Prox Dynamics, AS

of the order of "bird-sized" while NAVs are of the order of "insect-sized." While no exact demarcation exists, this loose definition will serve its purpose here.

To date, nano air vehicles still remain mostly a research endeavor. There are no examples of fixed wing NAVs at the size and scale previously mentioned. Prox Dynamics (http://www.proxdynamics.com/) has been successful in developing some of the world's smallest rotary wing NAVs, as depicted in Figure 3.6. A large research endeavor is currently ongoing at the time of writing in flapping wing technology specifically focused on MAVs and NAVs. One such example is depicted in Figure 3.7. While nature has demonstrated a keen ability of flapping-wing flyers to be quite adept but similarly scaled, human-engineered, flight vehicles still in early research and development stage.

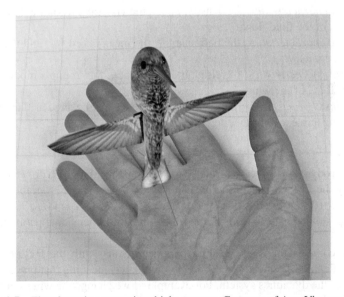

Figure 3.7   Flapping wing nano air vehicle concept. Courtesy of AeroVironment, Inc.

3.3 Technical Challenges for MAVs

Of course, the enabling of the MAV/NAV concept is not simply an exercise in miniaturization. The physics which enable flight and which are well understood at larger aircraft scales do not scale linearly nor proportionally at the very small "micro" scale.

Most notable is the Reynolds number which is the ratio of inertial to viscous force within a fluid. At large aircraft scale, the Reynolds number is on the order of millions. However, at the micro/nano scale, the Reynolds number is much lower, on the order of 1000–100,000. The implication of this is that the desirable airfoil and wing design experiences a departure from traditional designs at the large scale.

Unsteady aerodynamics plays a much more important role at the MAV/NAV scale. At traditional large aircraft sizes, the aerodynamics is largely treated in the "steady" regime. However, at the MAV and NAV scale, unsteady aerodynamics is the norm. This is especially true for natural flyers that rely on flapping flight for aerodynamic force production.

The scaling effect on weight places a strong influence in MAV designs. The weight of an airframe decreases as the cube of the scaling factor. That is, an airframe that is one-half the size of another will weigh one-eighth the weight, if scaled perfectly. Thus, the wings of the smaller vehicle need not produce as much lift in the scaled-down version and can therefore be smaller. The implications of this are that the structural design of the wing will also be a radical departure from large-scale aircraft. A complex monocoque wing structure no longer is necessary or ideal. Overall, as in nature, a thin-wing design is a preferred shape at the MAV scale.

Other important issues when conducting research in this regard is that there are a number of scaling parameters (Shyy *et al.* 2008a; Shyy *et al.* 2010). Consider the following relevant physical quantities:

1. *fluid and flow characteristics*: the density, ρ_f and the viscosity, μ, of the fluid; the reference velocity, U_{ref}, of the fluid flow;
2. *the geometric characteristics*: the half span, R, the mean chord, c_m, and the thickness, h_s, of the wing geometry;
3. *the structural characteristics*: the structural density, ρ_s, the Young's modulus, E, and the Poisson's ratio, v, of the wing;
4. *the kinematics characteristics*: the flapping amplitude, ϕ_a, the angular flapping frequency, ω, the pitching angle, α, of the wing kinematics.

The resulting aerodynamic force, F, is related to these characteristics via dimensionless groups, as governed by the Pi-theorem. In the present scenario, there are 13 variables and 3 dimensions leading to 10 non-dimensional parameters. With ρ_f, U_{ref}, and c_m as the basis variables, the dimensional analysis leads to the following non-dimensional parameters, shown in Table 3.1.

A major outcome is that these scaling parameters vary with the factors such as wing dimension and flapping frequency in different power laws, meaning that one cannot maintain the invariance of the dynamics system. For example, if we change the wing sizes and flapping frequency from the design to the laboratory scale to conduct wind tunnel testing, then the

Table 3.1 Non-dimensional parameters

Reynolds number	$Re = \dfrac{\rho_f U_{ref} c_m}{\mu}$	Ratio between the inertial and the viscous forces in the fluids
Aspect ratio	$AR = \dfrac{4R}{c_m}$	Wing span normalized with the chord
Normalized thickness	$h_s^* = h_s/c_m$	Thickness normalized with the chord
Density ratio	$\rho^* = \rho_s/\rho_f$	Ratio between the structural density and the fluid density
Poisson's ratio	v	Ratio between the transverse and the axial strain
Effective stiffness	$\Pi_1 \dfrac{E h_s^{*3}}{12(1-v)\rho_f U_{ref}^2}$	Ratio between the elastic bending forces and the aerodynamic force
Reduced frequency	$k = \dfrac{\omega c_m}{2U_{ref}}$	Measure of unsteadiness by comparing the spatial wavelength of the flow disturbance with the chord
Strouhal number	$St = kAR\phi_a$	Ratio between the flapping speed and the reference velocity
(effective) Angle of attack	α	Curvature of the streamlines leading to pressure changes on the wing surface
Force coefficient	$C_F = \dfrac{F}{1/2\rho_f U_{ref}^2(2c_m^2 AR)}$	Aerodynamic force normalized with the dynamic pressure and the wing surface area

above scaling parameters will assume different values, hence changing the definition of the problem. This matter has significant implications for vehicle development and performance testing.

3.4 Flight Characteristics of MAVs and NAVs

MAVs (and NAVs) are characterized by small size, light weight, very low moments of inertia, low flight speeds, and a high susceptibility to gusts and turbulence. For the roles and missions envisioned for MAVs, there is also a requirement to be able to hover and/or land precisely for long-term observation. All these characteristics make the flight mechanics' design and development of MAVs and NAVs extremely challenging.

One unique difference for MAV/NAV design is the emphasis on agility vs. stability. As detailed in the previous sections, MAVs will require the ability to perform aggressive maneuvers to avoid obstacles and reject gusts. Unlike a conventional aircraft design where there is a designed flight condition that will be optimized, MAVs will use a wide range of speeds and flight regimes. This will be enabled by their very small inertias and light weight. It stands to reason, then, that MAVs need to be more agile rather than stable. That is not to say that MAVs need to have destabilizing flight characteristics but rather have a reduced amount of stability in order to perform aggressive maneuvers. Achieving this balance between stability and agility will be influenced by different factors at the MAV/NAV scale vs. full scale.

Because of the aggressive maneuvering envisioned for MAVs and because of the very low Reynolds number regime in which they fly, MAVs will tend to operate in more of an unsteady aerodynamic condition than their larger air vehicle counterparts. Whereas a large aircraft enjoys a steady flow for a majority of its operations, MAVs will be in a near-constant unsteady flowfield condition. In fact, flight control of MAVs can be described as "management of unsteady aerodynamics." New autonomous flight control concepts and strategies will need to be developed specifically for this type of flight condition.

3.5 Bio-Inspired Morphing Concepts for MAVs

Because of the unique characteristics and flight regime of MAVs, it is clear that innovative airframe concepts are required to provide them with the capabilities needed for their envisioned missions. The ability to change the shape or configuration of an airframe while in flight has been shown to be a powerful technique to achieve multiple flight conditions (Niksch *et al.* 2008; Niksch *et al.* 2009).

Consider both the US F-111 and the F-14 fighter jets. The designers could not find a compromise wing platform that performed well at both low-speed and high-speed flight conditions. In order to meet performance specs, the designers of these aircraft chose to allow the wings to change sweep while in flight as shown in Figure 3.8. It was an enormous challenge to design this capability and the design and construction of the wing-box for each of these

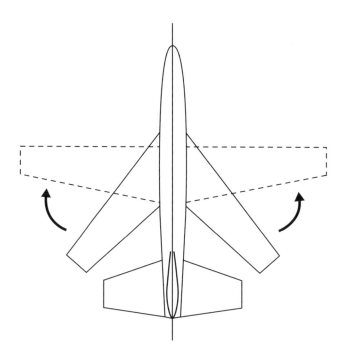

Figure 3.8 Swing wing concept of morphing

aircraft was a difficult endeavor. The additional weight of the swing-wing mechanism impacted the overall design of the aircraft but the performance pay-off was significant.

Fortunately, because of the small size of MAVs, the structural loading is greatly reduced. This allows much easier implementation of morphing concepts at this scale. That is not to say that morphing is not a challenge. If anything, the challenge is greater because of the wider range of morphing available at this scale which is simply not possible at larger scales. Given the size of MAVs which so closely match that of natural flyers, it makes sense to study and understand how natural flyers utilize morphing so that engineered systems can leverage these concepts.

"Morphing" refers to a change in the airframe configuration which results in a change in the performance of the vehicle. There are many types of morphing as well as a wide range in which morphing can be implemented. Already mentioned were the F-14 and F-111 which used wing sweep as a form of morphing. Here, in low-speed configurations, the wings will have little sweep for enhanced performance. As the speed of the aircraft increases, the wings are swept back. At the highest speeds, in the supersonic regime, the wings are fully swept back for optimal performance. The ability to change wing sweep while in flight is an extreme example of morphing reserved for high-performance military aircraft. However, nearly all aircraft have more subtle forms of morphing, such as flap deployment and retractable landing gear. In all of these cases, the morphing is referred to as "active." That is, the pilot or flight control system has control of the shape change and will initiate the change based upon pre-determined criteria.

"Passive" morphing is the change of the vehicle configuration with no control actuation from the pilot or control system. An example of passive morphing is wing deformation due to aerodynamic loading. If you have ever seen a B-52 parked on a ramp, you will notice how the wing tips nearly touch the ground. However, in flight, the aerodynamic loading on the wings makes them nearly horizontal. This is an example of a passive deformation. In most cases, this passive deformation of the structure due to aerodynamic loadings is known *a priori* and is incorporated into the system design. For instance, passive morphing can be the deformation of a pliant wing as the result of the distributed aerodynamic loads. Another example of passive morphing is the massive deformation of insect wings during the flapping cycle.

A more advanced passive form of morphing based upon bio-inspiration is the design of pliant wing MAVs to reduce flight disturbances. Here, a compliant or flexible wing is allowed to deform and bend as the wing is aerodynamically loaded in flight. Energy due to gusts is stored in the deformation of the wing and is released when the aero-loading is removed. The inspiration for this type of morphing is seen in Nature in a number of instances. In flapping wing examples, high speed photography has shown significant deformation of wings during the flapping cycle. This idea is in contrast to early attempts to understand flapping wing aerodynamics in which rigid flat plates were studied. Another example of fixed wing passive deformation is in that of birds. Cameras that have been carried by large birds and which have recorded wing movement during flight have shown deformations which zoologists believe are the results of passive deformation of the wing due to wing aerodynamic loading.

The merits of morphing are quite clear. If the structure can deform or change to produce optimal performance in different regimes, then the overall performance of the system will benefit. Oftentimes the design of an air vehicle is a compromise in performance. For instance, for low speed vehicles, long slender wings will have minimal induced drag; however, such a wing is difficult to construct because it needs a stiffer structure that increases the system weight. Therefore, overall aerodynamic performance is less than optimal.

There are numerous examples of biological-inspired morphing when it comes to MAVs. We will discuss several in this section.

3.5.1   Wing Planform

Every bird has the ability to fold its wings. The obvious advantages are for storage when not flying; otherwise, the birds could not function on the ground. The ability of the bird to fold its wings gives it a tremendous aerodynamic advantage as well. The bird can adjust the size of the wing planform to provide optimal performance. For instance, large raptors (eagles, falcons, etc.) can glide with their wings fully extended but they merely have to pull them in to perform a flight maneuver such as attacking prey. It has been noted that falcons can reach speeds of 300 mph when going into a vertical dive. Were the falcon not able to tuck its wings in, it would not be able to achieve these speeds. Additionally, in evasive maneuvers, a bird merely has to tuck one wing in to provide a rapid roll maneuver.

3.5.2   Airfoil Shape

Some natural flyers have the ability to change the airfoil profile during flight. Nearly all birds, insects, and bats have very thin wings in which there is a semi-rigid spar (bones in the case of birds and bats) and a compliant wing covering (e.g., feathers). At the low Reynolds number at which natural flyers operate, smooth airfoil shapes are not necessarily required for force generation. Dragonflies are a well known example, whose wings are of corrugated cambers. Furthermore, as in all natural systems, the parts of the organism serve many functions and no part is optimal in any one function. The surface structure of a bat wing largely consists of a very thin elastic membrane. This membrane deforms due to the wing loading during the flapping cycle. Most birds when gliding can splay their feathers to modulate the shape of the airfoil as well.

3.5.3   Tail Modulation

Among the natural flyers, birds have tail feathers to help provide directional control. Images have been captured in flight (Taylor *et al.* 2007) that clearly show the tail feathers splaying and moving constantly while the bird flies and maneuvers. The bird's tail feathers are very much akin to modern aircraft with empennages with the exception of the vertical stabilizer. Birds control both pitch and yaw through their movement of the tail to a large extent and their wings to a smaller extent.

3.5.4   CG Shifting

One of the oldest forms of flight control is the movement of the center of gravity (CG). Hang gliders rely on this form of modulation for control. While not really a strong morphing concept, the ability of a natural flyer to shift its center of gravity does give it enhanced agility. When birds begin a perch maneuver, they will typically throw their legs down to initiate a large pitch rate and the wings will feather as well.

3.5.5 Flapping Modulation

A mild form of morphing is the ability of a natural flyer to modulate its flapping parameters. Most insects when they want to maneuver will initiate some asymmetric flapping of their wings in order to produce a turning moment. Sometimes changing the flap amplitude will suffice to give a turning moment. Such an asymmetric flapping may occur over many flapping cycles but at the high flapping rates ($\sim$200 Hz for insects), it can produce fast turning.

3.6 Outlook for Morphing at the MAV/NAV scale

It has long been realized that the ability of an air vehicle to morph while in flight could provide tremendous performance benefits. However, at large aircraft scales, such capabilities often come at a high expense. On the other hand, due to the small weight associated with micro air vehicles, morphability is a much more achievable prospect. The added benefit is that at this scale, there is a wealth of natural flying systems from which to take inspiration.

However, the engineer must be cautious when looking to nature for inspiration. Natural flyers need to balance the various competing needs including, flight, mating, survival, feeding, etc. An aeronautical engineer might look at a bird or bat and make an inference that make sense in engineering terms yet is not correct in biological terms. For instance, if we look at birds and notice that they do not have vertical tails, an engineer might come to the conclusion that a vertical tail is not necessary or that the bird is an inefficient flyer. The fact may be that a vertical tail on a bird could be a hindrance when it is nesting and it adapts its flying without such a tail. This is where a biologist or zoologist who has formal training with natural flyers will be invaluable. Together the engineer and the zoologist can study the natural flyer and come to valid conclusions about the creature. Only then can true bio-inspiration at the MAV/NAV scale be realized.

3.7 Future Challenges

The main challenges for bio-inspired morphing of micro air vehicles include: understanding and quantifying the performance advantages of biological systems, developing materials and structures that leverage natural design, better understanding of fundamental physics at the MAV/NAV scale, and system control design.

Scientists and engineers need to work closely with biologists and zoologists to understand those features that enable natural flight. For instance, it is understood that wings produce the lift required for flight in natural systems but not all wing features are flight-related. Only by working across the scientific disciplines will scientists and engineers be able to uncover those features that enable the desired flight performance in natural flyers. This may result in engineered wings that have physical properties different from that of a natural flyer's wing but result in improved performance. This is bio-inspiration versus strict bio-mimicry.

Developing engineered systems that leverage biological designs is a challenge as well. Bird wings, bat wing membranes, insect wings, etc. have some interesting material properties that lend themselves to the ability to fly. The amount of deflection of a bat's wing is due to the skeletal structure and the material properties of the membrane. Engineers and scientists may be able to study the wings of natural flyers but may not be able to match the physical properties of nature with an engineered material. Much research is ongoing into the complex phenomena related to aerodynamics and aero-structural interactions of flapping wings (Shyy *et al.* 2008b), which will help quantify those features of a wing structure crucial to flight at the MAV/NAV scale. Yet more work will be needed for advanced materials to benefit from such insight.

There have been many efforts ongoing to increase our understanding of the fluid physics of biology-inspired mechanisms that simultaneously provide lift and thrust, enable hover, and grant high flight control authority, while minimizing power consumption. Detailed experimental efforts and first principles-based computational modeling and analysis capabilities are essential in support of the investigation of issues related to fluid-structure interactions, unsteady freestream (wind gust), and unsteady aerodynamics. Other issues for further research are:

1. In order to support the broad flight characteristics such as take-off, forward flight of varying speed, wind gust response, hover, perch, threat avoidance, station tracking, and payload variations, a variety of wing kinematics and body/leg maneuvers will need to be employed. Considering the variations in size and flapping patterns of natural flyers, there is significant potential and need for us to further refine our knowledge regarding the interplay between kinematics and aerodynamics.
2. It has been established that local flexibility can significantly affect aerodynamics in both fixed and flapping wings (Shyy *et al.* 2008b; Shyy *et al.* 2010). Furthermore, as already discussed, insects' wing properties are anisotropic, with the spanwise bending stiffness about 1 to 2 orders of magnitude larger than the chordwise bending one. As the vehicle size changes, the scaling parameters cannot all maintain invariance due to different scaling trends associated with them. This means that if necessary, for measurement precision, instrumentation preference, etc., that one cannot do a laboratory test of a flapping wing design using different sizes or flapping frequencies. A closely coordinated computational and experimental framework is needed in order to facilitate the exploration of the vast design space (which can have $O(10^2)$ or more design variables including geometry, material properties, kinematics, flight conditions, and environmental parameters) while searching for optimal and robust designs.
3. The implications of the dynamics and stability of a flapping vehicle, in association with flapping wing aerodynamics, are still inadequately understood. In particular, the vehicle stability via passive shape deformation due to flexible structures needs to be addressed.
4. Bio-inspired mechanisms need to be developed for the flapping wing. These mechanisms include, for example, joints and distributed actuation to enable flapping and morphing. Most importantly, these mechanisms should be capable of mitigating wind gust.
5. Vision-based sensing techniques will be very helpful for flight control as well as estimating the aero-elastic states of the vehicle. For example, both rigid-body and deformation states of a vehicle can be extracted by noting frequency-varying properties by optical means.

Finally, one last key challenge inspired by natural flyers is the sensor-rich characteristic of the system (Zbikowski 2004). Natural flying systems are rife with sensors that provide information about the state of the animal. Control concepts for MAVs may also need to be inspired by Nature as well. Most modern control approaches are a "model-based" approach in which the plant is well characterized. However, in a realm where unsteady aerodynamics is the norm, a neural-network or learning-type control concept may be a better choice (Lampton *et al.* 2009,

2010). Biological systems have many sensors and state estimation is performed by evaluating feedback from many inputs. Advanced control concepts will be required to accurately control MAVs in the complex environments for which they are envisioned.

3.8   Conclusion

Micro air vehicles will rely heavily on active and passive morphing for flight control. Scaling limitations preclude engineers from engineering MAVs in the same way as larger aircraft. Natural flyers have clearly shown that morphing is essential to agile flight performance at the micro scale. Inspiration from Nature will give us insight into how to manage the complex flight environment, but it is ultimately up to scientists and engineers to implement such concepts on man-made systems. Work in this area has recently begun, and it is clear that significant progress needs to be made before MAVs can perform real missions envisioned by the community.

References

Grasmeyer JM and Keennon MT 2001 Development of the Black Widow Micro Air Vehicle, AIAA Paper 2001-0127. Paper presented at the 39th AIAA Aerospace Sciences Meeting, Reno, NV, January.

Ifju, P., Jenkins, D., Ettinger, S., Lian, Y., Shyy, W., and Waszak, M. (2002). "Flexible Wing-Based Micro Air Vehicles," *AIAA 40th Aerospace Sciences Meeting & Exhibit*, Paper No. 2002-0705.

Lampton A, Niksch A, and Valasek J 2009 Reinforcement learning of morphing airfoils with aerodynamic and structural effects. *Journal of Aerospace Computing, Information, and Communication*, 6(1): 30–50.

Lampton A, Niksch A and Valasek J (2010) Reinforcement learning of a morphing airfoil-policy and discrete learning analysis. *Journal of Aerospace Computing, Information, and Communication*, 7(8): 241–260.

McMichael J M and Francis M S 1997 *Micro Air Vehicles: Toward a New Dimension in Flight*. DARPA, USA.

Niksch A, Valasek J, Strganac T, and Carlson L 2008 Morphing aircraft dynamical model: longitudinal shape changes, AIAA-2008-6567. In *Proceedings of the AIAA Atmospheric Flight Mechanics Conference*, Honolulu, HI, 19 August.

Niksch A, Valasek J, Strganac T, and Carlson L 2009 Six degree-of-freedom dynamical model of a morphing aircraft, AIAA-2009-5849. In *Proceedings of the AIAA Guidance, Navigation, and Control Conference*, Chicago, IL, 11 August.

Shyy, W., Berg, M., and Ljungqvist, D. (1999). "Flapping and Flexible Wings for Biological and Micro Air Vehicles," *Progress in Aerospace Sciences*, Vol. 35, pp. 155–205.

Shyy W, Aono H, Chimakurthi SK, Trizila P, Kang C-K, Cesnik CES, and Liu H 2010 Recent progress in flapping wing aerodynamics and aeroelasticity. *Progress in Aerospace Sciences*, 46: 284–327.

Shyy W, Lian Y, Tang J, Liu H, Trizila P, Stanford B, Bernal LP, Cesnik CES, Friedmann P and Ifju P 2008a Computational aerodynamics of low Reynolds number plunging, pitching and flexible wings for MAV applications. *Acta Mechanica Sinica*, 24: 351–373.

Shyy W, Lian Y, Tang J, Viieru D, and Liu H 2008b *Aerodynamics of Low Reynolds Number Flyers*. Cambridge University Press, New York.

Taylor GK, Bacic M, Carruthers AC, Gillies J, Ozawa Y, and Thomas ALR 2007 Flight control mechanisms in birds of prey, AIAA Paper 2007-0039. Paper presented at the 45th AIAA Aerospace Sciences Meeting, Reno, NV, January.

Zbikowski R 2004 Sensor-rich feedback control. *IEEE Instrumentation & Measurement Magazine*, 7(3): 19–26.

Part II

Control and Dynamics

4

Morphing Unmanned Air Vehicle Intelligent Shape and Flight Control

John Valasek[1], Kenton Kirkpatrick[1], and Amanda Lampton[2]
[1]*Texas A&M University, USA*
[2]*Systems Technology Incorporated, USA*

4.1 Introduction

Although there are several definitions and interpretations of the term morphing, it is generally understood that the concept can refer to both small-scale and large-scale shape changes or transfigurations. Two distinct classes of morphing have been identified: *Morphing for Mission Adaptation*, and *Morphing for Control* (Bowman *et al.* 2002). In the context of flight vehicles, Morphing for Mission Adaptation is a large-scale, relatively slow, in-flight shape change to enable a single vehicle to perform multiple diverse mission profiles. Conversely, Morphing for Control is often a small-scale or component level in-flight physical or virtual shape change, used to achieve multiple control objectives such as noise suppression, flutter suppression, load alleviation and active separation control. This chapter addresses the problem of Morphing for Mission Adaptation.

Morphing research to date has not adequately addressed or described the supervisory and control aspects of shape changing or morphing. In the context of intelligent systems, three essential functionalities of a practical Morphing for Mission Adaptation capability are

1. When to reconfigure.
2. How to reconfigure.
3. Learning to reconfigure.

When to reconfigure is driven by mission priorities/tasks, and leads to optimal shape being a system parameter. In the context of a reconfigurable vehicle such as an aircraft, each shape

---

results in performance values (speed, range, endurance, etc.) at specific flight conditions (Mach number, altitude, angle-of-attack, and sideslip angle). It is a major issue, as the inability of a given aircraft to perform multiple missions successfully can directly be attributed to shape, at least if aerodynamic performance is the primary consideration. This is because for a given task or mission, there is usually an ideal or optimal vehicle shape, e.g. configuration (Bowman *et al.* 2002). However, this optimality criterion may not be known over the entire flight envelope in actual practice, and the mission may be modified or completely changed during operation. *How* to reconfigure is a problem of sensing, actuation, and control (Scott *et al.* 1998). These problems are important and challenging since large shape changes produce time-varying vehicle properties, and especially, time-varying moments and products of inertia. The controller must therefore be sufficiently robust to handle these potentially wide variations. *Learning* to reconfigure is perhaps the most challenging of the three functionalities, and the one which has received the least attention. Even if optimal shapes are known, the actuation scheme(s) to produce them may be only poorly understood, or not understood at all; Reinforcement Learning is therefore a candidate approach. It is important that learning how to reconfigure is also life-long learning. This will enable the vehicle to be more survivable, operate more safely, and be multi-role.

Control law design for morphing air vehicles has seen a comparatively moderate level of research activity. Boothe *et al.* (2005) and Abdulrahim and Lind (2005) consider the case of variable wing dihedral in which a vortex lattice method is used to calculate the aerodynamics. Desired dynamics for each mission phase are chosen, and H_∞ model-following controllers are developed for each. This chapter develops a novel approach and methodology for intelligent control of a morphing unmanned air vehicle, starting with a high-level description of the functionality of the Adaptive-Reinforcement Learning Control (A-RLC) architecture. This is followed by detailed developments of the learning agent, air vehicle model and simulation, smart actuators, and adaptive controller. It is completed with simulation results and conclusions.

4.2   A-RLC Architecture Functionality

The Adaptive-Reinforcement Learning Control (A-RLC) technique first introduced in Valasek *et al.* (2005) addresses the optimal shape changing of an entire vehicle, rather than isolated components or individual actuation. Figure 4.1 shows that A-RLC is composed of two subsystems: Reinforcement Learning (RL) and Structured Adaptive Model Inversion (SAMI). The two sub-systems interact significantly during both the episodic learning stage, when the optimal shape change policy is learned, and the operational stage, when the plant morphs and tracks a trajectory. For either type of stage, the system functions as follows.

Considering the RL sub-system at the top of Figure 4.1 and moving counterclockwise, the RL module initially commands an arbitrary action from the set of admissible actions. This action is sent to the plant, which produces a shape change. The cost associated with the resultant shape change in terms of system states, parameters, and user defined performance measures, is evaluated with the cost function and then passed to the agent. The agent modifies its action-value function according to Equation 4.6. For the next episode, the agent chooses a new action based on the current policy and its updated action-value function, and the sequence repeats itself. The RL sub-system was improved by applying Sequential Function Approximation

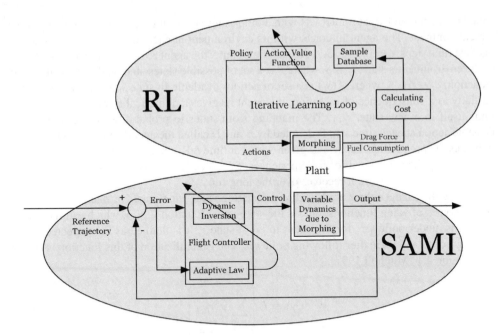

Figure 4.1   Adaptive-Reinforcement Learning Control architecture

to generalize the learning from previously experienced quantized states and actions to the continuous state-action space (Valasek *et al.* 2008).

Considering the SAMI sub-system at the bottom of Figure 4.1, shape changes in the plant due to actions generated by the RL agent cause the plant dynamics to change. By calculating commanded moments, the SAMI controller tracks a reference trajectory irrespective of the changing dynamics of the vehicle caused by these shape changes. SAMI is a nonlinear technique based on the concepts of Feedback Linearization, Dynamic Inversion, and Structured Model Reference Adaptive control. The dynamic inversion is approximate since the system parameters are assumed to be modeled inaccurately. An adaptive control structure is wrapped around the dynamic inverter to account for uncertainties in the system parameters (Subbarao 2001). SAMI has been shown to be effective for tracking reference trajectories of spacecraft (Subbarao *et al.* 2000), planetary entry vehicles (Restrepo and Valasek 2008), and aircraft (Subbarao *et al.* 2001). The SAMI approach has also been extended to handle actuator failures (Tandale and Valasek 2006; Marwaha and Valasek 2011), and to facilitate correct adaptation in the presence of actuator saturation (Tandale and Valasek 2004, 2007).

The following sections detail the individual components of the RL and SAMI sub-systems, and their interactions within the A-RLC architecture. The RL components are addressed first.

4.3   Learning Air Vehicle Shape Changes

4.3.1   *Overview of Reinforcement Learning*

Reinforcement Learning (RL) is a method of learning from interaction between an agent and its environment to achieve a specified goal (Mitchell 1997). The learner and decision-maker is called the agent, and what it interacts with, comprising everything outside the agent, is called the environment. The agent interacts with its environment at each instance of a sequence of discrete time steps, $t = 0, 1, 2, 3....$ At each time step t, the agent receives some representation of the environment's state, $s_t \in S$, where S is a set of possible states, and on that basis it selects an action, $a_t \in A(s_t)$, where $A(s_t)$ is a set of actions available in state s_t. One time step later, partially as a consequence of its action, the agent receives a numerical reward, $r_{t+1} = R$, and finds itself in a new state, s_{t+1}. The mapping from states to probabilities of selecting each possible action at each time step is denoted by π and is called the agent's policy. Thus $\pi_t(s, a)$ indicates the probability that $a_t = a$ given $s_t = s$ at time t. RL methods specify how the agent changes its policy as a result of its experiences. Specifically, the agent's goal is to maximize the total amount of reward it receives over the long run.

Almost all RL algorithms are based on estimating value functions. For one policy π, there are two types of value functions. One is the state-value function $V^\pi(s)$, which estimates how good it is, under policy π, for the agent to be in state s. It is defined as the expected return starting from s and thereafter following policy π. The generalization of this function is shown in Equation 4.1 (Mitchell 1997).

$$V^\pi(s_t) \equiv E\left[\sum_{k=0}^{\infty} \gamma^k r_{t+k}\right] \tag{4.1}$$

where γ is the discount factor and r_{t+k} is the sequence of rewards.

The other state-value function is the action-value function $Q^\pi(s, a)$, which estimates how good it is, under policy π, for the agent to perform action a in state s. It is defined as the expected return starting from s, taking action a, and thereafter following policy π. It is related to the state-value function by Equation 4.2, where $\delta(s, a)$ denotes the state resulting from applying action a to state s.

$$Q^\pi(s, a) \equiv r(s, a) + \gamma V^*(\delta(s, a)) \tag{4.2}$$

The process of computing $V^\pi(s)$ or $Q^\pi(s, a)$ is called policy evaluation. π can be improved to a better π' that, given a state, always selects the action, out of all possible actions, with the best value based on $V^\pi(s)$ or $Q^\pi(s, a)$. This process is called policy improvement. $V^{\pi'}(s)$ or $Q^{\pi'}(s, a)$ can then be computed to improve π' to an even better π''. The ultimate goal of RL is to find the optimal policy π^* that has the optimal state-value function, denoted by $V^*(s)$ and defined as $V^*(s) = max_\pi V^\pi(s)$, or the optimal action-value function, denoted by $Q^*(s, a)$ and defined as $Q^*(s, a) = max_\pi Q^\pi(s, a)$. This recursive way of finding an optimal policy is called policy iteration. As a result Q^* can be written in terms of V^*.

$$Q^*(s, a) \equiv E\left[r(s, a) + \gamma V^*(\delta(s, a))\right]$$
$$= E\left[r(s, a)\right] + E\left[\gamma V^*(\delta(s, a))\right]$$
$$= E\left[r(s, a)\right] + \gamma \sum_{s'} P(s'|s, a) V^*(s') \tag{4.3}$$

where $P(s'|s, a)$ is the probability of taking action a in state s will produce the next state s'.

To make this function more manageable, Q can be re-expressed recursively.

$$Q^* (s, a) = E \left[r (s, a)\right] + \gamma \sum_{s'} P \left(s'|s, a\right) \max_{a'} Q \left(s', a'\right)$$ (4.4)

Equation 4.4 can be further modified into a training rule that iteratively updates each $Q(s,a)$ as it is visited and converges to $Q^*(s, a)$. This training rule is defined in Equation 4.5.

$$Q_n (s, a) \leftarrow (1 - \alpha) Q_{n-1} (s, a) + \alpha \left[r + \gamma \max_{a'} Q_{n-1} \left(s', a'\right)\right]$$ (4.5)

There exist three major methods for policy iteration: Dynamic Programming, Monte Carlo methods, and temporal-difference learning. Dynamic Programming refers to a collection of algorithms that can be used to compute optimal policies given a perfect model of the environment as a Markov decision process (MDP). The key idea is the use of value functions to organize and structure the search for good policies. While classical Dynamic Programming algorithms (Bellman, 1957; Bellman and Dreyfus 1962; Bellman and Kalaba 1965) are very important from a theoretical point of view, they are of limited utility in RL, both because of their assumption of a perfect model and their great computational expense.

Monte Carlo methods are employed to estimate functions using an iterative, incremental procedure. The term "Monte Carlo" is sometimes used more broadly for any estimation method whose operation involves a significant random component. In the present context it represents methods which solve the RL problem based on averaging sample returns. To ensure that well-defined returns are available, they are defined only for episodic tasks, and it is only upon the completion of an episode that value estimates and policies are changed. By comparison with Dynamic Programming, Monte Carlo methods can be used to learn optimal behavior directly from interaction with the environment with no model of the environment's dynamics. They can be used with simulation, and it is easy and efficient to focus Monte Carlo methods on a small subset of the states. However, all Monte Carlo methods for RL have been developed only recently, and their convergence properties are not well understood.

Temporal-Difference methods can be viewed as an attempt to achieve much the same effect as Dynamic Programming, but with less computation and without assuming a perfect model of the environment. Sutton's method of Temporal-Differences is a form of the policy evaluation method in Dynamic Programming which attempts to choose a control policy π_0 (Sutton 1988). The prediction problem becomes that of learning the expected discounted rewards, $V^\pi (i)$, for each state i in S using π_0. With the learned expected discounted rewards, a new policy π_1 can be determined that improves upon π_0. The algorithm may eventually converge to some policy under this iterative improvement procedure, as in Howard's algorithm (Williams and Baird 1993).

Q-Learning is a form of the successive approximations technique of Dynamic Programming, first proposed and developed by Watkins (Watkins and Davan 1989). Q-learning learns the optimal value functions directly, as opposed to fixing a policy and determining the corresponding value functions, like Temporal-Differences. It automatically focuses attention to where it is needed, thereby avoiding the need to sweep over the state-action space. Additionally, it is the first provably convergent direct adaptive optimal control algorithm.

RL has been applied to a wide variety of physical control tasks, both real and simulated. For example, an acrobat system is a two-link, under-actuated robot roughly analogous to a gymnast swinging on a high bar. Controlling such a system by RL has been studied by many researchers (DeJong and Spong 1994: Boone 1997; Sutton 1995). In many applications of RL to control tasks, the state space is too large to enumerate the value function. Some function approximators must be used to compactly represent the value function. Commonly used approaches include neural networks, clustering, nearest-neighbor methods, tile coding, and cerebellar model articulator controller.

4.3.2 Implementation of Shape Change Learning Agent

The agent in the morphing wing problem is its RL agent. It attempts to independently maneuver from some initial state to a final goal state, characterized by the aerodynamic properties of the wing. To reach this goal, the agent endeavors to learn from its interaction with the environment the optimal policy that, given the specific aerodynamic requirements, commands the series of actions that changes the morphing wing's thickness state or camber state toward an optimal shape. The environment is the resulting aerodynamics to which the wing is subjected to. It is assumed that the RL agent has no prior knowledge of the relationship between actions and the thickness and camber of the morphing wing. However, the RL agent does know all possible actions that can be applied. It has accurate, real-time information of the morphing wing shape, the present aerodynamics, and the current reward provided by the environment.

The RL agent uses a 1-step Q-learning method, which is a common off-policy Temporal Difference (TD) control algorithm. In its simplest form it is a modified version of Equation 4.5 and is defined by

$$Q(s, a) \leftarrow Q(s, a) + \alpha \left\{ r + \gamma \max_{a'} Q(s', a') - Q(s, a) \right\} \qquad (4.6)$$

The Q-learning algorithm is illustrated as follows (Sutton and Barto 1998):

Q-Learning
- Initialize $Q(s,a)$ arbitrarily
- Repeat (for each episode)
  - Initialize s
  - Repeat (for each step of the episode)
    * Choose a from s using policy derived from $Q(s,a)$ (e.g. ϵ-Greedy Policy)
    * Take action a, observe r, s'
    * $Q(s, a) \leftarrow Q(s, a) + \alpha \left\{ r + \gamma \max_{a'} Q(s', a') - Q(s, a) \right\}$
    * $s \leftarrow s'$
  - until s is terminal
- return $Q(s,a)$

The agent learns the greedy policy, defined as:

$$\begin{aligned} &\varepsilon - \text{greedy policy} \\ &\text{if}(\text{probability} > 1-\varepsilon) \\ &a = \arg \max_a Q(s, a) \\ &\text{else} \\ &a = rand(a_i) \end{aligned} \qquad (4.7)$$

As the number of learning episodes increases, the learned action-value function $Q(s,a)$ converges asymptotically to the optimal action-value function $Q^*(s, a)$. The method is an off-policy one as it evaluates the target policy (the greedy policy) while following another policy. The policy used in updating $Q(s,a)$ can be a random policy, with each action having the same probability of being selected. The other option is an ϵ-greedy policy, where ε is a small value. The action a with the maximum $Q(s,a)$ is selected with probability 1-ε, otherwise a random action is selected.

If the number of the states and the actions of a RL problem is a small value, its $Q(s,a)$ can be represented using a table, where the action-value for each state-action pair is stored in one entity of the table. Since the RL problem for the morphing vehicle has states (the shape of the wing) in continuous domains, it is impossible to enumerate the action-value for each state-action pair. In essence, there is an infinite number of state-action pairs. One commonly used solution is to artificially quantize the states into discrete sets, thereby reducing the number of state-action pairs that the agent must visit and learn. This reduces the number of state-action pairs while maintaining the integrity of the learned action-value function. For a given problem, experimentation must be conducted to determine what kind of quantization is appropriate for the states. In this chapter several increasingly larger quantizations are considered to determine what the largest allowable step size is. For the problem at hand, this is very important to keep the number of state-action pairs manageable when more state variables are added to the existing thickness and camber states in the form of other morphing parameters.

4.4 Mathematical Modeling of Morphing Air Vehicle

4.4.1 Aerodynamic Modeling

To calculate the aerodynamic properties of the various wing configurations, a constant strength doublet-source panel method is used (Niksch 2009). This method was chosen over other CFD methods because of the success that the authors had using a panel method approach in predicting the aerodynamic effects on a morphing airfoil. The main assumptions are that the flow is incompressible and inviscid. Thus, the model is only valid for the linear range of angle-of-attack. The versatility of this type of model allows easy manipulation of morphing degrees-of-freedom and flight condition parameters. The morphing degrees-of-freedom and flight condition parameters in the model are:

- Wing thickness, t
- Maximum camber
- Location of maximum camber
- Root chord, c_r
- Tip chord, c_t
- Sweep angle, Λ
- Dihedral angle, Γ
- Wing span, b
- Wing angle-of-attack, α

Given this versatility there are also some limitations to the model. Since the model uses a panel method to determine the aerodynamics, it is very sensitive to the grid size, the location of the panels, and the number of panels created. The grid uses cosine spacing for both chordwise and spanwise panels. By utilizing cosine spacing, more panels are placed near the leading and trailing edges of the wing as well as at the root and tip. This type of grid is necessary because many aerodynamic changes occur near the leading and trailing edges as well as at the tips of the wing. As the number of panels decrease, the accuracy of the model also decreases. However, as the number of panels is increased, the computational time of the model increases as well. Thus, a balance is needed between accuracy and computational time. This balance is achieved by defining a set number of panels for which any increase from that number of panels yields a minimal increase in accuracy. For example, if the number of panels were doubled and the accuracy of the model increased by 10%, this increase in the number of panels would be deemed acceptable. However, if this set of panels were increased by 50% and the accuracy increased by less than 1%, then this increase in the number of panels would be deemed unnecessary.

The model also has a limitation on the different types of airfoil sections which can be used. Only NACA 4-Digit Series airfoils are considered here because there are explicit equations which easily describe the upper surface and lower surface geometries. These equations have defined thickness and camber variables, which makes them easy to examine and optimize to achieve the best possible wing shape.

4.4.2 Constitutive Equations

The wing is modeled using a constant strength doublet-source panel method. In order to obtain the equations for aerodynamic forces on a wing, basic potential flow theory is used. The basic equation of potential flow theory (Katz and Plotkin 2001) is Laplace's Equation

$$\nabla^2 \Phi = 0 \tag{4.8}$$

where ∇^2 is the Laplace operator and Φ is the velocity potential. This equation satisfies the inviscid and incompressible flow assumptions to the general conservation equations. Using Green's identity, a solution to Equation 4.8 is formed with a sum of source σ and doublet μ distributions along the boundary, SB.

$$\Phi = -\frac{1}{4\pi} \int_{SB} \left[\sigma \left(\frac{1}{r} \right) - \mu \mathbf{n} \cdot \nabla \left(\frac{1}{r} \right) \right] dS + \Phi_\infty \tag{4.9}$$

Assuming the wake convects at the trailing edge of the wing as a set of thin doublets, Equation 4.9 may be rewritten as

$$\Phi = \frac{1}{4\pi} \int_{Body+Wake} \mu \mathbf{n} \cdot \nabla \left(\frac{1}{r} \right) dS - \frac{1}{4\pi} \int_{Body} \sigma \left(\frac{1}{r} \right) dS + \Phi_\infty \tag{4.10}$$

The boundary condition for Equation 4.8 is the no-penetration condition, which requires the normal velocity of the flow at the surface to equal zero. This boundary condition must be specified by either a direct or indirect formulation. The direct formulation forces the normal velocity component to be zero and is defined as the Neumann problem. The indirect formulation specifies a value for the potential function on the boundary and, by doing so, the zero normal flow condition is indirectly satisfied. This method is defined as the Dirichlet problem. The morphing wing model uses the Dirichlet problem to enforce the zero normal flow boundary condition. Using the Dirichlet boundary condition, the potential must be specified at all points on the boundary. If a point is placed inside the surface, the inner potential, Φ_i, is defined by the singularity distributions along the surface.

$$\Phi_i = \frac{1}{4\pi} \int_{Body+Wake} \mu \frac{\partial}{\partial \mathbf{n}} \left(\frac{1}{r} \right) dS - \frac{1}{4\pi} \int_{Body} \sigma \left(\frac{1}{r} \right) dS + \Phi_\infty \qquad (4.11)$$

These integrals become singular as r approaches zero. In order to evaluate the integrals near this point, the no-penetration boundary condition must be enforced. In order to enforce this boundary condition, Φ_i is set to a constant value. If the direct formulation is used, it may be shown that Φ_i is a constant. Since Φ_i is a constant, Equation 4.11 is equal to a constant as well. The constant value of Φ_i is chosen to be Φ_∞. Thus, Equation 4.11 is reduced to a simpler form.

$$\frac{1}{4\pi} \int_{Body+Wake} \mu \frac{\partial}{\partial \mathbf{n}} \left(\frac{1}{r} \right) dS - \frac{1}{4\pi} \int_{Body} \sigma \left(\frac{1}{r} \right) dS = 0 \qquad (4.12)$$

Next, these integral equations are reduced to a set of linear algebraic equations. Let the system be divided into N panels for the surface and N_w panels for the wake. The boundary condition is specified at a collocation point, which for the Dirichlet boundary condition is inside the body and at the center of the panel. Equation 4.12 is rewritten for N collocation points for N panels. The integrands shown below only depend on the geometry of the respective panel, and thus can be evaluated.

$$\sum_{k=1}^{N} \frac{1}{4\pi} \int_{BodyPanel} \mu \mathbf{n} \cdot \nabla \left(\frac{1}{r} \right) dS$$

$$+ \sum_{l=1}^{N} \frac{1}{4\pi} \int_{WakePanel} \mu \mathbf{n} \cdot \nabla \left(\frac{1}{r} \right) dS - \sum_{k=1}^{N} \frac{1}{4\pi} \int_{BodyPanel} \sigma \left(\frac{1}{r} \right) dS = 0 \qquad (4.13)$$

Since the singularity elements μ and σ of each panel influence every other panel on the body, Equation 4.13 may be rewritten for each collocation point inside the body. Note that the variables preceding the singularity elements are the respective integrals evaluated for a particular panel and the respective collocation point. Thus,

$$\sum_{k=1}^{N} A_k \mu_k + \sum_{l=1}^{N} A_l \mu_l - \sum_{k=1}^{N} B_k \sigma_K = 0 \qquad (4.14)$$

where A is the doublet influence coefficient and B is the source influence coefficient. In order to eliminate the wake strength from Equation 4.14, a new relationship is introduced. The Kutta condition states that there is no circulation at the trailing edge of a wing section. By using the Kutta condition, one will find the doublet strength of the wake panel is equivalent to the difference between the trailing edge panels on the upper surface and the lower surface. By exploiting this relationship, the wake contribution may be eliminated from Equation 4.14 by substitution at the trailing edge panels only. Since the source strengths are known, Equation

4.14 reduces to a set of N equations with N unknown doublet strengths which may be solved by matrix inversion.

$$
\begin{pmatrix} a_{11} & \cdots & a_{1N} \\ \vdots & \ddots & \vdots \\ a_{N1} & \cdots & a_{NN} \end{pmatrix} \begin{pmatrix} \mu_1 \\ \vdots \\ \mu_N \end{pmatrix} = - \begin{pmatrix} b_{11} & \cdots & b_{1N} \\ \vdots & \ddots & \vdots \\ b_{N1} & \cdots & b_{NN} \end{pmatrix} \begin{pmatrix} \sigma_1 \\ \vdots \\ \sigma_N \end{pmatrix} \tag{4.15}
$$

Once the doublet strengths are found, it is possible to find the aerodynamic forces acting on each panel. The first step is to determine the tangential (l,m) and normal (n) perturbation velocity components for each of the panels.

$$
q_l = -\frac{\partial \mu}{\partial l}, q_m = -\frac{\partial \mu}{\partial m}, q_n = -\sigma \tag{4.16}
$$

With these velocities , the total velocity of each panel may be computed.

$$
Q_k = (Q_{\infty l}, Q_{\infty m}, Q_{\infty n})_k + (q_l, q_m, q_n)_k \tag{4.17}
$$

Note that these velocities are expressed in the local panel coordinate system. Using the velocities at each panel, the pressure coefficient at each panel is found using a modified form of Bernoulli's Equation.

$$
C_{p_k} = 1 - \frac{Q_k^2}{Q_\infty^2} \tag{4.18}
$$

Once the pressure coefficient has been determined, the non-dimensional aerodynamic forces are calculated for each panel. The total aerodynamic forces are found by summing the contributions from each panel.

$$
\Delta C_{F_k} = -\frac{C_{p_k} \Delta S}{S} \cdot \mathbf{n}_k \tag{4.19}
$$

All that remains now is to calculate the parasitic drag contribution, which by definition is drag that is not due to the production of lift. Roskam (1989) contains a method for calculating the parasitic drag coefficient C_{D_0}, based on wing area S and the equivalent parasite area f.

$$
C_{D_0} = \frac{f}{S} \tag{4.20}
$$

The equivalent parasite area is related to the wetted area by

$$
\log_{10} f = a + b \log_{10} S_{wet} \tag{4.21}
$$

The terms a and b are correlation coefficients related to the equivalent skin friction of the aircraft. The equivalent skin friction coefficient is estimated by using data from similar aircraft. The Oswald efficiency factor may be expressed as a function of aspect ratio AR, and is valid if the leading edge sweep angle of the wing is less than $30°$.

$$
e = 1.78(1 - 0.045AR^{0.68}) - 0.64 \tag{4.22}
$$

4.4.3   Model Grid

An important feature of the model is the ability to generate a grid which is easy to manipulate and permits many morphing degrees-of-freedom. The first step is to represent airfoil sections that allow camber and thickness changes, and which are suitable for incompressible flight conditions. There are many ways to accomplish this. One way is to create a table of known airfoil coordinates for table look-up whenever a reconfiguration occurs. The advantages of this type of representation are the wide variety of airfoils available for selection and the ease with which to transition from one type of airfoil to another. However, the major disadvantage of a table with multiple airfoil sections is not being able to have direct control over the thickness and camber of the airfoil. For the model developed here, the capability of direct, quick control for a change in thickness and camber is vital. Therefore, a set of airfoils which have equations that describe the upper and lower geometries of the airfoil section as a function of a thickness and camber is selected. This class of airfoils are the NACA 4-Digit series, which have blunt leading edges for either thick or thin airfoil sections, thereby making them ideal for subsonic flight conditions. Another important aspect of generating a grid around the wing is the assumption that the wing has the XZ (longitudinal) plane as a plane of symmetry. By assuming a symmetric wing, only half of the wing is modeled by the grid. This makes the definition of the influence coefficients simpler and makes the model less computationally intensive.

The method of spacing used to place the panels on the wing is also an important aspect of generating a grid. For this particular model, cosine spacing is utilized for both chordwise and spanwise paneling (Moran 1984).

$$x_{v_i} = \frac{c(y)}{2} \left(1 - \cos\left(\frac{i\pi}{N+1}\right)\right)$$
$$i = 1 : N$$

(4.23)

By using cosine spacing in the chordwise direction, more panels are placed near the leading and trailing edges of the wing. Cosine spacing in the spanwise direction places more panels at the span stations, which are near the tips of the wing. Figures 4.2, 4.3, and 4.4 show the effect of utilizing cosine spacing in both the spanwise and chordwise directions as well as some of

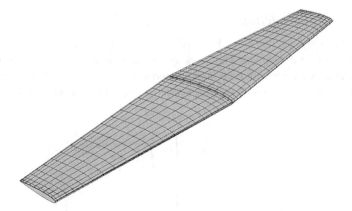

Figure 4.2   Straight tapered wing configuration with cosine spacing

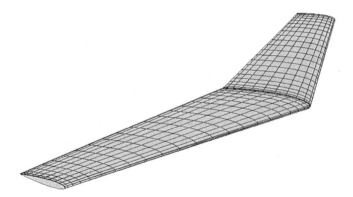

Figure 4.3   Swept wing configuration with cosine spacing

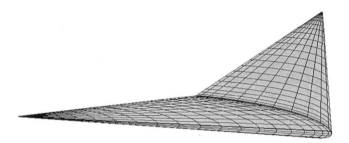

Figure 4.4   Delta wing configuration with cosine spacing

the different shapes that the aerodynamic model is able to represent. As shown in the figures, the four corner points of the wing have the most number of panels.

4.4.4   Dynamical Modeling

Starting with Newton's Second Law, $\mathbf{F} = m\dot{\mathbf{v}}^N$, the translational equations of motion for the morphing wing can be developed. The body axis system used here is defined in Figure 4.5. Consider a velocity vector $\mathbf{v}$ with body-axis components as defined in Figure 4.5 and a body-axis angular velocity vector ω with roll (p), pitch (q), and yaw (r) components respectively.

$$\mathbf{v} = \begin{pmatrix} u \\ v \\ w \end{pmatrix} \tag{4.24}$$

$$\omega = \begin{pmatrix} p \\ q \\ r \end{pmatrix} \tag{4.25}$$

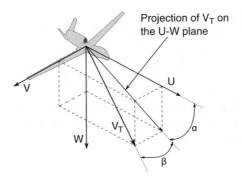

Figure 4.5   Body axis system definitions

The superscript N denotes an inertial reference frame and superscript B denotes a body-fixed reference frame. The inertial derivative of the velocity vector with respect to time yields

$$\dot{\mathbf{v}}^N = \dot{\mathbf{v}}^B + \omega \times \mathbf{v} = \begin{bmatrix} \dot{u} + qw - rv \\ \dot{v} + ru - pw \\ \dot{w} + pv - qu \end{bmatrix} \tag{4.26}$$

The forces acting on the morphing wing consist of gravitational (G), propulsive (T), and aerodynamic (X, Y, Z) forces. The gravitational forces are calculated using simple trigonometry. The propulsive force is assumed to be constant. The aerodynamic forces are calculated using the constant strength source-doublet panel method developed in the previous section. The force vector $\mathbf{F}$ can be expanded as

$$\mathbf{F} = \begin{bmatrix} X + T_x + G_x \\ Y + T_y + G_y \\ Z + T_z + G_z \end{bmatrix}$$

$$= \begin{bmatrix} -mg \sin(\theta) - D \cos(\alpha) \cos(\beta) + L \sin(\alpha) \cos(\beta) + T \\ mg \sin(\phi) \cos(\theta) + D \cos(\alpha) \sin(\beta) - L \sin(\alpha) \sin(\beta) \\ mg \cos(\phi) \cos(\theta) - D \sin(\alpha) - L \cos(\alpha) \end{bmatrix} \tag{4.27}$$

where ψ, θ, and ϕ are the standard Euler yaw, pitch, and roll attitude angles respectively, and α and β are aerodynamic angles defined in Figure 4.5. Substituting Equation 4.26 and Equation 4.27 into Newton's Second Law, the translational equations of motion are obtained.

$$m(\dot{u} + qw - rv) = -mg \sin(\theta) - D \cos(\alpha) \cos(\beta) + L \sin(\alpha) \cos(\beta) + T \tag{4.28}$$

$$m(\dot{v} + ru - pw) = mg \sin(\phi) \cos(\theta) + D \cos(\alpha) \sin(\beta) - L \sin(\alpha) \sin(\beta) \tag{4.29}$$

$$m(\dot{w} + pv - qu) = mg \cos(\phi) \cos(\theta) - D \sin(\alpha) - L \cos(\alpha) \tag{4.30}$$

where T, D, and L are the thrust, drag, and lift forces. Using Euler's Equations a relationship between the vector sum of the moments $\mathbf{L}$ and the angular momentum vector $\mathbf{h}$ can be determined as $\mathbf{L} = \dot{\mathbf{h}}^N$. With

$$\mathbf{h} = \mathbf{I}\omega \tag{4.31}$$

the inertia matrix $\mathbf{I}$ may be written as

$$\mathbf{I} = \begin{pmatrix} I_{xx} & -I_{xy} & -I_{xz} \\ -I_{xy} & I_{yy} & -I_{yz} \\ -I_{xz} & -I_{yz} & I_{zz} \end{pmatrix} \tag{4.32}$$

These moments of inertia are a function of the configuration, and thus the shape changes, that occur during flight. Therefore the moments are time-varying. Taking the time derivative of the angular momentum vector,

$$
\begin{aligned}
\dot{\mathbf{h}}^N &= \mathbf{I}\dot{\omega}^B + \dot{\mathbf{I}}^B\omega + \omega \times \mathbf{I}\omega \\
&= \begin{bmatrix}
I_{xx}\dot{p} - I_{xy}\dot{q} - I_{xz}\dot{r} + \dot{I}_{xx}p - \dot{I}_{xy}q - \dot{I}_{xz}r + p\left(-I_{xz}q + I_{xy}r\right) \\
+q\left(-I_{yz}q - I_{yy}r\right) + r\left(I_{zz}q + I_{yz}r\right) \\
I_{xy}\dot{p} - I_{yy}\dot{q} - I_{yz}\dot{r} + \dot{I}_{xy}p - \dot{I}_{yy}q - \dot{I}_{yz}r + p\left(I_{xx}r + I_{xz}p\right) \\
+q\left(-I_{xy}r + I_{yz}p\right) + r\left(-I_{xz}r - I_{zz}p\right) \\
I_{xz}\dot{p} - I_{yz}\dot{q} - I_{zz}\dot{r} + \dot{I}_{xz}p - \dot{I}_{yz}q - \dot{I}_{zz}r + p\left(-I_{xy}p - I_{xx}q\right) \\
+q\left(I_{yy}p + I_{xy}q\right) + r\left(-I_{yz}p + I_{xz}q\right)
\end{bmatrix} \tag{4.33}
\end{aligned}
$$

The moments are due to the aerodynamic and propulsive forces. The moments produced by the aerodynamic forces are calculated with the panel method described in the previous section. It is assumed that the thrust line is parallel to the body x-axis and acts at the center of gravity location, thereby not producing a moment. The aerodynamic moment vector is

$$\mathbf{L} = \begin{bmatrix} L_A \\ M_A \\ N_A \end{bmatrix} \tag{4.34}$$

with roll (L), pitch (M), and yaw (N) moments respectively. By substituting Equation 4.33 and Equation 4.34 into Euler's Equations, the rotational equations of motion for the morphing wing are

$$
\begin{aligned}
&I_{xx}\dot{p} - I_{xy}\dot{q} - I_{xz}\dot{r} + \dot{I}_{xx}p - \dot{I}_{xy}q - \dot{I}_{xz}r + p\left(-I_{xz}q + I_{xy}r\right) \\
&+q\left(-I_{yz}q - I_{yy}r\right) + r\left(I_{zz}q + I_{yz}r\right) = L_A
\end{aligned} \tag{4.35}
$$

$$
\begin{aligned}
&I_{xy}\dot{p} - I_{yy}\dot{q} - I_{yz}\dot{r} + \dot{I}_{xy}p - \dot{I}_{yy}q - \dot{I}_{yz}r + p\left(I_{xx}r + I_{xz}p\right) \\
&+q\left(-I_{xy}r + I_{yz}p\right) + r\left(-I_{xz}r - I_{zz}p\right) = M_A
\end{aligned} \tag{4.36}
$$

$$
\begin{aligned}
&I_{xz}\dot{p} - I_{yz}\dot{q} - I_{zz}\dot{r} + \dot{I}_{xz}p - \dot{I}_{yz}q - \dot{I}_{zz}r + p\left(-I_{xy}p - I_{xx}q\right) \\
&+q\left(I_{yy}p + I_{xy}q\right) + r\left(-I_{yz}p + I_{xz}q\right) = N_A
\end{aligned} \tag{4.37}
$$

The independent variables α and β can be expressed as a function of body-axis velocities and total velocity V_T from the geometric relationships

$$\tan(\alpha) = \frac{w}{V_T} \tag{4.38}$$

$$\tan(\beta) = \frac{v}{V_T} \tag{4.39}$$

Differentiating Equation 4.38 and Equation 4.39 with respect to time yields the desired relations

$$\dot{\alpha} = \frac{1}{V_T} \left(\dot{w} \cos(\alpha) - \dot{u} \sin(\alpha) \right) \tag{4.40}$$

$$\dot{\beta} = \frac{1}{V_T} \left(\dot{v} \cos(\beta) - \dot{u} \sin(\beta) \right) \tag{4.41}$$

4.4.5 Reference Trajectory

The aim of this work is to demonstrate that while changing shape, the A-RLC controller can ensure that the morphing wing can track reference trajectories which correspond to a variety of flight conditions, and the transitions between them. A complete reference trajectory consists of a sequence of common manuever segments, such as cruise, climb, descent, turn, climbing turn, etc. For the present work, only longitudinal maneuvers are considered and a reference trajectory is composed of three distinct segments. In the first segment, the morphing wing is flying at a steady, level, straight, $1g$ cruise condition. The second segment is a descent and level out to cruise at a lower altitude, and the third segment is a climb back up to a desired altitude, followed by leveling out into a cruise condition. Pitch attitude angle θ and altitude are given as discrete commands, and polynomials are fitted to make the combined reference trajectory smooth.

4.4.6 Shape Memory Alloy Actuator Dynamics

For morphing of an aircraft wing to be achieved, actuators must be used that are capable of inducing the deflections required while being light enough for several actuators to be available on board. Here, it is assumed that the actuators that will be used for morphing aircraft are composed of Shape Memory Alloy (SMA) wires. SMAs are a special class of alloy that exhibit a property known as the Shape Memory Effect (Waram 1993). When they are at low temperatures, they exist in a crystal phase of martensite. When heated, the SMA undergoes a crystal phase transformation to austenite. A SMA wire can be trained via heat treatments to "remember" a specific martensitic shape so that if it is loaded to a point of plastic deformation, it can return to its original undeformed shape by heating through the austenite phase and cooling again. This behavior is illustrated in Figure 4.6.

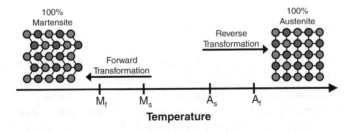

Figure 4.6 Shape memory effect

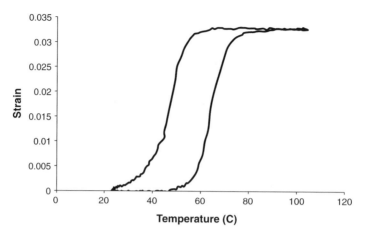

Figure 4.7   SMA hysteresis

During the crystal phase transformation to austenite, there is a very pronounced thermo-mechanical response that causes the SMA to become more compact. In the case of an SMA wire, this response results in the wire shortening. The wire then returns to its original length by cooling back to a phase of martensite. The relationship between temperature and strain can be experimentally determined, but it is difficult to model because there is a hysteresis in the curve (Lagoudas 2008). An example of this is shown in Figure 4.7. Controlling SMA wires through this thermomechanical response can result in lightweight actuators for morphing since the heating process can be performed by electrical resistive heating (Kirkpatrick 2009).

Considering that SMA actuators will be used for morphing actuation, it is important when simulating the morphing of the wing to have representative SMA actuator dynamics. Since the dynamics of the electrically induced thermomechanical response of SMAs is not information that is available, they had to be determined experimentally. The specimen used in experimentation was a NiTi SMA wire. The SMA crystal phase change demonstrated exponential decay in the strain-time history with no oscillatory motion. For this reason, it was decided to approximate the SMA dynamics as first-order. Equation 4.42 is the equation of motion for the SMA dynamics, where ε is the tensile strain of the SMA wire, ε_c is the commanded strain, and τ is the time constant.

$$\dot{\varepsilon} = \frac{\varepsilon_c - \varepsilon}{\tau} \tag{4.42}$$

It then becomes necessary to determine the time constant for these actuators. This is not so simple because just as there is a hysteresis in the temperature-strain relationship in SMAs, there is also hysteresis in the dynamics. The time constant for the SMA wire length varies depending upon the direction of the phase change, so different time constants are required for both the heating and cooling cycles. It was also determined upon finding these constants that they also change depending upon how far along the crystal phase transformation is. Thus, the time constant varies depending upon both directional changes and magnitude of current strain. For the experimental sample used, the equations for calculating the time constant during the heating and cooling cycles are shown in Equations 4.43 and 4.44 respectively.

$$\tau = 3.1e^{-200\varepsilon} + 1 \qquad (4.43)$$

$$\tau = e^{46\varepsilon} \qquad (4.44)$$

These equations can be used to calculate τ based on the current tensile strain, ε, and the sign of the first derivative of the tensile strain. It should be noted that these equations were derived from experimental data using a NiTi specimen under a constant tensile load of 120 MPa, and the maximum strain achieved (austenitic strain) was 3.5%. Using Equations 4.43 and 4.44 in Equation 4.42, the equations of motion for the SMA actuators become:

$$\dot{\varepsilon} = \begin{cases} \frac{\varepsilon_c - \varepsilon}{3.1e^{-200\varepsilon} + 1} & \text{if } \varepsilon_c < \varepsilon \\ (\varepsilon_c - \varepsilon)e^{46\varepsilon} & \text{if } \varepsilon_c > \varepsilon \end{cases} \qquad (4.45)$$

Equation 4.45 is the equation of motion that can be used in morphing simulations to represent the dynamics of SMA actuators.

4.4.7 Control Effectors on Morphing Wing

The morphing wing modeled in this work is essentially a free-body that can fly. Because of its shape changing or morphing capability, a morphing wing does not have conventional hinged-type control effectors such as elevons or flaps. Instead it has warping or shape changing control effectors that are non-affine functions in the control variable, i.e. the control does not appear linearly in the control effectiveness function. Traditional linear control methodologies require the control effectiveness functions to be affine in the control variable, so the only applicable control methodologies are nonlinear, and therefore very limited in number. To permit use of traditional control methodologies, which in this case will be adaptive control, the morphing wing is modeled with notional control effectors called pseudo-controls. A notional control effectiveness matrix is selected to represent the effectiveness of these pseudo controls. Thrust is assumed to be supplied by a notional jet engine, and only affects translational velocities u and w. Work is continuing on the design, modeling, and control of systems with non-conventional, non-affine control effectors such as camber or location of camber, to eventually use in replacement of the pseudo-controls.

4.5 Morphing Control Law

4.5.1 Structured Adaptive Model Inversion (SAMI) Control for Attitude Control

Equations of motion for the morphing wing are expressed as a nonlinear, six degree-of-freedom dynamical system that is affine in the control. When written in body-axes, the dynamics of most systems can be represented in the form of a second-order differential equation. This second-order differential equation can be separated into a structured form consisting of a kinematic diferential equation which is exactly known, and a momentum level differential equation containing uncertain parameters. The kinematic level states d_x, d_y, d_z, are the positions of the center of mass of the morphing wing along the inertial X_N, Y_N and Z_N axes. Rotational states at the kinematic level ψ, θ and ϕ are the 3-2-1 Euler angles which give the relative orientation of the body-axis with the inertial axis. The acceleration level states are the body-axis linear velocities u, v, w and the body-axis angular velocities p, q, r.

Following the approach in Subbarao (2001), equations representing the relation between kinematic and acceleration level states are

$$\dot{\mathbf{p}}_c = J_l \mathbf{v}_c \tag{4.46}$$

$$\dot{\boldsymbol{\sigma}} = J_a \boldsymbol{\omega} \tag{4.47}$$

where $\mathbf{p}_c = [d_x \quad d_y \quad d_z]^T$, $\mathbf{v}_c = [u \quad v \quad w]^T$, $\boldsymbol{\sigma} = [\phi \quad \theta \quad \psi]^T$ and $\boldsymbol{\omega} = [p \quad q \quad r]^T$
Matrices J_l and J_a are given as

$$J_l = \begin{bmatrix} C_\theta C_\psi & S_\phi S_\theta C_\psi - C_\phi S_\psi & C_\phi S_\theta C_\psi + S_\phi S_\psi \\ C_\theta S_\psi & S_\phi S_\theta S_\psi + C_\phi C_\psi & C_\phi S_\theta S_\psi - S_\phi C_\psi \\ -S_\theta & S_\phi C_\theta & C_\phi C_\theta \end{bmatrix}$$

$$J_a = \begin{bmatrix} 1 & S_\phi tan(\theta) & C_\phi tan(\theta) \\ 0 & C_\phi & -S_\phi \\ 0 & S_\phi sec(\theta) & C_\phi sec(\theta) \end{bmatrix} \tag{4.48}$$

and $C_\phi = cos(\phi)$, $S_\theta = sin(\theta)$ and so on. The differential equations at the acceleration level are

$$m\dot{\mathbf{v}}_c + \tilde{\omega}m\mathbf{v}_c = \mathbf{F} + \mathbf{F}_{aero} \tag{4.49}$$

$$I\dot{\boldsymbol{\omega}} + \dot{I}\boldsymbol{\omega} + \tilde{\omega}I\boldsymbol{\omega} = \mathbf{M} + \mathbf{M}_{aero} \tag{4.50}$$

where m is the mass of the morphing wing, $\mathbf{F}$ is the force generated by the control, $\mathbf{F}_{aero}$ represents aerodynamic forces, I is the body axis moment of inertia, $\mathbf{M}$ is the control torque, and $\mathbf{M}_{aero}$ represents aerodynamic moments. $\tilde{\omega}\mathbf{V}$ is the matrix representation of the cross-product between vector $\boldsymbol{\omega}$ and vector $\mathbf{V}$, in which

$$\tilde{\omega} = \begin{bmatrix} 0 & -r & q \\ r & 0 & -p \\ -q & p & 0 \end{bmatrix} \tag{4.51}$$

Note that compared to rigid-body equations of motion, there is an additional $\dot{I}\boldsymbol{\omega}$ term in Equation 4.50 due to shape changing. The shape change is responsible for speeding up or slowing down the rotation of the vehicle due to the time rate of change in the moment of inertia about a particular axis. SAMI does not directly address time-varying inertias since it is subject to the standard adaptive control assumption of slowly-varying parameters to constant values. Thus the $\dot{I}\boldsymbol{\omega}$ term is neglected.

For the present work only longitudinal dynamics are considered. Starting with σ representing Modified Rodrigues Parameters and ω representing angular velocity, $J(\sigma)$ is the nonlinear transformation relating $\dot{\sigma}$ and ω

$$\dot{\sigma} = J(\sigma)\omega \tag{4.52}$$

$$\dot{\omega} = -I^{-1}(\tilde{\omega}I\omega) + I^{-1}(u + M_{aero}) \tag{4.53}$$

Next the reference model is defined. It has a structure similar to that of the nonlinear plant, with states consisting of reference Modified Rodrigues Parameters (σ_r) and reference angular velocities (ω_r). Equations 4.47 and 4.50 can then be manipulated to obtain the form

$$I_a^*(\sigma)\,\ddot{\sigma} + C_a^*(\sigma,\,\dot{\sigma})\dot{\sigma} = P_a^T(\sigma)\mathbf{M} \tag{4.54}$$

where the matrices $I_a^*(\sigma), C_a^*(\sigma,\dot{\sigma})$ and $P(\sigma)$ are defined as

$$P_a(\sigma) \triangleq J_a^{-1}(\sigma) \tag{4.55}$$

$$I_a^*(\sigma) \triangleq P_a^T I P_a \tag{4.56}$$

$$C_a^*(\sigma,\dot{\sigma}) \triangleq -I_a^* \dot{J}_a P_a + P_a^T [\widetilde{P_a \dot{\sigma}}] I P_a \tag{4.57}$$

According to (Ahmed et al. 1998), the product of the inertia matrix I and a vector v can be written as

$$I v = \Lambda(v)\theta, \qquad \forall v \in \mathbb{R}^3 \tag{4.58}$$

where $\Lambda \in \mathbb{R}^{3\times6}$ is defined as

$$\Lambda(v) \triangleq \begin{bmatrix} v_1 & 0 & 0 & v_2 & v_3 & 0 \\ 0 & v_2 & 0 & v_1 & 0 & v_3 \\ 0 & 0 & v_3 & 0 & v_1 & v_2 \end{bmatrix} \tag{4.59}$$

Then the left-hand side of Equation 4.54 can be linearly parametrized as

$$I_a^*(\sigma)\ddot{\sigma} + C_a^*(\sigma,\,\dot{\sigma})\dot{\sigma} = Y_a(\sigma,\,\dot{\sigma},\,\ddot{\sigma})\theta \tag{4.60}$$

where θ is the constant inertia parameter vector defined as $\theta \triangleq [I_{11} \quad I_{22} \quad I_{33} \quad I_{12} \quad I_{13} \quad I_{23}]^T$ and $Y_a(\sigma,\dot{\sigma},\ddot{\sigma})$ is a regression matrix. The terms on the left-hand side of Equation 4.54 can be written as

$$\begin{aligned} I_a^*\ddot{\sigma} &= P_a^T I P_a \ddot{\sigma} \\ &= P_a^T \Lambda(P_a\ddot{\sigma})\theta \end{aligned} \tag{4.61}$$

$$\begin{aligned} C_a^*\dot{\sigma} &= -P_a^T I P_a \dot{J}_a P_a \dot{\sigma} + P_a^T [\widetilde{P_a\dot{\sigma}}] I P_a \dot{\sigma} \\ &= P_a^T \{-\Lambda(P_a \dot{J}_a P_a \dot{\sigma}) + [\widetilde{P_a\dot{\sigma}}]\Lambda(P_a\dot{\sigma})\}\theta \end{aligned} \tag{4.62}$$

Combining Equations 4.61 and 4.62 produces a linear minimal parameterization for the inertia matrix (Ahmed et al. 1998).

$$\begin{aligned} &I_a^*(\sigma)\ddot{\sigma} + C_a^*(\sigma,\dot{\sigma})\dot{\sigma} \\ &= P_a^T \{\Lambda(P_a\ddot{\sigma}) - \Lambda(P_a \dot{J}_a P_a \dot{\sigma}) + [\widetilde{P_a\dot{\sigma}}]\Lambda(P_a\dot{\sigma})\}\theta \\ &= Y_a(\sigma,\,\dot{\sigma},\,\ddot{\sigma})\theta \end{aligned} \tag{4.63}$$

Next, the attitude tracking problem is formulated. The aim is to make the error between the reference trajectory and the plant output zero. It is assumed that the desired reference trajectory is twice differentiable with respect to time. Let $\varepsilon \triangleq \sigma\text{-}\sigma_r$ be the tracking error. Differentiating twice and multiplying by I_a^* throughout gives

$$I_a^*\ddot{\varepsilon} = I_a^*\ddot{\sigma} - I_a^*\ddot{\sigma}_r \tag{4.64}$$

Adding $(C_{da} + C^*(\sigma, \dot{\sigma}))\,\dot{\varepsilon} + K_{da}\,\varepsilon$ on both sides, where C_{da} and K_{da} are user-defined design matrices,

$$I_a^* \ddot{\varepsilon} + (C_{da} + C_a^*(\sigma, \dot{\sigma}))\dot{\varepsilon} + K_{da}\varepsilon$$
$$= I_a^* \ddot{\sigma} - I_a^* \ddot{\sigma}_r + (C_{da} + C_a^*(\sigma, \dot{\sigma}))\dot{\varepsilon} + K_{da}\varepsilon \tag{4.65}$$

The right-hand side of Equation 4.65 can be written as

$$(I_a^* \ddot{\sigma} + C_a^*(\sigma, \dot{\sigma})\dot{\sigma}) - (I_a^* \ddot{\sigma}_r + C_a^*(\sigma, \dot{\sigma})\dot{\sigma}_r)$$
$$+ C_{da}\dot{\varepsilon} + K_{da}\varepsilon \tag{4.66}$$

From Equation 4.54 and the construction of Y_a similar to Equation 4.63, the right-hand side of Equation 4.65 can be further written as

$$P_a^T \mathbf{M} - Y_a(\sigma, \dot{\sigma}, \dot{\sigma}_r, \ddot{\sigma}_r)\theta + C_{da}\dot{\varepsilon} + K_{da}\varepsilon \tag{4.67}$$

From the preceding equation it is clear that the control law is

$$\mathbf{M} = P_a^{-T}\{Y_a(\sigma, \dot{\sigma}, \dot{\sigma}_r, \ddot{\sigma}_r)\theta - C_{da}\dot{\varepsilon} - K_{da}\varepsilon\} \tag{4.68}$$

This control law requires that the inertia parameters θ be known accurately, but θ may not be known in practice. So by using the certainty equivalence principle (Ioannou and Sun 1996), adaptive estimates for the inertia parameters $\hat{\theta}$ are used for calculating the control.

$$\mathbf{M} = P_a^{-T}\{Y_a(\sigma, \dot{\sigma}, \dot{\sigma}_r, \ddot{\sigma}_r)\,\hat{\theta} - C_{da}\dot{\varepsilon} - K_{da}\varepsilon\} \tag{4.69}$$

Substituting Equation 4.69 in Equation 4.54, the closed-loop dynamics become

$$I_a^* \ddot{\varepsilon} + (C_{da} + C_a^*(\sigma, \dot{\sigma}))\dot{\varepsilon} + K_{da}\varepsilon = Y_a(\sigma, \dot{\sigma}, \ddot{\sigma})\tilde{\theta} \tag{4.70}$$

where $\tilde{\theta} = \hat{\theta} - \theta$.

4.5.2 Update Laws

To determine the update law for $\hat{\theta}$ and to ensure stability of the system, a Lyapunov function is selected of the form

$$V = \frac{1}{2}\dot{\varepsilon}^T I_a^* \dot{\varepsilon} + \frac{1}{2}\varepsilon^T K_{da}\varepsilon + \frac{1}{2}\tilde{\theta}^T \Gamma^{-1}\tilde{\theta} \tag{4.71}$$

where Γ^{-1} is a symmetric positive definite matrix. Taking the time derivative of Equation 4.71

$$\dot{V} = \frac{1}{2}\dot{\varepsilon}^T \dot{I}_a^* \dot{\varepsilon} + \dot{\varepsilon}^T I_a^* \ddot{\varepsilon} + \dot{\varepsilon}^T K_{da}\varepsilon + \dot{\tilde{\theta}}^T \Gamma^{-1}\tilde{\theta}$$
$$\dot{V} = \frac{1}{2}\dot{\varepsilon}^T \dot{I}_a^* \dot{\varepsilon} + \dot{\varepsilon}^T (I_a^* \ddot{\varepsilon} + K_{da}\varepsilon) + \dot{\tilde{\theta}}^T \Gamma^{-1}\tilde{\theta} \tag{4.72}$$

and substituting the expression for $\ddot{\varepsilon}$ from Equation 4.70 produces

$$\dot{V} = \dot{\varepsilon}^T \left(\frac{1}{2}\dot{I}_a^* - C_a^*\right)\dot{\varepsilon} - \dot{\varepsilon}^T C_{da}\dot{\varepsilon} + (\dot{\varepsilon}^T Y(\sigma, \dot{\sigma}, \dot{\sigma}_r, \ddot{\sigma}_r) + \dot{\tilde{\theta}}^T \Gamma^{-1})\tilde{\theta} \tag{4.73}$$

The first term is a skew-symmetric relationship and is zero from Subbarao (2001). To make the last term zero, adaptive laws for θ should be selected as

$$\dot{\theta} = -\Gamma Y(\sigma, \dot{\sigma}, \dot{\sigma}_r, \ddot{\sigma}_r)\dot{\varepsilon} \tag{4.74}$$

which implies

$$\dot{\hat{\theta}} = -\Gamma Y(\sigma, \dot{\sigma}, \dot{\sigma}_r, \ddot{\sigma}_r)\dot{\varepsilon} \tag{4.75}$$

since θ is constant. Using this adaptive law for θ reduces the Lyapunov function to

$$\dot{V} = -\dot{\varepsilon}^T C_{da}\dot{\varepsilon} \leq 0 \tag{4.76}$$

4.5.3 Stability Analysis

From Equation 4.76 it is concluded that $V > 0$ and $\dot{V} \leq 0$. The Lyapunov function candidate is a function of $\tilde{\theta}$, ε, $\dot{\varepsilon}$ and $\dot{V}$ is a function of $\dot{\varepsilon}$. Hence, $\dot{\varepsilon} \in L_2 \cap L_\infty$. Additionally, $\tilde{\theta}$, ε, $\dot{\varepsilon}$ are all bounded. Since σ_r, $\dot{\sigma}_r$, ε and $\dot{\varepsilon}$ are bounded, σ, $\dot{\sigma}$ and the regression matrix are also bounded and $\in L_\infty$. Since $\dot{\varepsilon}$ is bounded, ε is uniformly continuous. Now $\ddot{\varepsilon}$ is bounded from previous arguments, so it is concluded that $\dot{\varepsilon} \to 0$ as $t \to \infty$. Since $V > 0$ and $\dot{V} \leq 0$, $\lim_{t \to \infty} V$ exists, which implies that the $\lim_{t \to \infty} \varepsilon$ exists, since $\lim \dot{\varepsilon} \to 0$. As ε is uniformly continuous, invoking Barbalat's lemma (Ioannou and Sun 1996) shows that the tracking error dynamics are asymptotically stable and hence $\varepsilon \to 0$ as $t \to \infty$.

4.6 Numerical Examples

4.6.1 Purpose and Scope

The objective is to demonstrate both the learning and trajectory tracking performance of the A-RLC architecture, and the utility of the vehicle model, for a series of prescribed maneuvers. The morphing wing in the examples is tasked with following a user-specified reference trajectory, and autonomously changing shape to achieve pre-determined aerodynamic goals. *It is important to note that only the trajectory is specified, not the shape the wing should morph into*; the shape of the morphing wing for a given flight condition, or for a given transition to a new flight condition, is learned *a priori* by the RL agent. Example 1 demonstrates the ability of the A-RLC architecture to learn how to morph the wing shape in order to achieve specified goals. The RL agent undertakes multiple episodic learning sequences to learn how to change from an arbitrary shape in the state-space, to a speciifc shape that meets a specified aerodynamic goal. Example 2 exploits two sets of previously learned goals to achieve several different *new* intermediate goals, without the need for additional learning. Since the shapes for maximum lift and minimum lift are already learned, it is possible to use these data to achieve intermediate goals and still maintain good trajectory tracking.

4.6.2 Example 1: Learning New Major Goals

The state-space consists of the shape parameters tip chord c_t, root chord c_r, span b, and leading edge sweep angle Λ. Table 4.1 shows the two goals the agent learns: a maximum lift coefficient

Table 4.1 Aerodynamic goals: Example 1

Time	C_L
$t \leq 40sec$	0.3 ± 0.05
$40sec < t \leq 80sec$	0.09 ± 0.05
$t > 80sec$	0.3 ± 0.05

of 0.3 ± 0.05 and a minimum lift coefficient of 0.09 ± 0.05. These goals can be thought of as the nominal goals. During the simulation the morphing wing must change shape to meet the nominal aerodynamic goals during the specified times listed in Table 4.1, while tracking the reference trajectory.

Figure 4.8 shows the translational motion time histories. The reference trajectory commands the vehicle to first descend, then level out and trim at constant altitude, followed by a climb to a commanded altitude and re-trim. For each of these transient flight conditions the aerodynamic goals corresponding to the shape are changed. Since the trajectory consists of only longitudinal maneuvers, only u, w, and θ are considered. Despite significant changes in shape the SAMI adaptive controller provides good tracking for all translational states. Figure 4.9 also shows good tracking of the rotational states, with only a small tracking error during the shape change transients due to the effect of changing inertias. However, the controller is able to handle these inertia changes and still regulate the tracking error to zero. Note that the time rate of shape

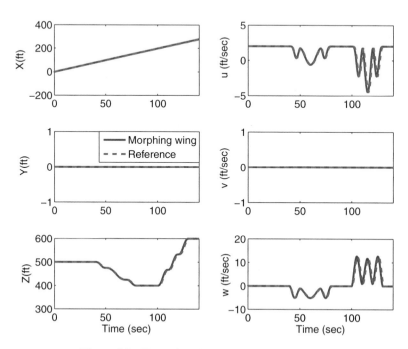

Figure 4.8 Example 1: Translational time histories

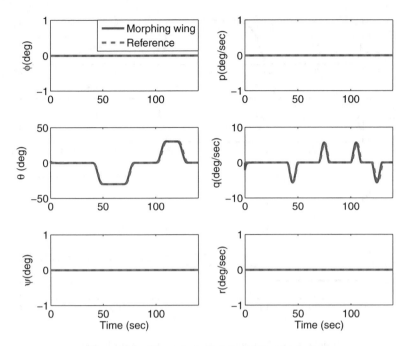

Figure 4.9   Example 1: Rotational time histories

change is large, and hence during the shape change the dynamics of the system also change, which accounts for the tracking errors during the transient responses. The simulation shows that error decreases with the decrease in the rate of shape change.

Figure 4.10 illustrates wing shape changes. The effect of the hysteretic SMA dynamics can be seen in the lagged response to reach steady-state at each configuration. When a morphing parameter increases, the slow cooling effect is reflected in a slow rise time and settling time. When a parameter is decreased, the fast heating effect is exhibited by a fast rise time and settling time. For the initial maximum nominal lift coefficient command, the shape parameters in Table 4.2 settle out to a tip chord of 0.5 ft, root chord of 4 ft, span of 10 ft, and leading edge sweep angle of 8 degrees. The wing selects this shape by consulting the shape learning data stored in the $Q(s, a)$ for $c_L = 0.3 \pm 0.05$. After 40 seconds the wing consults the learning data stored in the $Q(s, a)$ for $c_L = 0.09 \pm 0.05$ and chooses the shape of a tip chord of 1 ft, a root chord of 2 ft, a span of 5 ft, and a leading edge sweep angle of 15 degrees. Finally, after 80 seconds the wing again chooses a shape for maximum lift of tip chord of 0.5 ft, root chord of 4 ft, a span of 10 ft, and leading edge sweep angle of 17.5 degrees. This shape is different from that of the first 40 seconds because the starting state is different. The learning data tells the wing how to get from any state in the state-space to the closest shape in the space corresponding to the goal range. Since the wing configuration was different at 0 seconds and 80 seconds, the final shape chosen to meet the goal is not the same.

Figure 4.11 shows the forces and moments acting on the wing. Axial force and normal force change as the shape changes.

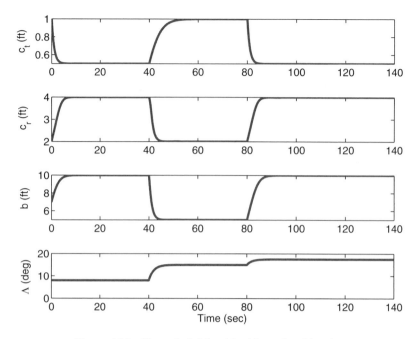

Figure 4.10   Example 1: Morphing/shape time histories

4.6.3   Example 2: Learning New Intermediate Goals

The series of aerodynamic goals for this example are listed in Table 4.3. The agent achieves these intermediate goals by judiciously choosing which set of learning data to consult. For example, initially the wing must find a maximum lift configuration so it just uses the maximum lift learning data. At the next time increment, the agent must find a configuration to achieve a lift coefficient of 0.2. Since the wing is starting from a maximum lift configuration, it can use the minimum lift learning data and just stop when the lift goal is achieved. A similar selection can be done when the wing needs to change from a minimum lift configuration to a 0.2 configuration.

The simulation time histories are shown in Figures 4.12, 4.13, 4.14, and 4.15. Figure 4.12 shows the translational time histories. The reference trajectory indicates a dive and climb in the same manner as Example 1. Despite the changes in shape, the adaptive controller maintains good tracking for all translational states except for small steady state errors during the shape change while tracking the altitude. Figure 4.13 also shows good tracking of the rotational

Table 4.2   Morphing parameters: Example 1

Time	c_t (ft)	c_r (ft)	b (ft)	Λ (deg)
$t \leq 40sec$	0.5	4.0	10	8.0
$40sec < t \leq 80sec$	1.0	2.0	5	15.0
$t > 80sec$	0.5	4.0	10	17.5

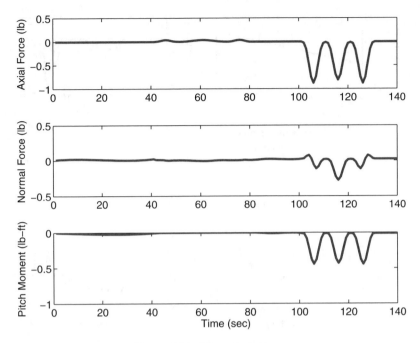

Figure 4.11   Example 1: Forces

states. Pitch attitude angle is commanded to 30 degrees and −30 degrees during the climb and dive, respectively. During the same time increment, the wing changes shape. Figure 4.14 illustrates the wing shape changes, and the hysteretic SMA dynamics are clearly visible. Table 4.4 lists the shape parameters for the shape chosen by the wing for each time segment. The shape parameters for the second time increment did not change from the first, even though the goal value of C_L changed. This is because the difference between the lower bound of the previous time segment and the upper bound of the second time segment are the same value, so the shape change required is negligible. The differences in shape for the 0.2 configuration can again be explained by the difference in starting configuration. The effects of these shape changes can be seen in Figure 4.15.

It should be noted that the reference trajectory selected for tracking is arbitrary. It just demonstrates three flight conditions of cruise, climb and dive. This trajectory is not optimally

Table 4.3   Aerodynamic goals: Example 2

Time	C_L
$t \leq 20sec$	0.3 ± 0.05
$20sec < t \leq 40sec$	0.2 ± 0.05
$40sec < t \leq 60sec$	0.09 ± 0.05
$60sec < t \leq 80sec$	0.2 ± 0.05
$t > 80sec$	0.3 ± 0.05

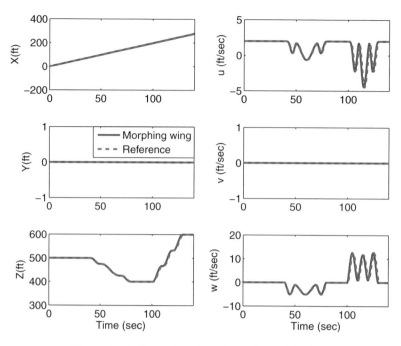

Figure 4.12   Example 2: Translational time histories

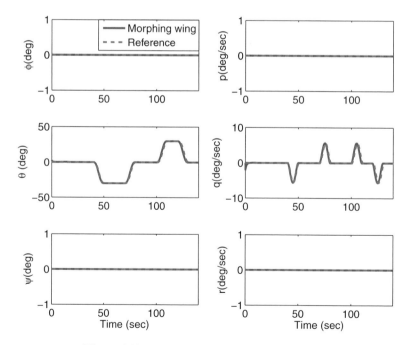

Figure 4.13   Example 2: Rotational time histories

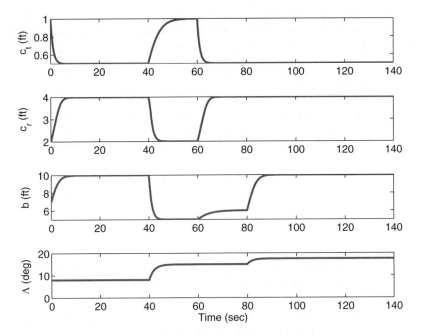

Figure 4.14 Example 2: Morphing/shape time histories.

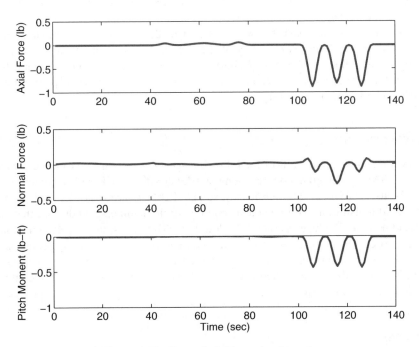

Figure 4.15 Example 2: Force time histories

Table 4.4   Morphing parameters: Example 2

Time	c_t (ft)	c_r (ft)	b (ft)	Λ (deg)
$t \le 20sec$	0.5	4.0	10	8.0
$20sec \le t < 40sec$	0.5	4.0	10	8.0
$40sec \le t < 60sec$	1.0	2.0	5	15.0
$60sec \le t < 80sec$	0.5	4.0	6	15.0
$t > 80sec$	0.5	4.0	10	17.5

calculated for these flight conditions. Extension of this work will include more realistic reference trajectories, which will give more insight into the maximum limits of rate of change of shape of the morphing wing.

4.7   Conclusions

This chapter detailed the development and application of an Adaptive-Reinforcement Learning Controller to a morphing wing that uses smart actuators. Tracking performance of the controller was investigated for transient flight conditions which induced vehicle shape changes. Two examples were presented. The first example demonstrated that the Adaptive-Reinforcement Learning Controller was able to command and control transitions between various flight conditions, using two sets of learned shape commands. Tracking errors were small, despite time-varying changes in forces and inertias. The second example demonstrated that the original learning data, generated from a specific set of pre-defined goals, can successfully be used to achieve new intermediate goals that were not part of the original set, without the need to re-learn from scratch. Two extreme sets of the orginal learning data were used. Together, the examples show that the Adaptive-Reinforcement Learning Controller and its associated architecture together are an excellent candidate for controlling both the shape of a morphing air vehicle and tracking its trajectory.

Acknowledgments

This work was sponsored (in part) by the following agencies: the Air Force Office of Scientific Research, USAF, under grant/contract number FA9550-08-1-0038 with technical monitors Dr. Scott Wells, Dr. William M. McEneaney, and Dr. Fariba Fahroo; the National Aeronautics and Space Administration with technical monitor Mark Hammerschmidt; and the National Science Foundation Graduate Research Fellowships. The views and conclusions contained herein are those of the authors and should not be interpreted as necessarily representing the official policies or endorsements, either expressed or implied, of the Air Force Office of Scientific Research, the National Aeronautics and Space Administration, the National Science Foundation, or the U.S. Government.

References

Abdulrahim M and Lind R 2005 Control and simulation of a multi-role morphing micro air vehicle. In *AIAA Guidance, Navigation, and Control Conference and Exhibit*, number AIAA-2005-6481, San Francisco, CA, 15–18 August.

Ahmed J, Coppola VT, and Bernstein DS 1998 Adaptive asymptotic tracking of spacecraft attitude motion with inertia matrix identification. *Journal of Guidance, Control, and Dynamics*, 21(5): 684–691.

Bellman RE 1957 *Dynamic Programming*. Princeton University Press, Princeton, NJ.

Bellman RE and Dreyfus SE 1962 *Applied Dynamic Programming*. Princeton University Press, Princeton, NJ.

Bellman RE and Kalaba RE 1965 *Dynamic Programming and Modern Control Theory*. Academic Press, New York.

Boone G 1997 Minimum-time control of the acrobot. In *International Conference on Robotics and Automation*. Albuquerque, NM, IEEE, pp. 3281–3287.

Boothe B, Fitzpatrick K, and Lind R 2005 Controllers for disturbance rejection for a linear input- varying class of morphing aircraft. In *AIAA/ASME/ASCE/AHS/ASC Structures, Structural Dynamics & Materials Conference*, number AIAA-2005-2374, Austin, TX, 18–21 April.

Bowman J, Weisshaar T and Sanders B 2002 Evaluating the impact of morphing technologies on aircraft performance. In *43rd AIAA/ASME/ASCE/AHS/ASC Structures, Structural Dynamics, and Materials Conference*, number AIAA-2002-1631, Denver, CO, 22–25 April.

DeJong G and Spong MW 1994 Swinging up the acrobot: An example of intelligent control. In *Proceedings of the American Control Conference*. American Automatic Control Council, pp. 2158–2162.

Ioannou PA and Sun J 1996 *Robust Adaptive Control*. Prentice-Hall, Inc., Upper Saddle River, New Jersey, pp. 10–11.

Katz J and Plotkin A 2001 *Low Speed Aerodynamics*. 2nd edn. Cambridge University Press, Cambridge, pp. 206–217.

Kirkpatrick K 2009 Reinforcement learning for active length control and hysteresis characterization of shape memory alloys. Master's thesis, Aerospace Engineering Department, Texas A&M University.

Lagoudas DC ed. 2008 *Shape Memory Alloys: Modeling and Engineering Applications*. Springer Science+Business Media, LLC, New York.

Marwaha M and Valasek J 2011 Fault tolerant control allocation for Mars entry vehicle using adaptive control. *International Journal of Adaptive Control and Signal Processing*, 25(2): 95–113.

Mitchell TM 1997 *Machine Learning*. The McGraw-Hill Companies, Inc., Boston, MA.

Moran J 1984 *An Introduction to Theoretical and Computational Aerodynamics*. John Wiley & Sons, Ltd, Chichester, pp. 126–128.

Niksch A 2009 Morphing airfoil and wing models with aerodynamic and structural effects. Master's thesis, Aerospace Engineering Department, Texas A&M University.

Restrepo C and Valasek J 2008 Structured adaptive model inversion controller for mars atmospheric flight. *Journal of Guidance, Control, and Dynamics*, 31 (4): 937–953.

Roskam, J 1989 *Airplane Design Part 1: Preliminary Sizing of Airplanes*. Roskam Aviation and Engineering Corporation, pp. 118–127.

Scott MA, Montgomery RC and Weston RP 1998 Subsonic maneuvering effectiveness of high performance aircraft which employ quasi-static shape change devices. In *Proceedings of the SPIE 5th Annual International Symposium on Structures and Materials*, San Diego, CA, 1–6 March.

Subbarao K 2001 Structured adaptive model inversion: theory and applications to trajectory tracking for non-linear dynamical systems. PhD thesis, Aerospace Engineering Department, Texas A&M University, College Station, TX.

Subbarao K, Steinberg M, and Junkins JL 2001 Structured adaptive model inversion applied to tracking aggressive aircraft maneuvers. In *Proceedings of the AIAA Guidance, Navigation and Control Conference*, number AIAA-2002-4456, Montreal,Canada, 6–9 August .

Subbarao K, Verma A, and Junkins JL 2000 Structured adaptive model inversion applied to tracking spacecraft maneuvers. In *Proceedings of the AAS/AIAA Space flight Mechanics Meeting*, number AAS-00-202, Clearwater, FL, 23–26 January.

Sutton RS 1988 Learning to predict by the method of temporal differences. *Machine Learning*, 3(1): 9–44.

Sutton RS 1995 Generalization in reinforcement learning: Successful examples using sparse coarse coding. In DS Touretzky, MC Mozer, and ME Hasselmo, eds., *Advances in Neural Information Processing Systems: Proceedings of the 1995 Conference*. MIT Press, Cambridge, MA, pp. 1038–1044.

Sutton R and Barto A 1998 *Reinforcement Learning: An Introduction*. MIT Press, Cambridge, MA.

Tandale MD and Valasek J 2004 Adaptive dynamic inversion control with actuator saturation constraints applied to tracking spacecraft maneuvers. *Journal of the Astronautical Sciences*, 54(4): 517–530.

Tandale MD and Valasek J 2006 Fault tolerant structured adaptive model inversion control. Journal of Guidance, Control, and Dynamics, 29(3): 635–642.

Tandale MD and Valasek J 2007 Solutions for handling control position bounds in adaptive dynamic inversion controlled satellites. *Journal of the Astronautical Sciences*, 55(2): 517–530.

Valasek J, Doebbler J, Tandale M, and Meade A 2008 Improved adaptive-reinforcement learning control for morphing unmanned air vehicles. *IEEE Transactions on Systems, Man, and Cybernetics: Part B*, 38(4): 1014–1020.

Valasek J, Tandale M, and Rong J 2005 A reinforcement learning-adaptive control architecture for morphing. *Journal of Aerospace Computing, Information, and Communication*, 2(4): 174–195.

Waram, T 1993 *Actuator Design Using Shape Memory Alloys*. Hamilton, Ontario, T.C. Waram.

Watkins CJCH and Dayan P 1989 Learning from delayed rewards. PhD thesis, University of Cambridge.

Williams RJ and Baird LC 1993 *Analysis of Some Incremental Variants of Policy Iterations: First Steps Toward Understanding Actor-Critic Learning Systems*. Technical Report NU-CCS-93-11, Boston.

5

Modeling and Simulation of Morphing Wing Aircraft

Borna Obradovic and Kamesh Subbarao
University of Texas - Arlington, USA

5.1 Introduction

Flight simulation of a morphing aircraft is a key step in the design process. Particularly in the early phases of design, efficient simulation methods of the full aircraft flight dynamics and aerodynamics are essential. The subject of this chapter is an analysis of modeling methodologies suitable for full, non-linear flight simulation of morphing aircraft. The morphing itself presents challenges for modeling of both aerodynamics and flight dynamics. Various modeling options will be discussed and compared, and the selected methods presented in greater detail. We will also carefully examine the morphing-induced actuator loads, and the resulting actuator power requirements. Finally, a study of a control system design for a morphing aircraft will be presented, utilizing the models and methods developed in the chapter. The resulting controller will also be useful in highlighting the actuator-load limitations of morphing.

5.1.1 Gull-Wing Aircraft

While numerous designs exist for morphing wings, we will primarily use a "Gull-wing" aircraft as our test subject (with some discussion of flexible morphing aircraft as well). The gull-wing aircraft used in this study is illustrated in Figure 5.1. Each wing consists of two segments, referred to as the main wing and the winglet. The wing sections are connected by an actuated, cylindrical joint. Likewise, the wing root is connected to the fuselage using the same type of joint. Each winglet also features an aileron, much like a conventional aircraft. Pitch and yaw control are established using a pair of ruddervons at the rear of the aircraft. The physical characteristics of the aircraft are summarized in Table 5.1.

Morphing Aerospace Vehicles and Structures, First Edition. Edited by John Valasek.
© 2012 John Wiley & Sons, Ltd. Published 2012 by John Wiley & Sons, Ltd.

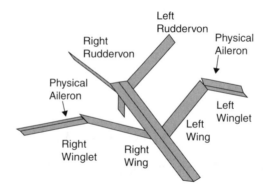

Figure 5.1   The gull-wing aircraft is illustrated with morphing and aileron actuators deflected

The gull-wing aircraft combines traditional control surfaces (ruddervons and ailerons) with the morphing wings. The physical ailerons are redundant (in principle), since morphing can be used to achieve roll moments (as will be shown in Section 5.2.3), but will be shown to be useful for managing overall actuator power (in Section 5.6.1). The available control surfaces are illustrated in Figure 5.2.

5.2   Modeling of Aerodynamics with Morphing

The aerodynamic effects of morphing are one of the key reasons for morphing in the first place, and must therefore be modeled as accurately as is practical. The aerodynamic model must be able to predict the lift, drag, and moments acting on the aircraft for any morphing configuration. Additionally, the effects of the morphing motion must be taken into account, if the morphing is not quasi-static. Another key consideration is the need to compute the aerodynamics throughout the trajectory of a full flight simulation. This requires careful balancing of accuracy vs. computational load. Numerous techniques have been developed, with varying degrees of accuracy and efficiency. The most commonly used methods are various analytical models (Nelson 1998; Stevens and Lewis 2003; Yechout and Morris 2003), Stripline theory (Katz and Plotkin 2001), steady and unsteady Vortex-Lattice Methods (VLM) (Bertin and Smith

Table 5.1   Gull-wing aircraft basic properties

Length	$2\ m$
Wingspan	$2\ m$
Area	$0.87\ cm^2$
Mass	$50\ kg$
I_{xx}	$10\ kg\ m^2$
I_{yy}	$17\ kg\ m^2$
I_{zz}	$11\ kg\ m^2$
I_{xz}	$-1.8\ kg\ m^2$
Mach Number (cruise)	$0.2 - 0.25$

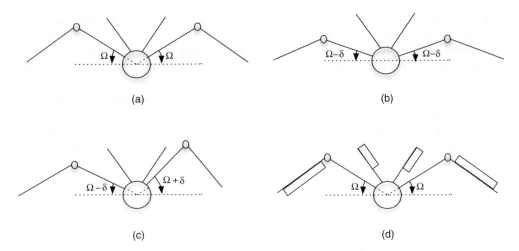

Figure 5.2 The control inputs to the gull-wing aircraft are illustrated; (a) nominal configuration; (b) symmetric deflection (morphing flap); (c) asymmetric deflection (morphing aileron); and (d) physical ailerons and ruddervons

1979; Katz and Plotkin 2001), and full Navier-Stokes CFD (NS) (Yue and Wang 2009). Their properties as pertains to morphing flight simulation are summarized in Table 5.2.

In Table 5.2, CPU time is a qualitative measure of the CPU effort required. Accuracy refers to the quality of the attainable simulation results over a wide range of flight/morphing conditions. "Predictivity" refers to the ability of the method to predict changes in aerodynamic properties due to changes in the aircraft structure. Fast morphing pertains to the accuracy of the method when morphing speed is comparable to the speed of forward flight. The Mach, Re number, α and β refer to the angle of attack and sideslip angle flight regime constraints for a given method. Note that we have not considered table-lookup. While this is certainly a useful and very commonly used method, the size of the lookup table required for a morphing aircraft makes this method less practical for early stages of analysis. The reason is that the number of entries in the table scales geometrically with the number of morphing variables (in addition

Table 5.2 Aerodynamics method tradeoffs

	Analytic	Stripline	Steady VLM	Unsteady VLM	NS
CPU Time	Low	Low	Medium	Medium	High
Accuracy	Low	Low-Medium	Medium	Medium	High
Predictivity	Low	Low	Medium	Medium	High
Fast Morphing	No	No	No	Yes	Yes
Mach Number	Any[1]	$0.1 < M < 0.3$	$0.1 < M < 0.3$	$M < 0.3$	Any
Re Number	Any[1]	$Re > 10^5$	$Re > 10^5$	$Re > 10^5$	Any
α, β	Any[1]	Small	Small	Small	Any

[1]Possible with special models/calibration, but generally difficult.

to the control surfaces and flight state variables), making table generation quite demanding of CFD or wind-tunnel time. Since we would like to be able to easily modify the aircraft and control system, table lookup is not really an option. Likewise, full flight simulation using Navier-Stokes with moving boundaries (due to morphing) is prohibitively expensive of CPU time.

At the opposite end of the complexity spectrum, standard analytic models tend to be too simplistic, given the unknown effects of morphing, and may require empirical calibration of parameters. Similarly, Stripline theory requires calibration of spanwise lift coefficients, making the predictivity low. This leaves various flavors of the Vortex-Lattice Method (VLM) as the most acceptable medium-fidelity solution. The VLM is therefore the method of choice for this work.

5.2.1   Vortex-Lattice Aerodynamics for Morphing

The Vortex-Lattice Method is a numerical solution to the laminar flow problem, i.e., a flow described by a potential function. The flow is assumed to be incompressible, irrotational (except at singular points on the surface of the aircraft), and inviscid. As such, it is applicable to low Mach number ($M < 0.3$) flows at small angles of attack. Since the flow is irrotational (except at the aircraft surface and the trailing vortex sheet), it can be described by a potential function as follows:

$$\mathbf{V} = \nabla \Phi \tag{5.1}$$

Applying Equation 5.1 to the steady-state continuity equation (with constant density) yields the equation for steady potential flow:

$$\nabla^2 \Phi = 0 \tag{5.2}$$

The flow equation (Equation 5.2) itself does not completely describe the flow; the boundary conditions of the problem must also be specified. For an aircraft flow problem, the required boundary condition is obtained by stipulating the "non-penetration-condition" of Equation 5.3, i.e., the air must flow around, not through, the aircraft. Far from the aircraft, the free-stream conditions are assumed to persist.

$$\hat{\mathbf{n}} \cdot \nabla \Phi = 0 \tag{5.3}$$

The symbol $\hat{\mathbf{n}}$ in Equation 5.3 signifies the local surface normal vector on the aircraft. Thus, Equation 5.3 requires that the flow immediately adjacent to the aircraft be parallel to the surface.

The basic idea of VLM is to obtain a solution to Equation 5.2 while satisfying the non-penetration condition of Equation 5.3 by composing the solution as a superposition of the unperturbed free-stream potential and the potential arising from a finite set of discrete sources. The strengths of the sources are chosen to satisfy the Laplace equation (Equation 5.2, and are typically singularity elements, such as vortices or doublets.

The values of the coefficients in the linear combination of the unperturbed free-stream potential and the discrete source potentials are determined   as follows. The condition of

Equation 5.3 is imposed on a finite set of collocation points (referred to as control points) on the surface of the aircraft; and the resulting system of equations is solved. The form of the solution is then given by:

$$\Phi(\mathbf{x}) = \sum_i \Gamma_i \phi_i(\mathbf{x}, \mathbf{x_i}) + \Phi_\infty \qquad (5.4)$$

where Φ represents the computed flow potential, and ϕ is the potential of the ith singlarity element. Also, $\mathbf{x}$ represents the evaluation point for the potential, while $\mathbf{x_i}$ is the location of the ith singularity element. The weighting coefficients to be determined are represented by Γ_i. Inserting Equation 5.4 into Equation 5.3, a system of linear equations is obtained:

$$\sum_j \left(\hat{\mathbf{n}}_i \cdot \nabla \phi_j\right) \Gamma_j = -\hat{\mathbf{n}}_i \cdot \nabla \Phi_\infty \qquad (5.5)$$

As it stands, Equation 5.5 is useful for quasi-static flows only. The flow velocity terms do not take into account the fact that the free-stream velocity is different at different control points of the aircraft. These differences arise due to the rotational and morphing motions. For example, as the aircraft rolls, the free-stream velocity experienced by the falling wing will be higher than that experienced by the rising wing. Likewise, the local angle of attack will shift. Similarly, if the aircraft morphs, and the planforms move within the body frame, the moving planforms will experience a modified free-stream velocity. This can be taken into account by modifying the non-penetration condition as follows:

$$\hat{\mathbf{n}}_i \cdot \left(\nabla \Phi + \nabla \Phi_\infty + [\tilde{\omega}]r_i + \mathbf{v}_i\right) = 0 \qquad (5.6)$$

The value of $[\tilde{\omega}]$ in Equation 5.6 is assumed to be an input to the vortex-lattice code. The positions and velocities of the panels r_i and v_i are also assumed to be computed elsewhere (discussed in Section 5.3) and provided as input to the vortex-lattice module. The complete system of equations used for vortex-lattice calculations in this work is then:

$$\sum_j \left(\hat{\mathbf{n}}_i \cdot \nabla \phi_j\right) \Gamma_j = -\hat{\mathbf{n}}_i \cdot \left(\nabla \Phi_\infty + [\tilde{\omega}]r_i + \mathbf{v}_i\right) \qquad (5.7)$$

For a given set of singularity functions $\{\phi\}$, a given set of control points $\{\mathbf{x}\}$, and specific free-stream conditions, the only unknowns in Equation 5.7 are the weighting coefficients $\{\Gamma\}$. Equation 5.7 can then be solved for the weighting coefficients. Clearly, the number of control points must be equal to the number of singularity elements for the system to be solvable. It is also clear that the choice and placement of the singularity elements are a matter of modeling. In addition to the surface of the aircraft, the singularity elements are also placed on the vortex wake trailing the aircraft. The vortex wake would not have been predicted by Equation 5.2, but it is known to exist, and can be modeled reasonably well by a sheet of singular source.

Table 5.3   VLM singularity element tradeoffs

	Horseshoe	VR	NQS VR	NQS Wake VR
CPU Time	Low	Low	Low	Medium-High
3-D Volumes	No	Yes	Yes	Yes
Fast Morphing	No	No	Yes	Yes

VR Vortex Ring, NQS Non Quasi-Static

The various lattice methods differ in the choice of singularity elements and the details of the treatment of the vortex wake. Numerous options exist in the literature, with various strengths and weaknesses. The key tradeoffs are described in Table 5.3.

5.2.2   Calculation of Forces and Moments

Forces and moments on the panels, planforms, and complete aircraft are computed by a summation of the Lorentz force across all the panels. Thus, we have:

$$\mathbf{F} = \sum_i \rho[\tilde{\mathbf{V}}_i]\mathbf{\Gamma}_i \tag{5.8}$$

$$\tau_{\mathbf{aero}} = \sum_i \rho[\tilde{\mathbf{r}}_i]\big([\tilde{\mathbf{V}}_i]\mathbf{\Gamma}_i\big) \tag{5.9}$$

where $\vec{r}_i$ is the position vector of the ith panel (relative to the origin of the body coordinate system), and $\vec{V}_i$ is the airstream velocity at the ith control point. The direct method used here requires more computation than methods based on vorticity or flow field alone, but it provides more detailed information about the distribution of the aerodynamic loads and three-dimensional forces and moments.

5.2.3   Effect of Gull-Wing Morphing on Aerodynamics

The dependence of aerodynamic moments on the control surfaces is illustrated in Figures 5.3 and 5.4. The l, m, and n moment coefficients refer to the moments induced about the body X,Y, and Z axes, respectively. The moment coefficients are plotted vs. the gull angle deflection (left figure), and the induced drag coefficient (right figure). As can be seen, the asymmetric wing configuration produces a roll moment and a (significantly weaker) yaw moment. This is qualitatively similar to the action of the ailerons. For equal deflection angles, the ailerons actually produce a larger roll moment. Comparing the y-axes of Figures 5.3 and 5.4, we see the physical ailerons are almost twice as effective at inducing aerodynamic moments, at matched deflection angles. However, this comes at the cost of increased induced drag. From Figures 5.3 and 5.4, it can be seen that wing morphing actually produces a higher roll moment than ailerons at matched induced drag. Furthermore, the modulation of induced drag with morphing is quite small (for the range of angles considered), whereas aileron deflection strongly impacts drag. It should be noted that only induced drag is computed; however, the difference is expected to be qualitatively the same for viscous and form drag.

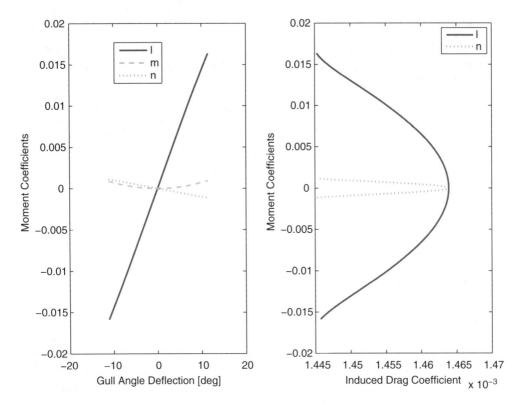

Figure 5.3   The aerodynamic effect of an asymmetric morphing deflection

5.3   Modeling of Flight Dynamics with Morphing

5.3.1   Overview of Standard Approaches

The conventional approach to modeling aircraft dynamics is to treat the aircraft as a rigid body. This is easily justified in most cases, since only small deformations of the aircraft are introduced by control surface deflections. Furthermore, if aeroelastic phenomena are not modeled, the elastic deformations of the aircraft due to applied loads can usually be neglected. Morphing aircraft, however, cannot generally be modeled as rigid. By definition, large structural changes are induced by morphing, and these are expected to modify the inertial properties and the dynamic behavior of the aircraft. The Rigid-Body Dynamics approach will fail if the deformations are large, or even if they are small but rapid (this will be explored in more detail in Section 5.3.2). We must therefore properly take the structural changes into account, if the aircraft behavior is to be modeled accurately.

A number of different approaches of varying levels of complexity and computational efficiency have been proposed and used. These can be roughly grouped into five categories:

- Rigid-Body Dynamics (RBD) with time-dependent inertia tensor
- Extended Rigid-Body Dynamics (ERBD) with full set of morphing forces and moments

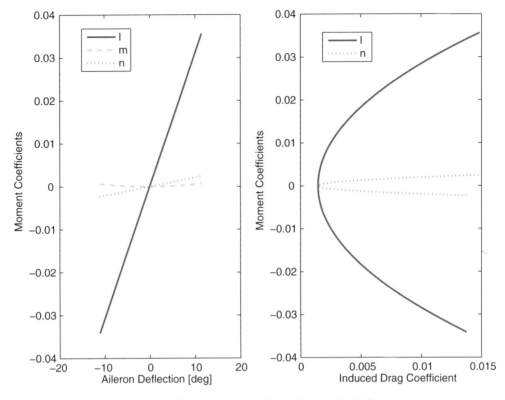

Figure 5.4   The aerodynamic effect of the physical ailerons

- Embedded Multi-Body Dynamics (Kane's Equations)
- Augmented Multi-Body Dynamics for systems of rigid bodies (Constrained Dynamics–CD)
- Augmented Multi-Body Dynamics for systems of flexible bodies (Flexible Constrained Dynamics–Flex CD)

The key choices to be made in determining the most suitable approach for a given problem are:

- acceptable CPU-time
- detailed morphing actuators, or morphing actuators as servoconstraints
- discrete-joint morphing, or continuum morphing
- type of linearized system - time-invariant, or explicitly time-varying

The tradeoffs are summarized in Table 5.4. As can be seen from Table 5.4, each method has its strengths and weaknesses. The CPU time is a qualitative assessment of the run time of a non-linear simulation based on each method. Rapid Morphing refers to the capability of the method to accurately model rapid changes in the aircraft structure. Continuum Morphing assesses the capability of the method to model large-scale continuum deformations, as opposed

Table 5.4　Flight dynamics model tradeoffs

	RBD	ERBD	Kane	CD	Flex. CD
CPU Time	Low	Low	Medium	Medium	High
Rapid Morphing	No	Yes	Yes	Yes	Yes
Continuum Morphing	Yes	Yes	No	No	Yes
Actuator Model	None	Servoconstraint	Full	Full	Full
Linearized System	LTV	LTI	LTI	LTI	LTI
Number of ODEs	12	$12 + 2n$	$12 + 2n$	$14n + m$	$> 10^3$

(n - Number of rigid bodies; m - Number of constraints

to morphing by discrete joints. The label Linearized System characterizes the system after linearization at a trim point as linear time-invariant (LTI), or linear time-varying (LTV). The Number of ODEs is a measure of the size of the system of differential equations required for non-linear simulation, with n being the number of bodies of which the system is comprised, and m being the number of constraints. Finally, the actuator model specifies how the morphing variables are handled. A full actuator model includes actuator dynamics which take into account the actual loads on the morphing joints. The behavior of the morphing joint is thus not prescribed, but is in fact computed based on control inputs and load dynamics. By contrast, a servoconstraint (Blajer 1997) prescribes the actuator dynamics using a simple model which is not a function of the joint loads, but only the control inputs (and the actuator state itself). In effect, the servoconstraint describes an actuator with a control system which mimics the behavior of a given simple model, and provides the necessary control forces and moments to track the model behavior in the presence of actuator loads. The required joint forces and moments can be computed as an inverse problem, as discussed in Section 5.4. If computational resources are no object, then Flexible Constrained Dynamics is the clearly the most effective solution. For an iterative design process of a control system or an initial design study, however, a more computationally efficient approach is preferable. Which method is selected will depend on the problem type.

5.3.1.1　Rigid-Body Dynamics with Time-Varying Inertia Tensor

Rigid body dynamics with a time-varying inertia tensor is a commonly employed technique (Chakravarthy *et al.* 2009; Davidson *et al.* 2003; Grant and Lind 2007; Grant *et al.* 2003; Niksch *et al.* 2008, 2009; Valasek *et al.* 2009; Yue and Wang 2009), whose primary merit is low CPU cost. The equations of motion are typically the standard Newton-Euler (Moon 2008; Shabana 2005) system for rigid bodies, with an explicitly time-varying inertia tensor. This approach is reasonable as long as the morphing rate is low compared to the slowest aircraft mode, i.e., quasi-static morphing. When morphing rates are higher, the dynamics need to be corrected. A commonly used correction term is the time derivative of the inertia tensor, i.e., starting with the expression:

$$\mathbf{L} \approx [\mathbf{J}]\omega \qquad (5.10)$$

and

$$\dot{\mathbf{L}} = \tau \tag{5.11}$$

time differentiation of Equation 5.10 yields:

$$[\mathbf{J}]\dot{\omega} + [\dot{J}]\omega = \tau \tag{5.12}$$

Equation 5.12 thus corrects the standard Euler equation with an additional term arising due to the time rate of change of the inertia tensor. However, Equation 5.12 is incomplete; this is due to the approximate nature of Equation 5.10 when applied to a non-rigid body in Equation 5.10 (would be exactly true in the rigid-body case). The full expression for the angular momentum of a non-rigid body is investigated in Section 5.3.2. It should be pointed out, however, that the correction term provided by Equation 5.12 is one of the less significant terms that need to be included (as is demonstrated in Section 5.2). Finally, morphing actuators are typically not modeled in this approach; instead, the moment of inertia tensor is made explicitly time-dependent in order to represent the effects of morphing. A consequence of this approach is that linearizing the aircraft equations of motion around a trim point results in a time-varying system of equations (LTV), which creates a challenging problem for control system design (Chakravarthy *et al.* 2009; Grant *et al.* 2003).

5.3.1.2   Multi-Body Dynamics

At the opposite end of the complexity spectrum are the various flavors of Multi-Body Dynamics (Kane and Levinson 1985; Moon 2008; Scarlet *et al.* 2006; Shabana 2005; Wittenburg 2002). The simplest of these is the Method of Virtual Power, or Kane's Equation (Kane and Levinson 1985; Moon 2008). The method is applied to a system of rigid bodies, using the principle of virtual power:

$$0 = \delta\dot{\mathbf{r}}^T \cdot ([\mathbf{m}]\ddot{\mathbf{r}} - \mathbf{F}) + \delta\dot{\omega}^T \cdot ([\mathbf{J}]\omega - \mathbf{M} - \tilde{\omega}[\mathbf{J}]\omega) \tag{5.13}$$

The vectors $\mathbf{r}$ and ω represent the positions of the center of mass (CM) and angular velocity of all the rigid bodies in the system. In order to use only independent degrees of freedom, $\mathbf{r}$ and ω are expressed in terms of generalized coordinates $\mathbf{q}$ as follows:

$$\dot{\mathbf{r}} = [\mathbf{a_1}]\dot{\mathbf{q}} + \mathbf{a}_{10} \tag{5.14}$$

$$\ddot{\mathbf{r}} = [\mathbf{a_1}]\ddot{\mathbf{q}} + \mathbf{b}_1 \tag{5.15}$$

$$\dot{\omega} = [\mathbf{a_2}]\dot{\mathbf{q}} + \mathbf{a}_{20} \tag{5.16}$$

$$\ddot{\omega} = [\mathbf{a_2}]\ddot{\mathbf{q}} + \mathbf{b}_2 \tag{5.17}$$

Upon substitution of the kinematic relations of Equation 5.17 into Equation 5.13, and recognizing that the terms $\delta\dot{\mathbf{q}}$ are independent, the final form of the Kane's equation is obtained:

$$[\mathbf{A}]\ddot{\mathbf{q}} - [\mathbf{B}] = 0 \tag{5.18}$$

Equation 5.18 is deceptively simple; the matrices $[\mathbf{A}]$ and $[\mathbf{B}]$ need to be recomputed at each time step (for non-linear simulation), recursively applying the kinematic expressions of Equation 5.17 across the entire system of rigid bodies. As can be seen from Table 5.4, the Kane's equation approach results in a small number of ODEs, since only independent degrees-of-freedom are used. By contrast, the Constrained Dynamics approach uses a large number of dependent degrees of freedom; six for each rigid body in the multi-body system. In addition to the Newton-Euler equations for each body, equations of constraint are formed for each joint in the system, as shown in Equation 5.19.

$$\begin{pmatrix} \mathbf{M} & \mathbf{C_q^T} \\ \mathbf{C_q} & 0 \end{pmatrix} \begin{pmatrix} \ddot{\mathbf{q}} \\ \lambda \end{pmatrix} = \begin{pmatrix} \mathbf{Q_e} \\ \mathbf{Q_d} \end{pmatrix} \tag{5.19}$$

In Equation 5.19, $\mathbf{M}$ is the generalized mass matrix, $\mathbf{Q_e}$ is the generalized applied force (non-constraint force), $\mathbf{C}$ is the constraint equation matrix, and λ is the vector of Lagrange Multipliers for the problem (Shabana 2005). Since these are typically algebraic (the constraint equation in Equation 5.19), the result is a Differential-Algebraic Equation (DAE) system, rather than the more straightforward system of ODEs. The underlying system of ODEs can be obtained by repeated differentiation (Fox *et al.* 2000). The result is a large, sparse system, given by Equation 5.20. Note that the constraints are satisfied approximately, since the constraint equation has been converted into differential form, and integrated with finite precision. The primary advantage of Constrained Dynamics over other methods is the relative ease of including elastic bodies.

$$\begin{pmatrix} \mathbf{I} & 0 & 0 \\ 0 & \mathbf{M} & \left(\frac{\partial \mathbf{C}}{\partial \mathbf{q}}\right)^T \\ 0 & \left(\frac{\partial \mathbf{C}}{\partial \mathbf{q}}\right) & 0 \end{pmatrix} \begin{pmatrix} \dot{\mathbf{q}} \\ \dot{\mathbf{v}} \\ \dot{\mu} \end{pmatrix} = \begin{pmatrix} \mathbf{v} \\ \mathbf{Q_e} \\ -(\mathbf{C_q\dot{q}})_q\dot{q} - 2\mathbf{C_{qt}\dot{q}} - \mathbf{C_{tt}} \end{pmatrix} \tag{5.20}$$

5.3.2   Extended Rigid-Body Dynamics

Extended Rigid-Body Dynamics (ERBD) (Obradovic 2009; Obradovic and Subbarao 2006), is a compromise between the simplicity of Rigid-Body Dynamics and the more complex but CPU-time-consuming Multi-Body Dynamics approaches. The key features of the method are the use of servoconstraints and the applicability to discrete-joint and continuum morphing. The final form of the ERBD equations is the Newton-Euler system for a rigid body, corrected by morphing forces and moments. This is somewhat analogous to the inclusion of the coriolis, transverse, and centrifugal forces in a non-inertial frame of reference. The equations of motion are derived by considering a multi-body (or flexible) aircraft, with a frame of reference attached to a fixed point in the body (typically a point in the fuselage), as shown in Figure 5.5. The morphing motion of the wings (or other morphing components) are described in this frame. We can now derive the Newton-Euler equations for this system.

5.3.2.1   Rotational Equations of Motion with Morphing

In order to derive the appropriate equations of motion (EOM), we start with rotational dynamics in the inertial frame. We then have the well-known result from Goldstein (2001):

$$\tau_{ext} = \dot{\mathbf{h}} + m\Delta\tilde{\mathbf{r}}_{cm}\dot{\mathbf{V}}_f \tag{5.21}$$

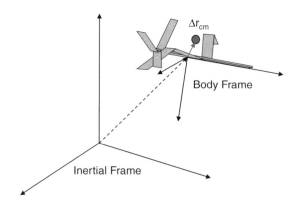

Figure 5.5   Displacement of the physical center of mass from the fuselage-fixed body frame

In Equation 5.21, τ_{ext} denotes the total applied moment, m is the total mass of the aircraft, $\Delta\tilde{\mathbf{r}}_{cm}$ is the displacement of the center of mass from the origin of the body frame (in skew-symmetric matrix form), and $\dot{\mathbf{V}}_f$ is the inertial-frame velocity of the body frame origin. The angular momentum in the body frame can be expressed as:

$$\mathbf{h} = \int \tilde{\mathbf{r}}([\tilde{\omega}]\mathbf{r} + \mathbf{v}')dm = [\mathbf{J}]\omega + \int \tilde{\mathbf{r}}\mathbf{v}'dm \tag{5.22}$$

The integration is taken over the entire mass of the aircraft. The term $[\tilde{\mathbf{r}}]$ is the skew-symmetric representation of the position of the mass element dm, $[\tilde{\omega}]$ is the skew-symmetric representation of the body frame angular velocity, and $\mathbf{v}'$ is the body frame morphing-induced velocity of the mass element dm. The final velocity term is unique to the morphing aircraft, and it results in the integral on the right-hand side of Equation 5.22. The term $[\mathbf{J}]\omega$ is simply the standard expression for angular momentum of a rigid body. The rate of change of the body frame angular momentum can then be expressed as:

$$[\mathbf{J}]\dot{\omega} + [\dot{\mathbf{J}}]\omega + \int ([\dot{\tilde{\mathbf{r}}}]\mathbf{v}' + [\tilde{\mathbf{r}}]\dot{\mathbf{v}}')dm + [\tilde{\omega}][\mathbf{J}]\omega + [\tilde{\omega}]\int [\tilde{\mathbf{r}}]\mathbf{v}'dm$$
$$= \tau_{ext} - m\Delta[\tilde{\mathbf{r}}_{cm}]\left(\dot{\mathbf{V}}_f + [\tilde{\omega}]\mathbf{V}_f\right) \tag{5.23}$$

The first term in the left-most integral vanishes, and we are left with the rotational equation of motion of the morphing aircraft in the body frame:

$$[\mathbf{J}]\dot{\omega} = \tau_{ext} - [\tilde{\omega}][\mathbf{J}]\omega - \left([\dot{\mathbf{J}}]\omega + m[\Delta\tilde{\mathbf{r}}_{cm}]\left(\dot{\mathbf{V}}_f + [\tilde{\omega}]\mathbf{V}_f\right) + [\tilde{\omega}]\int [\tilde{\mathbf{r}}]\mathbf{v}'dm\right.$$
$$\left. + \int [\tilde{\mathbf{r}}]\dot{\mathbf{v}}'dm\right) \tag{5.24}$$

The terms in parentheses on the RHS of Equation 5.24 are moments (referred to as "morphing moments" in this work) that are not present in the standard Newton-Euler equations for rigid body motion. Explicitly, they arise from the displacement of the CM from the body frame origin, the rate of change of the inertia tensor, and the body frame motion of mass within the aircraft. For the sake of notational compactness in subsequent sections, the morphing moments will be labeled as follows:

$$\mathbf{M_1} = -[\dot{\mathbf{J}}]\omega \tag{5.25}$$

$$\mathbf{M_2} = -m\Delta[\tilde{\mathbf{r}}_{cm}] \cdot \left(\dot{\mathbf{V}}_f + [\tilde{\omega}]\mathbf{V}_f\right) \tag{5.26}$$

$$\mathbf{M_3} = -[\tilde{\omega}] \int [\tilde{\mathbf{r}}]\mathbf{v}'dm \tag{5.27}$$

$$\mathbf{M_4} = - \int [\tilde{\mathbf{r}}]\dot{\mathbf{v}}'dm \tag{5.28}$$

For the special case of the rigid body, the morphing moments vanish, the inertia tensor is constant, and the rotational dynamics revert to the Euler equations. The final two terms involve non-trivial integrals. These can be treated analytically for simple cases, although general morphing requires a numerical treatement. (as described in Section 5.3). The relative importance of the various morphing moments will naturally depend on the aircraft as well as the flight conditions. This is studied in more detail on several morphing-induced turns in Section 5.5.

5.3.2.2 Translational Equations of Motion with Morphing

The translational dynamics are handled similarly to the rotational dynamics. The CM is not fixed at the body frame origin. The position, velocity, and acceleration of the CM in the inertial frame can be then be written as:

$$\mathbf{R}_{cm} = \mathbf{R}_f + \Delta\mathbf{r}_{cm} \tag{5.29}$$

$$\mathbf{V}_{cm} = \mathbf{V}_f + \Delta\dot{\mathbf{r}}_{cm} + [\tilde{\omega}]\mathbf{r}_{cm} \tag{5.30}$$

$$\dot{\mathbf{V}}_{cm} = \frac{\mathbf{F}_{ext}}{m} + \mathbf{g} \tag{5.31}$$

$$\dot{\mathbf{V}}_{cm} = \dot{\mathbf{V}}_f + [\tilde{\omega}]\mathbf{V}_f + \Delta\ddot{\mathbf{r}}_{cm} + 2[\tilde{\omega}]\dot{\mathbf{r}}_{cm} + [\dot{\tilde{\omega}}]\Delta\mathbf{r}_{cm} + [\tilde{\omega}][\tilde{\omega}]\Delta\mathbf{r}_{cm} \tag{5.32}$$

The equation of motion for the origin of the body frame then reads,

$$m\dot{\mathbf{V}}_f = \mathbf{F}_{ext} + m\mathbf{g} - m[\tilde{\omega}]\mathbf{V}_f$$

$$- \left(m\Delta\ddot{\mathbf{r}}_{cm} + 2m[\tilde{\omega}]\dot{\mathbf{r}}_{cm} + m[\dot{\tilde{\omega}}]\Delta\mathbf{r}_{cm} + m[\tilde{\omega}][\tilde{\omega}]\Delta\mathbf{r}_{cm}\right) \tag{5.33}$$

As was the case with rotational dynamics, the translational dynamics exhibit additional terms (in parentheses of Equation 5.33), as compared to the standard rigid body equations. The additional terms depend on the displacement of the CM (relative to the origin of the body frame), as well as on its 1st and 2nd derivatives. As in the case of the morphing moments, we define the morphing forces as:

$$\mathbf{F_1} = -m\Delta\ddot{\mathbf{r}}_{cm} \tag{5.34}$$

$$\mathbf{F_2} = -2m[\tilde{\omega}]\Delta\dot{\mathbf{r}}_{cm} \tag{5.35}$$

$$\mathbf{F_3} = -m[\dot{\tilde{\omega}}]\Delta\mathbf{r}_{cm} \tag{5.36}$$

$$\mathbf{F_4} = -m[\tilde{\omega}][\tilde{\omega}]\Delta\mathbf{r}_{cm} \tag{5.37}$$

This is a great simplification as compared to the rotational equations, since the morphing forces do not involve integration over the volume of the aircraft. Only CM displacement terms are involved.

5.3.3 Modeling of Morphing

In the ERBD formulation, morphing is modeled as the motion of mass in the body frame. The mass motion can occur either through discrete actuated joints, or by continuum deformation of aircraft components. In either case, we must be able to compute the following set of quantities:

- position, velocity, and acceleration of the CM in the body frame;
- position, velocity, and acceleration of the discrete set of panels that make up the aircraft, computed in the body frame;
- instantaneous inertia tensor and its derivative in the body frame;

Note that the computation of positions and velocities of aircraft panels is also required for the Vortex Lattice calculation. When used in conjunction with Vortex Lattice aerodynamics, ERBD adds the computation of the accelerations and inertia tensor, but inherits many other computations from the VLM.

The actuator deflections (whether driving a discrete joint or a continuum deformation) cannot occur instantaneously. As will be seen in Section 5.4, the deflection rates strongly influence the required moments and power, and ultimately determine the feasibility of a given morphing configuration. It is therefore necessary to model the actuator dynamics. To this end, we introduce state variables for the actuator displacements $\{q_1, q_2, \ldots, q_n\}$. These are generalized coordinates of the system, and can represent discrete rotation or translation, or parameterized continuum deformation. Since the equations of translational dynamics involve the 2nd derivative of the CM displacement (itself a function of the configuration variables), we need a 2nd order system to describe the dynamics of each configuration variable. Thus, we also define the state variables $\{p_1, p_2, \ldots, p_n\}$, with $p_i = \dot{q}_i$. The desired or control input set is then $\{q_{c1}, q_{c2}, \ldots, q_{cn}\}$. A suitable 2nd order system is simply:

$$\dot{p}_i = -2\xi_i\omega_i p_i - \omega_i^2 (q_i - q_{ci}) \tag{5.38}$$

$$\dot{q}_i = p_i \tag{5.39}$$

with the parameters ξ_i and ω_i chosen to model an appropriate delay in the particular deflection. Once the dynamics of the actuators have been defined, it becomes possible to compute the required kinematic and dynamic quantities. Specifically, the instantaneous coordinates of the CM are simply obtained as:

$$\mathbf{r}_{cm} = \frac{1}{m} \sum_i \mathbf{r}_i m_i \tag{5.40}$$

where r_i is the position of the CM of the ith planform of which the aircraft is comprised (also including the fuselage). The position of the CM of each planform is updated as the panel is rotated, translated, or stretched. The instantaneous moment of inertia tensor is computed as:

$$[\mathbf{J}'] = \sum_i \left[[\mathbf{R_i}]^T [\mathbf{J_i}][\mathbf{R_i}] + m_i [\mathbf{\Delta \tilde{r}_i}][\mathbf{\Delta \tilde{r}_i}]^T \right] \tag{5.41}$$

where $[\mathbf{J}']$ is the instantaneous moment of inertia in the body frame, $[\mathbf{J_i}]$ is the moment of inertia of the ith planform in the reference position (prior to rotation or translation), m_i is the mass of the ith planform, $[\mathbf{R_i}]$ is the rotation matrix of the ith planform relative to the inertial frame, and $[\mathbf{\Delta \tilde{r}_i}]$ is the position of the CM of the ith planform.

The equations of motion require the computation of the 1st and 2nd derivatives of the CM, panel coordinates, as well as the 1st derivative of the inertia tensor. Since the aircraft can be arbitrarily complex, an analytical solution is not practical. Instead, the derivatives are computed numerically. However, it is important to avoid using finite differencing in time to obtain the derivatives. This would introduce a time step-dependent truncation error into the derivatives; doing so would increase the truncation error of the ODE step. Instead, the derivatives are computed as follows (where $\mathbf{x_i}$ represents a panel coordinate vector or the CM vector):

$$\mathbf{x_i} = \mathbf{x_i}(q_1, q_2, \ldots, q_n) \tag{5.42}$$

$$\dot{\mathbf{x}_i} = \sum_k \frac{\partial \mathbf{x_i}}{\partial q_k} \dot{q}_k \tag{5.43}$$

$$\ddot{\mathbf{x}_i} = \dot{\mathbf{q}}^T [\mathbf{H_i}]\dot{\mathbf{q}} + \sum_k \frac{\partial \mathbf{x_i}}{\partial q_k} \ddot{q}_k \tag{5.44}$$

where the Hessian term $[\mathbf{H_i}]$ is defined as:

$$[\mathbf{H_i}]_{jk} = \frac{\partial^2 \mathbf{x_i}}{\partial q_j \partial q_k} \tag{5.45}$$

Note that each element of the matrix $[\mathbf{H_i}]$ in Equations 5.44 and 5.45 is a three-dimensional vector. Similarly, the time derivatives of the inertia tensor can be expressed as:

$$\frac{d[\mathbf{J}]}{dt} = \sum_n \frac{\partial [\mathbf{J}]}{\partial q_n} \dot{q}_n \tag{5.46}$$

Thus, the temporal derivatives of panel coordinates, planform and aircraft CM, as well as inertia tensor components, are computed using numerical differentiation with respect to actuator positional variables only. This effectively computes the virtual displacements of the independent coordinates q. Time derivatives are included implicitly in the state variables $\dot{q}_i$. Since the accuracy of the numerical derivatives with respect to the actuator kinematic variables is independent of the local ODE integration time step Δt, the order of the local truncation error with respect to Δt does not change. The actual computation of the Jacobians with respect to the actuator positions is carried out by performing a set of virtual displacements of the actuator positions at every time step and using central differences to compute the derivative values. Only a minimal computational overhead is incurred. Numerical integration is required for the final two morphing moments. These are:

$$\mathbf{M}_3 = [\tilde{\omega}] \int [\tilde{\mathbf{r}}]\mathbf{v}' dm \approx [\tilde{\omega}] \sum_i [\tilde{\mathbf{r}}]_i \mathbf{v}'_i \Delta m_i \tag{5.47}$$

and

$$\mathbf{M_4} = \int [\tilde{\mathbf{r}}]\dot{\mathbf{v}}'dm \approx \sum_i [\tilde{\mathbf{r_i}}]\dot{\mathbf{v}}'_i\Delta m_i \qquad (5.48)$$

The terms inside the integrals are the positions and velocities of the mass elements of the aircraft. Since there is no closed-form solution to the integrals for an arbitrary aircraft, the values of M_3 and M_4 are obtained numerically at each time step. A natural discretization of the moving planforms is already available for the Vortex-Lattice mesh. However, this potentially represents a large number of points for velocity and acceleration calculations, so the Vortex-Lattice panels are grouped into a smaller number of larger, non-trapezoidal panels. The positions, velocities, and accelerations of the CM of these shapes is then used for the computation of M_3 and M_4. Numerical tests indicate that the values of M_3 and M_4 converge with as few as six to eight panels per planform. The velocities and accelerations are computed based on the positions using Equations 5.43 and 5.44.

An essential step in the ERBD method is the computation of the displacements, Jacobians, and Hessians that result from morphing. The general procedure is illustrated in Figure 5.6, and is based on the assumption of a tree-like structure of the aircraft.

The general algorithm can be summarized as follows:

1. Loop over all changed actuator states.
2. For each changed actuator, recursively update all branches below the actuator.
3. Apply virtual displacement to each actuator, and recompute panel positions.
4. From virtual displacement of panels, compute Jacobian and Hessian terms.

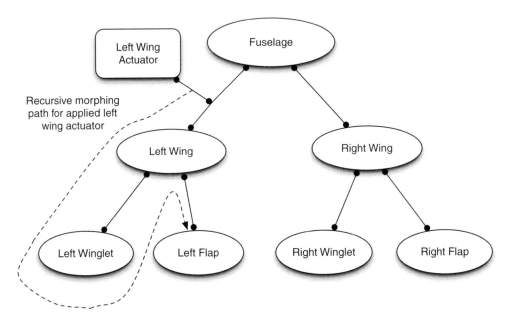

Figure 5.6   Depth-first recursive algorithm for the application of morphing

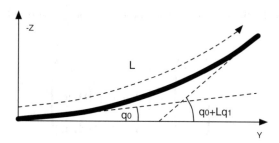

Figure 5.7 Two-parameter flexible morphing wing

Note that if the deformations are described analytically, the Jacobian and Hessian terms can be computed symbolically. This is particularly useful if the number of morphing panels of the aircraft is very large, such as in the case of continuum deformation. The continuum deformation case is illustrated on a flexible wing aircraft, which can morph the shape of the wing as illustrated in Figure 5.7.

A flexible morphing architecture, such as the one described by Figure 5.7, is most easily treated analytically. In the spirit of servoconstraints, the morphed shape is parameterized using (in this example) two parameters. This is in contrast to a Flexible Constrained Dynamics approach, in which the wing would have many finite-element degrees of freedom. The shape of the wing is characterized by the wing tangent angle as a function of the arc-length. The total length of the wing is assumed not to change by morphing. In the body frame coordinate system, the wing is oriented in the y-direction, and bends into the z-direction. The wing root angle q_0 and the arc-length rate of change of angle q_1 are used to parameterize the wing morphing. The differential equation describing the shape of the wing is then:

$$\frac{dz}{ds} = \sin(q_0 + q_1 s) \tag{5.49}$$

$$\frac{dx}{ds} = \cos(q_0 + q_1 s) \tag{5.50}$$

where the argument of the sin and cos functions represents the angular deflection of the wing at the span-wise coordinate s (as measured along the arc-length). The actuation variables $\{q_0, q_1\}$ are modeled using linear 2nd order systems, as given by Equations 5.38 and 5.39. The wing morphing Equation 5.50 can be solved analytically, giving the instantaneous wing shape:

$$z(s) = \frac{\cos(q_0) - \cos(q_0 + q_1 s)}{q_1} \tag{5.51}$$

$$y(s) = \frac{\sin(q_0) - \sin(q_0 + q_1 s)}{q_1} \tag{5.52}$$

The singularity at $q_1 = 0$ in Equation 5.52 is removable, and a Taylor series expansion of the numerator around $q_1 = 0$ is used for small values of q_1. The analytic formulation of the wing morphing (Equation 5.52) can be used to directly compute morphing moments M_3 and M_4 (as well as other quantities, such as CM displacement, etc.). As will be shown in Section 5.5, the most significant morphing term is the morphing moment M_4, so we examine it in more detail here in the context of the flexible wing. The body frame acceleration of a point on the wing can be expressed as:

$$\dot{\mathbf{v}}' = \begin{pmatrix} 0 \\ \frac{d^2 y}{dt^2} \\ \frac{d^2 z}{dt^2} \end{pmatrix} = \begin{pmatrix} 0 \\ \mathbf{J}_y \ddot{\mathbf{q}} + \dot{\mathbf{q}}^T [\mathbf{H}_y] \dot{\mathbf{q}} \\ \mathbf{J}_z \ddot{\mathbf{q}} + \dot{\mathbf{q}}^T [\mathbf{H}_z] \dot{\mathbf{q}} \end{pmatrix}$$ (5.53)

where the terms J and H are defined as the Jacobian and Hessian terms:

$$\mathbf{J}_i = \frac{\partial \mathbf{r}_i}{\partial \mathbf{q}}$$ (5.54)

$$^{nm}[\mathbf{H}]_i = \frac{\partial^2 \mathbf{r}_i}{\partial q_n \partial q_m}$$ (5.55)

The Jacobian and Hessian terms of Equation 5.55 are functions of the arc-length parameter s only, and can be computed analytically from Equation 5.52. The morphing moment M_4 is then given as:

$$M_4 = \int [\tilde{\mathbf{r}}] \dot{\mathbf{v}}' dm = \begin{pmatrix} \int (y \mathbf{J}_z - z \mathbf{J}_y) dm \, \ddot{\mathbf{q}} + \dot{\mathbf{q}}^T \int (y[\mathbf{H}_z] - z[\mathbf{H}_y]) dm \, \dot{\mathbf{q}} \\ \int (-x \mathbf{J}_z) dm \, \ddot{\mathbf{q}} + \dot{\mathbf{q}}^T \int (-x[\mathbf{H}_z]) dm \, \dot{\mathbf{q}} \\ \int (x \mathbf{J}_y) dm \, \ddot{\mathbf{q}} + \dot{\mathbf{q}}^T \int (x[\mathbf{H}_y]) dm \, \dot{\mathbf{q}} \end{pmatrix}$$ (5.56)

Equation 5.56 is a general expression for the morphing moment M_4, for a wing that morphs in the $Y-Z$ plane (as illustrated in Figure 5.7). Since the expressions for the morphing are analytic, all terms in Equation 5.56 can be evaluated in closed form. While this is somewhat tedious, it is computationally efficient, and needs only be done once. Anticipating the numerical results of Section 5.5, we expect M_4 to be dominated by the second temporal derivative term in the X-direction (for rapid morphing, second derivative terms tend to dominate, and the integration of the mass elements across the Y-oriented wing favors terms with y-products). Then, an approximate analytic expression for M_4, appropriate for 1st order deformations, is given as:

$$M_4 = \hat{\mathbf{x}} \int_0^L y[\mathbf{J}_z] \ddot{\mathbf{q}} \rho W \, dy = \hat{\mathbf{x}} \, m_w \frac{L}{2} (cos(q_0) \ddot{q}_0 + sin(q_0) \ddot{q}_1)$$ (5.57)

where m_w is the total mass of the wing, and L is the span. An additional contribution would come from the left wing, using generalized coordinates q_2, q_3. Equation 5.57 was obtained by considering the most important terms of Equation 5.56 and reducing to 1st order for the sake of obtaining intuitive understanding; the full expression of Equation 5.56 is used for numerical computations.

ERBD is a useful tool for theoretical analyses of this kind. Attempting to extract the most significant terms using a Flexible Constrained Dynamics approach for approximate analysis is not straightforward.

5.4 Actuator Moments and Power

The subject of actuator loading in morphing architectures is of critical importance, since excessive loads or power requirement may make a given morphing architecture impractical. The required loads may be beyond the capabilities of practical actuators, or may require a careful control system design to minimize the peak loads during maneuvers. This is particularly of concern with "fast" morphing, as used for maneuvering or aeroelastic control. Gradual morphing for mission optimization is less impacted.

From a computational standpoint, ERBD presents an interesting challenge for computing actuator loading. Since the actuators are modeled as servoconstraints, their dynamics are known, but the required moments and forces are not. Actuator loading is therefore formulated as an inverse problem in the context of ERBD. The equations of motion are constructed using Lagrange's equation of motion. Each actuator variable ("morphing" coordinate) is assigned to a generalized coordinate q^j. The overall Lagrangian includes additional generalized coordinates, but it is the morphing coordinates that are of interest for actuator dynamics. Lagrange's equation for the jth actuator can then be written as:

$$\frac{dP^j}{dt} = \frac{\partial T}{\partial q} + Q^j + Q^j_{aero} \qquad (5.58)$$

where Q^j is the generalized force associated with the jth generalized coordinate (one of the morphing state variables), and P^j is the associated generalized momentum. The generalized force Q^j_{aero} represents the aerodynamic portion of the load (including gravity), and it is computed explicitly from the Vortex-Lattice aerodynamics solution. Since the dynamics of the problem are known (the required generalized forces are post-processed after the dynamics at each time step), the term $\frac{dP^j}{dt}$ can be computed at run time from the state vector. Thus, Equation 5.58 can be simply rearranged to yield an expression for the generalized actuator force in terms of known (computable) quantities:

$$Q^j = \frac{dP^j}{dt} - \frac{\partial T}{\partial q} - Q^j_{aero} \qquad (5.59)$$

In order to use Equation 5.59, expressions for $\frac{dP^j}{dt}$ and $\frac{\partial T}{\partial q^j}$ are required. Using the definition of generalized momentum, we have:

$$\frac{dP^j}{dt} = \frac{d}{dt}\left(\frac{\partial T}{\partial \dot{q}^j}\right) \qquad (5.60)$$

The kinetic energy part of the Lagrangian is obtained as:

$$T = T_f + \frac{1}{2}\omega^T [J]\omega + T_{morph}(q, \dot{q}) \qquad (5.61)$$

where T_f is the kinetic energy of the translational velocity of the body frame, $\frac{1}{2}\omega^T J\omega$ is the rotational energy of the body frame, and T_{morph} is the kinetic energy of the intra-body-frame motion of the morphing aircraft components. Specifically, we have:

$$T = \int \frac{1}{2}||\mathbf{V_f} + \mathbf{v}||^2 dm = \int \frac{1}{2}\left(||\mathbf{V_f}||^2 + ||\mathbf{v}||^2 + 2\mathbf{V_f}\cdot\mathbf{v}\right)dm \qquad (5.62)$$

$$T = T_f + \int \left(\frac{1}{2}||\mathbf{v}||^2 + \mathbf{V_f}\cdot\mathbf{v}\right)dm \qquad (5.63)$$

The term $\mathbf{v}$ in Equation 5.63 represents the velocity of a mass element of the aircraft, including both the rotational velocity of the body frame and the intra-body-frame morphing velocity. The first term (T_f) is the kinetic energy due to the translational motion of the body frame, and it does not explicitly depend on any morphing state variables. Thus, it will not contribute directly to the generalized force. The second term in Equation 5.63 is further expanded as follows:

$$\int \frac{1}{2}||\mathbf{v}||^2 dm = \int \frac{1}{2}||[\tilde{\boldsymbol{\omega}}]r + \mathbf{v}'||^2 dm$$

$$= \int \frac{1}{2}\left[||[\tilde{\boldsymbol{\omega}}]r||^2 + ||\mathbf{v}'||^2 + 2[\tilde{\boldsymbol{\omega}}]r \cdot \mathbf{v}'\right] dm$$

$$= \frac{1}{2}\boldsymbol{\omega}^T[\mathbf{J}]\boldsymbol{\omega} + \frac{1}{2}\int ||\mathbf{v}'||^2 dm + \int ([\tilde{\boldsymbol{\omega}}]r) \cdot \mathbf{v}' dm \qquad (5.64)$$

The third and final term of Equation 5.63 can be further expressed as:

$$\mathbf{V_f} \cdot \int \mathbf{v} dm = \mathbf{V_f} \cdot \int \left([\tilde{\boldsymbol{\omega}}]r + \mathbf{v}'\right) dm$$

$$= \mathbf{V_f} \cdot \int \left([\tilde{\boldsymbol{\omega}}]r\right) dm + \mathbf{V_f} \cdot \int \mathbf{v}' dm$$

$$= \mathbf{V_f} \cdot m[\tilde{\boldsymbol{\omega}}]\Delta\mathbf{r}_{cm} + m\mathbf{V_f} \cdot \Delta\dot{\mathbf{r}}_{cm} \qquad (5.65)$$

Thus, the complete kinetic energy of the morphing aircraft can then be summarized as:

$$T = T_f + \frac{1}{2}\boldsymbol{\omega}^T[\mathbf{J}]\boldsymbol{\omega} + \frac{1}{2}\int ||\mathbf{v}'||^2 dm + \int ([\tilde{\boldsymbol{\omega}}]r) \mathbf{v}' dm$$

$$+ \mathbf{V_f} \cdot m[\tilde{\boldsymbol{\omega}}]\Delta\mathbf{r}_{cm} + m\mathbf{V_f} \cdot \Delta\dot{\mathbf{r}}_{cm} \qquad (5.66)$$

The first two terms in Equation 5.66 are recognized as the translational and rotational kinetic energy arising due to body frame motion and are present even for rigid aircraft. The remaining terms arise due to morphing. The generalized momentum associated with the jth state variable can then be expressed as:

$$P^j = \frac{\partial T}{\partial \dot{q}^j} = m\mathbf{V_f} \cdot \frac{\partial \Delta\dot{\mathbf{r}}_{cm}}{\partial \dot{q}^j} + \int ([\tilde{\boldsymbol{\omega}}]r) \frac{\partial \mathbf{v}'}{\partial \dot{q}^j} dm + \int \mathbf{v}' \frac{\partial \mathbf{v}'}{\partial \dot{q}^j} dm \qquad (5.67)$$

where only terms that are explicit functions of the morphing state variable derivatives are included. Noting that the term $\mathbf{v}'$ is the body frame temporal derivative of the position vector $\mathbf{r}$ and simplifying, we have:

$$P^j = m\mathbf{V_f} \cdot \frac{\partial \Delta\dot{\mathbf{r}}_{cm}}{\partial \dot{q}^j} + [\tilde{\boldsymbol{\omega}}]\int \mathbf{r}\frac{\partial \dot{\mathbf{r}}}{\partial \dot{q}^j} dm + \int \mathbf{v}' \frac{\partial \dot{\mathbf{r}}}{\partial \dot{q}^j} dm \qquad (5.68)$$

The joints are assumed to enforce holonomic constraints only. Applying "cancellation of dots," we have:

$$P^j = m\mathbf{V_f} \cdot \frac{\partial \Delta\mathbf{r}_{cm}}{\partial q^j} + \int \left([\tilde{\boldsymbol{\omega}}]r + \mathbf{v}'\right)\frac{\partial \mathbf{r}}{\partial q^j} dm \qquad (5.69)$$

Finally, in order to obtain the generalized force in Equation 5.58, the time derivative of Equation 5.69 is performed. The obtained result is:

$$\dot{P}^j = m\left(\dot{\mathbf{V}}_f + [\tilde{\omega}]V_f\right) \cdot \frac{\partial \Delta \mathbf{r}_{cm}}{\partial q^j} + m\mathbf{V_f} \cdot \left(\frac{\partial \Delta \dot{\mathbf{r}}_{cm}}{\partial q^j} + [\tilde{\omega}]\frac{\partial \Delta \mathbf{r}_{cm}}{\partial q^j}\right)$$

$$+ \int \left([\tilde{\omega}][\tilde{\omega}]r + 2[\tilde{\omega}]v' + [\dot{\tilde{\omega}}]r + \dot{v}'\right)\frac{\partial \mathbf{r}}{\partial q^j}dm$$

$$+ \int \left([\tilde{\omega}]r + \mathbf{v}'\right)\left(\frac{d}{dt}\frac{\partial \mathbf{r}}{\partial q^j} + [\tilde{\omega}]\frac{\partial \Delta \mathbf{r}_{cm}}{\partial q^j}\right)dm \tag{5.70}$$

From a computational standpoint with respect to geometrical derivatives, the various terms in Equation 5.70 can be grouped into five categories: (1) terms which depend on the geometrical derivatives of the CM; (2) the time derivative of the geometrical derivatives of the CM; (3) the geometrical derivatives of panel coordinates; (4) the time derivative of the geometrical derivatives of panel coordinates; and finally (5) a mixed term which combines panel derivatives and CM derivatives. As will be demonstrated in Section 5.5, the terms involving time derivatives of the geometric derivatives (i.e., $\frac{d}{dt}\frac{\partial \Delta r_{cm}}{\partial q^j}$) are negligible (but are included for completeness).

In order to finalize the computation of the generalized force, the partial derivative of the kinetic energy (2nd term on RHS of Equation 5.59) is derived next:

$$\frac{\partial T}{\partial q^j} = \int \mathbf{v}'\frac{\partial \mathbf{v}'}{\partial q^j}dm + \int [\tilde{\omega}]\frac{\partial \mathbf{r}}{\partial q^j}v'dm + \int [\tilde{\omega}]r\frac{\partial \mathbf{v}'}{\partial q^j}dm$$

$$+ m\mathbf{V_f} \cdot [\tilde{\omega}]\frac{\partial \Delta \mathbf{r}_{cm}}{\partial q^j} + m\mathbf{V_f} \cdot \frac{\partial \Delta \dot{\mathbf{r}}_{cm}}{\partial q^j} \tag{5.71}$$

In Equation 5.71, the first, third, and fifth terms on the RHS prove to be negligible (as shown in Section 5.5), since they represent mixed temporal and geometrical derivatives. The 3rd term of Equation 5.70 cancels the 4th term of Equation 5.71. Likewise, the 2nd term of Equation 5.70 cancels the last term of Equation 5.71. The 2nd term of Equation 5.71 is identical to the "Coriolis" term of Equation 5.70 to within a pre-factor, which, when added to Equation 5.71, converts the Coriolis pre-factor from two to three. Collecting the terms of Equations 5.70 and 5.71, and dropping the negligible and canceled terms, the various components of the generalized actuator force are summarized as:

$$Q_{CM} = m\frac{\partial \Delta \mathbf{r}_{cm}}{\partial q^j} \cdot \left(\dot{\mathbf{V}}_f + [\tilde{\omega}]V_f\right) \tag{5.72}$$

$$Q_{Panel} = \int \left([\tilde{\omega}][\tilde{\omega}]r + 3[\tilde{\omega}]v' + [\dot{\tilde{\omega}}]r + \dot{v}'\right)\frac{\partial \mathbf{r}}{\partial q^j}dm \tag{5.73}$$

$$Q_{Panel-Rate} = \int \left([\tilde{\omega}]r + \mathbf{v}'\right)\left(\frac{d}{dt}\frac{\partial \mathbf{r}}{\partial q^j}\right)dm \tag{5.74}$$

$$Q_{Mixed} = \int \left([\tilde{\omega}]r + \mathbf{v}'\right)[\tilde{\omega}]\frac{\partial \Delta \mathbf{r}_{cm}}{\partial q^j}dm \tag{5.75}$$

From a physical standpoint, Equations 5.72 through 5.75 contain two types of terms: those induced by morphing, and those that are purely inertial in nature. Terms which depend explicitly

Table 5.5 Summary of actuator generalized force properties

Term Type	Q_{CM}	Q_{Panel}	$Q_{Panel-Rate}$	Q_{Mixed}
Morphing	No	Yes	Yes	Yes
Inertial	Yes	Yes	No	Yes

on morphing velocities or accelerations are present only in morphing aircraft. Inertial terms, which do not depend on the derivatives of morphing terms, exist in any aircraft type. Note that the term $m\mathbf{V}_f \frac{\partial \mathbf{\Delta r}_{cm}}{\partial q^j}$ is not a purely morphing term. The partial derivative of the CM with respect to joint angles is non-vanishing, even when the CM is never displaced from its original position. The geometrical derivative $\frac{\partial \mathbf{\Delta r}_{cm}}{\partial q^j}$ represents a sensitivity parameter which determines the degree of coupling of the CM motion to virtual displacements of the wing actuators. *Thus, even for non-morphing aircraft, this formalism is useful for studying the induced joint moments, as the first step in a flexibility analysis.* The morphing and inertial contributions of the various Q-terms are summarized in Table 5.5.

Three types of derivatives appear in Equations 5.70 and 5.71: temporal derivatives of panel coordinates (or CM) such as $\dot{\mathbf{r}}_i$, purely geometrical derivatives such as $\frac{\partial \mathbf{r}_i}{\partial q^j}$, and time derivatives of the geometric derivatives, such as $\frac{d}{dt}\left(\frac{\partial \mathbf{r}_i}{\partial q^j}\right)$. The first two derivative types are handled in a straightforward manner; the latter is computed as follows:

$$\frac{d}{dt}\left(\frac{\partial \mathbf{X}}{\partial q^j}\right) = \sum_k \frac{\partial}{\partial q^k}\frac{\partial \mathbf{X}}{\partial q^j}\dot{q}^k = \sum_k = [\mathbf{H}]_{kj}\dot{q}^k \tag{5.76}$$

where the elements of the Hessian matrix $[\mathbf{H}]$ in Equation 5.76 are the purely geometric 2nd order partial derivatives given by:

$$[\mathbf{H}]_{kj} = \frac{\partial^2 \mathbf{X}}{\partial q^k \partial q^j} \tag{5.77}$$

and X is a placeholder for a panel coordinate, or the CM. Similarly, mixed temporal and geometrical derivatives appear in terms such as:

$$\frac{\partial \mathbf{\Delta\dot{r}}_{cm}}{\partial q^j} = \sum_k \frac{\partial^2 \mathbf{\Delta r}_{cm}}{\partial q^j \partial q^k}\dot{\mathbf{q}}^k \tag{5.78}$$

which also require the computation of Hessian terms. It can be anticipated that terms which include the Hessian will be of lesser importance (this is verified by explicit simulation in Section 5.5). These expressions represent the 2nd order terms in the Taylor series expansion of the functional dependence of panel coordinates (or the CM) on the morphing coordinates. Thus, we can write for a panel coordinate r_i:

$$\mathbf{r}_i(q_1, q_2, \ldots, q_n) = \mathbf{r}_i(q_{01}, q_{02}, \ldots, q_{0n}) + \nabla_q \mathbf{r}_i \cdot (dq_1, dq_2, \ldots, dq_n)$$

$$+ \sum_k \sum_j \frac{\partial^2 \mathbf{r}_i}{\partial q^j \partial q^k}dq^k dq^j + O(dq^3) \tag{5.79}$$

The 2nd order derivatives in Equation 5.79 are just the Hessians of Equation 5.45. Thus, neglecting the Hessian terms is equivalent to a 1st order Taylor expansion of the transformation between the body frame Cartesian coordinates and the morphing coordinates. When the shape of the aircraft is nearly in steady-state (such as in a trimmed flight condition), we can expect the 2nd order contributions to be small. Finally, the required power for each actuator can be computed simply as:

$$\frac{dW_k}{dt} = Q_k \dot{q}_k \tag{5.80}$$

5.5 Open-Loop Maneuvers and Effects of Morphing

Having formulated the approach to the modeling of morphing aerodynamics and flight dynamics, we are in a position to study the behavior of morphing aircraft using full non-linear flight simulation. To this end, we have developed a software suite consisting of a C++ aircraft geometry and VLM aerodynamics library, along with a MATLAB flight dynamics and control system implementation (Obradovic 2009; Obradovic and Subbarao 2006). The overall equations of motion are time-integrated using an adaptive-time step Runge-Kutta-Merson solver (Merson 1957). We first turn our attention to open-loop maneuvers, in order to simplify the interpretation of results. We are particularly interested in examining the dynamic role of morphing in rapid maneuvers.

5.5.1 Longitudinal Maneuvers

We first examine a longitudinal maneuver in which morphing is used to briefly increase the lift of the wings. The aircraft begins the maneuver with its wings in a symmetric gullwing configuration, in trimmed, level flight. At $t = 15s$, the wings are rapidly lowered to a (nearly) flat condition and then maintained in the lowered position for 5 s. The wings are then raised back into the symmetric gull-wing configuration. The simulated trajectory and aircraft configuration are shown in Figure 5.8. The 4th and 5th aircraft snapshots in Figure 5.8 illustrate the lowered wing configuration.

As expected, the increased lift with the flattened wings results in the aircraft pitching upwards and gaining altitude, after which a phugoid-like oscillation is observed. The detailed state of the aircraft during this maneuver is illustrated in Figure 5.9. Due to symmetry, only longitudinal variables are involved in the dynamics. The pitch rate behaves largely as expected, with the exception of the negative pitch rate at the very beginning of the maneuver. This initial negative pitch rate is a result of the morphing moment M_4 (illustrated in Figure 5.10).

As can be seen from Figure 5.10, the expected aerodynamic pitch moment is slightly preceded by the morphing moment M_4, which acts in the opposite direction (for both the initial and final morphing). The morphing moment M_4 (Equation 5.28) is associated with the acceleration of mass elements within the body frame attached to the aircraft. As the wings are lowered, mass elements of the wings accelerate downward. This implies a finite rate of change of angular momentum around the Y-axis, which cannot take place without an applied moment in the Y-direction. The morphing moment therefore suppresses this change of angular momentum (at least initially).

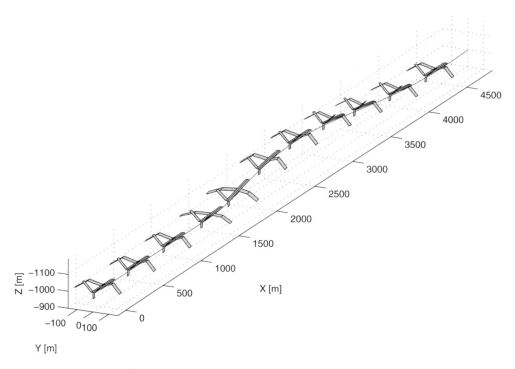

Figure 5.8   Trajectory with symmetric wing flattening

Since the M_4 moment is driven by acceleration of mass elements, while the aerodynamic moment is controlled by their displacement, the M_4 moment tends to precede the aerodynamic moment. The sign of M_4 depends on the details of the wing placement with respect to the CM of the aircraft. For the aircraft simulated here, most of the mass of the wings is behind the body frame origin (the CM of the aircraft prior to morphing), resulting in an initial negative morphing moment. *It is of interest to note that a similar effect was previously observed in Scarlet et al. (2006), although this was not explored in great detail.* The authors hypothesize that the pitching moment is an artifact of the control system (which may well be the case), but the configuration of the aircraft suggests that an implicitly modeled morphing moment may be responsible.

The overall behavior of the actuator moments for each joint during the entire 60 seconds of flight is illustrated in Figure 5.11. The abbreviations in Figure 5.11 stand for Left and Right Wing-Winglet and Wing-Fuselage joints. From Figure 5.11, it is apparent that there are five distinct time epochs that determine the qualitative behavior of the actuator moments: pre-morphing (up to t = 15s), first morphing (time period between t = 15s and t = 16s), inter-morphing (t = 16 to 20s) during which the effects of the morphed configuration are manifested, second morphing (t = 20 to 21s), and post-morphing (t = 21s and later), during which time the wings are in their original configuration. From Figure 5.11, ("Aerodynamic Joint Moments"), it is apparent that the aerodynamic joint moments are increased as the wings flatten. This is to be expected, since the overall lift is increased. The aerodynamic loads are therefore increased in the inter-morphing phase, and this is reflected in the actuator

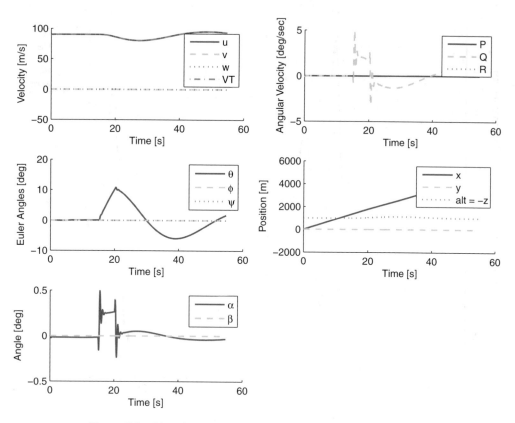

Figure 5.9 Aircraft state during symmetric wing-flattening maneuver

moments. The Wing-Fuselage joint moments are necessarily larger than the Wing-Winglet moments, since the Wing-Fuselage joints must carry the entire wing load. The aerodynamic loads depend on the instantaneous position of the wings, and the wing panel velocities. The latter are functions of the velocity of the aircraft body frame origin, the angular velocity, as well as the morphing velocities of the panels.

The inertial loads can be grouped into two categories: those with a significant non-morphing component, and those that are primarily morphing-induced. The only actuator moment in the former category is Q_{CM}, which is seen to be significant even in the post-morphing epoch. While some of the other moments do include purely inertial components (i.e., non-morphing) as summarized in Table 5.5, their inertial contribution is quite small. Furthermore, the moment $Q_{Panels-Rate}$ is seen to be negligibly small, as anticipated in Section 5.4. The Q_{CM} moment depends on the acceleration of the body frame origin (same for all actuators), modulated by a joint-dependent Jacobian term of the form $\frac{\partial \mathbf{r}_{cm}}{\partial q_k}$. The Jacobian term measures how much the CM of the aircraft shifts due to a perturbation of the generalized morphing variable q_k (in the case of the gull-wing aircraft, all q_k variables are rotation angles). The magnitudes of Q_{CM} are therefore longitudinally symmetric, but the Wing-Fuselage joints require a larger moment (due to the larger overall impact on the CM). The overall behavior is modulated by the body frame origin

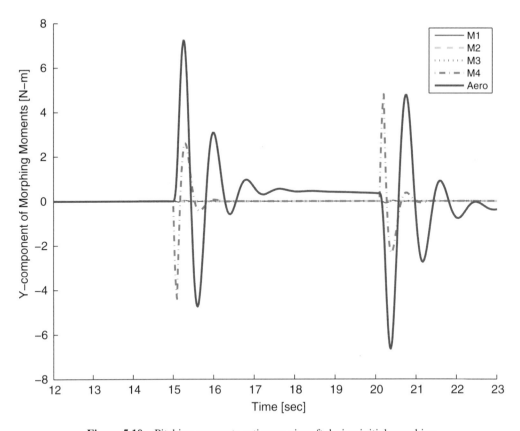

Figure 5.10   Pitching moments acting on aircraft during initial morphing

acceleration, which is identical for all joints. The sign of the Q_{CM} moment can be understood as follows: at the onset of morphing, the aircraft accelerates upward, due to increased lift. Inertial forces therefore tend to push the wings downward (beyond the acceleration dictated by the morphing model of Equation 5.38). The joint moment must therefore counter the inertial force and push the wings upward. In the sign convention used, upward rotation of the wings is considered positive. The positive joint moments persist during the inter-morphing period, as the aircraft continues to accelerate upward. The inertial term Q_{CM} therefore increases the overall load in this case (as evident from Figure 5.11, "Total Joint Moments").

After the second morphing event, the aircraft begins to accelerate downward (due to reduced lift), and the sign of the Q_{CM} reverses for all joints. Q_{CM} then oscillates during the post-morphing phase as the aircraft executes the phugoid-like flight mode.

The morphing motion of the wing results in moments Q_{Panels} and Q_{Mixed} (the latter also includes a contribution from the morphing-induced CM motion). In both terms, the dominant contribution arises due to the body frame acceleration of the wing panels. As the wings initially accelerate downward, the actuators must provide a negative moment (using the sign convention that positive angles increase the wing angle). As the wings slow down and settle into the flattened position, the required actuator moment becomes positive. The magnitudes of

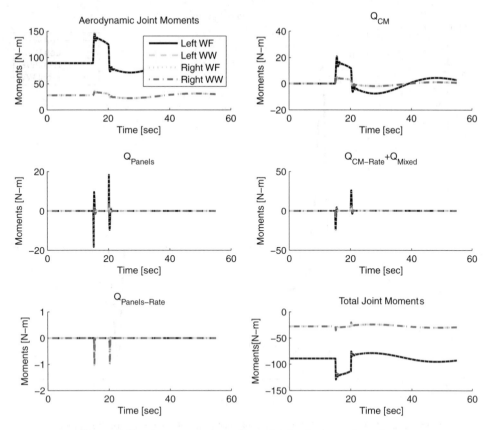

Figure 5.11 Actuator moments for each joint during entire trajectory

the morphing terms are comparable to the inertial (Q_{CM}) term in magnitude, but are of much shorter duration. The morphing terms are non-zero only during the morphing, whereas inertial terms are present whenever the body frame origin undergoes acceleration (and aerodynamic terms are present at all times).

The brief time period during which morphing takes place is particularly significant from the standpoint of power requirements. As is evident from Equation 5.80, actuator power is required only during morphing. However, all generalized forces contribute during this time—not just the morphing terms (the Q_k of Equation 5.80 is the total generalized force). The power required for the symmetric maneuver is illustrated in Figure 5.12. The sign of the required power in Figure 5.12 is at times negative, indicating work is done on the actuators. This is simply a consequence of the fact that, for a certain fraction of the time, the sum of aerodynamic and inertial forces is aligned with the desired acceleration of the wing panels (and the actuators consequently do negative work). However, this does not imply that the actuators are necessarily able to store this energy, unless a regenerative system is used. Thus, in general, energy will be expended during all phases of morphing motion, but the actual behavior during the negative power periods depends on the details of the actuators.

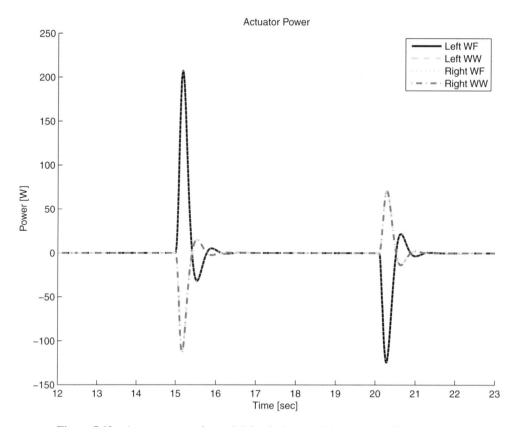

Figure 5.12   Actuator power for each joint during morphing portion of the trajectory

The magnitude of the required power depends on the morphing rate with (in principle) a super-linear dependence. At a minimum, Equation 5.80 contains a linear dependence of the morphing rate (through the $\dot{\mathbf{q}}_k$ term). The generalized force Q_k of Equation 5.80, however, is itself dependent on the morphing rate through the various morphing velocity and acceleration terms. Thus, we can expect the required power to be significantly decreased if the morphing rate is decreased. This is illustrated in Figure 5.13, where the actuator bandwidth was reduced by a factor of 2. The peak required power is noticeably decreased.

5.5.2   Turn Maneuvers

We now turn our attention to morphing-induced turn maneuvers. As was the case with longitudinal maneuvers, morphing moments and forces are expected to play a significant role in the dynamics. The particular maneuver we study involves asymmetric folding of wings, thereby inducing an aerodynamic roll moment. The aircraft begins the maneuver in trimmed, level flight, with symmetrically folded gull wings. At $t = 15$ s, only the left wing is lowered. The lift imbalance between the left and right wings produces a roll moment that results in a rapid turn, as illustrated in Figure 5.14.

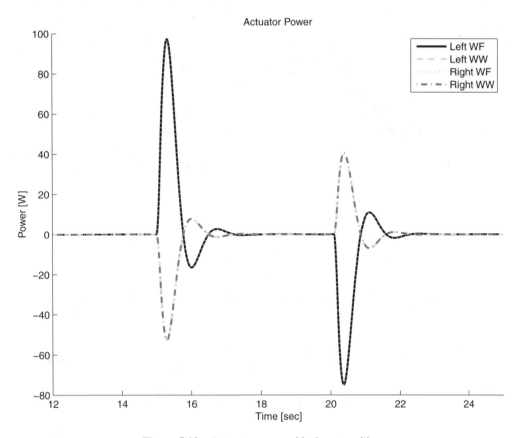

Figure 5.13   Actuator power with slow morphing

The overall behavior of the aircraft during the turn is illustrated in Figures 5.14 and 5.15. The angular velocity exhibits the expected spike in roll, induced largely by aerodynamic moments. Morphing moments (particularly M_4) also play a significant role in the dynamics, as shown in Obradovic and Subbarao (2006).

Much like the symmetric morphing case of the previous section, the behavior of the joint moments for the turn trajectory is best analyzed in three separate time epochs: the first 15 seconds before morphing, the 1.5 seconds of morphing, and the post-morphing remainder of the flight. Figure 5.16 illustrates all three epochs. From Figure 5.16, it is evident that during the first 15 seconds (trimmed, level flight), aerodynamic forces are the only source of joint moments. The joint moments are symmetric, and the Wing-Fuselage moments are $\approx 4x$ larger than the Wing-Winglet moments (the aerodynamic loads and moment arm are each $\approx 2x$ at the wing root).

During the morphing epoch, the aerodynamic moments change dramatically. As the left wing flattens, the lift on it increases, resulting in a sharp rise in the left wing root moment (and to a somewhat lesser extent in the left wing-winglet moment). During this period, morphing-induced moments appear as well. While all terms from Equation 5.70 contribute,

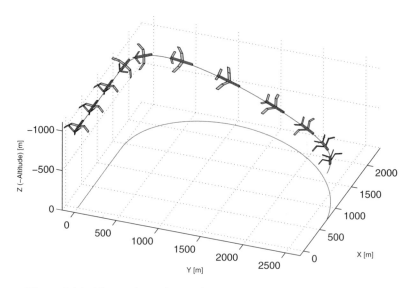

Figure 5.14   The turning trajectory induced by asymmetric wing morphing

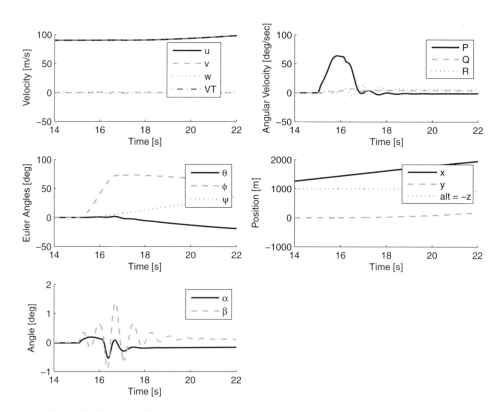

Figure 5.15   The full state of the aircraft during the morphing portion of the trajectory

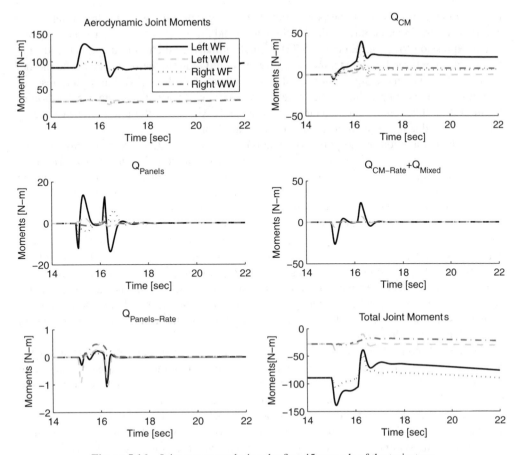

Figure 5.16 Joint moments during the first 45 seconds of the trajectory

the most significant are the terms involving the panel body frame accelerations (Q_{Panels}) and the acceleration of the body frame origin (Q_{CM}). The various joint moments are illustrated in Figure 5.16. The moment required to flatten the left wing is evident in Figure 5.16 (most evident in the Q_{Panels}). A negative moment is required to initiate the flattening, followed by a positive moment to stop it. At the end of the morphing state, the opposite sequence takes place, with a positive moment initiating the return to the symmetric gull-wing configuration and a negative moment ending it (also most clearly seen in Figure 5.16, Q_{Panels}). The dominant term in Equation 5.70 driving this effect is the panel acceleration term. Also, we see in Figure 5.16 the influence of inertial moments (Q_{CM}) on the right wing as well, in spite of the fact that it is not morphing. Particularly significant are the transverse acceleration (as the roll initiates) and the Y-direction motion of the CM (induced by the flattening of the left wing). Note that the effect is actually stronger on the right wing (which remains folded) than on the left wing (which flattens). This is caused by the larger coupling of the folded wing into the lateral motion of the CM. By the time the Q_{CM} moment peaks, the left wing is fully flattened. The acceleration vector during the turn is nearly parallel to the left wing, but the Jacobian for the left wing motion is nearly perpendicular to the wing (since the wing is almost flat at that point). Thus, the inner product of the Jacobian term and the acceleration vector which appears in the expression for Q_{CM} (Equation 5.72) is small. Finally, as the morphing epoch ends and the wings are returned to the symmetric gull-wing configuration, the influence of the inertial moments becomes more significant (as shown in Figure 5.16 by Q_{CM}) than at the onset of morphing. This is simply due to the increased velocity and, particularly, the acceleration of the aircraft at this point in the trajectory (Figure 5.15). As seen in the figure, both V_f and $\dot{V}_f$ are increased, due to the post-morphing dive and rapid turn.

After the completion of morphing, only aerodynamic and inertial forces contribute to the joint moments. As can be seen in Figure 5.16, the aerodynamic moments increase (become more positive, turning the wings upward). The actuator moments preventing the wing motion are negative for both wings as the aircraft velocity increases, as evidenced by the plot of "Total Joint Moments" (Figure 5.16). The actuator moments during this epoch can be understood intuitively. The aircraft is still executing a turn (even though morphing has ceased), and the aerodynamic moments are pushing the wings toward the center of the turn (requiring a negative actuator moment to prevent that motion). At the same time, the inertial acceleration of the body frame (Q_{CM}) is bending the wings downward (requiring a positive actuator moment). Thus, the required actuator moment during the non-morphing part of the turn is a balance between aerodynamic and inertial terms. The aerodynamic moment is dominant, but the net moment is significantly reduced during the turn, relative to what would have been predicted by aerodynamic loading alone.

The inertial moments on the various joints Q_{CM} are evidently quite different during the post-morphing epoch, in spite of the fact that the acceleration of the body frame is a common term for all of them. This is shown in Figure 5.16. Mathematically, the difference is caused by the coupling coefficients to the CM motion, or more specifically, how it projects onto the acceleration of the body frame origin. Physically, the behavior is clearly understood from the aircraft state during the turn. The bank angle remains large for most of the turn, while the wings are folded in the symmetric gull-wing configuration. This means the right wing and the left winglet are essentially parallel to the body frame acceleration vector. Conversely, the left wing and right winglet are almost perpendicular to the acceleration vector (this is an exaggeration for the purpose of illustration; the actual difference in angles is not as pronounced). As a consequence, the moments required by the left winglet and right wing joint are reduced, relative to those of the left wing and right winglet.

5.6 Control of Gull-Wing Aircraft using Morphing

While it is certainly possible to control a morphing aircraft in open-loop configuration (as demonstrated in the previous section), this is not desirable for two reasons. The first is that control of a morphing wing aircraft may be challenging for the operator, due to the non-intuitive nature of the controls and aircraft dynamics. The second is the significant possibility of actuator saturation due to excessive joint loads and power requirements. Simultaneously managing the flight dynamics and actuator loading is a challenging task, particularly for rapid maneuvers. Rather than flying open-loop, it is therefore desirable to provide a control system which simplifies the control of the aircraft, while at the same time minimizing the actuator

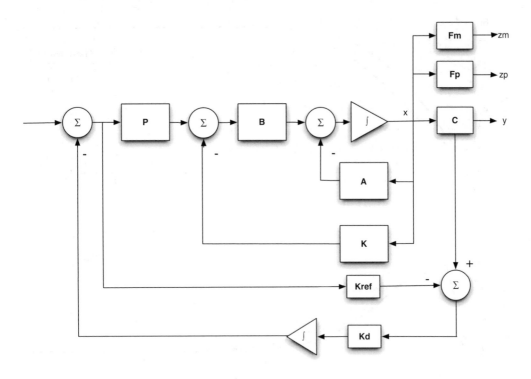

Figure 5.17   The block-diagram of the morphing-based SAS

loading, thereby preventing actuator saturation and energy waste. For this purpose, we turn our attention to a stability augmentation system (SAS) with actuator loading penalization. A useful by-product of this work is a study of conditions in which either morphing or conventional controls are preferable, from a performance/power tradeoff perspective.

5.6.1   Power-Optimal Stability Augmentation System using Morphing

The SAS in this work is an LQR-based linear control system (illustrated in Figure 5.17) with integral feedback. The system has full authority of only the bank angle, hence it is an SAS, rather than a CAS (Control Augmentation System). The control inputs are labeled Rudder, Elevator, Flap, Aileron, and Thrust, and are designed to mimic the behavior of standard control surfaces. Rudder and Elevator are realized as linear combinations of the ruddervon deflections, while the Flap and Aileron are achieved through combinations of symmetric and asymmetric morphing, as well as the conventional (physical) ailerons. Thrust is treated somewhat abstractly, with no physical model for the engine itself. Instead, it is treated as a body-axis aligned force with a second-order linear lag with respect to the commanded thrust. The morphing controls are illustrated in Figure 5.2. In Figure 5.17, block **A** represents the linearized aircraft dynamics, block **B** is the linearized input sensitivity. Block **P** represents the input mixing responsible for translating the Rudder, Elevator, Flap, and Aileron inputs into

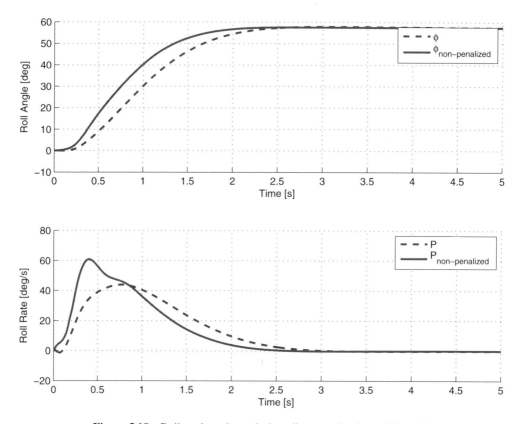

Figure 5.18 Roll angle and rate during aileron-assisted morphing roll

deflections of actual control surfaces. The LQR controller is represented by the **K** block, while the $\mathbf{K}_{ref}$ and $\mathbf{K}_d$ blocks form the integral feedback portion of the controller. The output matrix is given by the **C** block, while the $\mathbf{F}_m$ and $\mathbf{F}_p$ blocks represent the actuator moment and power outputs.

The SAS is tasked with providing stability and conventional aircraft-like handling. The integral feedback is used to make the steady-state bank angle function of the asymmetric input only, independent of the specifics of the control system. For this particular study, the aircraft is trimmed at level flight, with a forward velocity of 90 m/s (well within the limit of incompressible flow). The trim condition is established by adjusting the gull-wing angle (affecting lift and pitch moment), as well as ruddervon angle and thrust. The open-loop, rigid-body modes of the aircraft are stable, with the exception of the slightly unstable spiral mode.

Penalizing the morphing power tends to increase the reliance of the control system on physical ailerons. However, while the aileron deflection is increased (by 50%), the aircraft still relies heavily on morphing to achieve the required turn rate. The final morphing angle of the wing root is about 3x greater than the aileron deflection. Given that the aileron deflection

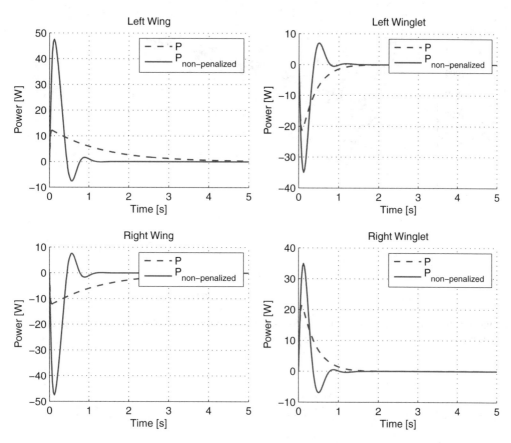

Figure 5.19 Actuator power during aileron-assisted morphing roll

is about twice as effective as gull-wing morphing at generating a roll moment (based on Figures 5.3 and 5.4), even the highly power-penalized aircraft is relying on morphing more than it is on the ailerons. However, while the reliance of morphing persists across all levels of power penalization, the morphing rate drops dramatically (Figure 5.21). This is not surprising, since the actuator power is very nearly linearly related to actuator deflection rates. The linear relationship is a consequence of the large and nearly constant aerodynamic moment component. In-plane morphing would minimize this component. As can be seen in Figure 5.21, the control system uses a high morphing deflection rate and no aileron deflection for minimal power penalization (high power). As the maximum allowed power is decreased, the morphing actuator rate is decreased and supplemented with increased aileron deflection rate. Thus, in the regime of low actuator power, the ailerons become the fast-response control surfaces, while the morphing actuators provide the steady state control. If actuator power is not a concern, the aircraft relies purely on morphing for both fast-response as well as steady-state control.

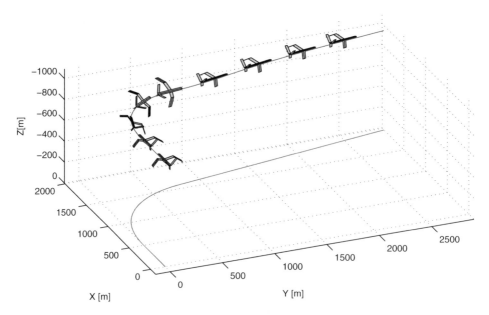

Figure 5.20 Aircraft trajectory during SAS-controlled turn. *Note*: Aircraft size exaggerated for visibility

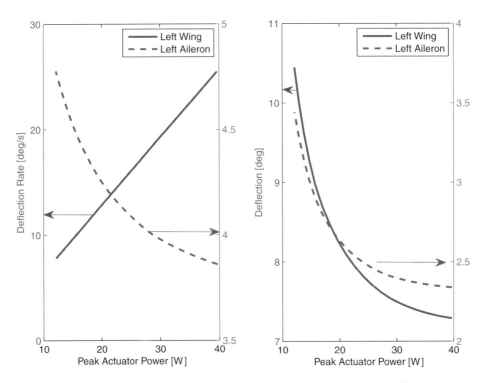

Figure 5.21 Effect of max actuator power on peak actuator deflections and deflection rates

5.7   Conclusion

We have described a complete set of models and a methodology for computationally-efficient simulation of morphing wing aircraft. The aerodynamics are modeled using an unsteady Vortex Lattice model, taking into account the motion of the morphing wing. In order to efficiently simulate the flight dynamics, we introduced a new approach, referred to as Extended Rigid-Body Dynamics (ERBD). The ERBD method accounts for the dynamic effects of morphing with a relatively small computational overhead beyond that required for purely rigid-body dynamics. Furthermore, the method is applicable to both jointed and flexible aircraft wings. It extends Rigid-Body Dynamics by adding morphing forces and moments as correction terms required to account for dynamic morphing effects. Furthermore, ERBD can be used to formulate analytic expressions (for sufficiently simple geometries), as well as fully numerical solutions. An example of the former is the bending-wing aircraft, while the gull-wing (jointed) aircraft represents the latter. Since the ERBD is based on the use of servoconstraints to model actuators and morphing, the dynamic actuator loads must be solved as an inverse problem. We provide a computational framework for computing the full actuator loads, which we classify as aerodynamic, inertial, and morphing-induced. Finally, the actuator power efficiency of gull-wing morphing was investigated. We observed that morphing is capable of producing roll moments more efficiently than ailerons, if compared at the same level of induced drag. However, the use of wing folding for maneuvering is energetically expensive, and a balance of aileron and morphing deflections must be maintained in order to prevent excessive actuator loads. It was also noted that the gull-wing architecture is particularly challenging from an actuator loading perspective. This is due to the large aerodynamic loads which the actuators must work against, even in the case of quasi-static morphing. An in-plane morphing geometry is therefore much preferable.

Appendix

$\mathbf{F}$	Net force acting on aircraft
$\mathbf{F}_1$	Morphing force associated with CM acceleration
$\mathbf{F}_2$	Morphing force associated with Coriolis force
$\mathbf{F}_3$	Morphing force associated with transverse
$\mathbf{F}_4$	Morphing force associated with centrifugal force
$[\mathbf{H}_i]$	Hessian matrix of i-th panel center with respect to morphing variables
$\mathbf{h}$	Angular momentum of aircraft
$[J]$	Moment of inertia tensor
τ_{ext}	Total external moment acting on aircraft
m	Mass of aircraft
$\mathbf{M}_j$	Morphing moment j ($j \in \{1, 4\}$)
$\hat{\mathbf{n}}_i$	Normal vector of the i-th panel
P^j	Generalized momentum associated with j-th actuator
Q_{CM}	Generalized actuator moment associated with CM motion
Q_{Panels}	Generalized actuator moment associated with panel motion
$Q_{CM-Rate}$	Generalized actuator moment associated with rate of CM motion
$Q_{Panels-Rate}$	Generalized actuator moment associated with rate of panel motion

$\mathbf{r}$	Position of a mass element within the body frame
$\tilde{r}$	Skew-symmetric matrix representation of r
$\mathbf{r}_{cm}$	Position of aircraft CM within body frame
$\mathbf{R}_f$	Position of body frame origin with respect to inertial frame
$\mathbf{R}_{cm}$	Position of aircraft CM with respect to inertial frame
Δr_{cm}	Displacement of aircraft CM from body frame origin
$\mathbf{V}_f$	Velocity of aircraft body frame origin
$\mathbf{v}'$	Velocity of a mass element in the body frame (body frame derivative of r)
$\mathbf{x}_i$	Position of center for the i-th aircraft panel in the body frame
Φ	Total velocity potential
Φ_∞	Freestream velocity potential
ϕ_i	Velocity potential induced by i-th panel
Γ_i	Induced vorticity of i-th vortex lattice element
$\boldsymbol{\omega}$	Angular velocity of body frame w.r.t the inertial frame
$[\tilde{\omega}]$	Skew-symmetric matrix representation of $\boldsymbol{\omega}$
ρ	Mass density (of air, or aircraft, depending on context)

References

Bertin J and Smith M 1979 *Aerodynamics for Engineers*. Prentice-Hall, Inc, Englewood Cliffs, New Jersey.

Blajer W 1997 Dynamics and control of mechanical systems in partly specified motion. *Journal of the Franklin Institute*, 334(3): 407–421.

Chakravarthy A, Grant D and Lind R 2009 Time-varying dynamics of a micro air vehicle with variable-sweep morphing. *AIAA Guidance, Navigation, and Control Conference*.

Davidson J, Chwalowski P and Lazos B 2003 Flight dynamic simulation assessment of a morphable hyper-elliptic cambered span winged configuration. *AIAA-2003-5301*.

Fox B, Jennings LS and Zomaya A 2000 *Constrained Dynamics Computations: Models and Case Studies*. vol. 16 edn. World Scientific Series in Robotics and Intelligent Systems, Singapore.

Goldstein H 2001 *Classical Mechanics*. Addison-Wesley: New York, NY.

Grant D, Chakravarthy A and Lind R 2003 Modal interpretation of time-varying eigenvectors of morphing aircraft. *AIAA Atmospheric Flight Mechanics Conference*.

Grant D and Lind R 2007 Effects of time-varying inertias on flight dynamics of an asymmetric variable-sweep morphing aircraft. *AIAA Atmospheric Flight Mechanics Conference and Exhibit*.

Kane TR and Levinson DA 1985 *DYNAMICS: Theory and Applications* 1 edn. McGraw-Hill, New York.

Katz J and Plotkin A 2001 *Low-Speed Aerodynamics* 2 edn. Cambridge University Press, New York, NY.

Merson RH 1957 An operational method for the study of integration processes. *Proc. Symp. Data Processing, Weapons Res. Establ. Salisbury*.

Moon FC 2008 *Applied Dynamics* 1 edn. WILEY-VCH, Singapore.

Nelson RC 1998 *Flight Stability and Automatic Control* 2 edn. McGraw-Hill, New York.

Niksch A, Valasek J, Strganac T and Carlson L 2008 Morphing aircraft dynamical model: Longitudinal shape changes. *Atmospheric Flight Mechanics Conference*, Honolulu, HI.

Niksch A, Valasek J, Strganac T and Carlson L 2009 Six degree-of-freedom dynamical model of a morphing aircraft. *AIAA Guidance, Navigation, and Control Conference*, Chicago, IL.

Obradovic B 2009 Modeling and simulation to the flight dynamics of morphable wing aircraft. Master's thesis. The University of Texas at Arlington.

Obradovic B and Subbarao K 2006 Modeling and simulation to study flight dynamics of a morphable wing aircraft, *AIAA Modeling and Simulation Technologies Conference*, Chicago IL.

Scarlet JN, Canfield RA and Sanders B 2006 Multibody dynamic aeroelastic simulation of a folding wing aircraft. *47th AIAA/ASME/ASCE/AHS/ASC Structures, Structural Dynamics, and Materials Conference*.

Shabana AA 2005 *Dynamics of Multibody Systems* 3 edn. Cambridge University Press, New York, NY.

Stevens BL and Lewis FL 2003 *Aircraft Control and Simulation*, 2 edn. John Wiley and Sons, New York.

Valasek J, Lampton A and Marwaha M 2009 Morphing unmanned air vehicle intelligent shape and flight control. *AIAA Infotech@Aerospace Conference*, Seattle, Washington.

Wittenburg J 2002 *Dynamics of Multibody Systems* 2 edn. Springer Verlag, New York.

Yechout TR and Morris SL 2003 *Introduction to Aircraft Flight Mechanics: Performance, Static Stability, Dynamic Stability and Classical Feedback Control*. AIAA Education Series.

Yue T and Wang L 2009 Multibody dynamic modeling and simulation of a tailless folding wing morphing aircraft. *AIAA Atmospheric Flight Mechanics Conference*.

6

Flight Dynamics Modeling of Avian-Inspired Aircraft

Jared Grauer and James Hubbard Jr.
University of Maryland and National Institute of Aerospace, USA

6.1 Introduction

A morphing vehicle can be defined as an aircraft that undergoes a radical shape change. The ability to morph the vehicle configuration enables one aircraft to take on the roles of several different aircraft, allowing, for instance, optimized flight over a large flight envelope instead of merely one flight condition. Morphing constitutes a considerable challenge due to several problems. The actuators required to perform large-scale shape changing often add weight to the vehicle to the point where performance increases due to the morphing are counter-balanced by the performance decreases due to additional payload. Morphing provides additional degrees of freedom to the system and has a huge influence on the stability and handling of a vehicle. There are certain configurations in which an otherwise stable vehicle could become unstable when morphed, or when morphed to quickly. Additionally morphing complicates the modeling and control process, changing discrete configuration variables such as wing span or dihedral angle, and adding other variables with spatial content including lift and chord distributions.

One interesting class of morphing vehicles is medium to large-scale flapping-wing aircraft, or ornithopters. These vehicles use large beating wings to excite unsteady aerodynamics and generate lift and thrust forces which propel the vehicle through the air. While most commercially available ornithopters today morph only with one degree of freedom, e.g. the wing angle, current research is aimed at applying fully morphing wings with differential control (Tummala *et al.* 2010), so that the ornithopter may become a more maneuverable and agile flight platform. However, even with only one morphing degree of freedom, the ornithopter exhibits several characteristics of morphing aircraft which significantly impact the manner in which they are designed, flown, and controlled. For instance, the wings carry a significant portion of the vehicle mass, so that their oscillation creates a moving center of mass and a periodic mass distribution.

Morphing Aerospace Vehicles and Structures, First Edition. Edited by John Valasek.
© 2012 John Wiley & Sons, Ltd. Published 2012 by John Wiley & Sons, Ltd.

Unmanned air vehicles, such as ornithopters, have the potential to fill a vacant niche in several applications. In the civilian world these vehicles work well as toys, hobby aircraft, and research flight platforms. They have been deployed in scenarios including wildlife population monitoring, atmospheric data collection, and airport wildlife control. They are expected to contribute to other applications including crop surveying and search and rescue missions. There are also several military applications for such a vehicle. They can be developed for missions such as autonomous intelligence, surveillance, and reconnaissance. They are expected to play a role in other missions including chemical plume detection.

An attractive vehicle choice for unmanned vehicle applications is the flapping wing. As the scale of the vehicle decreases, the three-dimensional, unsteady aerodynamic forces created by the flapping wings lead to improvements in aerodynamic efficiency over a steady airfoil. Recent results have shown that at small scales flapping-wing flyers are more efficient than fixed- or rotary-wing aircraft (Malhan *et al.* 2010; Pesavento and Wang 2009). It is expected that flapping-wing vehicles will best replicate the efficiency and agility seen in natural flyers, as well as serve as a robust flight platform with a high degree of contextual camouflage for completing selected mission profiles.

Several obstacles, however, stand in the way of accomplishing this goal. The unsteady aerodynamics which the flapping-wing ornithopters exploit are difficult to model, even using modern computational fluid dynamics tools (Shyy *et al.* 2007). Analytical models capture the basic mechanisms of flapping wing flight, including blade elements, quasi-steady regressors, and thin airfoil theory, but still fall short in fully describing flapping wing phenomenon (Dickinson *et al.* 1999). The flight motions for ornithopters are oscillatory due to the effects of the flapping wings, and are high in amplitude, complicating the analysis of flight dynamics models. Additionally like all miniature air vehicles, the ornithopter payload capacity is limited to MEMS-based avionics, which suffer from high noise levels and stochastic calibration parameters, and low mass and inertia give rise to higher wind-gust sensitivities.

This chapter is concerned with developing a flight dynamics model of ornithopter flight that can be used for simulation, system identification, and control design. Each of these steps is necessary to achieve an autonomous ornithopter, capable of completing real mission scenarios. Although applicable to a broad range of ornithopter designs, one particular ornithopter configuration is examined into order to carry out experiments and draw conclusions. The ultimate goal is to have a flight dynamics model that meets the following competing requirements:

- provides physical insight into the system dynamics to better design the vehicle;
- can be cast in a suitable form, e.g. state-space, to synthesize modern control algorithms;
- is efficient enough to accurately perform system identification;
- is low order to allow for the implement real-time control algorithms

This chapter presents work of the modeling of ornithopter flight dynamics in a way that captures the multibody effects, enables system identification from flight data and computer simulation, and facilitates the design of nonlinear flight control laws. Typically an ornithopter is modeled using conventional aircraft equations based on a six-degree-of-freedom model. Aerodynamics models are often experimentally validated by constraining the ornithopter to a load cell in a wind tunnel and time-averaging the force measurements. While these methods have led to hardware implementations capable of performing way-point navigation, the more challenging goals of indoor flight and perching require sophisticated models that better capture the behaviors observed in flight. As more research has been performed, it is apparent that a multibody model is necessary for the effective modeling of ornithopter flight dynamics.

In this chapter we begin with an introduction to flapping-wing flight and to the ornithopter research platform chosen for experimental investigation. Experiments into the aerodynamic characteristics, flight motions, and mass distribution are presented and lead to a nonlinear multibody model of the flight dynamics. These dynamics are then derived using energy-based methods and are cast in a canonical form that may be used in the nonlinear control of robots and spacecraft. System identification methods are employed to develop models of actuator dynamics and aerodynamic forces based on actual flight data. The model is then used to perform simulations and show the effectiveness of simple control laws.

6.2 Unique Characteristics of Flapping Flight

Flight using flapping wings is significantly different from flight using a fixed or a rotating set of wings. This section explores the characteristics of a flapping-wing vehicle and describes experimental characterizations that have led to the model development for the ornithopter. An ornithoptic research platform, used for experimental investigation herein, is first presented. Afterwards results from an investigation into the wing shape and force production of the ornithopter are described. Variation of the mass distribution with the vehicle configuration is also examined. Finally, inertial measurements taken in free flight are presented. This section concludes by suggesting the use of a nonlinear multibody model and a quasi-steady aerodynamic model for the ornithopter flight dynamics.

6.2.1 Experimental Research Flight Platform

The work shown in this chapter is applicable to any ornithopter platform and is thus ubiquitous in this sense. To engage in experimental work, a flight platform was obtained and modified for research purposes. The "Slow Hawk" ornithopter (made by Kinkade 2010), shown in Figure 6.1, was chosen for its durability, ease of piloting, and sensor payload-carrying capacity. The ornithopter has a 1.2 m wing span and a stock mass of 0.446 kg. This particular ornithopter is sized similarly to an osprey.

The fuselage is constructed from thin plies of carbon fiber. The wing sails and tail are constructed from a rip-stop polyester fabric membrane, reinforced with dacron tape and carbon fiber rods so as to maintain the wing shape. A primary wing spar is fitted through the leading edge of the wing and is connected to the flapping transmission. A secondary wing spar runs from the aft section of the wing root to the wing tip.

The ornithopter is controlled using standard radio equipment that is typically used to fly hobby airplanes and helicopters. A pilot launches the ornithopter and uses a transmitter to broadcast commands to an on board receiver, which then parses these commands to the respective actuators. The throttle stick controls the desired speed of a DC motor, which through a gear box and a four-bar linkage, flaps the wings. The faster the motor spins, the faster the wings flap, resulting in more lift and thrust force. The elevator stick controls a servo motor placed on the aft section of the fuselage which pitches the tail mechanism, and the aileron stick controls a second servo motor which rolls the tail flap. Orienting the tail flap relative to the

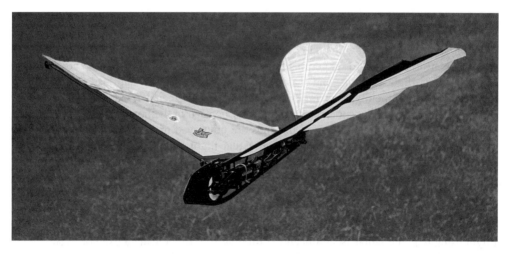

Figure 6.1   Experimental ornithopter flight platform

fuselage generates aerodynamic control torques on the aircraft, used to point the ornithopter in the desired direction.

6.2.2   Unsteady Aerodynamics

Flapping flight is characterized by the wing stroke, which is divided into the down stroke and the up stroke portions. The down stroke, the longer of the stroke phases, is where the majority of the lift and thrust forces are generated. In this phase the wing is moving downwards with a positive angle of attack, generating lift and thrust forces. Similarly during the recovering up stroke, the angle of attack is negative, so the wing can potentially generate negative lift, but usually also positive thrust. The down stroke needs to be shorter than the upstroke, and/or the vehicle needs to be flying with a net positive angle of attack, so that the beneficial lifting forces during the down stroke balance the detrimental forces generated during the down stroke. This vehicle has a stroke ratio of 1.18 and typically flies with a few degrees angle of attack.

The rapid movement of the wings generates unsteady aerodynamic forces not typically encountered in the modeling of conventional aircraft in steady flight conditions. It is known that in addition to Reynolds effects, mechanisms including leading edge vortices, dynamic stall, rapid pitch-up motions, and structural flexibility play a large role in the aerodynamics of flapping flight. Numerical studies employing computational techniques, for example (Shyy *et al.* 2007), have illustrated some of the underlying flow phenomenon. Wind tunnel testing (Krashanitsa *et al.* 2009) and hover tests (Dickinson *et al.* 1999) have also illustrated through experiment some of the flow physics and have quantified the degree to which each mechanism is responsible for the generated lift.

As model development directly from first principles is not currently accurate enough to model the aerodynamics of the ornithopter, an experimental study was performed to examine the aerodynamics. The ornithopter wings were fitted with roughly one hundred 1 mm diameter retro-reflective markers. A Vicon visual tracking system, consisting of eight cameras, was used to record measurements of the spatial position of each marker at a rate of 350 Hz. Additionally, the ornithopter was fixed to a 6 DOF load cell to measure lift and thrust forces.

Measurements of lift and thrust were synchronized in time with the marker position measurements, so that a data set of wing position and aerodynamic force was created. The position data was used as a prescribed input to the Reynolds-averaged Navier-Stokes CFD solver UMTURNS (Sitaraman and Baeder 2003). The solution was able to illuminate the flow field and show leading and trailing edge vortices, as well as predict time histories for the lift and thrust forces (Roget *et al.* 2009). The lift was accurately predicted, however, the thrust had significant errors due to resonance phenomenon not captured by the analysis. The position data was also used as an input for an analytical blade element model based on quasi-steady aerodynamics (Harmon *et al.* 2008). These results indicated that quasi-steady aerodynamics would be sufficient to model the lift and thrust production.

6.2.3 Configuration-Dependent Mass Distribution

In the case of fixed-wing aircraft, moving parts are generally small in mass and deflection angle, so that the aircraft is well approximated using an invariant mass distribution. Additionally, for small amounts of time, fuel usage does not significantly alter the mass distribution. In the case of rotary-wing vehicles, the rotor blades have less mass than the rest of the aircraft, and rotate at rates significantly higher than the rigid body dynamics of the aircraft. Hence for stability and control analysis, rigid body dynamics can be used to model the flight dynamics.

The same, however, cannot be said of the ornithopter. The wings and tail comprise approximately 23.5% of the aircraft mass, are located at the extremities of the vehicle, and flap at comparable rates to the expected rigid body modes. To compute the variation of the mass distribution with the configuration of the ornithopter, the center of mass and inertia tensor about the center of mass can be computed. For this work, the parts were modeled using a CAD package. It was found that the tail movement did not significantly impact the center of mass or the inertia tensor; however, the wing angle significantly altered both. Figure 6.2(a) shows the variation of the gross ornithopter center of mass location, as measured from the fuselage center of mass. As the wings move, the center of mass migrates vertically with the wings. The variation of the inertia tensor is shown in Figure 6.2(b). The off-axis products of inertia experience relatively small variations. However, the on-axis moments of inertia experience significant variations, especially in the pitching and yawing axes.

To adequately capture the effects of the mass distribution variation, this pose-dependence must be modeled. This can be achieved either using a single body model with a variable mass distribution, or rather with a multiple body model that encompasses several rigid bodies.

6.2.4 Nonlinear Flight Motions

While there is a growing amount of literature describing the development of lift and thrust forces for an ornithopter constrained in a wind tunnel, there is relatively little on the free flight dynamics of flapping-wing vehicles through the air. To investigate the dynamics in a free flight environment, a custom avionics unit was developed to record measurements as the ornithopter flew in straight and level mean flight.

The avionics unit is approximately 0.044 m by 0.070 m in dimension and has a 0.028 kg mass. On board is an inertial measurement unit, housing orthogonal triads of magnetometers,

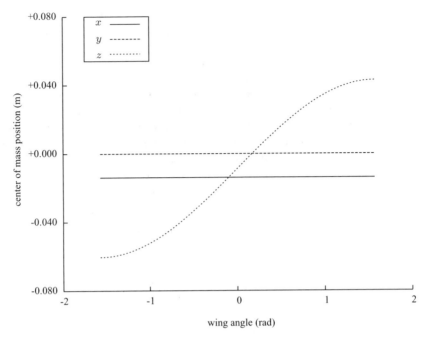

(a) Gross center of mass relative to the fuselage center of mass

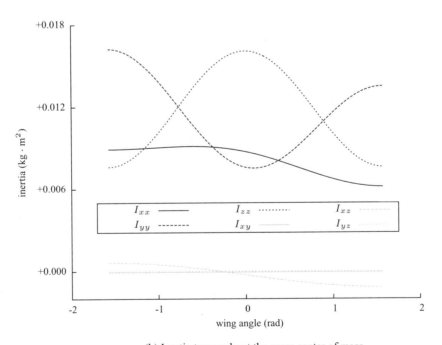

(b) Inertia tensor about the gross center of mass

Figure 6.2   Mass distribution variation with wing configuration

accelerometers, and gyroscopes. These sensors are common on aircraft and in autopilots, and are used for measuring orientation, linear motion, and rotational velocity. Additional sensors are also installed on the avionics board for measuring actuator commands and responses. The board is controlled using a reprogrammable PIC 18F8722 microprocessor.

A 6.4 second segment of flight data was recorded at 146 Hz during trimmed straight and level mean flight, and consisted of 28 complete wing strokes. As the recorded signals were periodic with the wing flap frequency, ensemble averaging techniques were applied to determine characteristic waveforms as well as statistics about the waveforms. Ensemble averages for some of the flight data signals are shown in Figure 6.3 with two standard deviation bounds, over the course of a normalized wing stroke period. The first plot shows the wing angle profile, which is approximately sinusoidal with a frequency of 4.7 Hz. The second plot shows the fuselage pitch rate, which oscillates up to 322 rad/s. The last plot shows the vertical heave acceleration, ranging up to 46.11 m/s^2.

These measurements, recorded in the most benign flight condition of straight and level mean flight, represent fast motions that are not characteristic of conventional aircraft. The fast and high amplitude oscillations are due to the flapping wings and would not be captured using a conventional aircraft model, suggesting the use of a nonlinear multibody model of flight dynamics. Additionally the high accelerations preclude the use of conventional attitude estimation methods, such as TRIAD or QUEST, and require a model-based state estimator to deduce attitude. The increase in variance near the transition part of the wing stroke alludes to unsteady aerodynamic effects.

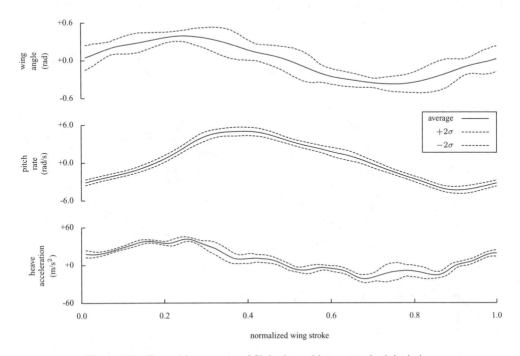

Figure 6.3   Ensemble averages of flight data with two standard deviations

6.3   Vehicle Equations of Motion

6.3.1   *Conventional Models for Aerospace Vehicles*

The dynamics of many aerospace vehicles are often well-approximated using the dynamics of a single rigid body. A diagram of a generic aircraft, modeled as a single rigid body, is illustrated in Figure 6.4. Vectors in this chapter are denoted using boldface lowercase symbols, where the subscripts denote the start and end points and where the superscripts denote which frame the vector is expressed in. Matrices are written as boldface uppercase symbols. An inertial coordinate frame is placed at an arbitrary point on the surface of the Earth C_I with the collection of "NED" unit vectors $K_I = \{\mathbf{e}_{xI}, \mathbf{e}_{yI}, \mathbf{e}_{zI}\}$ pointing in the north, east, and down directions. A body coordinate frame is placed at the center of the mass of the aircraft C_0 with unit vectors $K_0 = \{\mathbf{e}_{x0}, \mathbf{e}_{y0}, \mathbf{e}_{z0}\}$ pointing out the nose, right wing, and underside of the aircraft. The inertial frame is assumed to be a true inertial frame, fixed in one spatial location, while the body frame is fixed to the aircraft and moves with it.

The vector $\mathbf{r}_{0,I}$ describes the spatial position of the aircraft center of mass, relative to the inertial frame. The vector $\boldsymbol{\eta}_{0,I}$ is either a three- or four-element vector describing the orientation of the aircraft, relative to the inertial frame. In this chapter the orientation is parameterized using a unit quaternion

$$\boldsymbol{\eta}_{0,I}^{I} = \begin{bmatrix} \boldsymbol{\chi} \sin\left(\gamma/2\right) \\ \cos\left(\gamma/2\right) \end{bmatrix} = \begin{bmatrix} \boldsymbol{\epsilon} \\ \delta \end{bmatrix} \tag{6.1}$$

where the vector part $\boldsymbol{\epsilon}$ and the scalar part δ of the quaternion are derived from a single angular rotation γ about the Euler axis $\boldsymbol{\chi}$ (Hughes 2004). The quaternion is used because it is globally

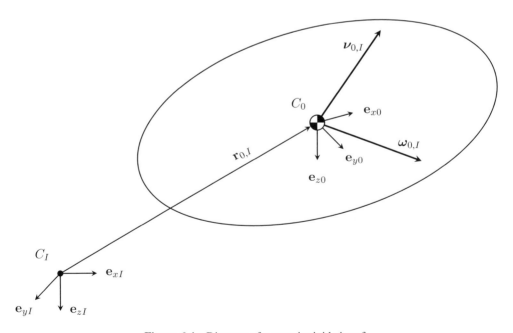

Figure 6.4   Diagram of a generic rigid aircraft

valid while the conventional Euler angles incur singularities at specific orientations (Kuipers 1998). The aircraft attitude (Equation 6.1) can be used to define a rotation matrix to transform quantities expressed in the inertial frame, e.g. gravity, into the body frame

$$\mathbf{R}^{0,I} = (\delta^2 - \boldsymbol{\epsilon}^T \boldsymbol{\epsilon})\mathbb{I} + 2\boldsymbol{\epsilon}\boldsymbol{\epsilon}^T - 2\delta S(\boldsymbol{\epsilon}) \tag{6.2}$$

where the skew operator is defined as

$$S(\mathbf{x})\mathbf{y} = \mathbf{x} \times \mathbf{y} = \begin{bmatrix} 0 & -x_3 & x_2 \\ x_3 & 0 & -x_1 \\ -x_2 & x_1 & 0 \end{bmatrix} \begin{bmatrix} y_1 \\ y_2 \\ y_3 \end{bmatrix} \tag{6.3}$$

and represents the matrix form of the cross-product operation for two vectors $\mathbf{x}, \mathbf{y} \in \mathfrak{R}^{3 \times 1}$.

The aircraft has translational velocity $\boldsymbol{v}_{0,I}$ and rotational velocity $\boldsymbol{\omega}_{0,I}$. These vectors are traditionally expressed in the body reference frame and denoted as $[u \quad v \quad w]^T$ for the translational velocities and $[p \quad q \quad r]^T$ for the rotational velocities.

The generalized position states of the aircraft are then

$$\mathbf{p} = \begin{bmatrix} \mathbf{r}_{0,I}^I \\ \eta_{0,I}^I \end{bmatrix} \tag{6.4}$$

expressed in the inertial frame, and the velocity states are

$$\mathbf{v} = \begin{bmatrix} \boldsymbol{v}_{0,I}^0 \\ \boldsymbol{\omega}_{0,I}^0 \end{bmatrix} \tag{6.5}$$

expressed in the body frame. Because the position and velocity states are written in different reference frames, the kinematic differential equations, which describe the evolution of the position states, have a non-flat relationship and are

$$\begin{bmatrix} \dot{\mathbf{r}}_{0,I}^I \\ \dot{\eta}_{0,I}^I \end{bmatrix} = \begin{bmatrix} \mathbf{R}^{I,0} & \mathbf{0} \\ \mathbf{0} & \mathbf{J}_\eta \end{bmatrix} \begin{bmatrix} \boldsymbol{v}_{0,I}^0 \\ \boldsymbol{\omega}_{0,I}^0 \end{bmatrix} \tag{6.6}$$

or rather more succinctly as

$$\dot{\mathbf{p}} = \boldsymbol{\Phi}\mathbf{v} \tag{6.7}$$

where $\boldsymbol{\Phi}$ depends on the vehicle orientation and has an inverse relation defined by the matrix $\boldsymbol{\Psi}$. For an attitude parametrization using quaternions, the attitude Jacobian matrix is

$$\mathbf{J}_\eta = \frac{1}{2} \begin{bmatrix} \delta\mathbb{I} - S(\boldsymbol{\epsilon}) \\ -\boldsymbol{\epsilon}^T \end{bmatrix}. \tag{6.8}$$

The dynamic differential equations describe the evolution of the velocity states as a function of the state variables and the applied forces on the system. For a single rigid body, these equations are most easily derived using the Newton-Euler equations

$$\frac{d}{dt} \begin{bmatrix} m\boldsymbol{v}_{0,I}^I \\ \mathbf{I}_0^I \boldsymbol{\omega}_{0,I}^I \end{bmatrix} = \begin{bmatrix} \mathbf{f}_0^I \\ \boldsymbol{\tau}_0^I \end{bmatrix} \tag{6.9}$$

and can be found in any book on flight dynamics (Klein and Morelli 2006; McRuer *et al.* 1973; Stevens and Lewis 2003). In Equation 6.9, m is the aircraft scalar mass, $\mathbf{I}_0$ is the aircraft inertia tensor, and $\mathbf{f}_0$ and $\boldsymbol{\tau}_0$ represent forces and torques on the aircraft, respectively.

Applying the differential operators and employing algebraic manipulations, Equation 6.9 can be written in the form

$$
\begin{bmatrix} m\mathbb{I} & 0 \\ 0 & \mathbf{I}_0^0 \end{bmatrix} \begin{bmatrix} \dot{v}_{0,I}^0 \\ \dot{\omega}_{0,I}^0 \end{bmatrix} + \begin{bmatrix} mS(\omega_{0,I}^0) & 0 \\ 0 & -S(\mathbf{I}_0^0\omega_{0,I}^0) \end{bmatrix} \begin{bmatrix} v_{0,I}^0 \\ \omega_{0,I}^0 \end{bmatrix} = \begin{bmatrix} \mathbf{f}_0^0 \\ \tau_0^0 \end{bmatrix} \tag{6.10}
$$

or more succinctly as

$$
\mathbf{M}(\mathbf{p})\dot{\mathbf{v}} + \mathbf{C}(\mathbf{p}, \mathbf{v})\mathbf{v} = \tau \tag{6.11}
$$

which is a canonical form for the simulation and nonlinear control design of Euler-Lagrange systems (Ortega and Loria 1998; Slotine and Li 1991). The matrix $\mathbf{M}(\mathbf{p})$ describes the generalized mass and inertia of the system as a function of its position variables. The matrix $\mathbf{C}(\mathbf{p}, \mathbf{v})$ contains nonlinear forces arising from centripetal and Coriolis accelerations. The vector τ describes the external forces, such as those arising from gravitational forces, aerodynamic forces, and control inputs.

As they stand, Equations 6.7 and 6.11 form a set of thirteen globally valid, ordinary differential equations (ODEs) which develop the position and velocity state variables of a rigid body vehicle. Using the position and velocity states it is a sufficient model with which to parametrize the flight dynamics of a conventional vehicle. However, there are several shortcomings of this model for modeling the flight dynamics of a flapping-wing ornithopter, or any other morphing vehicle. For instance, these equations were derived under the assumption of a rigid body with an invariant mass distribution. Relaxing this assumption in the derivation yields a new coupling matrix

$$
\mathbf{C}(\mathbf{p}, \mathbf{v}) = \begin{bmatrix} mS(\omega_{0,I}^0) + \dot{m}\mathbb{I} & 0 \\ 0 & -S(\mathbf{I}_0^0\omega_{0,I}^0) + \dot{\mathbf{I}}_0^0 \end{bmatrix} \tag{6.12}
$$

which adds accelerations resulting from a change in mass and a changing inertia tensor about the moving center of mass, which is now dependent on the aircraft configuration. While this augmentation would capture the gross effects of the changing mass distribution due to the wings flapping, it would not capture the internal reaction forces arising from flapping the wings. A multibody model is required to capture those reaction forces which generate the severe pitching rotations and heave oscillations.

6.3.2 Multibody Model Configuration

Due to the limitations of conventional aircraft models, a multibody model is needed to approximate the flight dynamics of a flapping-wing ornithopter. There are many methods of forming multibody equations of motion available. A designer must choose the method based on the goals of the model. For instance, the modeling process can be automated using computerized multibody codes (Masarati 2010). While these codes work well for simulation and analysis, they are often formed completely in the inertial frame and are difficult when used to parametrize the aerodynamic forces and develop models for stability and control analysis.

Analytical models, on the other hand, while more laborious to derive, provide the freedom to tailor a model to the specific goals of stability and control. Dynamics models can be categorized into classical methods and energy methods. Classical methods are based on using the Newton Euler equations (Equation 6.9) to form the rigid body equations of motion for each individual body in the multibody system. Algebraic constraint equations are then used to connect the individual linkages, resulting in a system of differential-algebraic equations (DAEs) that must be solved simultaneously. This method is the most general and straightforward, most often used in the multibody codes, but results in a large number of redundant state variables and a set of DAEs for which one must then use clever tricks to deduce the ODEs necessary for a stability and control analysis.

Another category of dynamics equations are those based on energy methods. These methods include the equations of Hamilton, Maggi, and Lagrange, which all stem from d'Alembert's principle of virtual work. In these methods the total scalar energy of the system is formed, and several differential operators are applied to find the dynamic equations of motion. Additionally the Gibbs-Appell equations (Greenwood 2003) and Kane's equation (Kane and Levinson 1985) use a similar approach with an "energy of acceleration" scalar quantity. While these methods require tedious computations of the state-dependent energy scalars and then several symbolic differentiations, they are preferred here for flight dynamics modeling because they admit ODEs with a minimum number of state variables, respecting the requirement for small but accurate models in control system design. Additionally the process requires no special tricks, computerized algebra software such as Mathematica can be used to automatically generate the equations. The energy scalars of the system also serve as inspiration for Lyapunov equations with which nonlinear controllers can be designed (Slotine and Li 1991).

The multibody configuration of the ornithopter consists of five rigid bodies, illustrated in Figure 6.5. A body is allocated for the fuselage, each wing, and each of the moving parts of the tail mechanism. Subscripts ij are used to denote each rigid body, where i is the linkage number and j is the chain number. Each rigid body has a coordinate frame K_{ij} placed at its local center of mass C_{ij}. Body fixed vectors l_{ij} and r_{ij} denote the locations of the inboard and outboard revolution joint positions relative to the local center of mass, which pass through axis vectors z_{ij} and $z_{(i+1)j}$, respectfully. Angles θ_{ij} indicate the rotation of the body ij about the axis z_{ij}, relative to its adjacent in-board body.

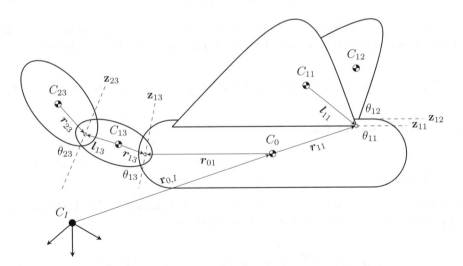

Figure 6.5   Multibody ornithopter schematic

6.3.3 Kinematics

The state variables for the ornithopter were chosen to parallel conventions used in both the aircraft and robot manipulator literature: a center fuselage with actuated linkages. The position states are

$$
\mathbf{p} = \begin{bmatrix} \mathbf{r}_{0,I}^{I} \\ \boldsymbol{\eta}_{0,I}^{I} \\ \boldsymbol{\theta} \end{bmatrix}
\tag{6.13}
$$

where $\mathbf{r}_{0,I}^{I}$ indicates the inertial position of the fuselage center of mass, $\boldsymbol{\eta}_{0,I}^{I}$ is the attitude quaternion for the fuselage, and the vector $\boldsymbol{\theta}$ concatenates the articulated joint angles of the wing $\theta_{11}, \theta_{12}, \theta_{13}$ and θ_{23}.

The velocity states of the ornithopter are

$$
\mathbf{v} = \begin{bmatrix} \boldsymbol{v}_{0,I}^{0} \\ \boldsymbol{\omega}_{0,I}^{0} \\ \dot{\boldsymbol{\theta}} \end{bmatrix}
\tag{6.14}
$$

where $\boldsymbol{v}_{0,I}^{0}$ and $\boldsymbol{\omega}_{0,I}^{0}$ are the translational and rotational velocities of the fuselage, and $\dot{\boldsymbol{\theta}}$ are the joint rates.

The center of mass position of link i on chain j has the position vector

$$
\mathbf{r}_{ij,I}^{I} = \mathbf{r}_{0,I}^{I} + \mathbf{R}^{I,0}\mathbf{r}_{0j}^{0} + \sum_{k=1}^{i-1} \mathbf{R}^{I,kj}(r_{kj}^{kj} - l_{kj}^{kj}) - \mathbf{R}^{I,ij}l_{ij}^{ij}
\tag{6.15}
$$

expressed in the inertial frame. The rotational velocity of the rigid body is

$$
\boldsymbol{\omega}_{ij,I}^{ij} = \mathbf{R}^{ij,0}\boldsymbol{\omega}_{0,I}^{0} + \mathbf{Z}_{ij}^{ij}\dot{\boldsymbol{\theta}}
\tag{6.16}
$$

in the body frame, where the matrix $\mathbf{Z}_{ij}$ extracts the appropriate axes of rotation for the joints. Differentiating the position vector (Equation 6.15) yields the translational velocity

$$
\boldsymbol{v}_{ij,I}^{0} = \boldsymbol{v}_{0,I}^{0} + S(\boldsymbol{\omega}_{0,I}^{0})\mathbf{r}_{0j}^{0} + \sum_{k=1}^{i=1} S(\boldsymbol{\omega}_{kj}^{0})\mathbf{R}^{0,kj}(r_{kj}^{kj} - l_{kj}^{kj}) - S(\boldsymbol{\omega}_{ij}^{0})\mathbf{R}^{0,ij}l_{ij}^{ij}
\tag{6.17}
$$

expressed in the fuselage frame.

6.3.4 Dynamics

Using the expressions for the velocities of each rigid body Equations 6.17 and 6.16, the kinetic energy of the system can be written using König's theorem

$$
T(\mathbf{p}, \mathbf{v}) = \frac{1}{2} \sum_{i=0}^{n_i} \sum_{j=0}^{n_j} m_{ij}(\boldsymbol{v}_{ij,I}^{0})^T(\boldsymbol{v}_{ij,I}^{0}) + (\boldsymbol{\omega}_{ij,I}^{ij})^T \mathbf{I}_{ij}^{ij}(\boldsymbol{\omega}_{ij,I}^{ij})
\tag{6.18}
$$

where n_j are the total number of kinematic chains and n_i are the number of linkages on chain j. Additionally the potential energy of the system is

$$U(\mathbf{p}) = -\sum_{i=0}^{n_i} \sum_{j=0}^{n_j} m_{ij} (\mathbf{r}_{ij,l}^I)^T \mathbf{g}^I \tag{6.19}$$

where $\mathbf{g}$ is the local gravitational acceleration vector. For this chapter, flight is assumed at standard sea level conditions, having a gravitational field strength of 9.81 m/s^2.

The Boltzmann-Hamel equations (Greenwood 2003) are then used to derive the system dynamic equations. These are a generalization of the Lagrange equations which accounts for the fact that the position and velocity variables are expressed in different reference frames. In matrix form these equations are

$$\frac{d}{dt} \left[\frac{\partial T}{\partial \mathbf{v}} \right]^T + \left(\sum_{k=1}^{n_v} \frac{\partial T}{\partial v_k} \boldsymbol{\Gamma}_k \right) \mathbf{v} - \boldsymbol{\Phi}^T \left[\frac{\partial T}{\partial \mathbf{p}} \right]^T = \boldsymbol{\tau} \tag{6.20}$$

where n_v are the number of velocity states, and where the Hamel coefficient matrices are defined as

$$\boldsymbol{\Gamma}_k = \boldsymbol{\Phi}^T \boldsymbol{\Lambda}_k \boldsymbol{\Phi} \tag{6.21}$$

with individual matrix elements

$$\{\boldsymbol{\Lambda}_k\}_{mn} = \frac{\partial \Phi_{km}}{\partial p_n} - \frac{\partial \Psi_{kn}}{\partial p_m}. \tag{6.22}$$

Equation (6.20) can be manipulated into the canonical form (Equation 6.11) using algebraic substitutions. Specifically, the kinetic energy can be written as the quadratic form

$$T(\mathbf{p}, \mathbf{v}) = \frac{1}{2} \mathbf{v}^T \mathbf{M_b}(\mathbf{p}) \mathbf{v} \tag{6.23}$$

which when substituted into Equation 6.20 and carrying out the differentiation, can be re-grouped as

$$\mathbf{M_b} \dot{\mathbf{v}} + \left(\dot{\mathbf{M}}_b + \sum_{k=1}^{n_v} \frac{\partial T}{\partial v_k} \boldsymbol{\Gamma}_k - \frac{1}{2} \boldsymbol{\Phi}^T (\mathbb{I} \otimes \mathbf{v}^T) \left[\frac{\partial \mathbf{M_b}}{\partial \mathbf{p}} \right]^T \right) \mathbf{v} = \boldsymbol{\tau} \tag{6.24}$$

where $\otimes$ is a Kronecker product operator (Brewer 1978).

The rigid body mass matrix $\mathbf{M_b}(\mathbf{p})$ is a summation of the mass matrices for each individual rigid body. Bodies with the same linkage number i have similar forms for the mass matrices. These matrices are found by taking the kinetic energy for each rigid body, and using algebraic manipulations to cast the energy in the form (Equation 6.23), from which the mass matrix is then obvious. The mass matrix of the fuselage body $i = 0$ is

$$\mathbf{M_b}(\mathbf{p}) = \begin{bmatrix} m_0 \mathbb{I} & \mathbf{0} & \mathbf{0} \\ \mathbf{0} & \mathbf{I}_0^0 & \mathbf{0} \\ \mathbf{0} & \mathbf{0} & \mathbf{0} \end{bmatrix} \tag{6.25}$$

which corresponds to the same as a conventional rigid body aircraft. Similar expressions can be found for the first linkage $i = 1$ (e.g. the wings) and the second linkage $i = 2$ (e.g. the tail flap) using this method.

The dynamic coupling matrix $C(p, v)$ can be found once the mass matrix has been determined. While the product $C(p, v)v$ is unique, the matrix $C(p, v)$ is not and can take several forms. In the nonlinear control of Euler-Lagrange systems, there is a specific formulation of the coupling matrix that satisfies the condition that $\dot{M}(p, v) - 2C(p, v)$ is a skew-symmetric matrix. This condition is often exploited in passivity control to design nonlinear controllers that do not cancel potentially helpful nonlinear system dynamics. The coupling matrix formulated in Equation 6.24 does not satisfy this property; rather by extension of Lewis *et al.* (2004), the coupling matrix

$$C(p, v) = \frac{1}{2}\dot{M}_b + \left(\sum_{k=1}^{n_v} \frac{\partial T}{\partial v_k}\Gamma_k\right) + \frac{1}{2}\left[\frac{\partial M_b}{\partial p}\right](v \otimes \mathbb{I})\Phi - \frac{1}{2}\Phi^T(\mathbb{I} \otimes v^T)\left[\frac{\partial M_b}{\partial p}\right]^T \quad (6.26)$$

facilitates these properties and is the formulation used in this chapter.

The full form of the rigid body ornithopter vehicle dynamics is

$$M_b(p)\dot{v} + C_b(p, v)v + g(p) + a(p, v) = \tau \quad (6.27)$$

where τ is a generalized force, $g(p)$ are the forces and torques due to gravitational acceleration, and $a(p, v)$ are the aerodynamic forces and torques that arise from flight. Gravitational effects are included vis

$$g(p) = \Phi^T\left[\frac{\partial U}{\partial p}\right]^T \quad (6.28)$$

and aerodynamic effects vector $a(p, v)$ will be discussed in later sections.

6.4 System Identification

In the previous section the rigid, multiple-body equations of motion were derived from first principles. In many instances, however, it may be necessary or beneficial to model a dynamical system using system identification techniques. System identification is the process of determining, using observations of inputs and outputs, a mathematical model that under specified conditions, behaves similarly to the physical system. Full texts on system identification have been written by Klein and Morelli (2006), Tischler and Remple (2006), and Ljung (1999). System identification is applied in this chapter to obtain models for actuator dynamics and aerodynamics, since their models were not known *a priori*.

After processing raw data from an experiment, there are two important steps to system identification: model structure determination and parameter estimation. Model structure determination is the process of cementing the form of a dynamical model, relating inputs to outputs. A model structure can be fixed using *a priori* knowledge or design requirements, or can be determined using statistical methods such as step-wise regression or orthogonal regressors (Klein and Morelli 2006).

Parameter estimation is then the process of determining the model parameters within the model, e.g. stability and control derivatives, based on the data. Parameter estimates ϕ are chosen to minimize a cost function

$$J(\boldsymbol{\phi}) = \frac{1}{2}(\mathbf{z} - \mathbf{y})^T \mathbf{R}^{-1}(\mathbf{z} - \mathbf{y}) \tag{6.29}$$

where $\mathbf{z}$ are measurements, $\mathbf{y}$ are model outputs, and $\mathbf{R}$ is a weighting matrix. Two popular simplifications of the maximum likelihood estimator are the equation-error and output-error methods. In the equation-error formulation, process error is assumed and the measurements specified are accelerations. In the output-error method, measurement error is assumed and the measurements are typically positions, velocities, and/or accelerations. Equation-error is often a linear estimation problem, having an analytical solution. Output-error, on the other hand, is in general a nonlinear estimation problem requiring an iterative solver; however, it has more realistic assumptions and is regarded as more accurate. In general, each estimation method may be performed in both the time and frequency domains.

6.4.1 Coupled Actuator Models

Laboratory testing and review of flight videos have shown that standard hobby actuators used on the ornithopter are not of good research quality and have non-ideal dynamics that would decrease closed-loop performance, such as lags. System identification was used to identify simple dynamical models for these actuators that improve the fidelity of the model.

On board the ornithopter are one brushless DC motor and two hobby servo motors. An experiment was conducted where the actuators were constrained to a torque cell while inputs were given and position or velocity outputs were measured (Grauer and Hubbard 2009a). Model structure determination was employed and resulted in the simple linear model structure

$$\mathbf{M_a}\dot{\mathbf{v}} + \mathbf{C_a}\mathbf{v} + \mathbf{G_a}\boldsymbol{\tau} + \mathbf{K_a}\mathbf{p} = \mathbf{B_a}\mathbf{u} \tag{6.30}$$

where here $\boldsymbol{\tau}$ are the joint torques and $\mathbf{u}$ are the pilot inputs. The matrix $\mathbf{M_a}$ describes the inertia of the actuator armatures. The matrix $\mathbf{C_a}$ models linear damping arising from viscous friction, electrical resistance, and back electro-magnetic force. The matrix $\mathbf{G_a}$ has along its diagonal the square inverse of the joint gear ratios. The matrix $\mathbf{K_a}$ describes the synthetic stiffness arising from proportional feedback in the servo motor control boards. The matrix $\mathbf{B_a}$ is control input coupling gains. No additional model accuracy was obtained using other types of friction models or additional control gains.

Parameter estimates were obtained in both the time domain and frequency domain using the equation-error and output-error methods for each actuator. Figure 6.6 shows the model fits to the data for each actuator using the time domain output-error method, as well as the residuals with a 95% confidence bound. The models matched the data well and the parameter estimates were accurate, as per the low error bounds on the respective parameters.

Solving the rigid body dynamics (Equation 6.27) for $\boldsymbol{\tau}$ and substituting into the actuator dynamics (Equation 6.30) couples the equations of motion and yields

$$[\mathbf{G_a}\mathbf{M_b} + \mathbf{M_a}]\dot{\mathbf{v}} + [\mathbf{G_a}\mathbf{C_b} + \mathbf{C_a}]\mathbf{v} + [\mathbf{G_a}\mathbf{g} + \mathbf{G_a}\mathbf{a} + \mathbf{K_a}\mathbf{p}] = \mathbf{B_a}\mathbf{u} \tag{6.31}$$

which remains in the canonical form for nonlinear control design

$$\mathbf{M}(\mathbf{p})\dot{\mathbf{v}} + \mathbf{C}(\mathbf{p}, \mathbf{v})\mathbf{v} + \mathbf{w}(\mathbf{p}, \mathbf{v}) = \mathbf{B}\mathbf{u}. \tag{6.32}$$

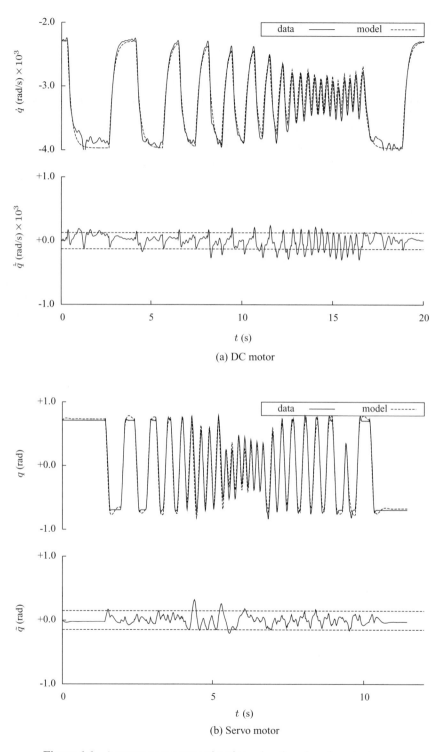

Figure 6.6   Actuator parameter estimation using time domain output-error

6.4.2 Tail Aerodynamics

A model for the tail aerodynamics was determined using conventional steady wind tunnel testing. The ornithopter was fixed to a load cell and placed in the test section of an open jet wind tunnel. Measurements of the lift and drag forces were recorded as the tail was cycled through a series of angles of attack and sideslip.

The method of orthogonal regressors (Klein and Morelli 2006) was used to determine the model structure of the lift and drag coefficients

$$C_L = C_{L_0} + C_{L_\alpha}\alpha + C_{L_{\alpha\beta}}\alpha\beta + C_{L_{\alpha^3}}\alpha^3 + C_{L_{\alpha^2\beta^2}}\alpha^2\beta^2 \tag{6.33}$$

$$C_D = C_{D_0} + C_{D_{\alpha^2}}\alpha^2 \tag{6.34}$$

based on the data. The equation-error method was used to estimate parameters in both the time and frequency domains. Model fits from the frequency domain analysis are shown in Figure 6.7 as surface response plots. The models matched very well and have small error bounds on the parameter estimates.

6.4.3 Wing Aerodynamics

In the dynamic equations of motion (Equation 6.31), the only unknown terms are the aerodynamic contributions $\mathbf{a}(\mathbf{p}, \mathbf{v})$. These terms can be isolated as

$$\mathbf{a}(\mathbf{p}, \mathbf{v}) = \mathbf{G_a}^{-1}[\mathbf{Bu} - \mathbf{M}(\mathbf{p})\dot{\mathbf{v}} - \mathbf{C}(\mathbf{p}, \mathbf{v})\mathbf{v} - \mathbf{G_a}\mathbf{g}(\mathbf{p}) - \mathbf{K_a}\mathbf{p}] \tag{6.35}$$

where the left side of the equation describes the aerodynamic forces and torques generated by the wings and tail, and where the variables on the right side are quantities that can be measured on the ground and during a flight test.

A flight test was conducted in order to perform system identification to determine the remaining aerodynamic contributions of the wings. Measurements of the position and velocity states were estimated from data gathered from a visual tracking system, which provided spatial positions of numerous retro-reflective markers placed on the ornithopter. Substitution of these measurements into Equation 6.35 then yields computed measurements of the aerodynamic effects, such as lift and thrust.

Step-wise determination was applied in the time domain to yield the model structure

$$C_L = C_{L_0} + C_{L_{v_x}}v_x + C_{L_{v_z}}v_z + C_{L_{\omega_y}}\omega_y + C_{L_{\dot\theta_{11}}}\dot{\theta}_{11} \tag{6.36}$$

$$C_T = C_{T_0} + C_{T_{\dot\theta_{11}}}\dot{\theta}_{11} + C_{T_{\theta_{11}^2}}\theta_{11}^2 + C_{T_{\dot\theta_{11}^2}}\dot{\theta}_{11}^2 \tag{6.37}$$

which is essentially a quasi-steady model for the lift and a parabolic model for the drag. Parameter estimates were computed in the time and frequency domains using the equation-error method. The time domain results are shown in Figure 6.8. The model captures the lift and thrust trends fairly well with a simple aerodynamic model.

System identification provided a key tool in developing the ornithopter flight dynamics model. While the rigid body vehicle dynamics were derived using first principles, aerodynamic and actuator models required an experiment and analysis. System identification resulted in low

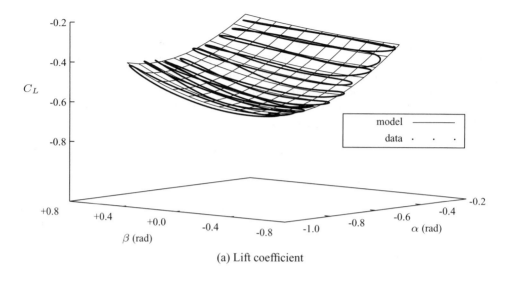

(a) Lift coefficient

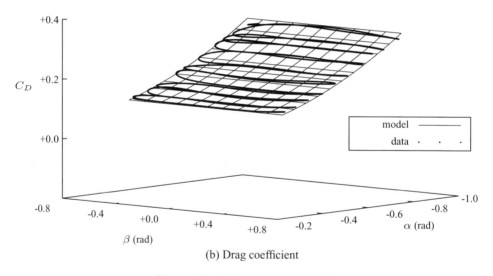

(b) Drag coefficient

Figure 6.7   Tail aerodynamic model

order models that were accurate enough for control system synthesis of complex phenomenon
including unsteady aerodynamics, membrane wing dynamics, and structural aeroelastic effects.

6.5   Simulation and Feedback Control

At this point a full nonlinear model of the ornithopter flight dynamics has been constructed
using a combination of analytical modeling and system identification from experimental data.
Computer models can be programmed to explore the dynamics in flight simulators and to test

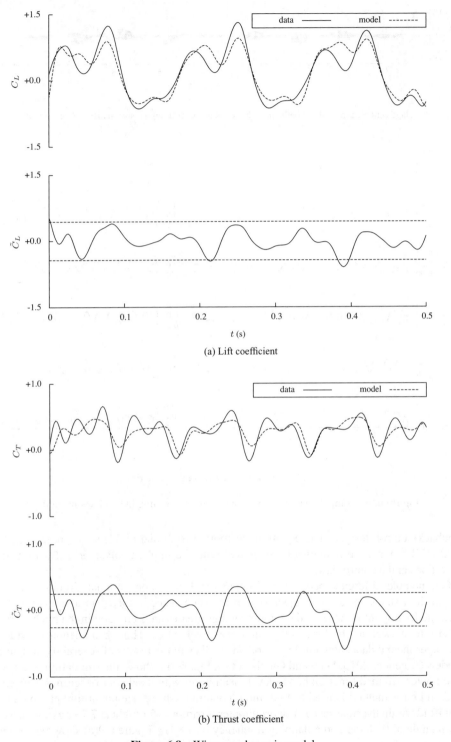

(a) Lift coefficient

(b) Thrust coefficient

Figure 6.8   Wing aerodynamic model

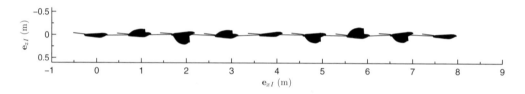

(a) Fuselage center of mass flight path and silhouettes of the ornithopter, shown at 0.125 second intervals

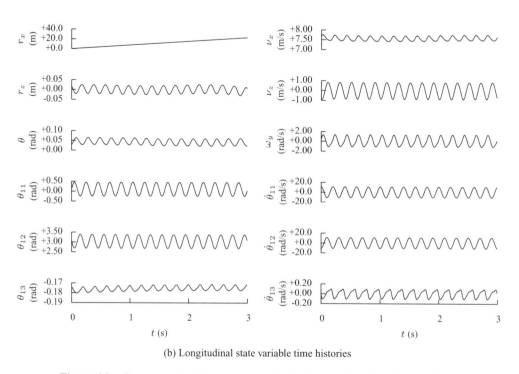

(b) Longitudinal state variable time histories

Figure 6.9   Computer simulation of an ornithopter in straight and level mean flight

feedback control designs. The equations of motion (6.7) and (6.32) were programmed into MATLAB® and were numerically integrated with the implicit solver ode15s from initial conditions and a control law.

One notable difference between ornithopters and other conventional aircraft is that their equilibrium states are closed trajectories in the state space, rather than a single point. The periodic forcing introduced by the flapping wings creates an oscillation in the pitch angle and pitch rate, as well as the longitudinal and heave velocities. This phenomenon is evident in the experimental data shown in Figure 6.3, as well as in the results of several flight dynamics models (Bolender 2010; Dietl and Garcia 2008). Figure 6.9 shows the simulation results of an ornithopter trimmed for straight and level mean flight with fixed control settings. Currently a trial and error method is used to find initial conditions that place the ornithopter on a stable manifold within the state space. The ornithopter is trimmed for flight at 7.79 m/s², with a mean pitch angle of 0.06 rad and a flapping frequency of 5.8 Hz. Figure 6.9(a) shows snapshots of

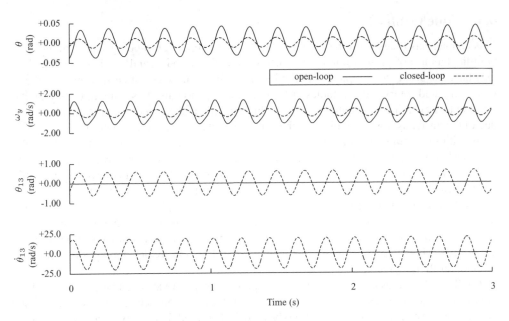

Figure 6.10 Simulation results in straight and level mean flight using a proportional control law that mixes the fuselage pitch rate with the longitudinal tail command

a rigid body animation of the ornithopter flight, made at time intervals of 0.125 seconds. The flight motions are consistent with what has been seen in video of flight tests and captures the phasing of the pitching and heaving motions of the ornithopter. The state variables displayed in Figure 6.9(b) have amplitudes that are consistent with measurements made using avionics hardware (Grauer and Hubbard 2009b).

Computer simulations also provide a good tool for testing and tuning feedback controllers before implementing on hardware. One simple goal of feedback control could be to damp out the pitching motion of the ornithopter. This could be useful for improving the overall efficiency of the flight, or for improving the quality of video camera images taken on board the ornithopter. The fuselage pitch rate, for instance, measured using a gyroscope, could be mixed with the pilot control input as

$$u_2 = u_2^* + k_p \omega_y \qquad (6.38)$$

where k_p is a proportional gain used to inject synthetic damping into the longitudinal dynamics. The control gain is chosen so that the actuator angle commands are large but remain within their hardware limits.

Computer simulation results using this simple proportional controller are shown in Figure 6.10 for the longitudinal pitch angle θ, the fuselage pitch rate ω_y, and the longitudinal tail position θ_{13}. These plots show that the pitch angle oscillation is attenuated from 0.0419 rad to 0.0128 rad, and the pitch rate oscillation is attenuated from 1.3921 rad/s to 0.4029 rad/s. The ornithopter flies more straight and a camera mounted to the fuselage would vibrate less.

6.6   Conclusion

This chapter has focused on the modeling of flight dynamics for flapping-wing ornithopters. Ornithopters are of present interest because we are able to build and fly these vehicles and they have the ability to complete useful missions at the small scales of current interest. While fixed-wing and rotary-wing vehicles are conventionally thought of as miniature air vehicles, ornithopters exhibit the potential to achieve highly agile and efficient flight at smaller scales due to the unsteady, low Reynolds number flows that characterize ornithopter flight.

As with most miniature air vehicles, one goal is to develop models of the flight dynamics using ordinary differential equations, based on techniques including first principles modeling, wind tunnel testing, and system identification from flight data. Afterwards flight control systems can be designed, simulated in software, and implemented in hardware. The ultimate goal of this work is to develop a fully autonomous ornithopter platform. This platform should be able to accomplish simple feats such as flight stabilization and way-point navigation, but also more complex tasks such as flight through cluttered indoor environments or perching on a tree limb. This chapter takes the first steps in that direction by developing a model of the ornithopter flight dynamics.

The flight dynamics model was based on experience with a representative ornithopter flight platform. Large mass distribution changes and fast flight motions, characteristic of morphing aircraft, suggested the use of a multibody model. The model was developed using energy methods via the Boltzmann-Hamel equations, and cast in a form convenient for nonlinear control design. Actuator models and aerodynamic models were extracted from flight test data. Simulations of straight and level mean flight, using a simple proportional feedback to dampen pitch rate oscillations were presented. These results show promise for the future control laws designed to achieve the project goals.

In the future the model will drive several works. Using blade element models of the wing aerodynamics, vehicle design trade-off studies can be performed in software. These studies will help guide design optimization through performance simulations, before hardware implementations are manufactured. The model reduction of the ornithopter flight dynamics may yield smaller models that can be more quickly computed for real-time control. Model linearizations about flight gaits may provide simpler models for tasks such as flight stabilization and way-point navigation. In future, hardware implementations of a Kalman filter and a passivity-based flight control law will be inserted in a custom autopilot to demonstrate the ornithopter system.

References

Bolender M 2010 Open-loop stability of flapping flight in hover number 2010-7552. In *Guidance, Navigation, and Control Conference*, AIAA, Toronto, Ontario.

Brewer J 1978 Kronecker products and matrix calculus in system theory. *IEEE Transactions on Circuits and Systems*, 25(9): 772–781.

Dickinson M, Lehmann F and Sane S 1999 Wing rotation and the aerodynamic basic of insect flight. *Science*, 284: 1954–1960.

Dietl J and Garcia E 2008 Stability in ornithopter longitudinal flight dynamics. *Journal of Guidance, Control, and Dynamics*, 31: 1157–1162.

Grauer J and Hubbard J 2009a Identification and integration of ornithopter actuator models number 2009-5937. In *Atmospheric Flight Mechanics Conference*, AIAA, Chicago, IL.

Grauer J and Hubbard J 2009b Inertial measurements from flight data of a flapping-wing ornithopter. *Journal of Guidance, Control, and Dynamics*, 32(1), 326–331.

Greenwood D 2003 *Advanced Dynamics*. Cambridge University Press, Cambridge.

Harmon R, Grauer J, Hubbard J, Conroy J, Humbert S, Sitaraman J and Roget B 2008 Experimental determination of ornithopter membrane wing shapes used for simple aerodynamic modeling number 2008-6237. AIAA.

Hughes P 2004 *Spacecraft Attitude Dynamics*. Dover Publications, New York.

Kane T and Levinson D 1985 *Dynamics: Theory and Applications*. McGraw-Hill, New York.

Kinkade S 2010 Hobby technik. www.hobbytechnik.com.

Klein V and Morelli E 2006 *Aircraft System Identification: Theory and Practice*. American Institute of Aeronautics and Astronautics, Reston, VA.

Krashanitsa R, Silin D and Shkarayev S 2009 Flight dynamics of a flapping-wing air vehicle. *International Journal of Micro Air Vehicles*, 1(1), 35–49.

Kuipers J 1998 *Quaternions and Rotation Sequences*. Princeton University Press, Princeton, NJ.

Lewis F, Dawson D and Abdallah C 2004 *Robot Manipulator Control: Theory and Practice*. Marcel Dekker, New York.

Ljung L 1999 *System Identification: Theory for the User*. Prentice Hall, Englewood Cliffs, NJ.

Malhan R, Benedict M and Chopra I 2010 Experimental investigation of a flapping wing concept in hover and forward flight for micro air vehicle applications. 66th Annual Forum American Helicopter Society.

Masarati P 2010 Mbdyn - multibody dynamics software. www.aero.polimi.it/ mbdyn/index.html.

McRuer D, Graham D and Ashkenas I 1973 *Aircraft Dynamics and Automatic Control*. Princeton University Press, Princeton, NJ

Ortega R and Loria A 1998 *Passivity-Based Control of Euler-Lagrange Systems*. Springer, New York.

Pesavento U and Wang Z 2009 Flapping wing flight can save aerodynamic power compared to steady flight. *Physical Review Letters*, 103(11), 1–4.

Roget B, Sitaraman J, Harmon R, Grauer J, Hubbard J and Humbert S 2009 Computational study of flexible wing ornithopter flight. *Journal of Aircraft*, 46(6), 2016–2031.

Shyy W, Lian Y, Tang J, Viieru D and Liu H 2007 *Aerodynamics of Low Reynolds Number Flyers*. Cambridge University Press, Cambridge.

Sitaraman J and Baeder J 2003 On the field velocity approach and geometric conservation law for unsteady flow simulations number 2003-3835. AIAA.

Slotine J and Li W 1991 *Applied Nonlinear Control*. Prentice Hall, Englewood Cliffs, NJ.

Stevens B and Lewis F 2003 *Aircraft Control and Simulation*. Wiley, New York.

Tischler M and Remple R 2006 *Aircraft and Rotorcraft System Identification*. American Institute of Aeronautics and Astronautics, Reston, VA.

Tummala Y, Wissa A, Frecker M and Hubbard J 2010 Design of a passively morphing ornithopter wing using a novel compliant spine number 3637. In *Conference on Smart Materials, Adaptive Structures, and Intelligent Systems*. ASME, Philadelphia, PA.

7

Flight Dynamics of Morphing Aircraft with Time-Varying Inertias

Daniel T. Grant, Stephen Sorley, Animesh Chakravarthy, and
Rick Lind
University of Florida, USA

7.1 Introduction

The moments of inertia of a body obviously have a profound influence on the dynamics and associated motion of that body. Certainly aerospace systems, with multiple degrees of freedom for translation and rotation, must properly account for inertia to a high level of accuracy in order to model the dynamics. The time-varying aspect of these inertias must be considered with similar accuracy to note the influence of variations in geometry and mass on the system.

Some extensive and rigorous evaluations of traditional causes of time-varying inertia, such as fuel expenditure and multi-body rotation, have been performed for space systems. The effects of translating mass within a space station are derived under an assumption of harmonic motion and used to compute librational stability (Spenny and Williams 1991). Moving mass was also included in the dynamics of a vehicle with a solar sail that could move for control purposes. The dynamics and associated time-varying inertia were modeled for a two-vehicle formation in which a Coulomb tether controlled the relative distance and mass distribution (Natarajan and Schaub 2006). Another study optimized a design for a two-vehicle formation with a flexible appendage whose motion altered the inertia properties (Oliver and Asokanthan 1997). The influence of thrusters, which expend mass through activation and thus vary the inertia, was investigated using a formulation of feedback and feedforward to cancel the effects (Thurman and Flashner 1996). The time-varying inertia due to thrusters was coupled with effects of fluid sloshing in another examination of spacecraft dynamics (Hill *et al.* 1988).

Morphing Aerospace Vehicles and Structures, First Edition. Edited by John Valasek.
© 2012 John Wiley & Sons, Ltd. Published 2012 by John Wiley & Sons, Ltd.

These traditional causes have also been examined with respect to their effects on aircraft although not necessarily to the same degree as spacecraft. Fuel burn is often neglected since its time constant is slower than the flight dynamics of many aircraft; however, the effects on time-varying inertia were shown for the case of aerial refueling in which mass was rapidly transferred from the tanker to the recipient (Venkataramanan and Dogan n.d.). On a smaller scale, the dynamics of a flapping-wing micro air vehicle were computed by noting the effect of wing motion (Vest and Katz n.d.).

The introduction of morphing, or shape-changing actuation, to an aircraft will alter the shape and mass distribution of the vehicle, thus introducing time-varying inertias. Many studies into morphing aircraft have focused on the steady-state benefits of altering a configuration for issues such as fuel consumption (Bowman n.d.), range and endurance (Gano and Renaud n.d.), cost and logistics (Bowman and Weisshar n.d.), actuator energy (Prock and Crossley 2002), maneuverability (Rusnell and Batill 2004) and airfoil requirements (Secanell and Gamboa 2005). Additionally, aeroelastic effects have been often studied relative to maximum roll rate (Khot and Kolonay 1997), (Gern and Kapania 2002), (Bae and Lee 2005) and actuator loads (Love and Chase 2004).

Morphing has also been introduced to micro air vehicles for the purpose of manuevering control. Specifically, an aircraft is designed that uses independent wing-sweep of inboard and outboard on both right and left wings (Grant and Lind n.d.). That aircraft is shown to use the morphing for altering the aerodynamics and achieve performance metrics related to sensor pointing. The wings are able to sweep on the order of a second; consequently, the temporal nature of the morphing must be considered.

This chapter investigates the effects of time-varying inertia for the variable-sweep aircraft. In particular, the flight dynamics are demonstrated during representative maneuvers to highlight the influence of the morphing and associated inertia variations. The concept of time-varying poles is utilized to properly account for the effect of the morphing.

7.2 Aircraft

7.2.1 Design

A vehicle which features the independent multi-joint capability is designed. The basic construction uses skeletal members of a prepregnated, bi-directional carbon fiber weave along with rip-stop nylon. The fuselage and wings are entirely constructed of the weave while the tail features carbon spars covered with nylon. The resulting structure is durable but lightweight.

The wings actually consist of separate sections which are connected to the fuselage and each other through a system of spars and joints. These joints, as shown in Figure 7.1, are representative of an elbow and wrist which serve to vary the sweep of inboard and outboard. The range of horizontal motion admitted by these joints is approximately ±30 deg.

It is noted that conventional aileron control surfaces are omitted from the aircraft's final design. This feature is a direct result of span-wise inconsistencies created by the dynamic range of morphing configurations. Therefore, the wrist joints are designed in such a manner that they allow both horizontal sweep and rolling twist (Abdulrahim and Lind 2005). This motion is accomplished by creating a floating joint that closely mimics the various ranges of motion attainable by an automobile's universal joint, as shown in Figure 7.2.

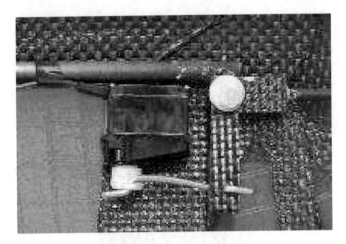

Figure 7.1 Joints on wing

The wing surface must be kept continuous for any configuration of sweep to reduce unexpected aerodynamic issues. This vehicle ensures such continuity by layering feather-like structures, as shown in Figure 7.3, within the joint.

These structures retract onto each other under the wing when both the inboard and outboard are swept back. Conversely, they create a fan-like cover across the ensuing gap when the inboard is swept back and the outboard is swept forward. The contraction and expansion of the surface area created by these structures are smoothly maintained by a tract and runner system implemented on the outer regions of each member, as seen in Figure 7.4.

Spars, formed from hollow shafts of carbon fiber, are placed along the leading edge of each wing. These spars act as both a rigid source to maintain the leading-edge curvature and a connection of each independent wing joint. The inboard spar is translated horizontally by a

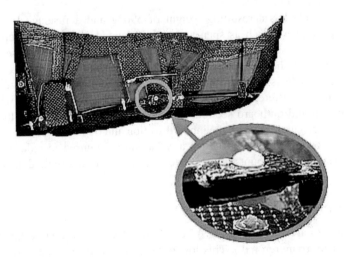

Figure 7.2 Floating elbow joint

Figure 7.3   Feather-like elements

servo-driven linear actuator located inside the fuselage. The inboard spar is then connected to the inboard wing section at the elbow joint located on the outside of the fuselage. The inboard spar then connects at the wrist joint to the outboard spar at roughly the quarter-span point. The outboard wing region is activated independently of the inboard region by means of a servo attached at the wrist. An illustration of the spar configuration, with corresponding attachment points, can be seen in Figure 7.5.

Overall, the vehicle has a resulting weight of 596 g and a fuselage length of 48 cm. The reference parameters, such as span and chord, depend on the sweep configuration. A representative set of these parameters are given in Table 7.1 for a limited set of symmetric configurations in which the left and right wings have identical sweep.

The resulting vehicle is able to achieve a wide range of sweep configurations. These configurations include different values of sweep for the right wing and left wing along with the inboard section and outboard section; however, this chapter will limit the morphing to only symmetric configurations with the inboard section and outboard section having the same sweep such as shown in Figure 7.6. Such a reduction is required to reduce the degrees of freedom to a manageable amount and facilitate presentation of the flight dynamics.

7.2.2   Modeling

The flight dynamics are analyzed using Athena Vortex Lattice (AVL) to estimate the aerodynamics (Drela and Youngren n.d.). This low-order code makes assumptions that the flow is incompressible and inviscid; however, it is widely used in the community and is particularly

Figure 7.4 Track and runner system

accurate for analyzing micro air vehicles with thin wings (Stanford *et al.* 2007), (Traub 2009), (Gopalarathnam and Norris 2009), (Cox and Hall 2009), (Boschetti *et al.* 2010), (Leong *et al.* 2010), (Royer and Jones 2010), (Stewart and Evers 2006), (Stewart and Salichon 2007), (Stewart and Abate 2008). The aerodynamics of the wings are estimated along with flow associated with slender bodies such as the fuselage.

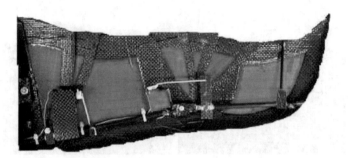

Figure 7.5 Underwing spar structure

Table 7.1 Reference parameters for symmetric sweep

Inboard (*deg*)	Outboard (*deg*)	Reference Span (*cm*)	Reference Chord (*cm*)	Reference Area (*cm*)
−15	−30	66.17	14.68	1028.11
−10	−20	73.97	13.12	1003.45
−5	−10	78.81	12.38	976.25
0	0	80.39	11.84	947.11
5	10	78.61	11.62	916.68
10	20	73.61	11.69	885.66
15	30	65.72	12.13	854.76

AVL assumes quasi-steady flow and therefore unsteady vorticity shedding is neglected. More precisely, it assumes the limit of small reduced frequency which means that any oscillatory motion must be slow enough so that the period of oscillation is much longer than the time it takes the flow to traverse an airfoil chord. This assumption is valid for virtually any expected flight maneuver of the vehicle. Also, the rates in roll, pitch and yaw used in the computations must be slow enough so that the resulting relative flow angles are small as judged by the dimensionless rotation rate parameters.

7.3 Equations of Motion

7.3.1 Body-Axis States

Standard measurements for an aircraft are based in either the Earth-fixed or the body-fixed coordinate system. Both of these coordinate systems use a right-handed axes framework that obeys cross-product rules. A representative illustration of these axes is given in Figure 7.7 along with the respective origins.

The body-fixed coordinate system has its origin located at the aircraft's center of gravity. The axes are oriented such that **x**, points directly out the nose, **y**, points directly out the right wing, and **z**, points directly out the bottom.

Figure 7.6 Different sweep configurations of MAV

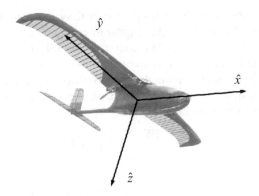

Figure 7.7 Body-fixed coordinate frame

The body-axis translational velocities are then defined as the forward velocity, u, along **x**, the horizontal velocity, v, along **y**, and the vertical velocity, w, along **z**.

The orientation angles of the aircraft are of particular interest for modeling a morphing-wing aircraft. The roll angle, ϕ, describes rotation about **x**, the pitch angle, θ, describes rotation about **y** and the yaw angle, ψ, describes rotation about **z**. The rates of change of these orientation angles are also of particular interest. The roll rate, p, is the angular velocity along **x**, the pitch rate, q, describes angular velocity along **y**, and the yaw rate, r, describes angular velocity along **z**.

Altogether, the state vector includes the three orientation angles (ϕ, θ, ψ), the three angular rates (p, q, r), the position vector ($[x \ y \ z]$), and the velocity vector ($[u \ v \ w]$).

7.3.2 Influence of Time-Varying Inertias

Flight dynamics are essentially governed by four sets of equations related to attitudes, velocities, forces, and moments as rigorously derived in many reports (Duke and Krambeer n.d.) and textbooks (Etkin and Reid 1996; Nelson 1998; Roskam 2001). The fundamental equations of motion are based on Newton's laws and thus are applicable to aircraft with fixed geometry and morphing geometry; however, the simplified expressions that describe linearized dynamics around a flight condition will have some variation. In particular, consider that morphing will vary the inertias which do not affect the force equations but certainly will affect the moment equations.

The expressions for a morphing aircraft are thus derived by starting with the fundamental expression for angular momentum, which applies to any aircraft, and then retaining terms that are typically ignored for traditional aircraft but must be considered for morphing aircraft. The expressions for force do not need such additional terms since, for example, the lift changes with sweep but not on the rate of change of sweep if unsteady aerodynamics are not considered.

7.3.3 Nonlinear Equations for Moment

Newton's second law is satisfied by equating the summation of moments to the total rate of change of the moment of angular momentum. A set of expressions are derived by assuming that all vectors are expressed in the body-fixed coordinate system, denoted by the subscript of B, unless explicitly noted. For example, the angular momentum vector as seen by an observer in the Earth-fixed frame but expressed in the body-fixed coordinate system is given as $\mathbf{H}$.

Traditionally, the angular momentum is computed from measurements taken in the body-fixed coordinate system. In order to properly describe the Earth-defined angular momentum vector, it is transformed into the inertially-fixed Earth frame. This transformation is accomplished by the transport theorem in Equation 1.1.

$$\frac{d\mathbf{H}}{dt} = \frac{d\mathbf{H}}{dt}\bigg|_{B} + {}^{E}\omega^{B} \times \mathbf{H} \tag{7.1}$$

The angular momentum, $\mathbf{H}$, is determined by multiplication of the inertial tensor and the angular rate vector. This tensor is expressed using the traditional variables for moments of inertia as expressed in the body-fixed coordinate system while the angular rates are expressed using body-fixed variables as in Equation 7.2 and Equation 7.3.

$$\mathbf{H} = \begin{bmatrix} I_{xx} & -I_{xy} & -I_{xz} \\ -I_{yx} & I_{yy} & -I_{yz} \\ -I_{xz} & -I_{yz} & I_{zz} \end{bmatrix} \begin{bmatrix} p \\ q \\ r \end{bmatrix} \tag{7.2}$$

$$= \begin{bmatrix} pI_{xx} - qI_{xy} - rI_{xz} \\ qI_{yy} - rI_{zz} - pI_{xy} \\ rI_{zz} - pI_{xz} - qI_{yz} \end{bmatrix} \tag{7.3}$$

A derivative of $\mathbf{H}_E$ is taken with respect to time to compute the moments. This derivative, expressed in Equation 7.4, notes the rate of change of the Earth-defined angular momentum vector as seen by an observer in the body-fixed coordinate system and represented in the body-fixed coordinate system.

$$\frac{d\mathbf{H}}{dt}\bigg|_{B} = \begin{bmatrix} \dot{p}I_{xx} - \dot{q}I_{xy} - \dot{r}I_{xz} + p\dot{I}_{xx} - q\dot{I}_{xy} - r\dot{I}_{xz} \\ \dot{q}I_{yy} - \dot{r}I_{yz} - \dot{p}I_{xy} + q\dot{I}_{yy} - r\dot{I}_{zz} - p\dot{I}_{xy} \\ \dot{r}I_{zz} - \dot{p}I_{xz} - \dot{q}I_{yz} + r\dot{I}_{zz} - p\dot{I}_{xz} - q\dot{I}_{yz} \end{bmatrix} \tag{7.4}$$

The rate of change of angular momentum is expressed by substituting Equation 7.4 into Equation 7.1 and introducing the cross-product of angular rates with the angular momentum of Equation 7.3. The resulting vector is given in Equation 7.5.

$$\frac{d\mathbf{H}}{dt} = \begin{bmatrix} \dot{p}I_{xx} - \dot{q}I_{xy} - \dot{r}I_{xz} + p\dot{I}_{xx} - q\dot{I}_{xy} - r\dot{I}_{xz} \\ \dot{q}I_{yy} - \dot{r}I_{yz} - \dot{p}I_{xy} + q\dot{I}_{yy} - r\dot{I}_{zz} - p\dot{I}_{xy} \\ \dot{r}I_{zz} - \dot{p}I_{xz} - \dot{q}I_{yz} + r\dot{I}_{zz} - p\dot{I}_{xz} - q\dot{I}_{yz} \end{bmatrix}$$
$$+ \begin{bmatrix} qrI_{zz} - qpI_{xz} - q^{2}I_{yz} - qrI_{yy} + r^{2}I_{yz} + rpI_{xy} \\ rpI_{xx} - qrI_{xy} - r^{2}I_{xz} - rpI_{zz} + p^{2}I_{xz} + qpI_{yz} \\ pqI_{yy} - rpI_{yz} - p^{2}I_{xy} - pqI_{xx} + q^{2}I_{xy} + rqI_{xz} \end{bmatrix} \tag{7.5}$$

The standard definition for the moments describing an aircraft is related to the rate of change of angular momentum as in Equation 7.6.

$$\frac{d\mathbf{H}}{dt} = \begin{bmatrix} L \\ M \\ N \end{bmatrix}_{E} \tag{7.6}$$

A full-order set of nonlinear equations describing the moments of an aircraft results by equating Equation 7.6 with Equation 7.5 to generate Equations 7.7–7.9.

$$L = \dot{p}I_{xx} - qrI_{yy} + qrI_{zz} + (pr - \dot{q})I_{xy} - (pq + \dot{r})I_{xz}$$
$$+ (r^2 - q^2)I_{yz} + p\dot{I}_{xx} - q\dot{I}_{xy} - r\dot{I}_{xz} \tag{7.7}$$

$$M = prI_{xx} + \dot{q}I_{yy} - prI_{zz} - (qr - \dot{p})I_{xy} + (p^2 - r^2)I_{xz}$$
$$+ (pq - \dot{r})I_{yz} + q\dot{I}_{yy} - p\dot{I}_{xy} - r\dot{I}_{yz} \tag{7.8}$$

$$N = -pqI_{xx} + pqI_{yy} + \dot{r}I_{zz} + (q^2 - p^2)I_{xy} + (qr - \dot{p})I_{xz}$$
$$- (pr + \dot{q})I_{yz} + r\dot{I}_{zz} - p\dot{I}_{xz} - q\dot{I}_{yz} \tag{7.9}$$

7.3.4   Linearized Equations for Moment

The moment equations are linearized by considering small disturbances around a trim condition. Expand the parameters for moments and states in a manner such that, for example, the pitch moment, M, is a sum of the pitch moment at trim, M_o, and a perturbation, ΔM, about that trim. The resulting equations are shown in Equations 7.10–7.15.

$$L = L_0 + \Delta L \tag{7.10}$$
$$= (r_0 \Delta q + q_0 \Delta r)(I_{zz} - I_{yy}) + (p_0 \Delta r + r_0 \Delta p - \Delta \dot{q})I_{xy}$$
$$- (p_0 \Delta q + q_0 \Delta p + \Delta \dot{r})I_{xz} + (2r_0 - 2q_0 \Delta q)I_{yz}$$
$$+ \Delta \dot{p} I_{xx} + \Delta p \dot{I}_{xx} - \Delta q \dot{I}_{xy} - \Delta r \dot{I}_{xz} \tag{7.11}$$

$$M = M_0 + \Delta M \tag{7.12}$$
$$= (r_0 \Delta p + p_0 \Delta r)(I_{xx} - I_{zz}) - (q_0 \Delta r + r_0 \Delta q + \Delta \dot{p})I_{xy}$$
$$+ (2p_0 \Delta p - 2r_0 \Delta r)I_{xz} + (q_0 \Delta p + p_0 \Delta q - \Delta \dot{r})I_{yz}$$
$$+ \Delta \dot{q} I_{yy} + \Delta q \dot{I}_{yy} - \Delta p \dot{I}_{xy} - \Delta r \dot{I}_{yz} \tag{7.13}$$

$$N = N_0 + \Delta N \tag{7.14}$$
$$= (p_0 \Delta q + q_0 \Delta p)(I_{yy} - I_{xx}) - (2q_0 \Delta q - 2p_0 \Delta p)I_{xy}$$
$$+ (r_0 \Delta q - q_0 \Delta r - \Delta \dot{p})I_{xz} - (r_0 \Delta p + p_0 \Delta r - \Delta \dot{q})I_{yz}$$
$$+ \Delta \dot{r} I_{zz} + \Delta r \dot{I}_{zz} - \Delta p \dot{I}_{xz} - \Delta q \dot{I}_{yz} \tag{7.15}$$

The linearized equations of motion that represent moments associated with perturbations around trim are presented in Equations 7.16–7.18. In this case, the trim condition is restricted to being unaccelerating straight-and-level flight.

$$I_{xx} \Delta \dot{p} - I_{xy} \Delta \dot{q} - I_{xz} \Delta \dot{r} = \Delta L - \dot{I}_{xx} \Delta p + \dot{I}_{xy} \Delta q + \dot{I}_{xz} \Delta r \tag{7.16}$$

$$-I_{xy} \Delta \dot{p} + I_{yy} \Delta \dot{q} - I_{yz} \Delta \dot{r} = \Delta M + \dot{I}_{xy} \Delta p - \dot{I}_{yy} \Delta q + \dot{I}_{yz} \Delta r \tag{7.17}$$

$$-I_{xz} \Delta \dot{p} - I_{yz} \Delta \dot{q} + I_{zz} \Delta \dot{r} = \Delta N + \dot{I}_{xz} \Delta p + \dot{I}_{yz} \Delta q - \dot{I}_{zz} \Delta r \tag{7.18}$$

Note that the inertial rates ($\dot{I}$ terms) are retained in the linearized moment equations. The retention of these terms is done in order to account for the fact that the aircraft is capable of morphing. The general formulations are also expressed as differential equations involving a single derivative as in Equations 7.19–7.21.

$$\Delta\dot{p} = \frac{P_p}{D}\Delta p + \frac{P_q}{D}\Delta q + \frac{P_r}{D}\Delta r + \frac{P_L}{D}\Delta L + \frac{P_M}{D}\Delta M + \frac{P_N}{D}\Delta N \tag{7.19}$$

$$\Delta\dot{q} = \frac{Q_p}{D}\Delta p + \frac{Q_q}{D}\Delta q + \frac{Q_r}{D}\Delta r + \frac{Q_L}{D}\Delta L + \frac{Q_M}{D}\Delta M + \frac{Q_N}{D}\Delta N \tag{7.20}$$

$$\Delta\dot{r} = \frac{R_p}{D}\Delta p + \frac{R_q}{D}\Delta q + \frac{R_r}{D}\Delta r + \frac{R_L}{D}\Delta L + \frac{R_M}{D}\Delta M + \frac{R_N}{D}\Delta N \tag{7.21}$$

The coefficients of the perturbation terms in Equations 7.19–7.21 are expressed as functions of the inertial moments, products and rates as in Equations 7.22–7.39.

$$P_p = -I_{yz}^2\dot{I}_{xx} + I_{zz}I_{yy}\dot{I}_{xx} - I_{xy}I_{zz}\dot{I}_{xy} - I_{xy}I_{yz}\dot{I}_{xz} - I_{xz}I_{yz}\dot{I}_{xy} - I_{xz}I_y\dot{I}_{xz} \tag{7.22}$$

$$P_q = I_{xy}I_{zz}\dot{I}_{yy} - I_{xy}I_{yz}\dot{I}_{yz} + I_{xz}I_{zz}\dot{I}_{yy} - I_{xz}I_{yy}\dot{I}_{yz} - I_{zz}I_{yy}\dot{I}_{xy} + I_{yz}\dot{I}_{xy} \tag{7.23}$$

$$P_r = -I_{xy}I_{zz}\dot{I}_{yz} + I_{xy}I_{yz}\dot{I}_{zz} + I_{yz}^2\dot{I}_{xz} + I_{xz}I_{yy}\dot{I}_{zz} - I_{xz}I_{yz}\dot{I}_{yz} - I_{yy}I_{zz}\dot{I}_{xz} \tag{7.24}$$

$$P_L = I_{yz}^2 - I_{zz}I_{yy} \tag{7.25}$$

$$P_M = -I_{xy}I_{zz} - I_{xz}I_{yz} \tag{7.26}$$

$$P_N = -I_{xy}I_{yz} - I_{xz}I_{yy} \tag{7.27}$$

$$Q_p = -I_{xx}I_{zz}\dot{I}_{xy} - I_{xx}I_{yz}\dot{I}_{xz} - I_{xz}I_{xy}\dot{I}_{xz} + I_{yz}I_{xz}\dot{I}_{xx} + I_{xz}^2\dot{I}_{xy} + I_{xy}I_{zz}\dot{I}_{xx} \tag{7.28}$$

$$Q_q = I_{xx}I_{zz}\dot{I}_{yy} - I_{xx}I_{yz}\dot{I}_{yz} - I_{xz}I_{xy}\dot{I}_{yz} - I_{yz}I_{xz}\dot{I}_{xy} - I_{xz}^2\dot{I}_{yy} - I_{xy}I_{zz}\dot{I}_{xy} \tag{7.29}$$

$$Q_r = -I_{xx}I_{zz}\dot{I}_{yz} + I_{xx}I_{yz}\dot{I}_{zz} + I_{xz}I_{xy}\dot{I}_{zz} - I_{yz}I_{xz}\dot{I}_{xz} + I_{xz}^2\dot{I}_{yz} - I_{xy}I_{zz}\dot{I}_{xz} \tag{7.30}$$

$$Q_L = -I_{yz}I_{xz} - I_{xy}I_{zz} \tag{7.31}$$

$$Q_M = -I_{xx}I_{zz} + I_{xz}^2 \tag{7.32}$$

$$Q_N = -I_{xx}I_{yz} - I_{xz}I_{xy} \tag{7.33}$$

$$R_p = I_{xy}^2\dot{I}_{xz} + I_{xz}I_{yy}\dot{I}_{xx} - I_{xx}I_{yz}\dot{I}_{xy} + I_{yz}I_{xy}\dot{I}_{xx} - I_{xz}I_{xy}\dot{I}_{xy} - I_{xx}I_{yy}\dot{I}_{xz} \tag{7.34}$$

$$R_q = -I_{xz}I_y\dot{I}_{xy} + I_{xy}^2\dot{I}_{yz} + I_xI_{yz}\dot{I}_y - I_{yz}I_{xy}\dot{I}_{xy} + I_{xz}I_{xy}\dot{I}_y - I_xI_y\dot{I}_{yz} \tag{7.35}$$

$$R_r = -I_{xz}I_y\dot{I}_{xz} - I_{xy}^2\dot{I}_z - I_{yz}I_{xy}\dot{I}_{xz} + I_xI_y\dot{I}_z - I_{xz}I_{xy}\dot{I}_{yz} - I_xI_{yz}\dot{I}_{yz} \tag{7.36}$$

$$R_L = -I_{xz}I_y - I_{yz}I_{xy} \tag{7.37}$$

$$R_M = -I_{xz}I_{xy} - I_xI_{yz} \tag{7.38}$$

$$R_N = -I_xI_y + I_{xy}^2 \tag{7.39}$$

A denominator term, D, affects every term in the differential equations of Equations 7.19–7.21. This term is described in Equation 7.40.

$$D = -I_{xx}I_{yy}I_{zz} + I_{xz}^2I_{yy} + I_{zz}I_{xy}^2 + I_{xx}I_{yz}^2 + 2I_{yz}I_{xy}I_{xz} \tag{7.40}$$

7.3.5   Flight Dynamics

7.3.5.1   Equations of Motion

A set of linearized equations characterize the flight dynamics of the aircraft about a trim condition. This set of 12 equations includes the three equations for moments, as described in Equations 7.19–7.21, along with an additional three sets of three equations.

A set of equations is determined by relating the force to mass and acceleration. In this case, the mass is considered constant in magnitude since the morphing is restricted to geometry changes. The resulting equations are given in Equations 7.41–7.43.

$$\Delta \dot{u} = \frac{1}{m}\Delta X - g\cos\theta_o\Delta\theta \tag{7.41}$$

$$\Delta \dot{v} = \frac{1}{m}\Delta Y + g\cos\theta_o\Delta\phi - u_o\Delta r \tag{7.42}$$

$$\Delta \dot{w} = \frac{1}{m}\Delta Z - g\sin\theta_o\Delta\theta + u_o\Delta q \tag{7.43}$$

The dynamics associated with the attitude present another set of equations. These equations relate the variations around trim to angles of roll, pitch and yaw as given in Equations 7.44–7.46.

$$\Delta \dot{\theta} = \Delta q \tag{7.44}$$

$$\Delta \dot{\phi} = \Delta p + \tan\theta_o\Delta r \tag{7.45}$$

$$\Delta \dot{\psi} = \sec\theta_o\Delta r \tag{7.46}$$

The remaining set of differential equations relates the changes in position of the vehicle. These equations note the effect of body-axis velocities and the orientation as in Equations 7.47–7.49.

$$\Delta \dot{x} = \cos\theta_o\Delta u - u_o\sin\theta_o\Delta\theta + \sin\theta_o\Delta w \tag{7.47}$$

$$\Delta \dot{y} = u_o\cos\theta_o\Delta\psi + \Delta v \tag{7.48}$$

$$\Delta \dot{z} = -\sin\theta_o\Delta u - u_o\cos\theta_o\Delta\theta + \cos\theta_o\Delta w \tag{7.49}$$

7.3.5.2   Aerodynamics

The linearized equations describe perturbations around a trim condition for states along with forces and moments; however, the perturbations to forces and moments can be described as functions of the perturbations to states. Taylor's expansion is adopted to generate the appropriate relationships using derivatives which are commonly generated using wind tunnels or computational algorithms.

The perturbations for forces are presented in Equations 7.50–7.52 as functions of perturbations to the states and control surfaces.

$$\Delta X = \frac{\partial X}{\partial u}\Delta u + \frac{\partial X}{\partial v}\Delta v + \frac{\partial X}{\partial w}\Delta w + \frac{\partial X}{\partial q}\Delta q + \frac{\partial X}{\partial p}\Delta p + \frac{\partial X}{\partial r}\Delta r$$
$$+ \frac{\partial X}{\partial \delta_a}\Delta \delta_a + \frac{\partial X}{\partial \delta_r}\Delta \delta_r + \frac{\partial X}{\partial \delta_e}\Delta \delta_e \tag{7.50}$$

$$\Delta Y = \frac{\partial Y}{\partial u}\Delta u + \frac{\partial Y}{\partial v}\Delta v + \frac{\partial Y}{\partial w}\Delta w + \frac{\partial Y}{\partial q}\Delta q + \frac{\partial Y}{\partial p}\Delta p + \frac{\partial Y}{\partial r}\Delta r$$
$$+ \frac{\partial Y}{\partial \delta_a}\Delta \delta_a + \frac{\partial Y}{\partial \delta_r}\Delta \delta_r + \frac{\partial Y}{\partial \delta_e}\Delta \delta_e \tag{7.51}$$

$$\Delta Z = \frac{\partial Z}{\partial u}\Delta u + \frac{\partial Z}{\partial v}\Delta v + \frac{\partial Z}{\partial w}\Delta w + \frac{\partial Z}{\partial q}\Delta q + \frac{\partial Z}{\partial p}\Delta p + \frac{\partial Z}{\partial r}\Delta r$$
$$+ \frac{\partial Z}{\partial \delta_a}\Delta \delta_a + \frac{\partial Z}{\partial \delta_r}\Delta \delta_r + \frac{\partial Z}{\partial \delta_e}\Delta \delta_e \tag{7.52}$$

Similarly, the perturbations to moments are presented in Equations 7.53–7.55 using perturbations to the states and control surfaces.

$$\Delta L = \frac{\partial L}{\partial u}\Delta u + \frac{\partial L}{\partial v}\Delta v + \frac{\partial L}{\partial w}\Delta w + \frac{\partial L}{\partial q}\Delta q + \frac{\partial L}{\partial p}\Delta p + \frac{\partial L}{\partial r}\Delta r$$
$$+ \frac{\partial L}{\partial \delta_a}\Delta \delta_a + \frac{\partial L}{\partial \delta_r}\Delta \delta_r + \frac{\partial L}{\partial \delta_e}\Delta \delta_e \tag{7.53}$$

$$\Delta M = \frac{\partial M}{\partial u}\Delta u + \frac{\partial M}{\partial v}\Delta v + \frac{\partial M}{\partial w}\Delta w + \frac{\partial M}{\partial q}\Delta q + \frac{\partial M}{\partial p}\Delta p + \frac{\partial M}{\partial r}\Delta r$$
$$+ \frac{\partial M}{\partial \delta_a}\Delta \delta_a + \frac{\partial M}{\partial \delta_r}\Delta \delta_r + \frac{\partial M}{\partial \delta_e}\Delta \delta_e \tag{7.54}$$

$$\Delta N = \frac{\partial N}{\partial u}\Delta u + \frac{\partial N}{\partial v}\Delta v + \frac{\partial N}{\partial w}\Delta w + \frac{\partial N}{\partial q}\Delta q + \frac{\partial N}{\partial p}\Delta p + \frac{\partial N}{\partial r}\Delta r$$
$$+ \frac{\partial N}{\partial \delta_a}\Delta \delta_a + \frac{\partial N}{\partial \delta_r}\Delta \delta_r + \frac{\partial N}{\partial \delta_e}\Delta \delta_e \tag{7.55}$$

7.4 Time-Varying Poles

7.4.1 Definition

A concept of poles for a linear time-varying system is derived from a factorization approach (Kamen 1988) and related to an argument using Parallel D Spectra and Series D Spectra (Zhu 1995). This concept is derived for n^{th}-order systems; however, the derivation for a 2nd-order system is useful as a tutorial to introduce the poles.

Consider a linear time-varying system as in Equation 7.56 that is equivalently written using operator notation of $D = \frac{d}{dt}$ as in Equation 7.57.

$$0 = \ddot{y} + a_1(t)\dot{y} + a_0(t)y(t) \tag{7.56}$$

$$= (D^2 + a_1(t)D + a_0(t))y(t) \tag{7.57}$$

The expression may be modified if there exist functions, $p_1(t)$ and $p_2(t)$, as in Equation 7.58 and the introduction of a non-commutative polynomial multiplication, o, as in Equation 7.59.

$$0 = (D - p_1(t))\{(D - p_2(t))y(t)\} \tag{7.58}$$

$$= \{(D - p_1(t))o(D - p_2(t))\}y(t) \tag{7.59}$$

An equation which determines $p_2(t)$ results from defining $Dop_2(t) = p_2(t)D + \dot{p}_2(t)$ as given in Equation 7.60.

$$p_2^2(t) + \dot{p}_2(t) + a_1(t)p_2(t) + a_0(t) = 0 \tag{7.60}$$

A corresponding expression is also derived for $p_1(t)$ in Equation 7.61.

$$p_1(t) + p_2(t) = -a_1(t) \tag{7.61}$$

The pair of $(p_1(t), p_2(t))$ form a pole set with $p_2(t)$ being called a right pole. Note that this pair is an ordered pole set. The poles of $p_1(t)$ and $p_2(t)$ may be complex; however, they need not in general be complex conjugates. Furthermore, uniqueness may be enforced on the poles by stipulating that the initial values of the time-varying poles are equal to the linear time-invariant poles that exist at $t = 0$.

A mode is associated with a time-varying pole. For the right pole, this mode is given as ϕ_{p2} in Equation 7.62.

$$\phi_{p2}(t, 0) = e^{\int_0^t p_2(\tau)d\tau} \tag{7.62}$$

The system actually has a pair of right poles and a pair of left poles. The pair of right poles results from solving Equation 7.60 using a pair of different initial conditions on these poles. Such a pair of initial conditions might be having $p_2(0)$ relate to a complex pole from the time-invariant dynamics before morphing is started and having $p_2(0)$ relate to the complex conjugate of that pole. Either way, the right poles are sufficient to describe the system since the left poles are simply their counterparts as described by Equation 7.61.

A set of eigenvectors are associated with each pole. Each eigenvector, v_i, and its pole, p_{2i}, must satisfy Equation 7.63.

$$(A(t) - p_{2i}(t))v_i(t) = \dot{v}_i(t) \tag{7.63}$$

Also, a mode is defined for each pole as ϕ_i as in Equation 7.64.

$$\phi_{2i}(t) = e^{\int_0^t p_{2i}(\tau d\tau} \tag{7.64}$$

The state response is finally written in Equation 7.65 in terms of these time-varying parameters. Note that this response depends on modes, which relates the integral of the poles, as opposed to depending directly on the pole.

$$x(t) = C_1\phi_{21}(t, 0) + C_2\phi_{22}(t, 0) \tag{7.65}$$

The decomposition of the states into the form of Equation 7.65 indicates the time-varying parameters essentially diagonalize the system. Consider that a matrix defined as $V(t) = [v_1(t)|v_2(t)]$ will diagonalize the system matrix as long as $V(t)$ is invertible and bounded.

The stability of the system is determined by the relationship in Equation 7.65. Essentially, the system has asymptotic stability for which states will tend to equilibrium if and only if the magnitude of the mode goes to zero as time increases. This condition, which is expressed as $|\phi_{2i}| \to 0$ as $t \to \infty$ for each $i = 1, 2$, is equivalent to a condition on the real part of the pole being $\int_0^\infty p_R(\tau)d\tau < 0$.

7.4.2 Discussion

Kamen's method involves computing a nth-order input-output difference equation with time-varying coefficients. This difference equation is based on the system's linear time-varying dynamics, and from it, an ordered pair of right and left eigenvalues can be calculated. The right eigenvalues are then used to describe the system's transient performance and stability. A few benefits of Kamen's method include:

- A right pole set, $p_{21}(t)$, $p_{22}(t)$, can be linked to the time-invariant system via initial conditions (frozen time eigenvalues at $t = t_{desired}$).
- The Vandermonde matrix, $V(t)$, diagonalizes the system matrix when $V(t)$ is invertible and bounded.
- The calculated LTV poles are unique for almost all initial conditions.
- Integrating the right pole set can influence the stability of the system.

whereas, the disadvantages include:

- LTV poles can sometimes have a finite-time singularity, resulting in $p_{21}(t)$, $p_{22}(t) \to -\infty$.
- Higher order systems are more difficult to convert into an input-output ordinary differential equation.

7.4.3 Modal Interpretation

The concept of modal parameters is used in the dynamic community to disseminate the behavior of a system in terms of a few common characteristics. The parameters of natural frequency and damping are commonly used as such characterizations of linear time-invariant systems. The evaluation of time-varying systems cannot immediately use these same definitions; however, related concepts of periodicity and decay envelope have essential similarity and are readily available.

Consider the oscillatory response of a 2-state system, as originally given in Equation 7.65, with the coefficients normalized to ease presentation as in Equation 7.66. Substitute the Equation 7.62 into Equation 7.66 to generate Equation 7.67. Also, assume the generalized poles to be complex conjugates such that $p_{21} = p_{22}^* = p_R + Jp_I$ as in Equation 7.68. The complex exponentials can then be expressed in terms of sines and cosines as in Equation 7.69

and combined to generate Equation 7.70.

$$x(t) = \phi_1(t) + \phi_2(t) \tag{7.66}$$

$$= e^{\int_0^t P_{21}(\tau)d\tau} + e^{\int_0^t P_{22}(\tau)d\tau} \tag{7.67}$$

$$= e^{\int_0^t (P_R(\tau) + JP_I(\tau))d\tau} + e^{\int_0^t (P_R(\tau) + JP_I(\tau))d\tau} \tag{7.68}$$

$$= \left[e^{\int_0^t P_R(\tau)d\tau} \cos\left(\int_0^t P_I(\tau)d\tau\right) + Je^{\int_0^t P_R(\tau)d\tau} \sin\left(\int_0^t P_I(\tau)d\tau\right) \right]$$

$$+ \left[e^{\int_0^t P_R(\tau)d\tau} \cos\left(\int_0^t P_I(\tau)d\tau\right) - Je^{\int_0^t P_R(\tau)d\tau} \sin\left(\int_0^t P_I(\tau)d\tau\right) \right] \tag{7.69}$$

$$= 2e^{\int_0^t P_R(\tau)d\tau} \cos\left(\int_0^t P_I(\tau)d\tau\right) \tag{7.70}$$

An oscillatory response with decay is demonstrated in Equation 7.70 to be generated by a pair of poles which are complex conjugates. The nature of the oscillations and the decay are both determined by the integrals of real and imaginary parts of these poles. Also, the equal-but-opposite nature of the imaginary parts of these poles means the response in Equation 7.70 is simply double the real part of the mode as noted in Equation 7.69.

The decaying nature of the response, which is similar to the damping ratio of a linear time-invariant system, is determined by the varying magnitude of the exponential in Equation 7.70. The resulting envelope is given in Equation 7.71 using only the real part of the pole and equivalently in Equation 7.72 by adding the complex-conjugate poles.

$$envelope(x(t)) = e^{\int_0^t P_R(\tau)d\tau} \tag{7.71}$$

$$= e^{\int_0^t \frac{P_{21}(\tau) + P_{22}(\tau)}{2}d\tau} \tag{7.72}$$

The oscillations occur with a frequency related to the imaginary part of the time-varying pole. A time-varying equivalent to natural frequency, $\omega(t)$, is generated by comparing the cosine term of Equation 7.70 to a standard term in dynamics of $\cos(\omega t)$. The time-varying equivalent to a natural frequency results from this comparison and is given in Equation 7.73. Note that any stable system will have ω tend to 0 as time increases.

$$\omega(t) = \frac{\int_0^t P_I(\tau)d\tau}{t} \tag{7.73}$$

The periodicity of the oscillations results directly from inverting the frequency of Equation 7.73 and is given in Equation 7.74. Alternatively, such periodicity can result simply by noting when the angle in the cosine term repeats itself as given in Equation 7.75.

$$T(t) = \frac{2\pi t}{\int_0^t P_I(\tau)d\tau} \tag{7.74}$$

$$= \max_{T > 0 \in \mathcal{R}} \left\{ \frac{2\pi}{2T} : \int_0^t P_I(\tau)d\tau = \int_0^{t+T} P_I(\tau)d\tau = 0 \right\} \tag{7.75}$$

Also, a time-varying equivalent to damping ratio is computed by relating the envelope of Equation 7.71 and the frequency in Equation 7.73. Essentially, the envelope is equivalent to $-\zeta \omega_n$ and the frequency is related to $\omega_n \sqrt{1 - \zeta^2}$. the resulting damping ratio is given in Equation 7.76.

$$\zeta(t) = \sqrt{\frac{1}{1 + \left(\frac{\int_0^t p_I(\tau)d\tau}{\int_0^t p_R(\tau)d\tau} \right)^2}} \tag{7.76}$$

7.5 Flight Dynamics with Time-Varying Morphing

7.5.1 Morphing

The flight dynamics of the vehicle shown in Figure 7.6 are analyzed during symmetric morphing from a backward sweep to having no sweep. Specifically, the sweep varied from +30 deg to 0 deg in 1 sec and then remains at a sweep angle of 0 deg for each wing. This morphing would be valuable when transitioning from a dive to straight-and-level flight similar in a manner to biological systems like gulls and hawks. This transition, especially when operating immersed in dense obstacles such as urban environments, may still require rapid maneuvering for positioning along with gust rejection so that the flight dynamics during the morphing remain of critical importance.

The response of the states are shown in Figure 7.8 as a result of the morphing. The aircraft is a linear time-varying systems for the initial 1 sec; however, the response still resembles the traditional modes for a linear time-invariant system. The pitch rate and vertical velocity show a high-frequency response that is heavily damped and thus resembles the short-period mode; conversely, the airspeed and pitch angle are dominated by a low-frequency response that is lightly damped and thus resembles a phugoid mode.

7.5.2 Model

A state-space model is formulated to represent the flight dynamics. This model results by combining the moment equations of Equations 7.19–7.21, the force equations of Equations 7.41–7.43 and attitude equations of Equations 7.44–7.46 along with the Taylor's expansions of forces in Equations 7.50–7.52 and moments in Taylor's Equations 7.53–7.55. Note the model dynamics are of primary interest so the position equations of Equations 7.47–7.49 are ignored since the flight dynamics are dependent on position.

The morphing is restricted to identical sweep angles for each wing. As such, the shape of the aircraft is symmetric about the fuselage. This symmetry simplifies the inertia sensor, and consequently the equations of motion, since $I_{xy} = 0$ and $I_{yz} = 0$. The expressions for forces and moments introduce additional simplifications to the equations since the longitudinal dynamics are independent of the lateral-directional dynamics. The derivatives of the longitudinal perturbations of ΔX, ΔY, ΔM are zero with respect to lateral-directional states of Δv, Δp, Δr, $\Delta \phi$ and similarly the derivatives of the lateral-directional perturbations of ΔY, ΔL, ΔN are zero with respect to longitudinal states of Δu, Δw, Δq, $\Delta \theta$.

The resulting equations of motion are represented in Equation 7.77 in state-space form. This representation uses traditional nomenclature of stability derivatives and control derivatives.

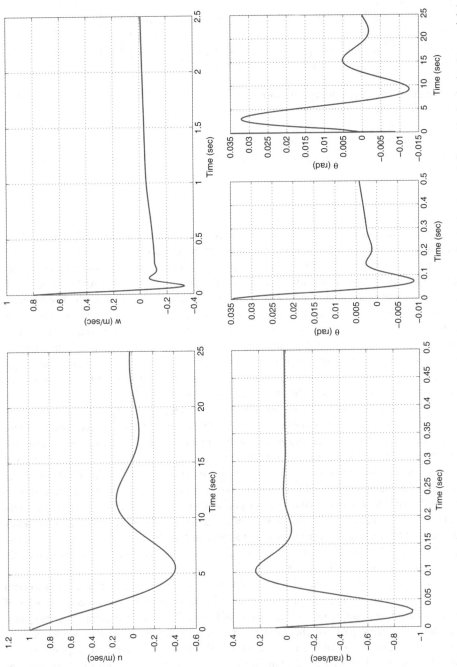

Figure 7.8 Longitudinal States during morphing from +30 deg to 0 deg over 1 sec: forward velocity (upper left), vertical velocity (upper right), pitch rate (lower left), pitch angle (lower right)

For example, $M_q = \frac{1}{I_{yy}} \frac{\partial M}{\partial q} - \frac{i_{yy}}{I_{yy}}$ is a term.

$$
\begin{bmatrix} \dot{u} \\ \dot{w} \\ \dot{q} \\ \dot{\theta} \end{bmatrix} = \begin{bmatrix} X_u & X_w & X_q & -g\cos\theta_0 \\ Z_u & Z_w(\mu) & u_0 & -g\sin\theta_0 \\ M_u(\mu) & M_w(\mu) & M_q(\mu) & 0 \\ 0 & 0 & 1 & 0 \end{bmatrix} \begin{bmatrix} u \\ w \\ q \\ \theta \end{bmatrix} \tag{7.77}
$$

Also, the dominant dependency on morphing is directly noted the model of Equation 7.77 using μ. The morphing affects every stability derivative; however, several of the terms vary negligibly. Only of four of the terms are found to have significant variations due to the morphing. Such lack of dependency is somewhat expected since the lift and drag at low airspeeds are not highly influenced by sweep so the moment equations show the highest dependency.

7.5.3 Poles

The time-varying poles associated with Figure 7.8 are computed and shown in Figure 7.9 along with the time-invariant poles that ignore the time-varying effects of morphing. These results indicate several characteristics of time-varying poles. Consider that the time-invariant poles associated with the short-period mode remain similar for any value of morphing; however, the time-varying poles of p_{41} and p_{42}, which are initially closest in value to the short-period poles, decay to zero at a rate similar to the decay of the state response due to damping. Also, note that the poles of p_{43} and p_{44} show the low magnitude and slow decay associated with a phugiod mode; however, these poles vary during the initial response which is dominated by a short-period response. As such, the time-varying poles differ in nature from time-invariant poles in that the short-period mode and phugoid mode are somewhat, but not completely, distinct and the magnitude of the poles decays as the response decays.

The modes defined in Equation 7.64 associated with each pole in Figure 7.9 are shown in Figure 7.10. The decomposition of the response actually depends on the eigenvectors and these modes, as opposed to the time-varying poles, so they must be considered when evaluating the flight dynamics. The indistinct separation between the short-period mode and the phugoid mode that is evident in the poles is also evident in the modes. The modes of ϕ_{41} and ϕ_{42} show the initial variation that would indicate a short-period response; however, these modes remain significant after the decay due to short-period damping and then show variation more consistent with the phugoid mode. The modes for ϕ_{43} and ϕ_{44} show some initial inconsistency around 1 sec but then are quite consistent with the phugiod mode. Indeed, the real parts of ϕ_{43} and ϕ_{44} are remarkably similar to the response of forward velocity, which is predominately due to the phugoid mode, in Figure 7.8.

The nature of the modes agrees with the mathematical properties that relate them to both the response and the poles. The responses of Figure 7.8 are oscillatory and indeed the poles of Figure 7.9 are complex conjugates so the modes of Figure 7.10 are also complex conjugates. The real and imaginary parts of the modes are noted in Equation 7.69 to be 90° out of phase and indeed this phase difference is seen for all times of the phugoid response of ϕ_{43} and the initial times of short-period response of ϕ_{41} until 0.2 sec when the damping has caused the response to decay. Also, the state response should be proportional to the real part of the mode as noted in Equation 7.70 which is demonstrated by the vertical velocity in

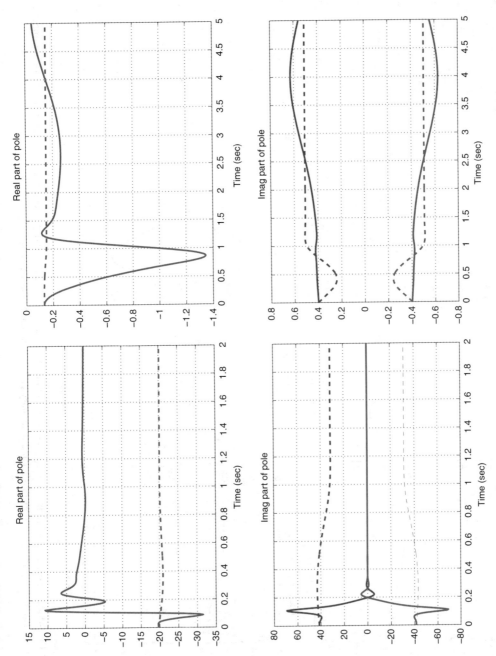

Figure 7.9 Linear time-varying poles (—) and linear time-invariant poles (– – –) during morphing from +30 deg to 0 deg over 1 sec: real part (upper left) and imaginary part (lower left) of p_{41} and p_{42}, real part (upper right) and imaginary part (lower right) of p_{43} and p_{44}

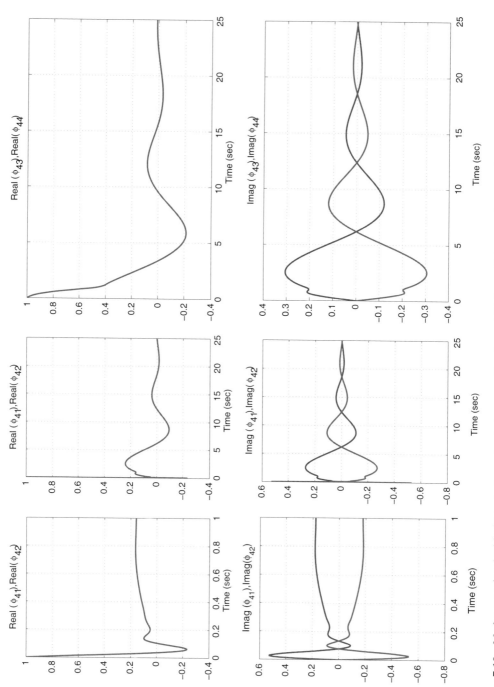

Figure 7.10 Modes associated with time-varying poles during morphing from $+30$ deg to 0 deg over 1 sec: real part (upper left) and imaginary part (lower left) of ϕ_{41} and ϕ_{42}, real part (upper right) and imaginary part (lower right) of ϕ_{43} and ϕ_{44}

Figure 7.8 matching the real part of ϕ_1 and the forward velocity in Figure 7.8 matching the real part of ϕ_3.

The issue of stability is directly indicated by the modes of Figure 7.10. These modes demonstrate that the system during this morphing trajectory has asymptotic stability since the magnitude of each mode decays to zero as time increases. This result correlates with the responses shown in Figure 7.8 that obviously return to equilibrium. Note that one guarantee of asymptotic stability is having negative real part for the time-varying pole. The real parts of the poles in Figure 7.9 that are predominately associated with the phugoid mode and are indeed always negative; however, the real parts of the poles that are predominately associated with the short-period mode are sometimes positive so the mode must be computed to ascertain stability.

Finally, the eigenvectors associated with each mode of Figure 7.10 are graphed in Figure 7.11 to show the relative response of each vehicle state as normalized by the vertical velocity. These eigenvectors, similar to the poles and modes, show both short-period characteristics and phugiod characteristics but each is clearly dominated by one type of dynamic. The eigenvector of v_1 initially shows short-period motion, with little variation in forward velocity and a phase difference of $90°$ between pitch rate and vertical velocity, until the damping decays that motion and the phugoid response is evident. The eigenvector of v_2 steadily transitions into the phugiod response which is primarily motion in forward velocity and pitch angle which are $90°$ out of phase. Also, note that these eigenvectors nearly converge to similar magnitudes and phases except for a $90°$ difference in phase of the pitch angle between v_1 and v_2.

7.5.4   Modal Interpretation

A modal interpretation of the poles in Figure 7.9 is conducted to relate these mathematical constructs to standard parameters associated with flight dynamics. The parameters are directly computed from the time-invariant poles while their counterparts from the time-varying poles result from interpretations that relate characteristics of the responses.

The natural frequencies as shown in Figure 7.12 have some commonalities but also some clear differences when comparing the time-varying poles and the time-invariant poles. The values are reasonably close for the entire trajectory when considering the poles associated with the phugoid mode; however, the values are only close for a short time when considering the short-period mode. The difference in natural frequencies for the short-period mode results from the relationship of the time-varying poles to the states. Essentially, the short-period pole is initially relating to the oscillatory behavior of the response but the significant decrease in response magnitude due to damping is actually reflected by the time-varying pole decaying to zero.

The envelope that limits the responses is shown in Figure 7.13. The parameters are similar for the phugoid mode but again, as with the natural frequency, the parameters differ for the time-varying poles and the time-invariant poles for the short-period mode. In this case, the envelope limits the response of the pitch rate and vertical velocity which dominate the short-period response but then, after that mode has damped out, the envelope reflects the bound on the pitch angle.

The damping ratio is shown in Figure 7.14 for the time-varying poles and time-invariant poles. These values are small for both types of poles and thus are reasonably close.

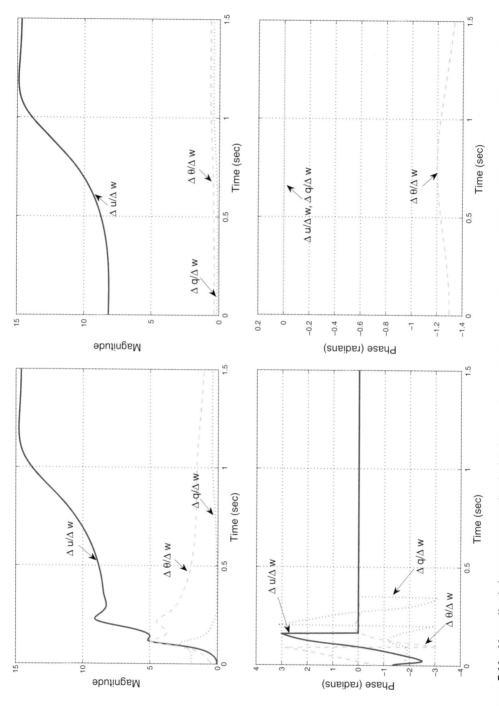

Figure 7.11 Normalized eigenvectors associated with time-varying modes during morphing from +30 deg to 0 deg over 1 sec: Magnitude (upper left) and phase (lower left) of v_1 and magnitude (upper right) and phase (lower right) of v_2

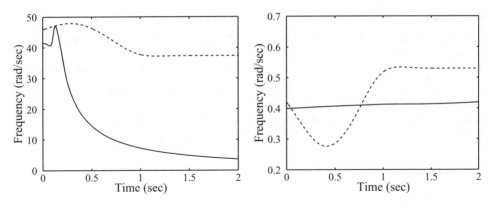

Figure 7.12   Natural frequency associated with linear time-varying poles (—) and linear time-invariant poles (− − −) during morphing from +30 deg to 0 deg over 1 sec: poles 1 and 2 (left) and poles 3 and 4 (right)

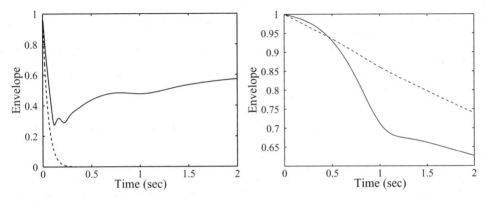

Figure 7.13   Envelope associated with linear time-varying poles (—) and linear time-invariant poles (− − −) during morphing from +30 deg to 0 deg over 1 sec: poles 1 and 2 (left) and poles 3 and 4 (right)

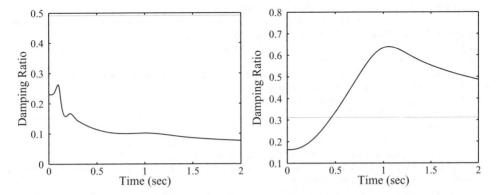

Figure 7.14   Damping ratio associated with linear time-varying poles (—) and linear time-invariant poles (− − −) during morphing from +30 deg to 0 deg over 1 sec: poles 1 and 2 (left) and poles 3 and 4 (right)

References

Abdulrahim MHG and Lind R 2005 Flight characteristics of shaping the membrane wing of a micro air vehicle. *Journal of Aircraft*, 42(1), 131–137.

Bae J, STID and Lee I 2005 Aerodynamic and aeroelastic considerations of a variable-span morphing wing. *Journal of Aircraft*, 42(2), 528–534.

Boschetti P, Cardena E and Arevalo A 2010 Stability and performance of a light unmanned airplane in ground effect *AIAA Aerospace Sciences Meeting*, AIAA–2010–293.

Bowman J n.d. Affordability comparison of current and adaptive and multifunctional air vehicle systems. *AIAA-2003-1713*.

Bowman JBS and Weisshar T n.d. Evaluating the impact of morphing technologies on aircraft performance. *AIAA-2002-1631*.

Cox AG and Hall C 2009 Development of stable automated cruise flap for an aircraft with adaptive wing. *Journal of Aircraft*, 46(1), 301–311.

Drela M and Youngren H n.d. AVL-aerodynamic analysis, trim calculation, dynamic stability analysis, aircraft configuration development. *Athena Vortex Lattice v3.15*.

Duke ELRA and Krambeer K n.d. Derivation and definition of a linear aircraft model. *NASA-RP-1207*.

Etkin B and Reid L 1996 *Dynamics of Flight*. John Wiley and Sons, Inc, New York.

Gano S and Renaud J n.d. Optimized unmanned aerial vehicle with wing morphing for extended range and endurance. *AIAA-2002-5668*.

Gern FHID and Kapania R 2002 Structural and aeroelastic modeling of general planform wings with morphing airfoils. *AIAA Journal*, 40(4), 628–637.

Gopalarathnam A and Norris R 2009 Ideal lift distributions and flap angles for adaptive wings. *Journal of Aircraft*, 46(2), 562–571.

Grant DT and Lind R n.d. Flight dynamics of a morphing aircraft utilizing independent multiple-joint wing sweep *AIAA Atmospheric Flight Dynamics Conference*, vol. AIAA-2006-6505.

Hill DE, Baumgarten JR and Miller JT 1988 Dynamic simulation of spin-stabilized spacecraft with sloshing fluid stores. *Journal of Guidance, Control and Dynamics*, 11(6), 597–599.

Kamen E 1988 The poles and zeros of a linear time varying system. *Linear Algebra and its Applications*, 98: 263–289.

Khot NS, EF and Kolonay R 1997 Method for enhancement of the rolling maneuver of a flexible wing. *Journal of Aircraft*, 34(5), 673–678.

Leong HIR Jager SK and Colgren R 2010 Development of a pilot training platform for UAVs using a 6dof nonlinear model with flight test validation *AIAA Modeling and Simulation Conference*, AIAA–2008–6368.

Love MH, Zink PS, Stroud RL, Bye DR and Chase C 2004 Impact of actuation concepts on morphing aircraft structures, vol. AIAA-2004-1724.

Natarajan A and Schaub H 2006 Linear dynamics and stability analysis of a two-craft coulomb tether formation. *Journal of Guidance, Control and Dynamics*, 29(4), 831–838.

Nelson R 1998 *Flight Stability and Automatic Control*. McGraw-Hill, New York.

Oliver R and Asokanthan S 1997 Control/structure integrated design for flexible spacecraft undergoing on-orbit maneuvers. *Journal of Guidance, Control and Dynamics*, 20(2), 313–319.

Prock BC, Weisshaar TA and Crossley WA 2002 Morphing airfoil shape change optimization with minimum actuator energy as an objective. AIAA-2002-5401.

Roskam J 2001 *Airplane Flight Dynamics and Automatic Flight Controls*. DARcorporation, Lawrence, KS.

Royer DA, Keshmiri S and Jones V 2010 Modeling and sensitivity analysis of the meridian unmanned aircraft *AIAA Infotech@Aerospace*, pp. AIAA–2010–3468.

Rusnell MT, Gano SE, Pérez VM, Renaud JE and Batill SM 2004 Morphing uav pareto curve shift for enhanced performance.

Secanell, M. SA and Gamboa P 2005 Design of a morphing airfoil for a light unmanned aerial vehicle using high-fidelity aerodynamic shape optimization, vol. AIAA-2005-1891.

Spenny C and Williams T 1991 Librational instability of rigid space station due to translation of internal mass. *Journal of Guidance, Control and Dynamics*, 14(1), 31–35.

Stanford B, Abdulrahim M, Lind R and Ifju P 2007 Investigation of membrane actuation for roll control of a micro air vehicle. *Journal of Aircraft*, 44(3), 741–749.

Stewart KGA and Evers J 2006 Flight mechanics and control issues for micro air vehicles. *AIAA Atmospheric Flight Mechanics Conference* AIAA–2006–6638.

Stewart KJ, Wagener GA and Salichon M 2007 Design of the Air Force Research Laboratory micro aerial vehicle research configuration. *AIAA Aerospace Sciences Meeting* AIAA–2007–667.

Stewart KK, Blackburn JWJC and Abate G 2008 Development and initial flight tests of a single-jointed articulated-wing micro air vehicle. *AIAA Atmospheric Flight Mechanics Conference* AIAA–2008–6708.

Thurman S and Flashner H 1996 Robust digital autopilot design for spacecraft equipped with pulse-operated thrusters. *Journal of Guidance, Control and Dynamics*, 19(5), 1047–1055.

Traub L 2009 Experimental investigation of annular wing aerodynamics. *Journal of Aircraft*, 46(3), 988–996.

Venkataramanan S and Dogan A n.d. Dynamic effects of trailing vortex with turbulence and time-varying inertia in aerial refueling. *AIAA-2004-4945*.

Vest M and Katz J n.d. Aerodynamic study of a flapping-wing micro UAV. *AIAA-99-0994*.

Zhu J 1995 A unified spectral theory for linear time-varying systems - progress and challenges In *Proceedings of the 34th IEEE Conference on Decision and Control*, pp. 2540–2546.

8

Optimal Trajectory Control of Morphing Aircraft in Perching Maneuvers

Adam M. Wickenheiser[1], and Ephrahim Garcia[2]
[1]*George Washington University, USA*
[2]*Cornell University, USA*

8.1 Introduction

Since the Wright Brothers' first successful designs, wing deformation has been critical in enabling stable flight. The brothers' aircraft used twist in the bending of the wings akin to the motion of birds, which twist their wings in order to generate differential lift between the wings, thus enabling roll control. Not only was this the first aircraft, it was also the first to incorporate morphing capabilities. As aircraft became heavier, wing twisting gave way to the use of ailerons. Here, we will explore morphing as a reconfiguration of critical aircraft components: wings, tail and fuselage. By defining new degrees of freedom for the aircraft—wing incidence, tail boom angle, and tail incidence—we can change aircraft configurations in-flight, giving the aircraft continuously variable mechanical and aerodynamic characteristics for increased maneuverability.

In the late 1990s, DARPA's Defense Sciences Office funded a program called the Smart Materials Demonstration Program (Sanders *et al.* 2004). Smart materials are a class of materials that can be activated by various forms of energy, such as electricity, heat and even light. In this program, Kudva *et al.* developed an aircraft with a seamless wing capable of changing its trailing edge continuously as a function of span (Kudva 2004). This new wing was unlike anything anyone had ever built before. Its ability to shape-change was not the small-scale deflection typically associated with transducers such as shape memory alloys or piezoelectric materials, but achieved using a distribution of lightweight ultrasonic motors along its trailing edge, coupled to mechanisms that created large deflections. Small-scale changes in geometry

Morphing Aerospace Vehicles and Structures, First Edition. Edited by John Valasek.
© 2012 John Wiley & Sons, Ltd. Published 2012 by John Wiley & Sons, Ltd.

proposed previously always lead to modest improvements in aerodynamic performance, but nothing radical and certainly nothing that enabled new mission capabilities.

In 2002, DARPA approved the creation of a Morphing Aircraft Structures program. Before this program started, there was an attempt at NASA Langley Research Center that focused mainly on materials development. The DARPA program focused on large-scale motion of aircraft wings to radically improve flight performance under a wide range of conditions. The outcome of previous studies showed that morphing could significantly improve disparate performance metrics of aircraft (Bowman *et al.* 2002). While concepts were put forth for entire vehicle morphological change, the first objective of the program was simply to morph the wing.

In this program, Lockheed-Martin (Bye and McClure 2007) and .NextGen Aeronautics (Flanagan *et al.* 2007) produced working prototypes of aircraft that underwent unprecedented morphological change. NextGen even went as far as to perform a flight test of their radical design, a mechanistic wing that expanded and contracted at the root while changing its aspect ratio and wing area. Each company pursued very different designs: Lockheed created a folding wing, and NextGen developed a stretching mechanism. However, both teams aimed to create an aircraft that could perform a hunter-killer mission. With this kind of aircraft, one configuration would be good for endurance and loiter and the other configuration, by reducing the wing aspect ratio and morphing to shorter wings, would be better suited to ground attack. The shorter wings would also reduce drag at higher speeds, thereby permitting a fast dash to a potential target area. These designs focused on reconfiguring an aircraft to change morphology to perform multiple missions better than any single design could.

While these projects proceeded directly to fabricate and demonstrate the possibilities of morphing, there was little in the way of analysis or foundations that engineers could use to model, design, and explore new regimes of flight. A series of papers has been developed that outlines a logical approach to modeling and utilizing morphological change to enable new capabilities for aircraft (Wickenheiser and Garcia 2006a; Wickenheiser and Garcia 2007a; Wickenheiser and Garcia 2007b). These papers utilize lifting line models for the aerodynamics, making morphing a tractable problem for trajectory optimization (Wickenheiser and Garcia 2006b). Critical findings showed that the degree of controllability of the aircraft can be improved by morphing the aircraft to maintain flight control surfaces properly aligned with the on-coming flow (Wickenheiser and Garcia 2007a). When studying the dynamics of morphing aircraft, it was determined that if a vehicle morphed too quickly, even from one stable state to another, it was possible to make the system unstable (Wickenheiser and Garcia 2007a).

Perching (Wickenheiser and Garcia 2007b) was an idea conceived by the authors to imitate the planted landing of bird flight using primarily lift and drag forces. Initially, the concept was created to preserve the Aerial Regional-Scale Environmental Survey (ARES) aircraft (Levine *et al.* 2003) after a short flight in the Martian atmosphere. It was conceived that if the ARES vehicle carried a few simple actuators that would permit shape change, perhaps using materials like shape memory alloys, then a configuration could be reached that would permit it to land like birds do, shedding kinetic energy using aerodynamic forces in a controlled manner (Wickenheiser and Garcia 2007b; McGahan 1973).

The concept of perching clearly has applications to Intelligence, Surveillance and Reconnaissance (ISR) missions as well. For ISR missions, persistence in-theater is paramount to mission success, especially when dealing with asymmetric warfare. The behavior and habits of adversaries must be kept under surveillance for long durations in a similar fashion to monitoring potential criminals in law enforcement. The key to this persistence is minimizing fuel consumption during ISR missions. Therefore, if one could land and observe the activities of an adversary, then the aircraft mission could go from being measured in hours to days. Perching on a power line, building ledge or even a tree branch would enable persistence in-theater, enabling active flight to be reduced to a small subset of the mission duration.

While perching seems an obvious solution to the problems of persistence in theater, little has been published on it previously. One earlier paper on the subject of perching by Crowther (Crowther 2000) examined the stalled landing of a fixed-frame aircraft. The trajectories developed in this study utilized a stall maneuver near the ground, allowing a small aircraft to drop a short distance to the ground. This strategy provided an interesting approach, but the aircraft did not achieve a true planted landing. Moreover, it only studied a fixed-frame aircraft and did not utilize morphological change to improve the maneuver.

In this chapter, we will present the aircraft design used to effect planted landings using a morphing, fixed-wing configuration. A model is developed to account for the dynamics of this morphing aircraft as it moves in the longitudinal plane. The aerodynamic model, based on a modified lifting-line theory for the wings and tail, is provided, which accounts for downwash from the wing on the tail and transient effects such as dynamic stall. Subsequently, the perching trajectory optimization problem is rigorously formulated to provide a framework for generating practical maneuvers for the ISR missions previously described, which means reducing the spatial requirements of the trajectory while respecting the capabilities of the aircraft. This chapter presents results of the optimization procedure for point-mass, fixed-configuration, and morphing airframes. Finally, several conclusions are offered regarding the important parameters of this problem and the variations in optimal solutions among these three classes of aircraft.

8.2 Aircraft Description

The particular aircraft used to develop the perching maneuver is based on the ARES Mars scout craft, an aircraft designed to unfold from a Viking derivative aeroshell and fly for approximately 81 minutes over a Martian landscape, collecting data on atmospheric chemistry, geology, and crustal magnetism (Levine *et al.* 2003). This design consists of a blended wing body (BWB) attached to a V-tail via booms. The idea to investigate perching stemmed from the challenge to save the ARES scout from a crash landing after its mission without resorting to the addition of high thrust capabilities, which would worsen its aerodynamics and consequently the duration of its flight. We propose to improve the vehicle's aerodynamic performance by modifying its configuration, fundamentally changing the aircraft from a fixed-frame to a reconfigurable one. As will be demonstrated, a practical perching maneuver with low thrust-to-weight ratio requires high angles of attack for aerobraking. The large drag forces induced by the flow at high angles of attack enable the aircraft to slow down rapidly; however, the control surfaces are stalled, significantly decreasing controllability. Thus, additional degrees of freedom (DOFs) are installed to create simultaneous regions of attached and separated flow over the aircraft through various flight regimes, thus enabling a controlled aerobraking maneuver. These DOFs are variable wing incidence, tail boom angle, and tail incidence, as shown in Figure 8.1. This aircraft also has ailerons on the trailing edges of the wings and ruddervators on the tail. The ruddervators can act as elevators when deflected symmetrically and as rudders when deflected

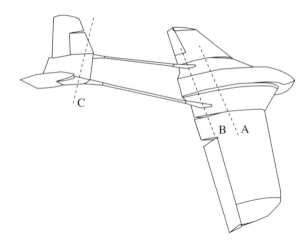

Figure 8.1 Three morphing actuations about the pitch axis: A) rotation of the wing incidence angle with respect to the fuselage body axis, B) rotation of the tail boom, and C) rotation of the horizontal stabilizer

antisymetrically. Thus, to maintain attached flow over the ailerons, the fuselage (equivalently, the inboard section of the BWB) is pitched up to high incidence, while the wings are rotated downward. Additionally, the tail is rotated down and out of the resulting unsteady wake of the body, and the horizontal stabilizer is actuated upward in order to keep the tail surface horizontal as the tail boom rotates. This change maintains attached flow over the wings and tail while pitching the fuselage up into a separated flow regime, as depicted in Figure 8.2.

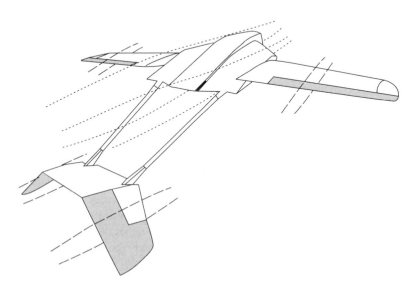

Figure 8.2 Regions of attached flow (dashed) and separated flow (dotted) over the aircraft and its control surfaces (shaded) at high angle of attack, after reconfiguration

Thus, the aileron and ruddervator surfaces remain effective at trimming and control through a wider range of flight conditions compared to a fixed-configuration design (Wickenheiser and Garcia 2006b).

8.3   Vehicle Equations of Motion

The aircraft used in this study is modeled as a blended wing body with rotating outboard wing sections, attached via rotating tail booms to a V-tail, as depicted in Figure 8.1. The fuselage and wings are considered one lifting body, and the tail is considered a second lifting body whose flow condition is affected by the downwash behind the wing. (The consequences of these assumptions on the aerodynamics are considered in section 8.4 on Aerodynamics.) The components of the aircraft are assumed to be rigid; thus, there is no deformation due to the loading. Furthermore, all of the control surface angles, including morphing and standard controls, and the thrust are assumed to be able to be prescribed at any given time. Thus, the dynamics of the actuators are not modeled. As a concession, all of the aircraft controls are limited in range and actuation rate, as discussed further in section 8.5 (Trajectory Optimization for Perching). Hence, although the EOMs are simplified by ignoring the actuator dynamics, these constraints on the optimization problem preclude solutions with unrealistic actuation rates. Finally, for this study, the thrust vector is assumed to be aligned with the chord line of the fuselage. Although thrust vectoring is a potentially useful capability for perching, it is beyond the scope of this research.

In this study, the motion of the aircraft is limited to the longitudinal plane. The practical reason for this simplification is because the available aerodynamic data and the chosen computational method are limited to the longitudinal plane. Large motion in the lateral direction requires a full 3-D aerodynamic analysis, which obviates the possibility of the computational reduction the lifting-line method offers. Although heuristic and empirical corrections can be added for small lateral deviations, these corrections are only applicable to standard configuration aircraft (Hoak 1978). Since the aircraft remains bilaterally symmetric for any morphing configuration and the ruddervators are only used symmetrically, the aircraft remains in the longitudinal plane in the absence of out-of-plane forces or moments. Consequently, this analysis must ignore the effects of wind disturbances and asymmetries in the aircraft layout. This simplification still yields the optimal trajectory under the stipulation that all disturbances and modeling errors are zero mean and small compared to the nonlinearities, so that they may be modeled as additive perturbation terms (Stengel 1994). These restrictions also constrain the candidate trajectories to the longitudinal plane. This constraint makes practical sense, since longitudinal maneuvers are easier to implement, and heading angle adjustments can be handled by a separate controller. It would seem that for a complicated landing maneuver, an aircraft might want to line up with a potential perch, rather than to approach it from random location in space. Furthermore, this focuses the research on the unique aspects of the perching maneuver while ignoring heading, roll, and yaw control, which are not pertinent to the problem.

To develop the equations of motion (EOMs) for this aircraft, consider the cross-sectional sketch shown in Figure 8.3. By definition, the velocity V is tangent to the flight path (i.e. trajectory) in the direction of motion, the lift force L is perpendicular to V and directed upward (in the local frame of the aircraft), and the drag force D is antiparallel to V. The thrust T is assumed to be parallel to the chord line of the aircraft in its plane of symmetry. The

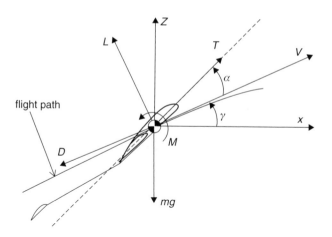

Figure 8.3   State variables of aircraft equations of motion

angle of attack α is measured between the velocity vector and the chord line of the aircraft, thus determining the orientation of the aircraft relative to the incoming air flow. The flight path angle γ is measured between the velocity vector and horizontal, indicating the extent to which the aircraft is climbing or diving. Using this geometry, a force balance in the x- and z-directions gives

$$m\ddot{x} = T \cos\theta - L \sin\gamma - D \cos\gamma \qquad (8.1a)$$

$$m\ddot{z} = T \sin\theta + L \cos\gamma - D \sin\gamma - mg \qquad (8.1b)$$

where $\theta \equiv \alpha + \gamma$ is the pitch angle, m is the aircraft mass, and g is the acceleration due to gravity. In this formulation, the pair (x, z) are the coordinates of the center of gravity of the aircraft, thus decoupling the rotational degree of freedom. Using the relationships $V^2 = (\dot{x})^2 + (\dot{z})^2$ and $\gamma = \tan^{-1}(\dot{z}/\dot{x})$, Equations 8.1a–8.1b can be written in terms of V and γ:

$$m\dot{V} = T \cos\alpha - D - mg \sin\gamma \qquad (8.2a)$$

$$mV\dot{\gamma} = T \sin\alpha + L - mg \cos\gamma \qquad (8.2b)$$

$$\dot{x} = V \cos\gamma \qquad (8.2c)$$

$$\dot{z} = V \sin\gamma \qquad (8.2d)$$

A balance of moments about the aircraft center of gravity (c.g.) gives

$$I_y \dot{q} = M - \dot{I}_y q \qquad (8.3)$$

where $q \equiv \dot{\theta}$ is the pitch rate, and I_y is the mass moment of inertia about the y-axis calculated about the c.g. Note that the last term in Equation 8.3 is necessary because the mass moment of inertia of the aircraft changes during morphing. In this formulation, the pitch angle θ is not fixed relative to any component of the aircraft in the general morphing case; it rotates relative

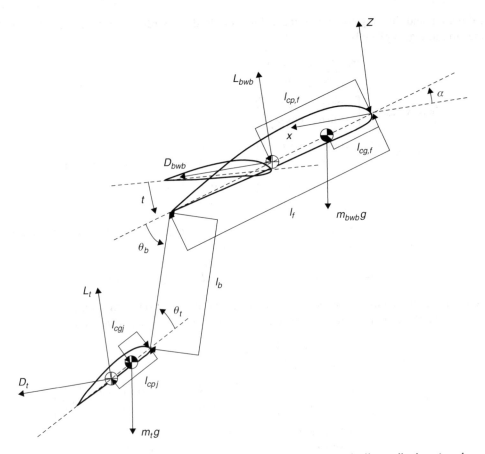

Figure 8.4 Breakdown of aerodynamic loads into blended wing body and tail contributions (not drawn to scale)

to the fuselage chord along with the principal axes of the inertia matrix as the aircraft deforms. (Hence, the angle of the thrust vector relative to θ must be adjusted accordingly.)

The net aerodynamic loads on the aircraft are resolved into lift and drag components and the pitching moment about the center of gravity. However, during the calculation of these loads, the blended wing body (fuselage and wings) and the tail are considered separately: the lift, drag, and center of pressure (where the lift and drag are applied) are calculated for each. These components and the salient dimensions for pitching moment calculation are shown in Figure 8.4. The overall lift and drag forces are given by $L = L_{bwb} + L_t$ and $D = D_{bwb} + D_t$ and mass by $m = m_{bwb} + m_t$; however, the pitching moment and mass moment of inertia calculations are more complicated because of the need to include the effects of shape change.

Equation 8.3 is a moment balance about the aircraft c.g.; thus, the location of the c.g. must be recalculated continuously as the aircraft morphs. It is convenient to place the origin of the local coordinate system at the leading edge of the root of the aircraft (i.e. the tip of the nose) and align the x-axis antiparallel to the velocity vector. Consequently, the lift force is in the

z-direction and the drag force is in the x-direction. In this coordinate system, the location of the aircraft c.g. is given by

$$\mathbf{x}_{cg} = \frac{m_{bwb}\mathbf{x}_{cg,bwb} + m_t\mathbf{x}_{cg,t}}{m_{bwb} + m_t} \tag{8.4}$$

where $\mathbf{x}_{cg,bwb} = \begin{bmatrix} \cos\alpha & \sin\alpha \\ -\sin\alpha & \cos\alpha \end{bmatrix} \begin{bmatrix} l_{cg,f} \\ 0 \end{bmatrix}$

and $\mathbf{x}_{cg,t} = \begin{bmatrix} \cos\alpha & \sin\alpha \\ -\sin\alpha & \cos\alpha \end{bmatrix} \begin{bmatrix} l_f \\ 0 \end{bmatrix} + \begin{bmatrix} \cos(\alpha+\theta_b) & \sin(\alpha+\theta_b) \\ -\sin(\alpha+\theta_b) & \cos(\alpha+\theta_b) \end{bmatrix} \begin{bmatrix} l_b \\ 0 \end{bmatrix}$

$$+ \begin{bmatrix} \cos(\alpha+\theta_b-\theta_t) & \sin(\alpha+\theta_b-\theta_t) \\ -\sin(\alpha+\theta_b-\theta_t) & \cos(\alpha+\theta_b-\theta_t) \end{bmatrix} \begin{bmatrix} l_{cg,t} \\ 0 \end{bmatrix}$$

Once the c.g. location is calculated using Equation 8.4, the mass moment of inertia about the c.g. can be found using the Parallel-Axis Theorem:

$$I_y = I_{y,bwb} + m_{bwb}\left(\mathbf{x}_{cg} - \mathbf{x}_{bwb}\right)^2 + I_{y,t} + m_t\left(\mathbf{x}_{cg} - \mathbf{x}_t\right)^2 \tag{8.5}$$

To compute the pitching moment about the c.g., first the location of the centers of pressure (c.p.) of the BWB and tail must be calculated, analogously to the c.g. calculations:

$$\mathbf{x}_{cp,bwb} = \begin{bmatrix} \cos\alpha & \sin\alpha \\ -\sin\alpha & \cos\alpha \end{bmatrix} \begin{bmatrix} l_{cp,f} \\ 0 \end{bmatrix}$$

and $\mathbf{x}_{cp,t} = \begin{bmatrix} \cos\alpha & \sin\alpha \\ -\sin\alpha & \cos\alpha \end{bmatrix} \begin{bmatrix} l_f \\ 0 \end{bmatrix} + \begin{bmatrix} \cos(\alpha+\theta_b) & \sin(\alpha+\theta_b) \\ -\sin(\alpha+\theta_b) & \cos(\alpha+\theta_b) \end{bmatrix} \begin{bmatrix} l_b \\ 0 \end{bmatrix}$

$$+ \begin{bmatrix} \cos(\alpha+\theta_b-\theta_t) & \sin(\alpha+\theta_b-\theta_t) \\ -\sin(\alpha+\theta_b-\theta_t) & \cos(\alpha+\theta_b-\theta_t) \end{bmatrix} \begin{bmatrix} l_{cp,t} \\ 0 \end{bmatrix}$$

Then the pitching moment is given by

$$M = L_{bwb}\left(x_{cg} - x_{cp,bwb}\right) + L_t\left(x_{cg} - x_{cp,t}\right) - D_{bwb}\left(z_{cg} - z_{cp,t}\right) - D_t\left(z_{cg} - z_{cp,t}\right) \tag{8.6}$$

Thus, Equations 8.5 and 8.6 can be substituted into Equation 8.4 for integration of the aircraft EOMs.

Although it is assumed that the morphing DOFs – the relative angles between the fuselage, wings, tail boom, and tail – can be prescribed as functions of time, additional calculations must be made to determine the motion of each member relative to the pitch angle θ due to the morphing actuation. Let $\Delta\theta_1$ and $\Delta\theta_2$ be the angles of two joining members relative to θ. The dynamics of these two variables are governed by conservation of angular momentum, since external torques only affect θ itself (Equation 8.4). Hence the relative rotations of two joining members (e.g. wing and fuselage, or fuselage and tail boom) are governed by

$$\frac{\left[I_{y,1} + \dfrac{m_1 m_2}{m_1 + m_2}l_1^2 - \dfrac{m_1 m_2}{m_1 + m_2}l_1 l_2 \cos(\Delta\theta_1 - \Delta\theta_2)\right]\Delta\ddot{\theta}_1 + \dfrac{1}{2}i_{y,1}\Delta\dot{\theta}_1}{\left[I_{y,2} + \dfrac{m_1 m_2}{m_1 + m_2}l_2^2 - \dfrac{m_1 m_2}{m_1 + m_2}l_1 l_2 \cos(\Delta\theta_1 - \Delta\theta_2)\right]\Delta\ddot{\theta}_2 + \dfrac{1}{2}i_{y,2}\Delta\dot{\theta}_2} = 1 \tag{8.7}$$

which can be obtained from a moment balance about the hinge axis between the two members. In Equation 8.7, $I_{y,i}$ is the mass moment of inertia of member i, m_i is the mass of member i, and l_i is the perpendicular distance between the c.g. and the hinge axis of member i. Thus, if $\Delta\theta_1 - \Delta\theta_2$ is prescribed at time t, then Equation 8.7 can be integrated to find $\Delta\theta_1(t)$ and $\Delta\theta_2(t)$.

Since the EOMs are to be integrated within a trajectory optimization routine, it is important that each of the states be of the same order of magnitude. Proper scaling helps maximize the convergence rate towards an optimal solution and minimize any numerical errors from poor matrix conditioning in the optimization algorithm (Betts 2001). Hence, the longitudinal EOMs (Equations 8.2a–8.3) are converted into the following nondimensional form:

$$\dot{V} = T\cos\alpha - C_D V^2 \sin\gamma \tag{8.8a}$$

$$\dot{\gamma} = \frac{T}{V}\sin\alpha + C_L V - \frac{\cos\gamma}{V} \tag{8.8b}$$

$$\dot{q} = \frac{\kappa C_m V^2 - \dot{I}_y q}{I_y}, \quad \kappa = \frac{2\bar{c}m^2}{\rho S} \tag{8.8c}$$

$$\dot{x} = V\cos\gamma \tag{8.8d}$$

$$\dot{z} = V\sin\gamma \tag{8.8e}$$

where V is in units of $\sqrt{gl}$, t is in units of $\sqrt{g/l}$, T is in units of mg, and x and h are in units of l, where $l = 2m/\rho S$ is the characteristic length. Additionally, ρ is atmospheric density, $\bar{c}$ is the mean aerodynamic chord of the BWB, and S is the planform area of the BWB. With angles measured in radians, all of the aircraft's states are now of unit order of magnitude.

8.4   Aerodynamics

For the purposes of this study, the aircraft is modeled in the longitudinal plane only, that is, roll, yaw, and sideslip dynamics are not considered. This assumption simplifies the aerodynamics and vehicle dynamics substantially while still providing an environment for studying the richness and qualitative behavior of the perching maneuver. As will be described, this restriction enables the 3-D aerodynamic problem to be decoupled into a finite coupled system of 2-D problems based on pre-computed airfoil data.

During the perching maneuver, the aircraft experiences regions of attached and separated flow over its surface. Indeed, this combination is a phenomenon to be exploited by this morphing aircraft design. Whereas rapid, computationally inexpensive tools exist for thin wings at low angles of attack, post-stall flows over lifting surfaces are significantly more difficult to compute. Therefore, in order to create a low-order aerodynamic model that is inexpensive enough for inclusion in an optimization routine and accurate over a wide range of angles of attack, a mixed numerical/empirical method is developed. This method blends a numerical potential flow method at low angles of attack with empirical airfoil data at high angles of attack. The form of the blending can be summarized by the following equation, inspired by the separation point calculations of Goman and Khrabrov (1994):

$$C_X(\alpha, \dot{\alpha}) = C_{X,\text{att}}(\alpha) \cdot p(\alpha, \dot{\alpha}) + C_{X,\text{sep}}(\alpha) \cdot [1 - p(\alpha, \dot{\alpha})] \tag{8.9}$$

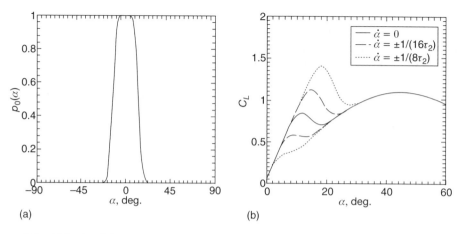

Figure 8.5   (a) Static mixing parameter as a function of angle of attack. (b) Wing lift coefficient variation for positive and negative angle of attack rates

where C_X can represent the lift, drag, or pitching moment coefficient. The subscript $(\cdot)_{att}$ indicates a result obtained from the attached flow regime (i.e. low angle of attack) analysis, and the subscript $(\cdot)_{sep}$ indicates a result obtained from the separated flow regime (i.e. high angle of attack) analysis. Equation 8.9 must be computed separately for the fuselage, wings, and tail because the degree of flow separation over each may be different.

The parameter p in Equation 8.9 varies between 0 and 1 and indicates the relative weighting between the attached and separated flow-based aerodynamic coefficients: 0 indicates fully separated and 1 indicates fully attached. When angle of attack is stationary, the variation of p with respect to α is denoted by $p_0(\alpha)$ and defined by the equation

$$p_0(\alpha) = \mathrm{sech}\left[\left(\frac{15\alpha}{\pi}\right)^3\right] \tag{8.10}$$

which represents the quasi-steady transition between attached and separated flow. This function is shown in Figure 8.5a. As constructed, it is nearly 1 at low angles of attack, indicating that the attached flow contribution is dominant, and nearly 0 at high angles of attack, indicating that separation effects dominate. The function $p_0(\alpha)$ is called the static mixing parameter because it specifies the extent of flow separation over the lifting surface when it is held fixed at a particular angle of attack.

When a lifting surface is rotating with respect to the oncoming flow, a lag develops between the motion of the solid boundary and the fluid due to the finite convection speed of the disturbance through the flow field. These fluid dynamics cause the phenomenon of dynamic stall and can be modeled as a first-order lag state (Goman and Khrabrov 1994):

$$\tau_1 \dot{p} = p_0(\alpha - \tau_2 \dot{\alpha}) - p \tag{8.11}$$

The model for the mixing parameter given by Equations 8.10–8.11 realistically accounts for static and dynamic stall effects. The $(\alpha - \tau_2 \dot{\alpha})$ term accounts for time delays in flow separation and reattachment caused by boundary-layer convection lag, which is roughly proportional to $\dot{\alpha}$. The $\tau_1 \dot{p}$ term accounts for the transient response of the flow to disturbances; this is

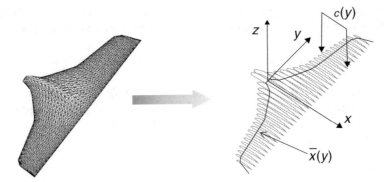

Figure 8.6   The decoupling of the 3-D wing into 2-D airfoils and the local coordinate system and geometry used in the lifting-line theory

simply modeled as a first-order dynamical system. Both time constants τ_1, τ_2 scale with the characteristic time scale ($\bar{c}/V$).

Figure 8.5b shows the effects of dynamic stall on the lift coefficient of the wings. The $\dot{\alpha} = 0$ curve portrays the effect of the static mixing parameter p_0 plotted in Figure 8.5a. As this parameter transitions from 1 to 0, the lift coefficient transitions from the linear dependence predicted by thin airfoil theory to the post-stall dependence. For positive angle of attack rates, the separation is delayed, resulting in the persistence of the linear region into higher angles of attack. The opposite effect occurs when the angle of attack rate is negative; the separated flow lift coefficient curve persists into lower angles of attack.

The aerodynamic forces on the aircraft components in the attached flow regime are calculated using a modified version of Weissinger's method (Weissinger 1947) developed by Wickenheiser and Garcia (2007a). This method is based on classical lifting-line techniques that are derived from potential flow theory; however, corrections are made to account for experimental (i.e. viscous) airfoil data. The 3-D wing is effectively broken into a series of 2-D airfoils joined by their quarter-chord curve (the curve connecting points on each airfoil's chord line a quarter of the distance between the leading and trailing edges), as depicted in Figure 8.6. The aerodynamic forces acting on each wing section are influenced by the circulation generated by each of the other sections and the vortex wake behind the body.

As in Prandtl's classical lifting-line theory, the wing is modeled as a "bound" vortex along the quarter-chord curve and a sheet of "free" vortices extending from the bound vortex to $x = \infty$ to model the wake behind the body. Using the Biot-Savart Law, which gives a formula for the velocity induced by a vortex curve, and the geometry shown in Figure 8.6, the velocity in the vertical direction w can be found in the xy-plane:

$$w(x, y) = \frac{1}{2\pi} \int_{-y_o}^{y_o} \frac{\Gamma'(\bar{y})}{y - \bar{y}} d\bar{y} + \frac{1}{4\pi} \int_{-y_o}^{y_o} \frac{\Gamma'(\bar{y})}{y - \bar{y}} \left[\frac{x - \bar{x}(\bar{y})}{\sqrt{(x - \bar{x}(\bar{y}))^2 + (y - \bar{y})^2}} - 1 \right] d\bar{y}$$

$$+ \frac{1}{4\pi} \int_{-y_o}^{y_o} \Gamma(\bar{y}) \frac{x - \bar{x}(\bar{y}) + \bar{x}'(\bar{y})(\bar{y} - y)}{\left[(x - \bar{x}(\bar{y}))^2 + (y - \bar{y})^2 \right]^{3/2}} d\bar{y} \qquad (8.12)$$

where $\Gamma(y)$ is the strength of the bound vortex at y.

To generalize the solution and improve the numerical accuracy when evaluating Equation 8.12, the variables are made non-dimensional by the following substitutions:

$$\eta = \frac{y}{y_0}, \quad \bar{\eta} = \frac{\bar{y}}{y_0}, \quad G = \frac{\Gamma}{y_0 U_\infty}, \quad \bar{\xi} = \frac{\bar{x}}{c}, \quad \alpha = \frac{w}{U_\infty} \quad (8.13)$$

According to the Pistolesi-Weissinger condition (Pistolesi 1937; Weissinger 1947), the overall wind velocity should be tangent to the plane of the wing at the wing's $\frac{3}{4}$-chord line. In other words, along this line the downwash angle is equal to the local airfoil's angle of attack, which is the sum of the wing's geometrical twist and its overall angle of attack. Thus, the downwash velocity w in Equation 8.12 should be evaluated at $x = \bar{x}(y) + c(y)/2$, which is half a chord length behind the quarter-chord line. Making these substitutions transforms Equation 8.12 into

$$\alpha(\eta) = \frac{1}{2\pi} \int_{-1}^{1} \frac{G'(\bar{\eta})}{\eta - \bar{\eta}} d\bar{\eta} + \frac{1}{4\pi} \int_{-1}^{1} P(\eta, \bar{\eta}) G(\bar{\eta}) d\bar{\eta} + \frac{1}{4\pi} \left(\frac{y_0}{c(\eta)}\right)^2 \int_{-1}^{1} R(\eta, \bar{\eta}) G(\bar{\eta}) d\bar{\eta}$$

$$(8.14)$$

where

$$P(\eta, \bar{\eta}) \equiv \frac{1}{\eta - \bar{\eta}} \left[\frac{\bar{\xi}(\eta) - \bar{\xi}(\bar{\eta}) + 1/2}{\sqrt{\left(\bar{\xi}(\eta) - \bar{\xi}(\bar{\eta}) + 1/2\right)^2 + (y_0/c(\eta))^2 (\eta - \bar{\eta})^2}} - 1 \right]$$

$$R(\eta, \bar{\eta}) \equiv \frac{\bar{\xi}(\eta) - \bar{\xi}(\bar{\eta}) + 1/2 + \bar{\xi}'(\bar{\eta})(\bar{\eta} - \eta)}{\left[\left(\bar{\xi}(\eta) - \bar{\xi}(\bar{\eta}) + 1/2\right)^2 + (y_0/c(\eta))^2 (\eta - \bar{\eta})^2\right]^{3/2}}$$

In order to solve Equation 8.14, the unknown function $G(\eta)$ is parameterized by its value at m points along the span of the lifting surface. Additionally, a collocation approach is typically taken, in which the local angle of attack function $\alpha(\eta)$ is also evaluated at these points. This approach generates a system of m linear equations that is solved for $G(\eta_i)$, $i = 1, 2, \ldots, m$, which are then used to reconstruct the entire function $G(\eta)$.

This analysis assumes that the cross-sections are ideal thin airfoils with a lift curve slope of 2π and zero camber. In order to incorporate the actual airfoil section data–C_l, C_d and C_m as functions of angle of attack–the effective angle of attack at each section must be evaluated. By Munk's analysis (Munk 1921), the downwash angle induced by the vorticity at each section is given by half the downwash angle at an infinite distance downstream. This angle is calculated by taking half the limit of Equation 8.14 as $x \to \infty$:

$$\alpha_i(\eta) = \frac{1}{4\pi} \int_{-1}^{1} \frac{G'(\bar{\eta})}{\eta - \bar{\eta}} d\bar{\eta} \quad (8.15)$$

Then the effective angle of attack is given by $\alpha_{\text{eff}}(\eta) = \alpha(\eta) - \alpha_i(\eta)$. This angle can then be used in a look-up table for the section aerodynamic coefficients.

For the aircraft used in this study, three airfoils are chosen from the catalog of low-speed airfoil data provided by the University of Illinois at Urbana-Champagne (McGranahan and Selig 2004). These airfoils are chosen for the fuselage centerline, the wing root (where the "wing" and "fuselage" sections of the BWB meet), and the wing tip. In between these span locations, the wing cross-sections are lofted (i.e. interpolated) linearly (see Raymer 1999).

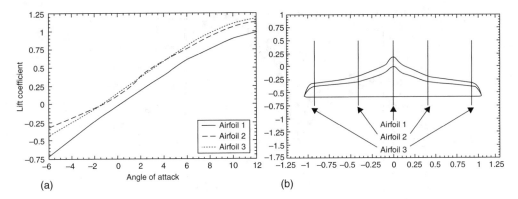

Figure 8.7 (a) Section lift coefficient vs. angle of attack for three cross-sections of BWB. (b) Spanwise stations of these cross-sections.

Figure 8.7 shows the span-wise locations of these airfoils (with the wing span normalized) and their lift coefficient curves.

Finally, the influence of the BWB on the tail must be computed. Since the tail is located in the wake of the BWB, the shed vortices induce a downwash angle on the tail $\alpha_{i,bwb \to t}$. The method of Phillips *et al.* (2002)) is used to calculate the downwash angle on the tail as a function of its position and the strength of the circulation around the BWB:

$$\alpha_{i,bwb \to t}(x, z) = \frac{\kappa_v \kappa_p \kappa_s}{\kappa_b} \frac{C_L}{AR} \qquad (8.16)$$

where C_L is the lift coefficient of the BWB and AR is its aspect ratio (defined by $AR = b^2/S$, where b is the wing span and S is the planform area). The coefficients appearing in Equation 8.16 are given by

$$\kappa_v = 1 + \sum_{n=2}^{m} \frac{a_n}{a_1} \sin\left(\frac{n\pi}{2}\right),$$

$$\kappa_b = \frac{1}{\kappa_v}\left[\frac{\pi}{4} + \sum_{n=2}^{m} \frac{n a_n}{(n^2 - 1)a_1} \cos\left(\frac{n\pi}{2}\right)\right],$$

$$\kappa_p = \frac{2\kappa_b^2}{\pi^2(z^2 + \kappa_b^2)}\left[1 + \frac{x(x^2 + 2z^2 + \kappa_b^2)}{r^2\sqrt{r^2 + \kappa_b^2}}\right],$$

$$\kappa_s = \left[1 + \frac{x - s}{t} + \frac{x(r + t)(t_0^2 - x^2)}{rt(rt + r^2 - xs)}\right]\left[1 + \frac{x(r^2 + t_0^2 - x^2)}{r^2 t_0}\right]^{-1}$$

where $r^2 = x^2 + z^2$, $s = \kappa_b \tan\Lambda$, $t^2 = (x - s)^2 + z^2 + \kappa_b^2$, and $t_0^2 = x^2 + z^2 + \kappa_b^2$. The parameter Λ is the average quarter-chord sweep angle of the BWB, and x and z are the coordinates of the aerodynamic center of the tail with respect to the aerodynamic center of the BWB. The coefficients $a_1, \ldots, a_m$ are the sine series coefficients of the nondimensional circulation distribution $G(\eta)$ found from the lifting-line analysis.

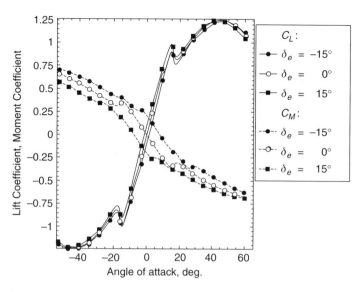

Figure 8.8   Lift and pitching moment coefficients for several elevator deflection angles

The aerodynamic forces on the aircraft components in the separated flow regime are calculated using empirical high angle of attack data (Sheldahl and Klimas 1981). A single set of aerodynamic data is used for every section, a simplification that is not unreasonable since the specific airfoil shape becomes less significant after the flow has detached, as shown experimentally in (Sheldahl and Klimas 1981). The aerodynamic model for fully separated flow is summarized in the following equations:

$$C_{l,\text{sep}} = 1.1 \sin(2\alpha) \tag{8.17}$$

$$C_{d,\text{sep}} = .9(1 - \cos(2\alpha)) \tag{8.18}$$

$$\left(\frac{x_{cp}}{c}\right)_{\text{sep}} = .04095\alpha + .0857 \tag{8.19}$$

where the center of pressure in Equation 8.19 is measured aft of the quarter-chord point. These section coefficients are integrated over the wing and tail planforms where the flow is separated.

To summarize the aerodynamic model, Figure 8.8 plots static C_L and C_M versus angle of attack for several values of elevator deflection δ_e. In the attached flow region, C_L and C_M are approximately linear with respect to angle of attack for each elevator deflection, and the negative C_M slope indicates static pitch stability. (As angle of attack increases, a negative moment is generated to reduce the angle of attack.) At stall, lift decreases rapidly over the aircraft, and the restoring moments begin to level out. This means that less control effort is required to pitch the aircraft further than if the flow had remained attached. When the aircraft has a non-zero angle of attack rate, the transition region between attached and separated flow is enlarged, and hysteresis occurs, as previously discussed regarding Figure 8.5. The combination of the nonlinear static aerodynamics and the dynamic stall effects constitutes the complete aerodynamic model used throughout this study.

A look-up table of all the possible values for lift, drag and moment for all possible shapes of the aircraft is assembled to simulate the motion of the vehicle. As the morphing parameters change so do the coefficients of lift, drag and moment. The range of motion for the vehicle and a reasonable discretization of the range of parameters, such as shown in Figure 8.8, caused the model to have more than 9500 permutations.

8.5 Trajectory Optimization for Perching

The main problem that this study addresses is how to land an aircraft at a point with zero (or very small) velocity, starting from straight and level flight, i.e., a cruising or loitering state. This problem differs from existing aircraft landing problems in two fundamental ways: (1) it is not assumed that there is substantial ground length after the aircraft touches down over which to bring it to a complete halt; and (2) the thrust is not assumed to be sufficient to land the aircraft vertically like a helicopter or Vertical Take-Off and Landing (VTOL) aircraft. Thus, the trajectory optimization problem is formulated as a two-point boundary value problem between a cruising state and a perching state at a specified point. This means that aspects of the initial state and the final state of the aircraft are specified, but how the aircraft flies from the initial to the final state is unknown. The known quantities and possible trajectories are shown in Figure 8.9. The position and velocity of the aircraft are specified at the landing site, but its orientation (i.e. pitch angle) is unspecified. The aircraft is initially assumed to be cruising/loitering, meaning it is trimmed in straight and level flight. Since an aircraft has an infinite number of straight and level trim states, a choice must be made to select one. Although this choice is somewhat arbitrary, in this study the trim condition for maximum endurance is chosen as the initial state, which is practical given the possible applications. The velocity for maximum endurance is given by

$$V = \sqrt{\frac{2mg}{\rho S} \sqrt{\frac{K}{3C_{D_0}}}} \qquad (8.20)$$

where it is assumed that the drag coefficient can be written as a quadratic: $C_D = C_{D_0} + KC_L^2$ (Raymer 1999). The initial position of the aircraft relative to the landing site ((r, h) in Figure 8.9) is unspecified since it is unknown beforehand how close the aircraft can be before

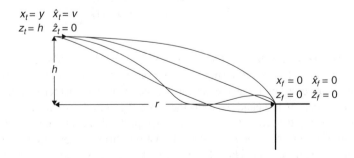

Figure 8.9 Perching trajectory optimization boundary value problem

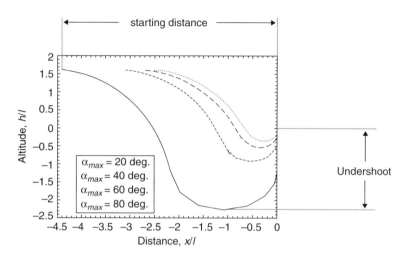

Figure 8.10 Optimal trajectories of varying maximum angle of attack for a point-mass aircraft, $T/W = 0.1$

it starts its landing maneuver. Indeed, minimizing this distance is a practical optimization goal that is discussed below.

Preliminary studies have considered optimizing the trajectory minimum starting distance for a point-mass aircraft using the method described below (Wickenheiser and Garcia 2007b). In those studies, the pitch dynamics are ignored, and the angle of attack is considered to be a control parameter in lieu of the elevator deflection, which indirectly controls the angle of attack. This simplification provides an upper bound or "best-case scenario" for the optimal solution, since pitch maneuverability is essentially unlimited. Figure 8.10 shows plots of optimal trajectories for point-mass aircraft with varying constraints on maximum angle of attack. In all cases, the thrust-to-weight ratio T/W is set to 0.1, and the distances are made nondimensional using the same characteristic scales as Equations 8.8a–8.8c. It is immediately apparent that each trajectory has an "undershoot", or a region in which it dives below the altitude of the landing site. To study this phenomenon further, each term in Equation 8.8a is examined:

$$\dot{V} = \underbrace{T\cos\alpha}_{+} + \underbrace{-C_D V^2}_{-} + \underbrace{-\sin\gamma}_{\substack{-,\gamma > 0 \\ +,\gamma < 0}}$$

The first term is always positive in the range $-90° < \alpha < 90°$, indicating that thrust can only increase velocity. The second term, the drag contribution, is always negative; however, it decreases in magnitude rapidly as the aircraft slows down. The last term is the contribution from the gravity force; it is negative when the aircraft is climbing and positive when it is diving. In order to bring the aircraft to zero velocity rapidly, there must be a contribution from the gravity term. Furthermore, for $T < 1$ (recall that the thrust is normalized by weight), the gravity contribution is necessary. Thus, for low thrust-to-weight ratio aircraft, the undershoot in the perching trajectory is necessary. It is somewhat surprising that this undershoot, which

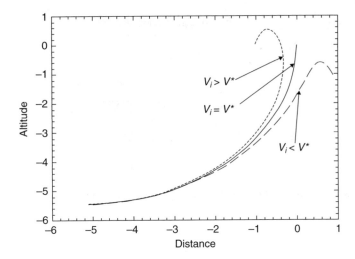

Figure 8.11 The final climbing phase of trajectories with varying initial velocities starting from level flight

explains why larger birds roost in aeries (McGahan 1973), arises "naturally" as a result of this preliminary trajectory optimization.

Subsequently, the effects of varying the final velocity are studied, since intuitively this has a great impact on the maximum undershoot of the trajectory. The speed of the aircraft is very slow throughout a large part of the climbing phase just before landing; therefore, gravity is the primary mechanism through which the kinetic energy of the aircraft is reduced here, not drag. By permitting a larger final kinetic energy (i.e. velocity), less change in gravitational potential is required. If the final velocity is specified as 0, then the aircraft must be flying vertically at the end of the trajectory, since lift and drag also go to 0. For practical purposes, this can be considered undesirable since it requires the aircraft to fly vertically very close to the structure upon which it is landing. Conversely, if the final velocity is greater than 0, then the final approach will be horizontal for minimum undershoot. This improvement can be seen in Figure 8.11, where trajectories of different initial kinetic energy (i.e. velocity) are plotted.

In Figure 8.11, V^* is the initial velocity required to reach $V = 0$ at the origin from the given starting position. This trajectory is a borderline case in the sense that it lies at a point of qualitative trajectory bifurcation with respect to initial velocity. As shown, a greater velocity causes the aircraft to overshoot the landing site and loop back on itself, whereas a lesser velocity causes it to stall (i.e. begin to lose altitude) before it reaches $V = 0$. In all three cases the minimum velocity occurs at the peak of the trajectory, and the minimum velocities for the dashed trajectories are equal and greater than 0. If the required final velocity is allowed to be greater than zero, then the lower trajectory ($V_i < V^*$) can be shifted upward until the peak is at the origin, thus satisfying the final condition on the trajectory. Hence, the undershoot of this trajectory is less than the $V_i = V^*$ trajectory. It is therefore apparent from these simple simulations that increasing the allowable landing speed must decrease the maximum undershoot. Furthermore, increasing the allowable landing speed eliminates the need to fly vertically below the landing site.

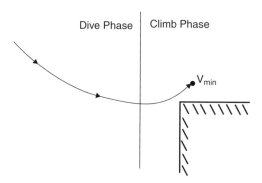

Figure 8.12   Division of the perching trajectory optimization problem into two phases

For this study, a cost function is chosen to minimize the spatial bounds of the trajectory, thus addressing two major concerns: minimizing the undershoot and horizontal distance from the perch site required to start the landing maneuver. Both goals have great practical value. Minimizing the undershoot is important due to spatial limitations, since the landing site may be close to ground level or may be obstructed by objects in the environment. Furthermore, the utility of the aircraft is increased if it can land on shorter structures. Minimizing the required distance to start the maneuver is important because on-board sensors such as CCD cameras, radar, or infrared range finders have a finite range at which they can accurately identify and track the landing site. Increasing these sensors' ranges generally means increasing their size and weight, thereby increasing the demands on the aircraft design. Decreasing this starting distance also means that the aircraft can be given the command to land when it is closer to the landing site.

The persistent undershoot in the trajectories at low thrust-to-weight ratios motivates the division of the problem into two halves. For this study, the goal of minimizing undershoot is given higher priority; thus, the problem can be divided and solved sequentially. These two halves, called the dive phase and the climb phase, are depicted in Figure 8.12. The climb phase can be solved first for minimum undershoot by integrating the EOMs from the lowest point of the trajectory (where $\gamma = 0°$) to the landing site. The global (over all possible trajectories) minimum undershoot is a function only of the climb phase, since only the dynamics here determine how quickly the aircraft can pull up to the landing site with the specified final speed. The dive phase then connects the initial condition to the starting point of the climb phase. This proposition assumes that the initial condition of the climb phase is a reachable end condition of the dive phase. The objective of the dive phase is to minimize the horizontal starting distance required to attain a final condition that matches the initial condition of the climb phase, which is stipulated to be the aircraft's straight and level trim point for maximum endurance. Thus, the cost functions for the two phases can be written as

$$J_{\text{dive}} = z_i - z_f \tag{8.21}$$

$$J_{\text{climb}} = - \min_{t \in [t_0, t_f]} h(t) \tag{8.22}$$

Table 8.1   Aircraft state and control constraints used in trajectory optimization

	Name	State Constraints Range		
α	angle of attack	$-90° - 90°$		
γ	flight path angle	$-90° - 90°$		
T	Thrust	>0		
V_t	initial velocity	Equation 8.20		
(x_f, z_f)	final position	$(0, 0)$		
V_f	final velocity	$0.05 V_i$		
		Actuator Constraints Nominal value	Range	Maximum Rate
ι	wing incidence angle	$0°$	$-90° - 90°$	$\pm 20°/s$
θ_b	tail boom angle	$-15°$	$-15° - 90°$	$\pm 20°/s$
θ_t	tail incidence angle	$-15°$	$-15° - 90°$	$\pm 20°/s$
δ_e	elevator angle	$0°$	$-20° - 20°$	$\pm 40°/s$

The requirement to minimize maximum undershoot (Equation 8.22) determines the optimal trajectory for the climb phase, which in turn determines the end condition of the dive phase. Thus, the solution for the dive phase is only optimal among the set of trajectories that match up with the optimal trajectory for the climb phase. Although the solution to the dive phase may be suboptimal over all possible trajectories for this phase, the overall solution is optimal given the constraint of minimizing the maximum undershoot. Thus, the computed optimal trajectory minimizes the undershoot over all possible trajectories and minimizes the starting distance over all trajectories that minimize the undershoot.

The state and actuator (control) constraints are listed in Table 8.1. The angle of attack and flight path angle constraints are enforced in order to eliminate looping or spinning trajectories and to ensure that the aircraft lands right-side up. The thrust constraints ensure that no negative thrusts are generated. The final velocity is specified to be 5% of the initial velocity, in accordance with the discussion of Figure 8.9. As previously discussed, the initial velocity is specified to be the velocity for maximum endurance. The origin of the coordinate system is placed at the landing site for convenience. No constraints are placed on the duration of the maneuver.

The *direct shooting method* of solving optimization problems is used to convert the nonlinear optimization problem into an equivalent nonlinear programming problem (Enright and Conway 1992). This procedure involves converting the continuous control time histories into a simple functional form that can be parameterized by a (relatively) small number of constants. Several parameterizations were tested before selecting a piecewise cubic Hermite interpolation. This method of interpolation can be designed to preserve the monotonicity and extrema of the underlying data, as well as providing continuity and continuous differentiability of the time series (Fritsch and Carlson 1980). Preserving the extrema of the control signals is especially significant since the optimal control strategies tend to be only piecewise continuous due to constraints, which might be violated by any overshoot in the interpolating polynomial. The control vector is given by the following for the morphing aircraft case:

$$\mathbf{u}(t) = [T(t) \quad \delta_e(t) \quad \iota(t) \quad \theta_b(t) \quad \theta_t(t)]^T \tag{8.23}$$

which are the thrust, elevator deflection angle, wing incidence angle, tail boom angle, and tail incidence angle, respectively. When optimizing the trajectory for fixed-configuration aircraft, the latter three controls are held to their nominal values listed in Table 8.1.

The nonlinear programming method used in this study is a combination of simulated annealing (Atiqullah 2001) and sequential quadratic programming (Powell 1978). These methods are used together in order to balance robustness against local minima and speed of convergence. Several methods for discretizing and numerically integrating the dynamics have been considered; however, Matlab's 4th–5th order adaptive Runge-Kutta algorithm (Dormand and Prince 1980) has been chosen for its robustness in the face of fast dynamics (i.e. pitch dynamics) coupled with slow dynamics (i.e. translational dynamics). The state vector for these dynamics is given by

$$\mathbf{x}(t) = [V(t) \quad \gamma(t) \quad q(t) \quad \theta(t) \quad x(t) \quad z(t) \quad p_{\text{fuse}}(t) \quad p_{\text{wing}}(t) \quad p_{\text{tail}}(t)]^T \tag{8.24}$$

for the EOMs given by Equations 8.8a–8.8e, 8.11. Note that a separation state is given for each lifting surface (fuselage, wing, and tail) since their local angles of attack may differ.

8.6 Optimization Results

Although the point-mass aircraft problem described above provides an adequate picture of the qualitative behavior of the perching problem, the bounds of the computed trajectories (i.e. the undershoot and the starting distance) are unrealistically small (Wickenheiser and Garcia 2007b). This is due to the fact that the aircraft can pitch as fast as necessary to optimize the trajectory, without regard to rotational inertia or actuator limits. With the addition of the pitch dynamics governed by Equation 8.11, the pitch rate is now limited by the maximum achievable pitch moment and the rotational inertia of the aircraft. The pitch moment coefficient C_M in Equation 8.8c is a function of the aircraft's angle of attack and its morphing state. There is an additional pitch damping term, traditionally denoted C_{M_q}, proportional to the pitch rate q, that effectively smooths out rapid changes in pitch angle. As the aircraft rotates, the local velocity and angle of attack on the tail increase, thereby increasing the drag on the tail. This force serves to resist the rotation of the tail and thus constitutes a damping-like effect on the rotational dynamics. Whereas this effect is desirable for gust alleviation, it is undesirable for rapid maneuvers like perching since the aircraft must produce greater moments from its control surfaces in order to achieve faster changes in pitch.

The maximum thrust-to-weight ratio is the first parameter to be varied since it has a huge impact on the engine size and ultimately the power required for long endurance flight. Intuitively, greater thrust makes the perching maneuver "easier" in some sense because if $T/W > 1$, then the aircraft can land vertically like a VTOL aircraft. Variations in maximum T/W are depicted in Figures 8.13 and 8.14, alongside a representative result from the point-mass analysis of Wickenheiser and Garcia (2007b). As shown in Figure 8.13, a higher thrust-to-weight ratio permits lower undershoot. Physically, this seems counterintuitive—after all, the objective is to minimize the kinetic energy of the system, whereas thrust can only increase it—but additional thrust allows the aircraft to fly at a slower speed (at a higher angle of attack)

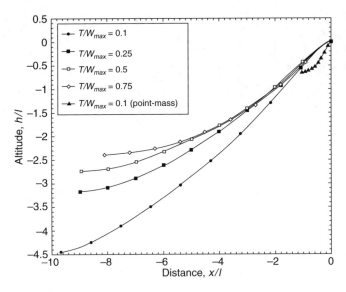

Figure 8.13 Climb phase trajectories of varying maximum thrust-to-weight ratio

while still climbing, since the thrust line is not aligned with the velocity vector at nonzero angles of attack. Additionally, the component of the thrust normal to the trajectory enables the aircraft to pull up out of its dive more sharply. Thus, the additional work done on the aircraft by the component of thrust along the trajectory is more than offset by the reduction in the required initial velocity (i.e. kinetic energy). The thrust control drops rapidly to 0 at the end of the trajectory, once the aircraft has reached a sufficiently steep climb to enable gravity to remove the remainder of its kinetic energy.

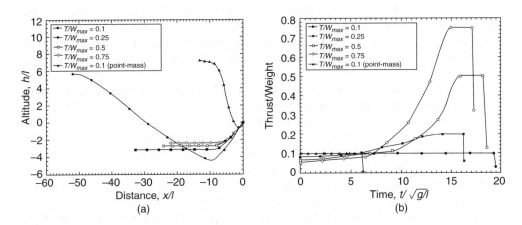

Figure 8.14 (a) Full trajectories of varying maximum thrust-to-weight ratio and (b) the thrust (normalized by weight) control histories for these trajectories

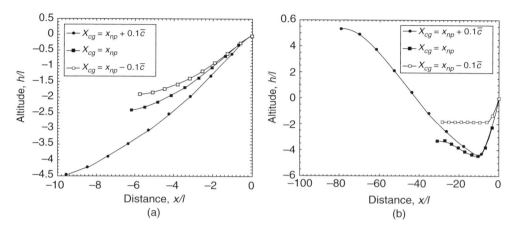

Figure 8.15 (a) Climb phase trajectories of varying center of gravity location $T/W = 0.1$. (b) Full trajectories of varying center of gravity location $T/W = 0.1$

Complete trajectories of various maximum thrust-to-weight ratios are shown in Figure 8.14a. The dive phase for each variation is adjoined to its corresponding climb phase, with the end of each climb phase set to $(0, 0)$. For each thrust-to-weight ratio, the dive phase is optimized for minimum altitude necessary to reach the required velocity at the start of the climb phase. For the cases shown here in which $T/W \geq 0.25$, the aircraft does not need to dive at all since with this much available thrust the aircraft can trim at the required velocity to start the climb. For smaller thrust-to-weight ratios, an initial dive is required to gain the kinetic energy needed to start the climb. Figure 8.14b indicates that maximum thrust is applied throughout the entire maneuver in the $T/W = 0.1$ case, and, in the other cases, high thrust is only utilized towards the end of the maneuver when the aircraft is climbing. The thrust is also throttled right before landing, causing the aircraft to pitch down so that its final velocity is purely horizontal. The effects of the pitch dynamics can be seen by comparing the trajectories in Figures 8.13 and 8.14 against the point-mass case. As predicted, the trajectories bear the same qualitative shape with much larger spatial bounds. Since the aircraft cannot pitch up as rapidly, it requires significantly more distance in which to complete the climb phase. Thus, while illustrative, a point-mass aircraft assumption does not capture the key physics required to generate practical maneuvers.

In Figure 8.15, maximum thrust-to-weight ratio is held constant while the center of gravity position is varied in the x-direction with respect to the aircraft's neutral point (n.p.). (The neutral point is defined as the point at which the aircraft would be marginally stable in the pitch axis if the c.g. were located there.) These plots indicate that the unstable aircraft ($x_{cg} = x_{np} - 0.1\bar{c}$) has a lower-cost (i.e. spatially smaller) optimal trajectory than the marginally stable and stable aircraft. Since the unstable aircraft naturally pitches up when perturbed nose-up from its equilibrium, it is able to pitch faster with less elevator deflection. This means the unstable aircraft can generate the same moment at lower speeds compared to the other aircraft; thus, it is able to fly slower and still climb in order to complete the maneuver. This lower flight speed requirement translates directly into smaller spatial bounds of the trajectory; hence, the aircraft's relative pitch stability plays a major role in its perching capability.

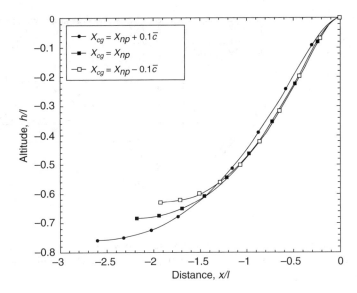

Figure 8.16 Climb phase trajectories of varying center of gravity location for the aircraft with morphing, $T/W = 0.1$

In-flight morphing allows the aircraft's dynamics to approach the point-mass case much more closely by enabling larger possible pitching moments. This is because the morphing actuator ranges are much larger than the elevator's, as listed in Table 8.1, and they cover a larger planform area, so they are able to generate a larger pitching moment per degree of rotation. Therefore, the lifting surfaces are able to rotate to higher magnitude angles of attack in order to generate larger pitching moments. By comparing the climb phase trajectories in Figures 8.15a and 8.16, the direct results of these greater pitching moments can be seen by noting the reduced undershoot in the morphing case. The morphing actuators are able to generate a larger moment at a lower speed, similar to the unstable aircraft case discussed in the previous subsection. Since, for the morphing aircraft, the wings are not generating a large moment due to drag at high angles of attack, their position with respect to the center of gravity is less significant compared to the tail's position. Thus, the morphing aircraft is less sensitive to changes in the center of gravity location compared to the fixed-configuration case, as seen by comparing Figures 8.15a and 8.16. Figure 8.17a shows full trajectories of the morphing aircraft with varying thrust-to-weight ratios. For the dive phase, the aircraft must morph from its cruise configuration to the configuration in which it begins the climb phase over the shortest distance. As previously discussed, additional thrust enables the aircraft to fly at much lower speeds, thereby shortening this distance. Figure 8.17b depicts the time histories of the morphing parameters for these trajectories. In these simulations, the elevator deflection is held at 0 to isolate the effects of vehicle reconfiguration. The wing incidence time history indicates that the wings should be pitched down as the fuselage pitches up, thereby maintaining attached flow over the wings throughout the maneuver. This is beneficial for maintaining aileron effectiveness and for maximizing the pitching moment contribution of the wings. The wing incidence and tail incidence increase monotonically over this phase,

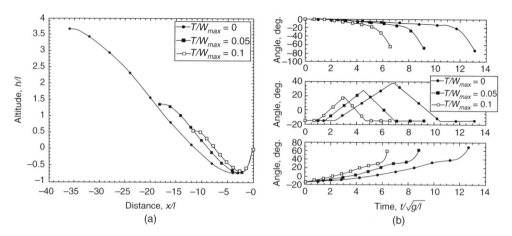

Figure 8.17 (a) Full trajectories of varying maximum thrust-to-weight ratio and (b) the morphing angle time histories for these trajectories: wing incidences (top), tail boom angle (middle), and tail incidence (bottom)

indicating a transition from one trim state at cruise to another at the bottom of the trajectory. The tail boom is swung down and then back up again, which serves to pitch the aircraft down in order to gain speed for the climb phase. During the climb phase, the tail boom remains fixed at its lower bound, which produces the largest moments due to down force and drag on the tail. The tail incidence angle is gradually increased, thereby producing an increasingly negative tail angle of attack. At first, this produces a large down force on the tail, pitching the aircraft up. As the aircraft approaches the landing site, the angle of attack decreases further, thereby increasing the drag and slowing and pitching down the aircraft. Figure 8.18 presents

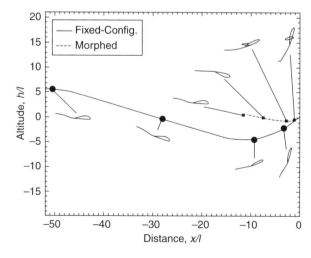

Figure 8.18 Comparison of fixed-configuration and morphing aircraft perching trajectories, $T/W = 0.1$

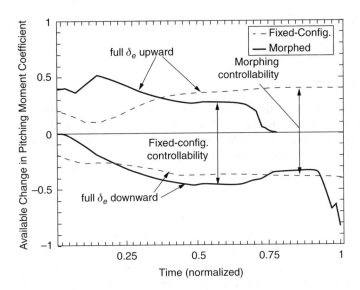

Figure 8.19 Comparison of fixed-configuration and morphing aircraft perching trajectories, $T/W = 0.1$

a direct comparison between a fixed-configuration and a morphing aircraft of the same thrust-to-weight ratio, indicating the orientation of the aircraft at several points along the trajectory. It is apparent that morphing dramatically increases the maneuverability of the aircraft, thus enabling it to perch within a much shorter distance.

Finally, the controllability of the aircraft during the perching maneuver is studied. Specifically, the effectiveness of the elevators is discussed, since the aircraft is only simulated in the longitudinal plane and the pitch dynamics have been shown to play a crucial role in the trajectory optimization solution. Figure 8.19 depicts the maximum change in pitching moment coefficient from the nominal along the trajectory due to elevator deflection in the upwards and downwards directions. Thus, this plot represents the additional pitch control authority—useful for disturbance rejection, for example—available throughout the maneuver. In Figure 8.19, the cases in which the maximum thrust-to-weight ratio is 0.1 and the center of gravity is located at the neutral point are compared between morphing and fixed-configuration aircraft. Since these two maneuvers have different durations, time is normalized from 0 to 1, respectively representing the beginning and the end of the maneuvers. In general, the morphed case maintains high control authority in both directions (i.e. pitch-up and pitch-down) throughout the maneuver. At the beginning and at the end of the maneuver, the fixed-configuration case only has authority in one direction because the elevators are fully deflected in order to track the optimal trajectory. The morphed case is worse around 15% through the maneuver because the tail boom is briefly rotating the elevators into the stalled regime in order to pitch the aircraft downwards; this problem could be alleviated by factoring in controllability into the cost function. If a specified level of control authority is added as a constraint, then the elevator time history could be optimized along with the morphing degrees of freedom in order to improve the trajectory further while maintaining adequate disturbance rejection capability. Indeed, this flexibility is one of the hallmarks of adding additional morphing degrees of freedom to the airframe.

8.7 Conclusions

The morphology presented herein represents non-traditional configuration changes for an aircraft, with the added degrees of freedom being wing incidence and tail manipulation. The change of morphology produced by these degrees of freedom is rigorously modeled and produced significant changes to the aircraft dynamics. A new lifting line theory for these computations is presented and its utility for computing over 9500 permutations is made evident. These degrees of freedom are proven capable of permitting a highly maneuverable trajectory such that an aircraft can, for all intents and purposes, perch on a structure. Studies are performed to evaluate this maneuver with limitation on control surface rates of motion, as would exist in any real aircraft. Additionally, the considerations such as the thrust-to-weight ratio of the vehicle and changes in its center of gravity are also considered. It is shown that as the thrust-to-weight ratio increases, the maneuvering space required for perching decreases. Interestingly, biomimetic dynamics reveal themselves from the optmization as well, including a final dip right before perched landing. This study has characterized the motion of a aircraft undergoing a perching maneuver and has considered a number of parameters that could play a key role in design such a system.

References

Atiqullah MM 2001 Tuned annealing for optimization. *Lect. Notes Comp. Sci.*, 2074, 669–679.

Betts JT 2001 *Practical methods for optimal control using nonlinear programming*. Philadelphia, PA, SIAM.

Bowman J, Sanders B and Weisshaar T 2002 *Evaluating the impact of morphing technologies on aircraft performance*. AIAA2002-1631.

Bye DR and McClure P D 2007 *Design of a morphing vehicle*. AIAA-2007-1728.

Crowther WJ 2000 Perched Landing and Takeoff for Fixed Wing UAVs. In *NATO symposium on unmanned vehicles for aerial, ground, and naval military operations* Ankara, Turkey.

Dormand JR and Prince PJ 1980 A family of embedded Runge-Kutta formulae. *J. Comp. Appl. Math.*, 6: 19–26.

Enright PJ and Conway BA 1992 Discrete approximations to optimal trajectories using direct transcription and nonlinear programming. *J. Guid. Contr. Dyn.*, 15(4), 994–1002.

Flanagan JS, Strutzenberg RC, Myers RB and Rodrian JE 2007 Development and flight testing of a morphing aircraft, the NextGen MFX-1. AIAA2007-1707.

Fritsch FN and Carlson RE 1980 Monotone piecewise cubic interpolation. *SIAM J. Num. Anal.*, 17(2), 238–246.

Goman M and Khrabrov A 1994 State-space representation of aerodynamic characteristics of an aircraft at high angles of attack *J. Aircraft*, 31(5), 1109–1115.

Hoak DE *et al.* 1978 The USAF stability and control datcom. TR-83-3048.

Kudva JN 2004 Overview of the DARPA Smart Wing Program. *J. Intell. Materl Sys. Struc.*, 15(4), 261–267.

Levine JS, Blaney DL, Connerney JEP, Greeley R, Head JW, Hoffman JH, Jakosky BM, McKay CP, Sotin C and Summers ME 2003 Science from a Mars airplane: The Aerial Regional-Scale Environmental Survey (ARES) of Mars. AIAA2003-6576.

McGahan J 1973 Gliding flight of the Andean condor in nature. *J. Exp. Biol.*, 58, 225–237.

McGranahan B and Selig M 2004 UIUC low-speed airfoil tests. URL: http://www.aae.uiuc.edu/m-selig/uiuc_lsat.html [cited 19 February 2004].

Munk MM 1921 *The minimum induced drag of airfoils*. NACA Report 121.

Phillips WF, Anderson EA, Jenkins JC, and Sunouchi S 2002 Estimating a low-speed downwash angle on an aft tail. *J. Aircraft*, 39(4), 600–608.

Pistolesi E 1937 Considerations respecting the mutual influence of systems of airfoils. In *Collected lectures of the 1937 principal meeting of the lilienthal society*. Berlin.

Powell MJD 1978 A Fast Algorithm for Nonlinearly Constrained Optimization Calculations. In GA Watson, ed., *Numerical Analysis* **630**, pp. 144–157. Springer Verlag.

Raymer DP 1999 *Aircraft Design: Conceptual Approach*. Reston, VA, AIAA.

Sanders B, Crowe R, and Garcia E 2004 Defense Advanced Research Projects Agency: Smart Materials and Structures Demonstration Program Overview. *J. Intell. Materl Sys. Struc.*, 15(4), 227–233.

Sheldahl RE and Klimas PC 1981 *Aerodynamic characteristics of seven symmetrical airfoil sections through 180-degree angle of attack for use in aerodynamic analysis of vertical axis wind turbines*. Sandia National Laboratories Report SAND80-2114.

Stengel RF 1994 *Optimal control and estimation*. Mineola, NY, Dover.

Weissinger J 1947 The lift distribution of swept-back wings. NACA TM-1120.

Wickenheiser A and Garcia E 2006 Longitudinal dynamics of a perching aircraft. *J. Aircraft*, 43(6),1386–1392.

Wickenheiser A and Garcia E 2006b Optimization of perching maneuvers through vehicle morphing. *J. Guid. Contr. Dyn.*, 31(4),815–823.

Wickenheiser A and Garcia E 2007 Aerodynamic modeling of morphing wings using an extended lifting-line analysis. *J. Aircraft*, 44(1),10–16.

Wickenheiser A and Garcia E 2007b Perching aerodynamics and trajectory optimization. In *Proc. SPIE*, 6525, 65250O.

Part III

Smart Materials and Structures

9

Morphing Smart Material Actuator Control Using Reinforcement Learning

Kenton Kirkpatrick and John Valasek
Texas A&M University, USA

9.1 Introduction to Smart Materials

Research in the fields of both structures and controls engineering has led to a point where it becomes necessary for materials to do more than simply provide structural support. Materials are needed that can span the gap between engineering disciplines and enable a variety of functions. Historically, materials have been researched and created for the purpose of filling some of these needs (Lagoudas 2008). The demand for vehicles that can travel through the air and even beyond the atmosphere led to the creation of materials that are both light and strong. Similarly, new demands on aerospace structures require new materials and research for the provision of multifunctional behavior.

Smart materials are a special class of materials that have the capability to act as both actuators and sensors. For example, they provide coupling between mechanical deformation and changes in temperature, electric current, and/or magnetic fields. These materials behave as energy transformers and can be engineered to act as sensors by converting variations in mechanical deformation into a non-mechanical response (e.g., thermal or electrical). Likewise, the opposite relationship allows them to act as actuators. By applying a non-mechanical input such as voltage, a smart material can respond with a mechanical deformation, even under substantial loads.

There are many classes of smart materials that have been created and researched. This chapter deals primarily with those that are considered most useful for structural morphing as applied to morphing aerospace vehicles. Control of electrical current is one of the easiest and lightest ways to actively deform smart materials that are thermally actuated. So, the smart materials described here are ones that are easily actuated through the use of only an electrical

Morphing Aerospace Vehicles and Structures, First Edition. Edited by John Valasek.
© 2012 John Wiley & Sons, Ltd. Published 2012 by John Wiley & Sons, Ltd.

response. These materials include but are not limited to piezoelectrics and shape memory alloys (SMAs).

9.1.1 Piezoelectrics

Piezoelectrics are one of the best-known classes of smart materials that provide coupling between electric current and mechanical deformation. There are several different types of piezoelectric materials, each with its own individual properties. Piezoelectric ceramics provide small deformations and load when actuated (Lagoudas 2008); their usefulness as actuators in aerospace structural morphing is therefore limited. Piezoelectric polymers have a much higher actuation strain, but have similarly low stress response (Lagoudas 2008). Piezoelectrics are typically used as actuators by embedding them within or bonding them to the surface of a structure, and are most effective when many small actuators are used together rather than a few large ones (Crawley and de Luis 1987). While it may be possible to achieve the deformations required by morphing in this manner, the need for many actuators leads to the problem of increased complexity of control, and possibly an infeasible number of separate voltage supplies for the mounted systems on UAVs. Thus piezoelectrics are not considered capable of achieving the structural deformations necessary for the large-scale shape changes required by morphing aerospace vehicles, and this chapter will not consider them further.

9.1.2 Shape Memory Alloys

A promising class of smart materials for the purpose of large-scale morphing is considered to be SMAs (Kirkpatrick and Valasek 2009). SMAs have a much higher actuation energy density than most smart materials, and they are capable of both relatively high actuation strain and stress (Lagoudas 2008). Shape memory alloys are metallic alloys that exhibit a unique property known as the shape memory effect (Waram 1993; Sofla et al. 2008). This material can be put under a stress that leads to a deformation that would normally be considered plastic, and then fully recover its original shape after heating it to a high temperature. The ability to withstand high strains (8–10%) makes SMAs useful for structures that undergo large deformations, such as morphing aircraft (Mavroidis et al. 1999). SMAs begin in a crystal phase of austenite and undergo a phase change to martensite when the alloy is cooled through its transformation range. This phase transformation realigns the atoms, and the alloy returns to its original austenitic shape when heated, recovering the SMA from the apparent plastic strain.

SMAs have been used as actuators in a variety of applications. Mabe et al. (2005) have successfully designed and implemented SMA-actuated chevrons that change shape at different altitudes to reduce engine noise and increase efficiency. They have also been used in the medical field for a variety of applications including cardiovascular stents, orthopedics, and dentistry (Duerig et al. 2000; Mantovani 2000). This material is considered to be particularly useful for aircraft wing morphing because it can behave as an actively controlled actuator by having a control system command changes in the temperature of the material, resulting in a mechanical response. This can be accomplished by varying the voltage for heating, and using convection for cooling. The benefit of using SMAs in this manner is that an actuator can be simply composed of voltage leads to a single SMA wire. Without any complex mechanisms to drive the actuator, the weight is significantly reduced.

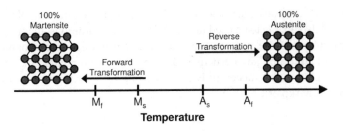

Figure 9.1   Thermally induced crystal phase change

9.1.3   Challenges in Controlling Shape Memory Alloys

SMA-based actuators pose a challenge from a control standpoint because of the highly non-linear, hysteretic response during the crystal phase change. When an SMA wire under a tensile load undergoes a phase transformation, it changes length. The phase transformation from martensite to austenite (heating) causes a decrease in length, while the reverse process extends it back to its original length. The relationship between temperature and strain exhibits a hysteresis because the phase transformation begins and ends at different temperatures depending upon the sign of the temperature change (Mavroidis *et al.* 1999). The relationship between temperature and strain is not only hysteretic, but is also highly nonlinear. Figures 9.1 and 9.2 demonstrate this behavior, where in Figure 9.1 M_s is the martensitic starting temperature, M_f is the martensitic finishing temperature, A_s is the austenitic starting temperature, and A_f is the austenitic finishing temperature.

The hysteresis behavior of SMAs in temperature-strain space is most often simulated through the use of constitutive models that are based on material parameters or by models resulting from system identification (Lagoudas *et al.* 2001). Other methods that simulate this behavior are phenomenological models (Lagoudas *et al.* 1996; Bo and Laogudas 1999; Malovrh and Gandhi 2001), micromechanical models (Patoor *et al.* 1987; Falk, 1989), and empirical models based on system identification (Banks *et al.* 1987; Webb *et al.* 1998). These models are quite accurate,

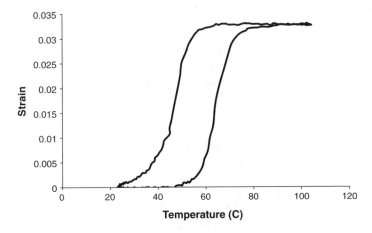

Figure 9.2   Example of SMA hysteresis

but some only work for particular types of SMAs and most require complex computations. Many of them are also unable to be used in dynamic loading conditions, making them unusable in the case of morphing. Since a parametric model is not available for development of a control policy, it is important to find an alternative. One computational method that has been shown in previous research to work successfully is the casting of SMA control as a Reinforcement Learning problem (Kirkpatrick 2009).

9.2   Introduction to Reinforcement Learning

The field of machine learning is a specialization of artificial intelligence research that focuses primarily on developing algorithms that attempt to mimic a human's ability to learn (Russell and Norvig 2003). Presently, machine learning is limited to algorithms that are tailored to recognize specific patterns or achieve desired goals. In the context discussed here, machine learning refers primarily to the ability of an algorithm to use given data to learn how to achieve a goal specified by a user. Although computers have developed to a point where they have dramatically faster processing capabilities than humans, they are still far from able to achieve the complexity of the human brain; machines are not yet able to decide problems and goals for themselves.

Machine learning methods use a variety of approaches that each have strengths in learning to solve certain classes of problems. Artificial neural networks are a popular branch of machine learning algorithms that learn specific tasks or patterns by simulating a complex network of human-inspired neurons (Yegnanarayana 2006). Kernel-based learning approaches have also been investigated extensively, such as support vector machines (Cristianini and J. Shawe-Taylor 2000). From decision trees (Quinlan 1986) to Bayesian network classifiers (Friedman 1997), from instance-based methods (Aha *et al.* 1991) to genetic algorithms (Goldberg 1989), many approaches have been developed to handle the need for automated learning of patterns and system behaviors. One method that shows particular promise for determining control policies for SMA actuators is Reinforcement Learning (Kirkpatrick 2009).

9.2.1   The Reinforcement Learning Problem

One limitation of some popular methods like artificial neural networks is that they must learn by repeatedly feeding previously obtained training data through their networks. In many instances, it is necessary to learn how to navigate an environment without the aid of previously obtained data for training. Reinforcement Learning (RL) is an approach to machine learning that does not require training data, but rather learns by interaction with a specified environment online. RL methods learn from experience by exploring a state-space and determining a proper mapping of states to actions so that they can maximize a numerical reward (Sutton and Barto 1998). It is the design of the state- and action-spaces that describes an environment, and the proper goals to be achieved are handled through the specification of how the agent can obtain rewards.

One fundamental element to describing a RL problem is the value function. Value functions are essentially the cerebrum of the RL agent: they maintain the memory. When the agent interacts with its allotted environment, it uses the rewards that it receives to update a value function. This value function becomes a guide for later recall so that the agent can know which choices have led to the most reward in the past. State-value functions are concerned only with the state itself. The value of being in a particular state is considered, and the agent attempts to move toward the states that lead to the highest cumulative award. Action-value functions are spatially more complex, but they assign values for both states and actions. For the purposes of shape memory alloy control, it is more practical to consider the action-value function. The benefit of using an optimal action-value function for control is that it maintains memory of which actions are necessary to achieve the goal for each state.

The goal of RL methods is to learn the optimal policy, which is the policy that maximizes the value function. The learning done by RL is performed episodically, where an episode is defined as some significant period of the learning process defined by the programmer. Episodes can be based on periods of time, goal achievement, numbers of actions selected, or whatever the programmer believes to be a good choice for the problem at hand. There are many algorithms that have been designed to solve RL problems. Dynamic programming and Monte Carlo methods are both classes of algorithms that are capable of solving RL problems. However, the algorithms that are considered to be most efficient at solving RL problems are Temporal-Difference methods (Sutton and Barto 1998).

9.2.2 Temporal-Difference Methods

Temporal-Difference methods are a special class of RL solution algorithms that are particularly useful for situations when the learning agent has no prior knowledge of the dynamics of the environment (Sutton and Barto 1998). In comparison to other algorithms for solving RL problems, Temporal-Difference algorithms are the most versatile. Dynamic programming requires a perfect model of the environment to determine an optimal policy, while Temporal-Difference needs no model. Another class of methods, Monte Carlo methods, require waiting to the end of an episode to learn any new information. Temporal-Difference methods have the ability to learn as they go along.

There are many different algorithms that fall under the category of Temporal-Difference, but most are variations of three base algorithms. These are Actor-Critic, Sarsa, and Q-learning. They all learn episodically, where an episode is some significant portion of the learning experience. This is user-defined and can either be preset intervals or described by certain achievements. Actor-Critic methods were widely used when Reinforcement Learning systems were first being implemented, but recently Sarsa and Q-learning have been receiving far more attention. For this reason only Sarsa and Q-learning are discussed in this section, but full details about all of these methods can be found in works by Sutton and Barto (1998).

9.2.2.1 Sarsa

Sarsa is an on-policy form of Temporal Difference, meaning that at every time interval the action-value function is evaluated and improved. Sarsa updates the action-value function by using the current state, current action, future reward, future state, and future action to dictate the transition from one state/action pair to the next (Sutton and Barto 1998). This is actually from where Sarsa gets its name (state-action-reward-state-action). The action-value function is updated as learning progresses, and the final optimal action-value function can be used as a control policy. The action-value function update rule for Sarsa is:

$$Q_k(s, a) \leftarrow Q_k(s, a) + \alpha \delta_k \tag{9.1}$$

where s is the current state, a is the current action, Q is the action-value function, and the k subscript signifies the current policy. The α term is a parameter that is used to "punish" the RL algorithm when it repeats itself within each episode. The term δ_k is defined as:

$$\delta_k = r_{k+1}(s', a') + \gamma Q_{k+1}(s', a') - Q_k(s, a) \tag{9.2}$$

The term s' refers to the future state, a' is the future action, $k+1$ corresponds to the future policy, and γ represents a constant that is used to optimize the rate of convergence by weighting the future policy. Equations (9.1) and (9.2) can be combined to form the detailed action-value function:

$$Q_k(s, a) \leftarrow Q_k(s, a) + \alpha[r_{k+1}(s', a') + \gamma Q_{k+1}(s', a') - Q_k(s, a)] \tag{9.3}$$

The reward given for each state/action pair is defined by r, and the reward that is given for each situation is a user-defined parameter. For example, the user could use $+1$ for achieving the goal, -1 for breaking rules, and 0 for all neutral achievements. This action-value function creates the policy that can be used to learn the parameters of the system being explored through RL. The Sarsa method uses a simple algorithm to update the policy using the action-value function provided in Equation (9.3). This is outlined in Algorithm 9.1.

Algorithm 9.1 Sarsa Algorithm (Sutton and Barto 1998)

- Initialize $Q(s,a)$ arbitrarily
- Repeat for each episode:
  - Initialize s
  - Choose a from s using policy derived from $Q(s,a)$ (e.g., ε-Greedy)
  - Repeat for each time step:
    * Take action a, observe r, s'
    * Choose a' from s' using policy derived from $Q(s,a)$ (e.g., ε-Greedy)
    * $Q(s,a) \leftarrow Q(s,a) + \alpha [r + \gamma Q(s',a') - Q(s,a)]$
    * $s \leftarrow s', a \leftarrow a'$
  - Until s is terminal

9.2.2.2   Q-learning

The most commonly used method of Temporal Difference is known as Q-learning. Q-learning is an off-policy form of Temporal Difference that utilizes an action-value function update rule that is very similar to Sarsa. The differences between the algorithms for Q-learning and Sarsa are slight, but the result can dramatically affect the results of the learning process. During an episode, Q-learning updates one value function while following a different one. This is what is meant by stating that it is "off-policy". At the end of an episode, the value function to be followed by the policy is replaced by the one that was recently learned so that both value functions are initially identical. Similar to Sarsa, the update rule for the action-value function is defined by the following equation:

$$Q_k(s, a) \leftarrow Q_k(s, a) + \alpha \delta_k \qquad (9.4)$$

where s is the current state, a is the current action, Q is the action-value function, and the k subscript signifies the current policy. The α term is a parameter that is used to "punish" the RL algorithm when it repeats itself within each episode. The term δ_k is what differs from the Sarsa definition. This term is defined as:

$$\delta_k = r_{k+1}(s', a') + \gamma \max_a Q_{k+1}(s', a') - Q_k(s, a) \qquad (9.5)$$

The term s' refers to the future state, a' is the future action, $k+1$ corresponds to the future policy, and γ represents a constant that is used to optimize the rate of convergence by weighting the future policy. Equations (9.4) and (9.5) can be combined to form the detailed action-value function:

$$Q_k(s, a) \leftarrow Q_k(s, a) + \alpha[r_{k+1}(s', a') + \gamma \max_a Q_{k+1}(s', a') - Q_k(s, a)] \qquad (9.6)$$

The reward given for each state/action pair is defined by r, and the reward that is given for each situation is a user-defined parameter. The rewards are defined by the user for the problem at hand. For example, the user could use $+1$ for achieving the goal, -1 for breaking rules, and 0 for all neutral achievements. This action-value function creates the policy that can be used to learn the parameters of the system being explored through RL. The Q-learning method uses a simple algorithm to update the policy using the action-value function provided in Equation (9.6). This algorithm can be viewed in Algorithm 9.2.

Algorithm 9.2 Q-learning Algorithm (Sutton and Barto 1998)

- Initialize $Q(s,a)$ arbitrarily
- Repeat for each episode:
  - Initialize s
  - Repeat for each time step:
    * Choose a from s using policy derived from $Q(s,a)$ (e.g., ε-Greedy)
    * Take action a, observe r, s'
    * $Q(s,a) \leftarrow Q(s,a) + \alpha [r + \gamma \max_{a'} Q(s',a') - Q(s,a)]$
    * $s \leftarrow s'$
  - Until s is terminal

9.2.3   Action Selection

When using one of the previously described Temporal-Difference Methods, it is required that an appropriate choice be made for how the actions are selected at each time step. The policy that the learner follows is what determines the action to be selected given the present state.

There are many policies that could be followed, and it is necessary that a method of action selection be defined that makes the most sense for the problem.

9.2.3.1 Exploration

One of the simplest methods of action selection is pure exploration. If the RL agent is programmed to follow a purely exploratory policy, the action-value function is not required as part of the policy. There are many ways of choosing to explore. One method is to simply choose an action at random at every time step. Another is to maintain a history of all states visited and choose an action that has not previously been attempted while in the current state. The most commonly used form of exploration tends to be the former, since it can be easily exploited without carrying around historical data. The action selection part of the algorithm for a purely exploratory policy is as shown in Equation (9.7).

$$a \leftarrow random \tag{9.7}$$

Using a purely exploratory policy is very limited. Since it does not actually exploit any knowledge gained along the way, it continues to blindly search regardless of how much the agent has learned. This tends to require the agent to undergo many more learning episodes for convergence to occur.

9.2.3.2 Greedy

Another commonly used policy for action selection is the greedy method. Greedy action selection implies that the most current form of the action-value function is best and is exclusively used. Given an action-value function, $Q(s,a)$, the action chosen for each state, s, is that which has the highest value. At times during the learning process when more than one state-action pair is the maximum (such as in the early stages), the proper action can be selected randomly from those that are tied for the highest value. The action selection part of the algorithm for a greedy policy is reflected in Equation (9.8).

$$a \leftarrow \max_a Q(s, a) \tag{9.8}$$

Exploiting knowledge gained along the way helps to reinforce the path with highest action-values more quickly, but can be limited by focusing solely on paths that have already been established. In the early learning episodes, the agent must explore since it does not have a path of higher values. Once a path that reaches the goal is established, the learner will be biased toward the direction of the path already taken. When enough episodes have been completed so that a full path from beginning to goal has been singled-out through reinforced values, a greedy policy will not allow for any other paths to be explored. While a greedy policy will still allow learning of a feasible policy, it will not necessarily be optimal.

9.2.3.3 ε-Greedy

Since both extremes of exploration and exploitation have limitations that inhibit the learning process, it is beneficial to rather choose a middle ground instead of one or the other. The method commonly referred to as ε-Greedy accomplishes just that (Sutton and Barto 1998). An ε-Greedy policy simply uses a predefined probability, ε, that determines whether to explore or exploit each time a new action must be taken. This allows the best of both worlds to be utilized. While in any case the agent is forced to explore in the early episodes due to lack of knowledge, the later learning becomes more efficient. Learned information is reinforced during exploitation actions, while still allowing for exploratory actions in case the present action-value function is suboptimal (Whiteson *et al.* 2007). This method can be implemented during the action selection portion of one of the previously mentioned Temporal-Difference algorithms in the following manner:

Algorithm 9.3 ε-Greedy Action Selection Algorithm

- Choose $\varepsilon \in [0\ 1]$
- Repeat for each action selection:
  - Generate random value $\beta \sim U(0, 1)$
  - If $\beta \geq 1 - \varepsilon$
    * $a \leftarrow$ random
  - If $\beta < 1 - \varepsilon$
    * $a \leftarrow \max_a Q(s,a)$

The choice of the value of ε affects the number of episodes required for convergence, and can be chosen either to be a constant value or a varying parameter. It is often beneficial to choose a high chance of exploration in early episodes, and have the value of ε decrease as more episodes are encountered. By decreasing ε as more episodes are completed, exploration is encouraged more in the early episodes and exploitation is encouraged more in later episodes. However, it is typically important to maintain a nonzero probability of exploration during late learning (e.g., $\varepsilon = 0.05$) so that the possibility of discovering a better path is available.

9.2.4   Function Approximation

One key limitation to using an action-value function for control is that in most cases it cannot capture the entirety of the state-space. The action-value function, $Q(s,a)$, is a discrete table of values with states and actions representing rows and columns. If the state-space is continuous, this matrix does not adequately capture the entire state-space due to its discrete nature. Even if the environment being explored is discrete, it may have too many possibilities of states and actions to experience every possibility as feasible. It is therefore required that some functional characterization of the action-value function be made.

There are many possibilities when choosing to approximate an action-value function, so the fundamental decision required is to determine the best approximation for the RL problem being investigated. In some cases, appropriate basis functions can easily be seen by the user and directly applied. In general, it is not so obvious and may require the use of other machine learning algorithms to learn the general behavior. Three machine learning methods that have classically been employed for the approximation of the action-value function, $Q(s,a)$, are discussed below.

9.2.4.1 *k*-Nearest Neighbor

Perhaps the simplest machine learning method is known as *k*-Nearest Neighbor. The *k*-Nearest Neighbor method is an instance-based method that is driven by the basic assumption that all instances are most alike to their nearest points in Euclidean space (Mitchell 1997). The Euclidean distance between instances is simply the geometric distance between objects in *n*-dimensional information space. This can be directly applied to a problem with continuous states (such as morphing parameters) by approximating the values associated with states that fall between discrete values of the Q matrix. This method acts as an interpolation algorithm, and can be used in function approximation by providing the interpolated values between the discrete states. The distance between states can be calculated by Equation (9.9) and then the *k*-nearest states are kept (Mitchell 1997).

$$d(x_i, x_j) = \sqrt{\sum_{r=1}^{n} (s_r(x_i) - s_r(x_j))^2} \tag{9.9}$$

In Equation (9.9), d is the Euclidean distance, x_i and x_j are the instances, r is the state dimension index, n is the dimension of the state-space, and s_r is the value of the rth state. By calculating the Euclidean distance between the present state and all discrete states represented in Q, the values for the actions associated with the current state can be approximated by the average values of the *k*-nearest neighbors, where k is a user-defined positive integer. This simple algorithm is very easy to implement, it needs very little tuning, and generally performs well (Russell and Norvig 2003).

9.2.4.2 Artificial Neural Networks (ANN)

One of the most popular methods of machine learning today is the artificial neural network (ANN). Artificial neural networks learn hidden behavioral patterns between inputs and outputs by attempting to simulate the complex interactions of neurons in the human brain. The basic unit of the ANN is called a perceptron (analogous to a neuron), and is represented in Figure 9.3.

$$X = \sum_{i=0}^{n} w_i I_i \tag{9.10}$$

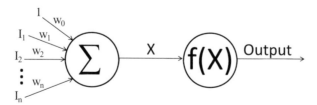

Figure 9.3 Perceptron

The various inputs, $I_0 - I_n$, are combined by a weighted sum, with $I_0 = 1$ always present to eliminate an inherent bias. The weighted sum, represented in Equation (9.10), is provided as an input to a normalizing function. This function is often a step function (Output $= +1$ if X is positive, -1 if X is negative, 0 if X $= 0$), but many other functions have been used in its place (e.g., sigmoid). Sometimes, no normalizing function is present at all, and the output is simply the weighted sum X. The choice of this function is entirely up to the user, and benefits vary depending upon the problem.

An ANN is composed of a network of these perceptrons that are comprised of at least two layers, but usually more. An input layer is necessary, where each input is given a separate node, and a similar output layer is composed of a single node for each output. The middle layers are called the "hidden layers," and are chosen according to user design. Once the structure of the network has been set, the network is trained by feeding training data through the network and adjusting the weights to determine the most appropriate relationship for minimizing the output error. There are several different algorithms available to train a neural network; one of the most widely used is the backpropagation algorithm. This algorithm first propagates a single training case through the network, and then uses the errors between the training data output and the network output to work backward and adjust weights accordingly (Mitchell 1997). ANNs have a reputation for being both highly accurate and fast when compared to other complex machine learning methods.

9.2.4.3 Genetic Algorithms

Genetic algorithms are a class of machine learning algorithms that attempt to mimic the genetic behavior behind the theory of survival of the fittest. The idea is to provide a "population" of hypotheses that are used to approximate an unknown function, where the best hypothesis is initially unknown. The notion of which hypothesis is best depends upon a fitness function that the user defines. This fitness function is used to test individual hypotheses and provide a score based on its evaluated fitness (Mitchell 1997).

In the first generation, hypotheses that make up the population are usually randomly generated. A single hypothesis is typically represented as a binary string, where different bit combinations represent different functions. The fitness function is designed to check how well the hypothesis approximates the function, and then generates a probability according to the following equation:

$$p(h_i) = \frac{F(h_i)}{\sum_{j=1}^{n} F(h_j)} \tag{9.11}$$

In Equation (9.11), $p(h_i)$ is the probability of selecting hypothesis h_i, $F(h_i)$ is the fitness function evaluated for h_i, and n is the total number of hypotheses in the population. This probability is used to determine which hypotheses are chosen for repopulation, and then they either perform crossover operations (two hypotheses are combined to form two new hypotheses), or they mutate (one hypothesis has a single bit changed to make the new hypothesis). Once the new generation is completed, the process continues until a single hypothesis is discovered that has a fitness greater than the user-defined minimum.

These are just a few of many machine learning methods that can be used in conjunction with Temporal-Difference RL algorithms to approximate the action-value function. In theory, any instance-based or pattern-learning method could be used for function approximation. Examples of how these methods can be used for function approximation are available in works by Kirkpatrick and Valasek (2009), Poggio and Girosi (1990), and Lampton (2009).

9.3 Smart Material Control as a Reinforcement Learning Problem

Casting the control of smart materials as an RL problem requires an appropriate representation of the states, actions, rewards, and goals. These are entirely dependent upon the level of localization, as well as the task being performed. In the case of structural morphing, the use of these materials as actuators is anticipated.

The development which follows will be for actuators composed of an SMA wire. The concepts can easily be extrapolated to consider similar types of actuators composed of other types of smart materials. Some of the difficulties that are involved in controlling these actuators are discussed, as well as how each portion of the problem should be cast. There are several requirements that must be met, including defining the parameters of the system, choosing an appropriate action-selection policy, and use of function approximation.

9.3.1 State-Spaces and Action-Spaces for Smart Material Actuators

To solve an RL problem, the first step must be to properly define the state-space and action-space. There are nearly limitless dimensions that could be considered in these spaces. One could include stress, strain, temperature, mass density, martensitic volume fraction, or Gibbs free energy to name a few. What matters for defining the problem is which parameters are both *relevant* and *easily measured*. The larger the state- and action-spaces, the greater the complexity of the environment that the RL agent must explore and interact with. It is therefore crucial to measure and consider only those states and actions which are necessary for goal achievement.

9.3.1.1 States

When the problem considered is the position control of an SMA-based actuator, the first state that is necessary is obvious: length. If the agent is to learn how to control the length of an SMA wire, it must receive length measurements. However, length is a parameter that is specific to the size of the actuator, and so a learned policy that controls wire length would not be effective for similar SMA wires that are shorter or longer than the one used for learning. It is therefore more beneficial to non-dimensionalize and consider tensile strain, rather than length. The tensile strain can easily be calculated by:

$$\varepsilon_t = \frac{L_m - L}{L_m} \tag{9.12}$$

In Equation (9.12), ε_t is the tensile strain, L is the present length of the SMA wire, and L_m is the length of the SMA wire in the crystal phase martensite (i.e., room temperature). Another state that must be included in the state-space is the SMA wire temperature. The actuation of this material is accomplished through the thermally-induced crystal phase transformation between martensite and austenite, so the coupling of strain with temperature is key to controlling the strain.

A third state that should be considered is tensile stress. Although it is desired to exploit the temperature-strain relationship for control, the tensile stress of the SMA wire has a major effect on both its longevity and the maximum strain that can be achieved. For example, a specific sample of SMA wire under a stress of 120 MPa may have a maximum strain of 3.5%, while the same sample under a stress of 150 MPa may experience a maximum strain of 5%. The need to include stress in the state-space depends upon how the tensile stress is treated in the control. If the restoring force used is constant, perhaps with the use of a dead-weight, then the stress need not be considered by the RL agent. However, if the stress is variable, then it should also be included in the state-space.

There are many other parameters that could be included in the state-space due to their contributions to the crystal phase change. These parameters include martensitic volume fraction, mass density, Gibbs free energy, and hardening energy to name a few (Hartl 2009). While these parameters are essential for determining parametric models of SMA crystal phase change behavior, they are not easy to measure. The RL agent must be able to receive the state-space parameters in real-time as it interacts with the environment. Also, the resulting policy from the agent is a black box control policy, not a parametric one, so these additional material parameters are not required. This leaves the user with a choice between two state-spaces, which depend upon the manner in which the actuator's stress is handled. A two-dimensional state-space is used with tensile strain and temperature if the restorative tensile stress is kept constant. If the tensile stress is varied, a three-dimensional state-space description with tensile strain, temperature, and tensile stress is required.

9.3.1.2 Actions

The next step is to determine the action-space of the agent. The actions are the tools that the agent uses to interact with and alter the state-space to achieve a desired goal. It is necessary to choose only those actions that affect the state-space in an easy, real, and controllable way. In this case, there are two options for the action-space: desired temperature and voltage. Heating is controlled by applying a voltage difference across the wire, but the conversion between temperature and voltage is not trivial. The relationship depends upon differential equations based on material parameters that are not constant during the crystal phase transformation. It is therefore much simpler to use desired temperature for the action-space when performing a numerical simulation, but simpler to consider the voltage when learning on an actual SMA actuator. In either case the action-space is one-dimensional for this RL problem, and the choice of control parameter is dependent upon whether the actuator is simulated or real.

9.3.1.3 Approximation Needs for Finite Time

A major limitation of using Q-learning is that convergence is only guaranteed for the situation where the RL agent is able to explore every possible combination of states and actions infinitely many times (Sutton and Barto 1998). The instruments used for measurement and voltage application are also important as it may not be possible to achieve a specified goal strain precisely due to limitations in either the sensitivity of measurements or voltage application.

These problems lead to a need to implant certain approximations in the environment itself so that a "good enough" sub-optimal policy can be determined in finite time. The level of approximation is unique to the hardware being used because accuracy of measurements and sensitivity of the voltage supply differ. Regardless, some consideration must be made for the level of discretization. It is also important to allow for some tolerance in the achievement of the goal. If the specified goal that the RL agent attempts to achieve is either not measurable or unattainable with the voltage supply, it can never learn how to even come close to that goal. In reality, when dealing with a continuous state-space the probability of observing an exact state is low. Some tolerance is required to reach the goal, and the size of the tolerance is mainly dependent upon the instruments used. This is usually handled in RL by altering the reward structure so that a positive reward is given for falling within the goal tolerances.

9.3.2   Function Approximation Selection

Choosing an appropriate approximation for the action-value function depends largely upon the state-space of the problem. The action-value function is a discrete table of values, so the function approximation is only necessary for RL problems for which the discrete Q matrix does not fully capture the entirety of the state-space and action-space. This is always the case when the state-space or action-space is continuous, and both are true in the problem of SMA actuator control.

Any of the methods discussed in Section 9.2.4 can be used to approximate the action-value function, Q, for smart material-based actuator control. While theoretically any machine learning method could be utilized, it is important to remember that in this application the dimensions of the state-space and action-space are very low in comparison to many RL applications of n-dimensional space. When RL is used in problems with high dimensionality, it is typically necessary to use a sophisticated machine learning algorithm to approximate the action-value function. In this case, the state-space is two- or three-dimensional, and the action-space is one-dimensional. Also, the continuous nature of each of the states and actions considered are such that one can accurately assume that an individual discrete state has the most in common with those states closest to it in Euclidean space. Thus, it is both convenient and accurate to utilize the k-Nearest Neighbor algorithm discussed in Section 9.2.4.

9.3.3   Exploiting Action-Value Function for Control

Once the RL agent has learned a proper near-optimal policy, and an appropriate function approximation method has been used, the end result is a near-optimal action-value function. One of the key reasons that RL methods are good for this problem is that the action-value function can easily be exploited for control purposes. The resulting action-value function is structured as a discrete table of values. The problem is that just like information stored chemically in the brain, the values themselves require some kind of translation to be physically meaningful. A separate action-value function is required for each goal to be reached, so to learn how to reach any goal it must be crafted so that the resulting Q matrix is of the size (states $\times$ actions $\times$ goals). When choosing a particular goal, g, to reach, one will analyze the (states $\times$ actions) slice of this Q matrix that represents goal g. This is illustrated in Figure 9.4, where g^* is the selected goal. The proper action required to reach goal g can then be determined by

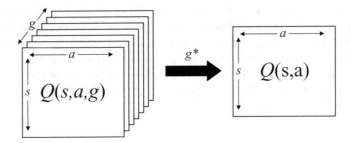

Figure 9.4 Slice taken from Q-matrix

choosing the row corresponding to the current state of the system, s, and finding the column that has the highest value in row s. This reveals which action has led to the most cumulative rewards from past experience when the SMA wire was in state s and attempted to reach state g. By programming the system to do this automatically every time a new actuator position needs to be reached, the action-value function acts as the actuator control policy. This policy provides a direct input-output mapping of the present state of the system to the actions required to reach the desired state of the system.

9.4 Example

This section explores casting the characterization and control of a NiTi shape memory alloy wire as a Reinforcement Learning problem, with the Sarsa algorithm employed to find a near-optimal solution. This example was constructed to demonstrate the capability of using these methods to determine control policies for smart material-based actuators. The research findings for this example have been published in works by Kirkpatrick, Valasek, and Haag (Kirkpatrick and Valasek 2009; Kirkpatrick 2009; Haag *et al.* 2005). The goal is to determine a policy that can be used to control a NiTi SMA wire once learning has been completed, and to achieve that goal, an agent must be constructed that can apply actions to the SMA and in return sense the states. The agent must also receive rewards for its actions to encourage or discourage certain behavior. There are two possibilities to be considered. The first is to define a two-dimensional state-space of tensile strain and present temperature with an action-space of desired temperature. Changes in temperature alter the length of the SMA wire, so temperature could essentially be used for control. The second approach would be to use a two-dimensional state-space composed of strain and temperature with an action-space of voltage. Since the the temperature of the wire is controlled by electrical resistance, conversions between temperature and voltage can be eliminated by this approach. In both cases, a positive reward $(+1)$ is given only to reach the target strain, while a negative reward is given for exceeding the bounds of the state-space (-1). Neutral rewards are given for reaching any other state in the system $(+0)$.

In this section, both methods will be explored. First, a numerical simulation will be used to solve this RL problem, and it will be conducted using the first method. Because temperature and voltage do not have a simple conversion relationship, simulating how voltage affects the temperature is difficult. Therefore, desired temperature will make up the actions in simulation. Second, this approach will be used in experimentation, but will use applied voltage as the actions. Not only will this accomplish the same goal of eliminating conversions between voltage and temperature, but it is also more directly useful in a control law. In both cases, the action-selection policy followed is an ε-Greedy method where the value for ε decreases episodically from $\varepsilon = 0.7$ to $\varepsilon = 0.05$, providing greater exploration encouragement in early learning episodes and greater exploitation in later episodes. The function approximation used in both cases is the simple 1-Nearest Neighbor algorithm, representing a subclass of the k-Nearest Neighbor algorithm where $k = 1$.

9.4.1   Simulation

Validation of the agent's ability to learn SMA hysteresis input-output characteristics online is conducted on a simulated SMA wire. The model used here for the SMA hysteresis is based on a hyperbolic tangent function described later. The agent is to learn and update the action-value function over an arbitrarily selected number of 24,000 episodes, where each episode consists of 10 commanded goal states. Within each episode, a current goal is held constant until 225 actions have been attempted, and then the agent moves on to a new goal. Refinement in learning the temperature-strain behavior is accomplished for a control policy consisting of no initial knowledge, and for multiple desired strain states. The SMA wire simulated here is based upon an experimentally characterized NiTi sample.

In this simulation, the desired strain trajectory includes multiple randomly generated goal states. The state space S is a two-dimensional discrete Cartesian space with $S = [10, 35]$, where the columns represent temperatures ranging from $30-130\,^\circ$C with $10\,^\circ$C increments, and the rows represent strains ranging from $0-3.5\%$ with 0.1% increments. Thus, with one state representing all conditions outside these acceptable boundaries, there are a total of 351 states. The action-space A consists of desired temperatures ranging from $30-130\,^\circ$C with $10\,^\circ$C increments, thus resulting in 10 possible actions per state. Rewards used to update the action-value function at time t are: $+1$ for moving to the goal state, 0 for moving to any other permissible states, and -1 for moving to any restricted states.

9.4.1.1   The tanh Model

To perform a dynamic task, the SMA must experience a cycle of heating and cooling which induces cyclic deformation. This can be accomplished with any type of applied heating, but most often with resistive heating. The Shape Memory Effect occurs due to a temperature and stress dependent crystal phase transformation in the material between the martensite- and austenite-phases. The change that occurs within the SMA crystalline structure results in temperature hysteresis due to energy dissipation from internal friction and the creation of micro-structural defects (Mavroidis *et al.* 1999). This temperature hysteresis translates directly into hysteresis in the temperature-strain relationship; this hysteresis behavior makes it challenging to develop accurate models and control schemes for an SMA actuator. Unlike the voltage-temperature relationship, the temperature-strain relationship is governed by algebraic, not differential, equations.

Here a hysteresis model based on the hyperbolic tangent function is developed. Note that this model is not used to design control laws, but only to model the hysteresis behavior because it does not capture dynamics. The temperature-strain relationship not only has a

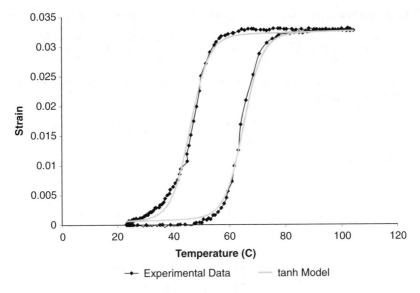

Figure 9.5 Validation of modeled SMA hysteresis

major hysteresis loop, but exhibits minor hysteresis loops if the direction of the change in temperature is reversed in between the minimum and maximum temperatures (T_l and T_r respectively) spanned by the major hysteresis loop. This behavior is explained in detail below in the modeling of the respective hysteresis loops.

The major hysteresis loop is modeled as a combination of two hyperbolic tangent functions M_r and M_l. The system follows path M_r when the temperature increases, and follows path M_l when the temperature decreases. This can be seen in Figure 9.5. The subscript l refers to the lowering, or left, side of the curve. The subscript r refers to the rising, or right, side of the curve.

$$M_l = \frac{H}{2} \tanh((T - ct_l)a) + s\left(T - \frac{ct_l + ct_r}{2}\right) + \frac{H}{2} + c_s \qquad (9.13)$$

$$M_r = \frac{H}{2} \tanh((T - ct_r)a) + s\left(T - \frac{ct_l + ct_r}{2}\right) + \frac{H}{2} + c_s \qquad (9.14)$$

In Equations (9.13) and (9.14), H, ct_l, ct_r, a, s and c_s are non-parametric constants which dictate the shape-determining parameters of the major hysteresis loop, such as width, height, location, and slope of the lines. By appropriately selecting these constants so that the curves match experimentally determined data, this model of the major hysteresis loop can represent a wide range of hysteresis behaviors. For simulation, a simple trial-and-error approach can be used to get a "good enough" fit to an experimental SMA wire.

It is assumed here that the minor hysteresis loops follow generally similar shapes as the major hysteresis loops, so the minor loops are modeled with similar equations but with a different height constant h. Also, all of the minor loops converge with the major loop lines beyond the temperatures T_l and T_r. The equation for a rising minor loop is

$$m_r = \frac{h}{2}\tanh((T - ct_r)a) + s\left(T - \frac{ct_l + ct_r}{2}\right) + H - \frac{h}{2} + c_s \qquad (9.15)$$

where h is calculated by considering that the current state is the intersection of the previous curve and the current minor loop, so that

$$h = \frac{h_{prev}(\tanh((T - ct_l)a) + 1) - 2H}{\tanh((T - ct_r)a) - 1} \qquad (9.16)$$

and h_{prev} is the height parameter h for the previous curve. Similarly, the equation for a lowering minor loop is

$$m_l = \frac{h}{2}\tanh((T - ct_l)a) + s\left(T - \frac{ct_l + ct_r}{2}\right) + \frac{h}{2} + c_s \qquad (9.17)$$

with h calculated as

$$h = \frac{h_{prev}(\tanh((T - ct_r)a) - 1) + 2H}{\tanh((T - ct_l)a) + 1} \qquad (9.18)$$

For the temperature-strain relationship, the hyperbolic tangent model employs constants H, ct_l, ct_r, a, s and c_s, which are manually tuned to represent any range of hysteresis loops that can exist in the domain of SMA behavior. The hyperbolic tangent-based model used in this example simulates the temperature-strain behavior of a one-dimensional NiTi SMA wire. Figure 9.5 shows a validation of the simulation employing the hyperbolic tangent model by comparing the major loop to an experimentally determined major hysteresis behavior for a NiTi SMA wire. The experimental data for the SMA specimen was obtained via the direct application of electrical current to a NiTi wire. The voltage was increased until the upper limit temperature was reached, and then the voltage was decreased until the initial length was attained. Note that Figure 9.5 only shows the major hysteresis loop of the SMA wire, but based on the assumed dependence of minor loops on the major loop and the percent composition of each crystalline phase (which can be determined from the strain and the upper age limit hysteresis temperature), the minor loops are also approximately known. The results indicate that the hyperbolic tangent SMA model can be used to approximate the temperature-strain relation of an experimental SMA wire, thereby verifying the temperature-strain SMA behavior.

9.4.1.2 Simulation Results

To demonstrate the RL agent's ability to converge to a near-optimal control policy, a simulation was designed using the hyperbolic tangent model discussed in Section 9.4.1. This simulation was allowed to run for an arbitrarily selected large number of episodes (24,000), where an episode for this simulation is defined as 10 commanded goal states spaced evenly over a total time period of 2,250 seconds. Figure 9.6 demonstrates the learning refinement and how the agent's knowledge of hysteresis behavior evolves over time. The time that this learning through interaction encompasses is dependent upon the size of the action-value function $Q(s,a)$. Thus, as the size of the temperature-strain mesh is enlarged, the number of states and actions increases, and the required learning time increases. During early learning episodes the agent

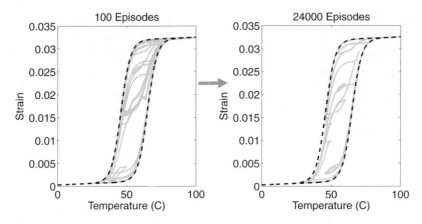

Figure 9.6 Learning refinement for a simulated tanh SMA model

experiences most of the possible actions at each state, regardless of the outcome. Thus several major and minor hysteresis loop paths which do not lead to the goal are experienced. As time progresses, the agent reduces the number of exploration actions and exploits the knowledge it has obtained. This later learning shown in Figure 9.6 (24,000 episodes) demonstrates that when the agent learns how to find the goals, the paths followed are very different than they were initially. After 24,000 learning episodes have been completed by the agent, it has learned most of the SMA temperature-strain behavior and yet remained in the acceptable strain range in all exploiting actions thereafter.

Figure 9.7 shows a time history of a fully exploiting RL agent which has experienced 24,000 episodes. The action is desired temperature and the state is strain. The allowed error for each goal strain was chosen to be ± 0.002. Due to the hysteresis, some states are unattainable with only one action, so they result in requiring one or two extra actions to achieve the goal. Also, there can exist some small changes within the goal range that occur as a result of all states within the range being equally rewarding for the learning agent. The transition from goal 4 to goal 5 shows that the agent leaves the goal range early but then returns permanently. This behavior is the result of early reinforcement that has not been corrected after these 24,000 episodes, but could be overcome by more learning episodes. By comparing the behavior around the first and second goals verses the penultimate and ultimate goals in Figure 9.7, it is seen that the agent makes the same choices. This demonstrates that when encountering an identical current state-to-goal state transition, the agent chooses the same actions. Overall, these simulation results demonstrate that the agent is capable of achieving the goal strains quickly, and then holding position at the commanded strain.

9.4.2 Experimentation

It is desirable to demonstrate that while these methods work in a simulated setting, they are still effective in an experimental setting. In this subsection, Sarsa is used to learn an optimal control policy in voltage-strain space in an experimentation. The aim is to demonstrate the ability to use Sarsa to learn the optimal control policy for an SMA wire.

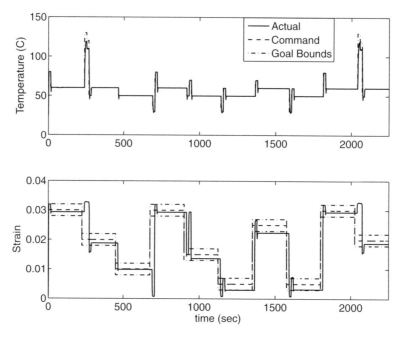

Figure 9.7   Time histories of temperature actions and strain state responses

The control policy determined for this SMA specimen is able to control the length of a NiTi SMA wire for two specific goal strains, within an error range of ±0.005. A tolerance of 0.005 represents 15.2% of the full range of motion, and is considered to be acceptable. The wire used for this experiment has an initial effective length of 13 cm, so with a maximum strain possible of 3.3%, the total operating range of motion was 4.29 mm. Since the control policy learned is able to reach its goal within a range of ±0.5%, the error range allowed is ±0.65 mm.

Under these specified conditions, the RL agent is executed for 100 episodes using specified alternating goal strains of 2.7% and 0.1%, providing 50 episodes per goal. Each episode in this experiment consists of a 450-second duration of seeking a single goal, where the RL agent is called every 15 seconds. This provides 30 new actions per episode for the learning agent.

The first goal presented is 2.7% strain. This goal is chosen for experimentation because it represents a partially actuated state for which the maximum strain of 3.3% falls outside of the allowed tolerance range of ±0.5%. This ensures that it cannot achieve the goal by simply applying the maximum voltage available. Under these conditions, the final control policy is tested and the resulting strain history can be seen in Figure 9.8.

Figure 9.8 shows that the control policy developed by the RL agent is capable of taking an SMA wire to the desired goal from multiple initial positions. It is this capability that makes morphing actuators possible. In Figure 9.8, initial voltages are applied before the time history recording begins so that the control policy can be tested at several different initial strains. The initial strains chosen for testing here are 0.1%, 3.2%, 1.2%, and 2.7%. The actual exploitation of the control policy begins at t = 0 seconds in each case, and the two horizontal lines represent the goal range of 2.7% ± 0.5% strain. The initial strains of 0.1% and 3.2% are chosen so

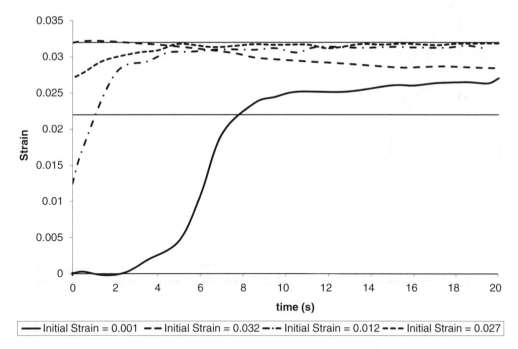

Figure 9.8   Strain-time histories of learned policy for strain goal = 2.7%

that the control policy can be tested from initial strains corresponding to fully un-actuated and fully actuated states, respectively. The initial strain of 1.2% is selected to test from an initially intermediate strain, and the goal strain of 2.7% is also chosen as an initial strain to show that the agent can learn how to stay within the specified range when the specimen is there initially. As Figure 9.8 shows, the control policy is successful in achieving its goal of 2.7% ± 0.5% in all four test cases.

This example showed that the Sarsa method was capable of learning to achieve an interior position in the hysteresis space, since the maximum strain of 3.3% lies outside the goal range of 2.7% ± 0.5%. Using RL to learn a control policy capable of achieving a strain that rests within the interior of the transformation curve is important because it greatly increases the range of functionality of SMA actuators. If the only values learned by the agent are those that correspond to maximum and minimum strains, an SMA actuator would be limited to only two possible positions. Learning these interior goals is also far more complicated than learning the extreme values because all that would be required for the latter would be to apply the maximum and minimum voltages every time.

The second goal chosen for experimental learning is 0.1%. This goal is chosen because it represents a state that is not quite on the boundary of the system, but effectively is on the boundary because the lower bound is encompassed by the tolerance range. While it can achieve its goal by applying 0 volts, it is not limited to this action. Figure 9.9 shows the results of testing the control policy for a goal of 0.1% strain.

Like the previous case, initial voltages are applied to reach initial strain conditions, and the control policy exploitation begins at t = 0 seconds. In Figure 9.9 the horizontal black

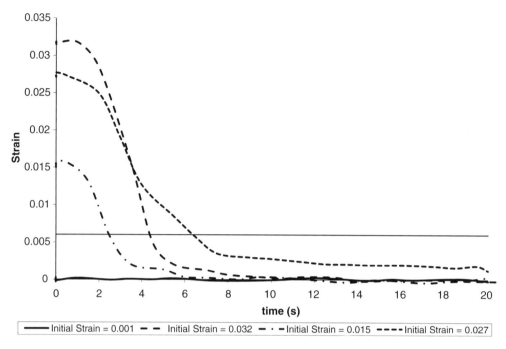

Figure 9.9   Strain-time histories of learned policy for strain goal $= 0.1\%$

line represents the upper bound of the tolerance range while the lower bound corresponds to a strain of 0. The initial strains chosen for Figure 9.9 are 0.1%, 3.2%, 1.5%, and 2.7%, which are nearly identical to the initial strains chosen in Figure 9.8. The 0.1% strain is chosen because it demonstrates the ability of the system to remain at the goal strain when already there, and 3.2% is selected because that is the other system boundary. The other strains are chosen because they nearly match the initial strains used in the previous test. Figure 9.9 shows that for each of these initial strains, the control policy is able to achieve its specified goal, but here it is accomplished for the goal of $0.1\% \pm 0.5\%$ strain.

Just as it was important to show that this approach allows for the ability to control SMAs in the interior of the transformation process, it was also important to reveal that the control policy is not limited to commands in the interior. By demonstrating that the control policy is able to also learn how to move the SMA wire back to its initial position, it has been demonstrated that using a RL approach provides the ability to learn both the extreme positions and the interior positions. It follows from these tests that controlling SMA actuators using RL methods for the purpose of developing morphing aircraft shows promise.

9.5   Conclusion

Smart material-based actuators provide the means to morph, or shape change, aircraft components. Of the smart materials currently available, shape memory alloys appear to hold the most promise. The problem then arises of how these actuators would be controlled, because shape memory alloys have a hysteretic relationship in the thermomechanical response. Conventional control methods that require accurate models of the dynamics are difficult to use since shape memory alloy modeling effort is time-consuming and does not capture dynamics well. By turning to Machine Learning methods, it is possible to find ways to control individual actuators without the need of a dynamic model. Reinforcement Learning methods provide the tools needed to accurately learn an optimal control policy without requiring any prior knowledge of shape memory alloy dynamics.

In this chapter, a Reinforcement Learning agent was designed to determine a control policy capable of controlling a shape memory alloy wire. This was first tested in a simulation setting using a hyperbolic tangent model for the simulated shape memory alloy wire. The results showed that the agent was capable of learning to control the simulated wire, so the agent was then tested in an experimental setting. The Reinforcement Learning agent proved capable of learning to control a real shape memory alloy wire, without being limited to either the interior or the boundary of the hysteresis curve. By using Reinforcement Learning to determine control policies for shape memory alloy actuators, the application of these actuators to morphing aerospace vehicles becomes possible.

References

Aha DW, Kibler D, and Albert MK 1991 Instance-based learning algorithms. *Machine Learning*, 6(1): 37–66.

Banks H, Kurdila A, and Webb G 1997 Modeling and identification of hysteresis in active material actuators, part (ii): Convergent approximations. *Journal of Intelligent Material Systems and Structures*, 8(6).

Bo Z and Lagoudas DC 1999 Thermomechanical modeling of polycrystalline SMAs under cyclic loading, part i–iv. *International Journal of Engineering Science*, 37.

Crawley E F and de Luis J 1987 Use of piezoelectric actuators as elements of intelligent structures. *AIAA Journal*, 25(10): 1373–1385.

Cristianini N and Shawe-Taylor J 2000 *An Introduction to Support Vector Machines: and Other Kernel-Based Learning Methods*. Cambridge University Press, Cambridge.

Duerig TW, Tolomeo DE, and Wholey M 2000 An overview of superelastic stent design. *Minimally Invasive Therapy and Allied Technologies*, 9: 235–246.

Falk F 1989 Pseudoelastic stress strain curves of polycrystalline shape memory alloys calculated from single crystal data. *International Journal of Engineering Science*, 27: 277.

Friedman N 1997 Bayesian network classifiers. *Machine Learning*, 29(2–3): 131–163.

Goldberg DE 1998 *Genetic Algorithms in Search, Optimization, and Machine Learning*. Addison-Wesley, Reading, MA.

Haag C, Tandale M, and Valasek J 2005 Characterization of shape memory alloy behavior and position control using reinforcement learning. In *AIAA Infotech@Aerospace Conference*, Arlington, VA, 26–29 September.

Hartl D 2009 Modeling of shape memory alloys considering rate-independent and rate-dependent irrecoverable strains. PhD thesis, Texas A&M University.

Kirkpatrick K 2009 Reinforcement learning for active length control and hysteresis characterization of shape memory alloys. Master's thesis, Texas A&M University.

Kirkpatrick K and Valasek J 2009 Reinforcement learning for characterizing hysteresis behavior of shape memory alloys. *Journal of Aerospace Computing, Information, and Communication*, 6(3): 227–238.

Lagoudas DC ed. 2008 *Shape Memory Alloys: Modeling and Engineering Applications*. Springer Science+Business Media, LLC, New York.

Lagoudas D, Bo Z, and Qidwai MA 1996 A unified thermodynamic constitutive model for SMA and finite element analysis of active metal matrix composites. *Mechanics of Composite Materials and Structures*, 3(153).

Lagoudas D, Mayes J, and Khan M 2001 Simplified shape memory alloy (SMA) material model for vibration isolation. In *Smart Structures and Materials Conference*, Newport Beach, CA, 5–8 March.

Lampton A 2009 Discretization and approximation methods for reinforcement learning of highly reconfigurable systems. PhD thesis, Texas A&M University.

Mabe JH, Cabell R, and Butler G 2005 Design and control of a morphing chevron for takeoff and cruise noise reduction. In *26th Annual AIAA Aeroacoustics Conference*, Monterey, CA, 2005.

Malovrh B and Gandhi F 2001 Mechanism-based phenomenological models for the pseudoelastic hysteresis behavior of shape memory alloys. *Journal of Intelligent Material Systems and Structures*, 12: 21–30.

Mantovani D 2000 Shape memory alloys: properties and biomedical applications. *Journal of Minerals, Metals, and Materials Society*, 52: 36–44.

Mavroidis C, Pfeiffer C, and Mosley M 1999 Conventional actuators, shape memory alloys, and electrorheological fluids. *Automation, Miniature Robotics and Sensors for Non-Destructive Testing and Evaluation*, pp. 10–21, April.

Mitchell TM 1997 *Machine Learning*. The McGraw-Hill Companies, Inc., Singapore.

Patoor E, Eberhardt A, and Berveiller M 1987 Potential pseudoelastic et plasticité de transformation martensitique dans les mono-et polycristaux métalliques. *Acta Metall*, 35(11): 2779.

Poggio T and Girosi F 1990 Networks for approximation and learning. In *IEEE*, Cambridge, MA.

Quinlan JR 1986 Induction of decision trees. *Machine Learning*, 1(1): 81–106.

Russell S and Norvig P 2003 *Artificial Intelligence: A Modern Approach*. Pearson Education, Inc., Upper Saddle River, NJ.

Sofla AYN, Elzey DM, and Wadley HNG 2008 Two-way antagonistic shape actuation based on the one-way shape memory effect. *Journal of Intelligent Material Systems and Structures*, 19: 1017–1027.

Sutton R and Barto A 1998 *Reinforcement Learning: An Introduction*. The MIT Press, Cambridge, MA.

Waram T 1993 *Actuator Design Using Shape Memory Alloys*. Hamilton, Ontario, T.C. Waram.

Webb G, Kurdila A, and Lagoudas D 1998 Hysteresis modeling of SMA actuators for control applications. *Journal of Intelligent Material Systems and Structures*, 9(6): 432–447.

Whiteson S, Taylor ME, and Stone P 2007 Empirical studies in action selection with reinforcement learning. *Adaptive Behavior*, 15: 33–50.

Yegnanarayana B 2006 *Artificial Neural Networks*. Prentice-Hall of India, New Delhi.

10

Incorporation of Shape Memory Alloy Actuators into Morphing Aerostructures

Justin R. Schick, Darren J. Hartl and Dimitris C. Lagoudas
Texas A&M University, USA

> *This mechanical (shape) memory, which is otherwise unknown in engineering alloy systems, furnishes design engineers with the opportunity to design on the basis of an entirely new principle*
>
> — (Jackson *et al.* 1972)

Shape memory alloys (SMAs) have become a key enabling technology in the development of many new morphing aerostructure designs. This chapter provides a fundamental introduction to SMAs, including their unique engineering behaviors. In particular, the shape memory effect and its ability to convert thermal energy into mechanical output has shown promise for aerospace applications. Following the introduction, a description of some recent aerospace applications that incorporate SMAs into active structures is presented. Some of the proposed applications discussed include SMAs as actuators in morphing wings, rotor blades, and deployable space structures. The experimental methods pertaining to material characterization are also presented. An understanding of these methods is essential both to assess the material performance capabilities and to calibrate the analytical tools used for the development of SMA applications. Finally, this chapter describes the current state-of-the-art in analytical tools for modeling SMA-based applications, and example results are provided.

10.1 Introduction to Shape Memory Alloys

Shape memory alloys are a special class of active metals able to undergo large amounts of apparent plastic deformation that can be substantially recovered upon heating (Otsuka and

Morphing Aerospace Vehicles and Structures, First Edition. Edited by John Valasek.
© 2012 John Wiley & Sons, Ltd. Published 2012 by John Wiley & Sons, Ltd.

Wayman 1999; Lagoudas 2008). The ability of SMAs to sustain such high strains (sometimes 8–10%) without permanently deforming is due to a diffusionless solid-to-solid phase transformation between their two primary phases (Wang *et al.* 1965). These two phases are the *austenitic* phase, which exists at higher temperatures, and the *martensitic* phase, which exists at lower temperatures. For each phase the atomic structure is different. The most commonly used alloy (NiTi), for example, has a body-centered cubic structure in the austenitic phase, or parent phase, and a monoclinic structure in the martensitic phase (Wang *et al.* 1965; Eckelmeyer 1976). This difference in the atomic structure of each phase and the repeatable motion of atoms from one configuration to the other account for the unique ability of SMAs to undergo large reversible deformations.

Though some investigations of shape-memory behaviors occurred earlier (Chang and Read 1951), the first discovery of SMA properties that led to continued study was at the Naval Ordinance Lab in 1962 by William J. Buehler and co-workers (Buehler *et al.* 1963). Since then, the number of applications for SMAs has continued to grow. This is especially true in the medical industry, which uses SMAs in a wide range of applications including stents, dental drills, and eye glass frames, among others (Otsuka and Wayman 1999; Duerig *et al.* 1990). More recently, the aerospace industry has begun to show increased interest in implementing SMAs into aircraft and spacecraft structures (Hartl and Lagoudas 2007b). SMAs can be used to replace hydraulic systems with solid-state actuators, thereby reducing the complexity and risk of failure of certain aircraft components. Also, small SMA actuators exhibit a high energy density, and thus can perform large amounts of work, potentially reducing both actuator weight and installation volume. This is advantageous in many aerospace applications.

Concepts such as underlying mechanisms, unique engineering effects, and the different types of SMA material compositions will be discussed in this introductory section. Section 10.2 will describe some current aerospace applications in development or production that rely on the solutions provided by SMAs. Next, experimental techniques for characterizing SMAs and modeling techniques for predicting their behavior will be presented in Section 10.3. Finally, the current challenges and the future of SMAs will be discussed in Section 10.4.

10.1.1   Underlying Mechanisms

As previously mentioned, the key to many of the unique capabilities of SMAs is the diffusionless, solid-to-solid phase transformation between the austenite and martensite phases. This reversible process from one phase to the other is referred to as *martensitic transformation*. *Forward transformation* is the process by which the austenite (parent) phase transforms into the martensite phase, while *reverse transformation* describes the conversion of martensite back into austenite. As shown in Figure 10.1, there are two important temperatures associated with the forward and reverse transformations occurring in the absence of any applied load. The temperature at which forward transformation begins (when martensite begins to develop) is the martensite start temperature (M_s); transformation is complete (100% martensite exists) at the martensite finish temperature (M_f). Similarly, for reverse transformation the austenite start temperature (A_s) indicates when martensite begins transforming into austenite, and an austenite finish temperature (A_f) indicates when the transformation is complete (100% austenite).

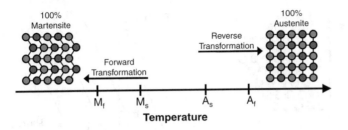

Figure 10.1 Martensitic transformation

During forward transformation, the high-symmetry austenite phase (e.g. a cubic structure) changes to a low-symmetry martensitic phase (for the most common SMA, NiTi, a monoclinic structure). When forward transformation occurs under stress-free conditions, martensitic variants form in many different crystal orientations such that the observable macro-scale deformation may be negligible. Martensite with such mixed variants is known as "self-accommodated," or sometimes "twinned" martensite. However, when a sufficient biasing force is applied to such a martensitic configuration, "reorientation" will occur as the net applied stress favors variants of some orientations at the expense of others. The result is an observable change in the shape of the material structure; this is sometimes referred to as "detwinning." Even after complete removal of the applied force, the change in shape will remain in the material as long as its temperature is maintained below A_s. Once the material is heated above A_s, it will begin to transform back toward the crystal structure of the austenite phase at the atomic scale, and thus its original shape at the macroscopic scale. The material will completely regain its original, undeformed shape when it reaches the austenite finish temperature (A_f); this process is presented in Figure 10.2.

An important tool in SMA design is the *phase diagram*; this diagram describes the temperature and applied stress states needed to induce/complete forward and reverse transformation in a given SMA composition with a given processing history. A typical phase diagram is shown in Figure 10.3. In general, as the magnitude (compression or tension) of the applied stress increases on an SMA, so do the corresponding transformation temperatures.

10.1.2   Unique Engineering Effects

The phase diagram in Figure 10.3 shows three different loading paths that are of particular interest for engineering applications. Path 1 will be described first. This path represents a

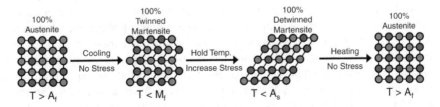

Figure 10.2 Detwinning of martensite

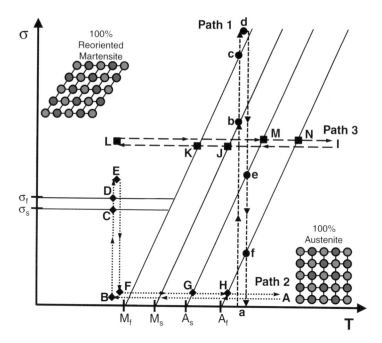

Figure 10.3 Phase diagram with pseudoelastic loading path (Path 1) and shape memory effect loading paths (Paths 2 and 3)

pseudoelastic cycle. Path 2 and Path 3 represent different methods of achieving the *shape memory effect.* Many SMA applications, some of which will be discussed later in this chapter, take advantage of either the pseudoelastic or shape memory effects.

Pseudoelastic Effect: The ability of SMAs to generate large amounts of seemingly irrecoverable strain under increased loading and then recover their shape upon unloading is known as the *superelastic effect,* or the *pseudoelastic effect.* A typical SMA pseudoelastic loading path is shown in Figure 10.3 by Path 1, where the corresponding stress-strain ($\sigma - \varepsilon$) response of a tested SMA is shown in Figure 10.4. It is important to note that a true pseudoelastic cycle with full recovery is only possible if the SMA is maintained at a temperature greater than A_f, otherwise the material configuration upon unloading will include some amount of reoriented martensite. At point a, in Figures 10.3 and 10.4 the SMA is completely in austenite; as the stress is increased the SMA responds elastically until the stress reaches point b. This point corresponds to the stress level at which the austenite phase begins to transform into reoriented martensite (for the given constant temperature). Between points b and c, the SMA is forward transforming and generates large amounts of inelastic strain. Once transformation is complete and the stress exceeds point c (σ^{M_f}), the martensitic phase responds nearly elastically as the stress increases to point d. Upon unloading, the SMA responds elastically until it reaches point e. At this point the stress is low enough for reverse transformation to initiate (σ^{A_s}), and the SMA recovers the strain generated during forward transformation. Transformation is complete at point f (σ^{A_f}). As the stress decreases to zero, the SMA responds elastically.

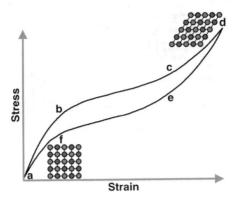

Figure 10.4   Pseudoelastic effect: experimental stress-strain response of an SMA

Ideally, upon full unloading the material will recover all strain, elastic and inelastic, generated during loading.

Repeating this process at different temperatures above A_f (e.g. $A_f + 10°C$, $A_f + 20°C$) will result in different points of transformation (σ^{Ms}, σ^{Mf}, σ^{As}, σ^{Af}), as shown by the slopes on the phase diagram presented Figure 10.3. As the temperature of the specimen increases, it takes increasing levels of stress during forward transformation to force the austenite phase to transform into the martensite phase. Likewise, upon reverse transformation, the higher temperature will cause the austenite to develop at higher stress levels. This characteristic of transforming materials is known as the "Clausius-Clapeyron relation" (Wollants *et al.* 1979).

Shape Memory Effect: The *shape memory effect* (SME) describes the capability of an SMA that has exhibited apparently irrecoverable deformations to return to its austenitic shape after the imposition of sufficient thermal inputs (i.e. heating) to above A_f. Two different loading paths that produce the shape memory effect are presented in Figure 10.3 (loading paths). The first, Path 2, is shown in a strain-stress-temperature ($\varepsilon - \sigma - T$) space in Figure 10.5. Starting at point A, the SMA is cooled to point below M_f (point B), causing the material structure to change from austenite to self-accommodated martensite. The martensitic variants

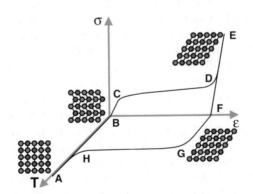

Figure 10.5   Shape memory effect: stress-strain-temperature response (Path 2)

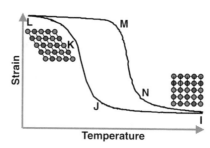

Figure 10.6 Shape memory effect: experimental temperature-strain response of an SMA (Path 3)

form in many different directions due to the lack of applied stress. The combined effect of these formations produces no net deformation in the material. Next, the SMA is subjected to an increasing stress to which it responds elastically until it reaches σ_s (point C), this being the stress sufficient to initiate the reorientation of martensite. While there are multiple self-accommodated variants, the applied stress favors the growth of some variants (aligned with the loading) over others (not favorably aligned with the loading). For example, as reorientation occurs under the application of uniaxial tension, tension-favored variants grow at the expense of all others, and the SMA elongates in the direction of the loading path. Reorientation is completed at point D and the SMA responds elastically to the increased loading once again up to E. The SMA recovers some elastic strain upon unloading down to F, but it retains the inelastic strains generated during reorientation. The SMA is then heated, and at point G (A_s) reverse transformation begins and is completed by point H (A_f). As the SMA goes through this reverse transformation, it recovers all strain generated during reorientation and returns to its original shape (point A). It should be noted that a very similar path can be produced if the material is initially cooled to a temperature just below A_s and then loaded, unloaded, and heated. Here, the mechanism of inelastic strain generation is not the reorientation of martensite, but rather the stress-induced forward transformation of austenite into martensite.

Another loading path that produces the shape memory effect is Path 3 in Figure 10.3. This path represents the ability of an SMA to perform as an actuator, reverting to its original shape under substantial loading. An experimental example of this response is shown in Figure 10.6 in a strain-temperature space. Starting at point I, the SMA is cooled until transformation begins at point J (M_s^σ). During this first step, there is some change in strain due to thermal contraction, but it is small relative to the subsequent transformation strain. Because there is stress being applied to the SMA during transformation, it will develop favored martensitic variants and thus avoid the formation of fully self-accommodated martensite. The SMA will continue to develop strain in the direction of the applied load until transformation is complete at point K (M_f^σ). The only change in strain that will be observed at temperatures below M_f is thermal contraction. At L the temperature is reversed and the phase of the SMA is unchanged until M, where reverse transformation begins, and the SMA begins to recover its shape (A_s^σ). The SMA will continue to recover its shape until transformation is complete at point N (A_f^σ).

While the SMA does recover most of the strain generated during forward transformation, there is some strain that is not recovered. This remaining unrecovered strain due to cycling under stress has been generated due to *transformation induced plasticity* (TRIP) (Bo and Lagoudas 1999; Lagoudas and Entchev 2004), though it may be due in large part to blocked martensite that accumulates over cycles and no longer participates in transformation (Favier and Liu 2000; Kumar and Lagoudas 2010). If an SMA design only calls for one or two actuation cycles, this effect will not lead to major design restrictions. However, for SMA actuators that are designed for repeated cycles, TRIP needs to be minimized so that consistent actuation can be achieved. To minimize TRIP, SMA actuators are subjected to *training*, sometimes referred to as *shakedown*, before they are implemented into a working design (Sun *et al.* 2008; Mertmann and Vergani 2008). Training SMAs serves to eliminate the large irrecoverable strains sometimes observed in initial cycles and thus stabilizes the material for actuation use. Depending on the material, applied stress, and design constraints, most SMAs can be trained in 100–1000 thermal cycles. Training can be performed either by thermal cycling under constant stress or pseudoelastic cycling until a stable material response is achieved (Morin and Trivero 1995). It should be noted that while TRIP can be greatly reduced through training, in most materials it cannot be completely eliminated and should be accounted for in any SMA application.

Training can also result in the *two-way shape memory effect* (TWSME), which is observed in some alloy composites after sufficient stabilization. While the shape memory effect (or one-way shape memory effect) describes the ability of SMAs to recover the macroscopic shape of the parent phase upon heating, alloys with the two-way effect also exhibit a return to the reoriented martensitic shape upon cooling in the absence of applied stress. During training, such a material develops internal stress fields that favor certain martensitic variants over others (Schroeder and Wayman 1977). The result is that when the SMA is thermally cycled in the absence of applied stress, it will change its shape as it changes its phase.

10.1.3   Alternate Shape Memory Alloy Options

There are many materials that have been discovered or designed to exhibit shape memory properties. The following section provides discussion on some of the more commonly studied SMAs; further information is provided in the literature (Otsuka and Wayman 1999; Funakubo 1987; Lagoudas 2008).

Equiatomic NiTi is the most widely used and thus most well understood of all current shape memory alloys. NiTi exhibits pseudoelasticity, provides large SME strains (5–8%), TWSME, and through the proper heat treatment, its transformation temperatures can be adjusted for a wide range of applications. The workability, corrosion resistance, and biocompatibility of NiTi have led to a large number of applications in the medical industry (usually based on pseudoelastic response), with products ranging from stents, to dental drills, to flexible frames for glasses (Otsuka and Wayman 1999; Duerig *et al.* 1999; Morgan 2004). More recently the automobile, energy, and aerospace industries have been looking into using NiTi thermally activated actuators (Hartl and Lagoudas 2007a; Sun *et al.* 2008; Gore *et al.* 2008).

The performance capabilities of NiTi can be altered by changing the balance of the two constituent elements. Generally, increased titanium leads to increased transformation temperatures (Otsuka and Wayman 1999). Increasing the amount of nickel in the material will lead to the development of nickel-rich precipitates that act to stabilize the thermomechanical cycles more quickly, reducing TRIP, though at the cost of lower transformation strains (Mabe *et al.* 2006). The addition of niobium (Nb) to NiTi has been observed to widen the hysteresis and maximize the difference between the M_s and A_s temperatures (Duerig and Melton 1989). On the other hand, the addition of copper (Cu) to the NiTi system can reduce the size of the SMA hysteresis (Proft *et al.* 1989). While this makes NiTiCu favorable for actuator applications, the addition of copper slightly reduces the maximum actuation strain in these alloys when compared to equiatomic NiTi (Miller and Lagoudas 2000).

The addition of certain elements to the NiTi system can also result in *high temperature shape memory alloys* (HTSMAs), which have transformation temperatures over 100°C. The addition of palladium (Pd) or platinum (Pt) to NiTi has been found to bring transformation temperatures up to 400–1000°C (Golberg *et al.* 1995; Tian and Wu 2003; Rios *et al.* 2005). More recent studies have found that the addition of hafnium (Hf) to NiTi provides comparable high temperature properties, but at a lower material cost than palladium or platinum (Meng *et al.* 2000; Firstov *et al.* 2004; Meng *et al.* 2008). However, NiTiHf transformation temperatures are not as high as the Pd or Pt enriched NiTi alloys (200–400°C) (Lagoudas 2008).

Other notable SMA compositions exist which are not NiTi-based. Two examples are copper-based SMAs and iron-based SMAs. Copper-based SMAs (e.g. CuAlBe) are capable of similar performance characteristics as NiTi-based SMAs. These alloys also have improved electrical conductivity, thermal conductivity, and ductility compared to NiTi SMAs (Otsuka and Wayman 1999). However, these alloys have limited actuation capabilities at higher stress levels and their transformation temperatures are highly sensitive to composition. For some copper-based SMAs, tolerances on composition must be maintained within the order of $10^{-3} - 10^{-4}$ at.% (atomic percentage) if consistent transformation temperatures are to be assured (Lagoudas 2008). Examples of these alloys include CuZnAl, CuAlNi, and CuAlMn (Morin and Trivero 1995; Contardo and Guenin 1990; Cingolani *et al.* 1998; Sutou *et al.* 2003; Guerioune *et al.* 2007). Iron-based SMAs have also shown potential as a cheap alternative to NiTi SMAs. After training, FeMnSi can achieve transformation strains of 2.5–4.5% and FeNiCoTi exhibits a thermal hysteresis width of 150°C (Lagoudas 2008). While iron-based SMAs have shown potential, they are still in the development phase and have not been incorporated into any current applications.

10.2 Aerospace Applications of SMAs

Having developed an understanding of SMAs, engineers can design applications that exploit their behaviors to the fullest. The subsequent section will present some current examples of how SMAs have been successfully implemented into aerospace morphing applications.

Incorporating morphing structures into aircraft is not a new idea. In fact, the first powered aircraft to take flight, the *Wright Flyer*, was based on a wing design intended to smoothly deform, or morph. The wings were constructed of a spruce wood framework with a cloth skin. This relatively compliant structure was warped during flight by control wires attached to the outboard trailing-edge, providing roll control. As aircraft increased in capability, stronger materials were needed to support ever-increasing performance requirements, including heavier, more powerful engines. These materials (e.g. aluminum and other lightweight, high-strength alloys) were far too rigid to allow warping, and thus morphing wings were quickly replaced by rigid wings with hinged control surfaces.

In the last couple of decades, advances in materials have made it feasible to create robust morphing aerospace structures once again. Implementing SMAs as solid-state actuators has been a key enabling technology in the development of many morphing applications. This section will introduce some proposed morphing designs for fixed-wing aircraft, rotorcraft, and spacecraft.

10.2.1   Fixed-Wing Aircraft

In an ongoing effort to increase the efficiency and capability of modern aircraft, SMAs are being implemented in both novel applications and the replacement of conventional devices with alternatives that are more compact, more powerful, and less complicated. While some designs have focused on morphing entire aerodynamic structures (e.g. wings), others have taken a more focused approach and addressed more localized deflections. These local actuation applications also result in improved aircraft performance, yet are easier to implement in the short-term. Examples of local actuation include tabs, flaps, and engine inlets/nozzles. At these locations an SMA component can eliminate the hinges found in conventional installations or permit actuator installation in an otherwise undersized volume. Examples of current morphing aerostructures for fixed-wing aircraft follow.

SMA actuators are energy dense (40–70 J/kg for Ni-rich NiTi (Gravatt *et al.* 2010)), so they are ideal for providing actuation while conserving both space and weight. These are important concepts in aircraft design (Song and Ma 2007; Hutapea *et al.* 2008). To this end, SMA actuated flaps have been studied, where some designs have incorporated SMA springs and SMA wires. While some actuator systems require a return spring to counter the SME and return the actuator to the deformed position, these designs eliminate the need for such a spring by installing opposing SMA actuators that pull the flaps in both directions. In designing this type of setup, the actuating SMA is used to "reset" the non-actuating SMA by forcing it back to its deformed position. The associated prototypes are shown in Figure 10.7.

Although incorporating SMA actuators into conventional hinged controls can be advantageous in terms of space and weight, such control solutions still lead to non-continuous wing

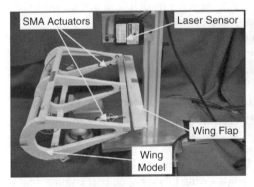
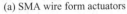
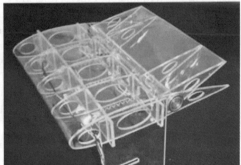

(a) SMA wire form actuators   (b) SMA spring form actuators

Figure 10.7 Advanced wing prototypes with SMA controlled flaps. (a) Reprinted from Figure 10.3a from "Robust control of a shape memory alloy wire actuated flap" by G. Song and N. Ma. Copyright 2007. Reproduced by permission of IOP Publishing and G. Song; (b) Reprinted from "Development of a smart wing" by P. Hutapea, J. Kim, A. Guion, C. Hanna, and N. Heulitt. Copyright 2008. Reproduced by permission of Parsaoran Hutapea, Temple University

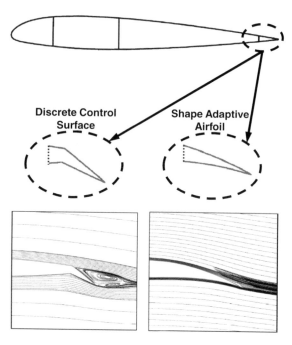

Figure 10.8   Predicted airflow over a wing with a flap (left) and with a continuous wing surface (right) (Roh *et al.* 2009). Reprinted from "Shape adaptive airfoil actuated by a shape memory alloy and its aerodynamic characteristics" by J. Roh, K. Kim, and I. Lee. Copyright 2009. Reproduced by permission of I. Lee

surfaces. To improve aircraft wing performance, discrete control surfaces and associated hinge lines should be eliminated. Figure 10.8 shows this through the modeling of airflow over continuous and discontinuous wing surfaces. In comparing the two simulations, it is clear that the wing with the hinged flap induces separation at the point of surface discontinuity, whereas the wing with the continuous surfaces delays or prevents air flow separation (Roh *et al.* 2009).

One example of a continuous surface with variable geometry is a morphing wing. Perhaps the first well-documented attempt to create a full morphing wing based on SMA actuation was the DARPA Smart Wing project. The goal of this project was to create a continuous wing that could exhibit the variable twist needed to optimize the wing for various flight regimes (Kudva *et al.* 1997). The use of conventional actuators in such an application with complex multi-component support systems (e.g. the pumps and reservoirs in a hydraulic system) would lead to significant weight and balance issues. Compared to conventional actuation systems, energy dense SMAs provide the force needed to twist a wing in a very compact volume. In the Smart Wing study, an equiatomic NiTi torque tube was used to twist a 1/16 scale F-18 wing, shown in Figure 10.9. Since the reaction time of the actuator was slower than is necessary for continuous in-flight adjustments, the role of the actuator to twist the wing was limited to take-off and landing and was found to improve the performance of the wing in those regimes (Kudva *et al.* 1999; Jardine *et al.* 1999). Another approach to controlling the continuous wing shape is to form an underlying structure with distributed SMA active components. One such

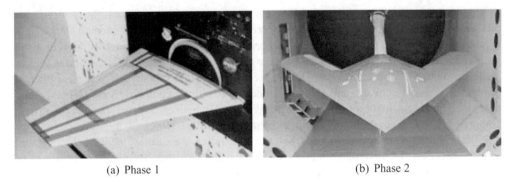

(a) Phase 1   (b) Phase 2

Figure 10.9   DARPA Smart Wing wind tunnel model (Sanders *et al.* 2004)

application is bio-inspired and mimics a complex vertebrate structure (Elzey *et al.* 2003). The idea behind this design, shown in Figure 10.10, is the fabrication of an internal structure that is stiff and light when passive, but is flexible when actuated. Changing the camber or twisting the wing was accomplished by the installation of SMA sheets in particular locations to apply the proper moments to the vertebrate structure. Morphing of the wing camber and span wise

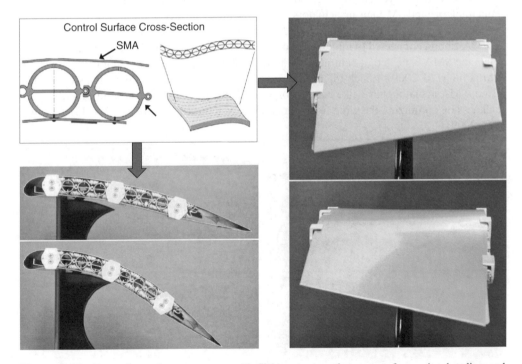

Figure 10.10   Internal vertebrate structure with SMA actuators that can perform wing bending and wing twisting without generating discrete surfaces (Elzey *et al.* 2003). Reprinted from "A bio-inspired, high-authority for shape morphing structures" by D. Elzey, A. Sofla, and H. Wadley. Copyright 2003. Reproduced by permission of SPIE and Dana M. Elzey

twisting are shown in Figure 10.10. Many aerodynamic configurations can be achieved for this wing by properly controlling how the opposing SMA components are heated and cooled.

SMAs can be used as passive elements in morphing wing structures as well, by exploiting the large recoverable deflections provided by the pseudoelastic effect. *Compliant cellular trusses* made up of beams and cables can change their shape if the proper cables are lengthened or shortened using conventional actuators. The hyper elliptic cambered span (HECS) wing developed by NASA incorporates an octahedral unit cell which can change shape in expansive, compressive, and shear directions (Ramrakhyani *et al.* 2005). However, the limited ability of the elastic beam components to bend or twist constrains the displacement of the unit cell in each direction. To increase deflection, pseudoelastic SMA rods are placed in positions of highest local deformation within the unit cell. As a result, less truss unit cells are required for the overall HECS structure, reducing weight.

While smoothly changing the profile of an entire wing can be advantageous during flight, smaller changes in wing geometry can be valuable as well. This is especially true at transonic speeds, where the accumulation of shockwaves on the wing can increase drag. Shifting the location of shockwaves further back on the wing can reduce this drag. Manipulation of the boundary layer over the upper surface of the wing can drive such a change in shockwave location, resulting in the associated decrease in drag. Two studies investigated the use of SMA actuators to create a "ridge" over the upper surface of a wing, which has been shown to be an effective boundary layer control method (Barbarino *et al.* 2009; Dong *et al.* 2008). The first setup implemented SMA spring actuators to raise the upper surface of the airfoil. The prototype is shown in Figure 10.11(a) (Dong *et al.* 2008). The second, shown in Figure 10.11(b), used an SMA ribbon connected to hinges at either of its ends to force the skin of the wing to bend. When the SMA is heated, it contracts and pulls on the hinges, creating a moment on the skin (Barbarino *et al.* 2009). Bench-top prototypes of each design have been built and successfully tested. SMA actuators have also been incorporated into similar designs for altering the wing thickness by optimizing the wing for flight at lower Mach numbers ($M = 0.2$–0.35) (Georges *et al.* 2009).

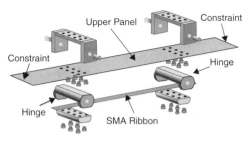

(a) SMA spring device (Dong *et al.* 2008)   (b) SMA ribbon and hinge device (Barbarino *et al.* 2009)

Figure 10.11   Upper wing surface boundary layer manipulation prototypes

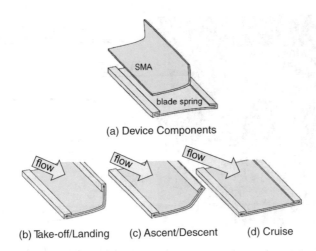

(a) Device Components

(b) Take-off/Landing   (c) Ascent/Descent   (d) Cruise

Figure 10.12   Passively controlled SMA vortex generator (Ikeda *et al.* 2007). Reprinted from "Small vortex generator transformed by change in ambient temperature and aerodynamic force" by T. Ikeda, S. Masuda, and T. Ueda. Copyright 2007. Reproduced by permission of SPIE and Tadashige Ikeda

An alternative approach to controlling the boundary layer considers implementing vortex generators that can be used to delay boundary layer separation from the wings during take-off and landing. A current design under consideration employs SMA-controlled vortex generators to delay separation from the wings. The SMA in these devices is activated by the higher temperatures in the lower atmosphere (during take-off and landing). Then, at the low temperatures observed at cruise altitude (i.e. about 9100 meters (30000 feet)), the SMA transforms into martensite while a return spring drives it toward a flattened configuration (Ikeda *et al.* 2007). The design for this passively controlled SMA vortex generator is presented in Figure 10.12.

The morphing and tuning of engine-related secondary structures is another way in which SMAs can improve aircraft performance. Current engine configurations are optimized for one flight regime, thus compromising performance in others. For example, engines are often designed for optimum efficiency at cruise, but this comes at the cost of increased noise and decreased performance at take-off and landing. However, if SMAs are implemented into the engine structural design, efficiency could be improved across all flight regimes. The Smart Aircraft and Marine System Projects Demonstration (SAMPSON) program was one of the first to implement SMAs in an attempt to improve engine performance (Dunne *et al.* 1999). SMAs were used to control three different elements of an F-15 inlet cowl. A bundle of equiatomic NiTi wires were used to rotate the inlet cowl, optimizing the inlet flow at various angles of attack (Pitt *et al.* 2002a). SMA wires were also used to optimize the inlet shape for subsonic and supersonic flight. In subsonic flight conditions, maximum airflow into the engine is needed, so the lower inlet lip was streamlined. However, in supersonic conditions, the air entering the engine needed to be slowed to increase efficiency (Pitt *et al.* 2001). This was achieved by actively curving the lower lip through the use of piezoelectric motors, while incorporating SMAs in a passive role. Due to the large surface strains generated when the lip was activated, the pseudoelastic effect of NiTi was taken advantage of to create a lip cover that exhibited

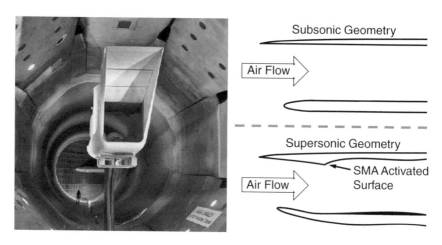

Figure 10.13   SAMPSON F-15 adjustable inlet (Pitt *et al.* 2002a)

large elastic strains. At the same time, another set of SMA wires activated a ramp on the upper surface of the inlet. The combination of lip and ramp slowed the air and directed it into the engine to increase supersonic performance. This F-15 inlet system, shown in Figure 10.13, underwent full-scale testing at NASA Langley and successfully showed that SMAs could be integrated into existing propulsion systems (Pitt *et al.* 2002b).

SMAs have also been considered for the active alteration of engine exhaust and engine bypass flows. NASA and Boeing have each designed, built, and tested SMA activated trailing edge *chevrons* with the intent of reducing engine noise during take-off and landing by inducing free stream and engine exhaust flow mixing (Turner *et al.* 2004; Mabe *et al.* 2006). Mixing is achieved by heating SMA components, which bend the chevrons into the flow. However, the drag resulting from this mixing reduces aircraft efficiency at cruise. To reduce drag, the SMAs are allowed to cool, thus relaxing and allowing the underlying chevron structure to straighten, no longer impeding the engine bypass air flow. Boeing has flight tested the active chevron system, where a decrease in engine noise of 3-5 dB was demonstrated during take-off and landing (Mabe *et al.* 2006).

More recently the chevron concept has been generalized and extended to the morphing of entire trailing edge panels (as opposed to triangular chevrons only), allowing the active tailoring of the engine exhaust area. Boeing has proposed a *variable area nozzle* that can change its area by up to 20% (Mabe 2008). This active nozzle provides two advantages to jet engines: varying nozzle outlet area can improve engine operational efficiency in different flight regimes and the reduction in exit velocity resulting from increased area has been shown to reduce engine noise. While Boeing has implemented SMA actuators directly into the nozzle structure, other designs have proposed that remotely installed SMA wires be used to control a separate mechanism for changing the nozzle area (Song *et al.* 2007). This removes the SMA from areas of heat, relaxing constraints on the selection of alloys based on their transformation temperatures. Figure 10.14 presents two of these designs for SMA-actuated engine outlets.

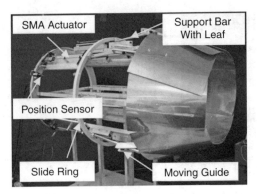

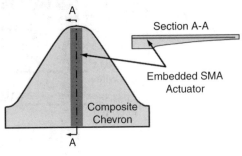

(a) SMA controlled variable area jet nozzle
(Song *et al.* 2007)

(b) NASA's SMA-enabled adaptive chevron
(Turner *et al.* 2004)

Figure 10.14 Engine nozzle morphing applications of SMAs. (a) Reprinted from "Design and control of a proof-of-concept variable area exhaust nozzle using shape memory alloy actuators" by G. Song, N. Ma, H. Lee, and S. Arnold, Figure 10.2. Copyright 2007. Reproduced by permission of IOP and Gangbing Song; (b) Reprinted from "Design, fabrication and testing of SMA enabled adaptive chevrons for jet noise reduction" by T. Turner, R. Buehrle, R. Cano, and G. Fleming. Copyright 2004. Reproduced by permission of SPIE and T. Turner

10.2.2 Rotorcraft

Aerospace applications incorporating SMAs are not limited to fixed wing aircraft; several are also under development for rotorcraft. Most research into rotorcraft morphing structures has concentrated on improving rotor blade performance as this component provides both lift and propulsion. It has been shown that actively controlling rotor blade twist during flight can reduce vibrations and decrease noise (Straub *et al.* 2004). With their high energy density, SMAs are ideal actuators for such applications given the limited installation space that is characteristic in these structures. Further, the robust solid-state nature of shape memory components allows reliable operation even under substantial radial g-forces.

Applications of particular interest include SMA-activated tabs and SMA-twisted rotor blades. Although they are fabricated using precise automated production processes, each rotor blade can perform differently during flight, and these dissimilarities between blades can generate large vibrations (Epps and Chopra 1999). The current method for limiting these vibrations is to manually adjust the pitch links and trailing edge tabs of each rotor blade between flights. This time-consuming process ensures that each individual rotor blade remains in the plane shared by the others, which is known as *tracking*. Provided that such adjustments are made, vibrations are reduced, rotor blade fatigue life is extended, and the rotorcraft exhibits improved overall performance (Singh *et al.* 2003). However, the passive (manually adjusted) trailing edge tabs can be made active by the incorporation of SMAs, and constant tracking adjustments can be performed in flight by the further addition of a control system. This eliminates the need for costly on-ground adjustments and maintains the performance of the rotor blade continuously during flight. As with the flap designs described earlier, these proposed tab systems are controlled by two SMA wires or torque tube actuators operating antagonistically

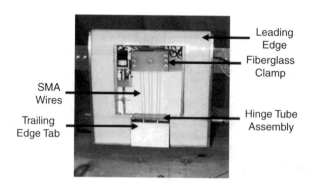

Figure 10.15 An example rotorcraft application of SMAs: full-scale actuated tracking tab (Epps and Chopra 1999). Reprinted from "In-flight tracking of helicopter rotor blades using shape memory alloy actuators" by J. Epps and I. Chopra, Figure 10.13. Copyright 1999. Reproduced by permission of IOP and I. Chopra

(Straub *et al.* 2004; Epps and Chopra 1999; Singh *et al.* 2003). An example of an SMA wire-driven active tab system is presented in Figure 10.15.

For rotorcraft, hover mode and forward flight require different rotor blade twists for optimum performance, especially in tilt-rotor configurations such as the V-22 Osprey (Mabe *et al.* 2004). SMAs in the form of torque tubes can provide the torque needed to twist a stiff rotor blade (Bushnell *et al.* 2008; Mabe *et al.* 2004; Prahlad and Chopra 2007). While earlier designs considered a single tube to vary blade twist in a smooth, continuous manner, more recent designs have recognized that actuating fully and directly from one discrete twist angle (e.g. during hover) to another (e.g. during cruise) provided a stiffer and more robust solution (Mabe *et al.* 2004). In the Boeing design, two SMA torque tubes are used to drive a bi-stable spring/gear device that then applies torque to the blade structure (Bushnell *et al.* 2008). The two tubes oppose each other, driving this bi-stable device from one twist state to the other. Thus, either optimal hover or cruise blade twists can be selected.

10.2.3 Spacecraft

SMAs are also well suited for spacecraft applications, where size and weight considerations can be critical to mission success (Godard *et al.* 2003). One popular example is the SMA-controlled dust wiper utilized on the early Mars rover missions (Fernandez *et al.* 2007). On the surfaces of other planets and moons, dust could potentially reduce the efficiency of solar panels or diminish the effectiveness of optical sensors. Further, the fine particles pose a threat to conventional electromechanical servos. A lightweight, compact, and robust device is needed for dust removal actuation, and SMAs are well suited for such an application.

Deployable structure applications incorporating SMAs have been considered as well. Solar arrays, for example, have been designed with SMA hinges between panels that take advantage of the SME for deployment (Carpenter and Lyons 2001; Beidleman *et al.* 2007). Prior to launch, the solar panels are packed into a compact configuration forcing the SMA hinges into their deformed (martensitic) configuration. Once the spacecraft is in orbit, the SMA hinges

(a) Solar array assembly

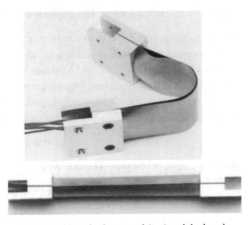

(b) SMA hinge in the stowed (top) and deployed (bottom) positions

Figure 10.16   SMA deployed solar array (Carpenter and Lyons 2001)

connecting the solar panels are heated, returning to their original (austenitic) configuration and deploying the solar panels. An example of an SMA-deployed solar array is presented in Figure 10.16. Similarly, deployable antennas have been developed that consist of SMA truss elements packed into a compact configuration and then deployed when heated (Hassan *et al.* 2008; Peng *et al.* 2008; Sofla *et al.* 2009). SMAs can also be used to morph inflatable structures; these structures present obvious advantages due to their light weight at launch and large usable volume upon deployment (Lee *et al.* 2006; Tian *et al.* 2009).

Another unique application that has been proposed is an SMA-based heat engine for solar energy conversion (Bombardelli and Menon 2008). In such a design, panels of SMA actuators (i.e. arrays of wires) are tethered to a central point, and each cyclically contracts and then expands when exposed to solar radiation and then shade. The resulting change in shape induces rotation of the panels, which creates mechanical energy for the spacecraft. SMAs have also been used to create non-explosive release devices for space applications (Johnson *et al.* 2008; Zhang *et al.* 2010). Conventional explosive release devices can cause damage to spacecraft if they prematurely detonate and induce large shock loads even when operated properly. SMA devices provide a robust, safe, and smooth method of release in a zero-g environment without damaging the spacecraft on which they are installed.

10.3   Characterization of SMA Actuators and Analysis of Actuator Systems

The following section provides a brief introduction to experimental procedures and analysis methods pertaining to the understanding of SMA materials and components. Both are critical tools for engineers designing SMA-based morphing aerospace applications.

10.3.1 Experimental Techniques and Considerations

Whether the end goal is the motivation or accurate calibration of analytical models, prediction of component response, or increased understanding of material behaviors, careful experimental characterization of SMA materials is an essential component of any research and development effort. Standard experimental methods have been established for SMAs, but the careful researcher must also consider some important details regarding material history and the repeatability and reliability of derived responses.

10.3.1.1 Experimental Methodology

Recall that we have discussed the following SMA characteristics: *i*) these materials are structural alloys that transform from one phase to another, each phase exhibiting an elastic response under certain thermomechanical loading conditions, *ii*) the criteria for transforming from one phase to another can be described in terms of material stress and temperature conditions (see Figure 10.3), and *iii*) during forward transformation (austenite to martensite), an inelastic strain of some magnitude is generated, while during reverse transformation (martensite to austenite), this strain is recovered. It then follows that a complete experimental characterization of an SMA material should describe and quantify each of these responses. The following experimental methodology has been shown throughout the literature to satisfy this goal:

1. Approximate the critical temperatures to complete full forward and reverse transformation under stress-free conditions (M_f and A_f, respectively),
2. Given this information, assess the thermoelastic response of pure martensite (i.e., at a temperature below M_f), and of pure austenite (i.e., at a temperature well above A_f),
3. Induce multiple full transformation cycles in the material under differing thermomechanical conditions, monitoring the conditions at which the two transformations (forward and reverse) begin and end as well as the deformation generated and recovered during the transformation.

This systematic approach to SMA characterization is well suited for the development of SMA morphing applications, and each step will be described in more detail.

To provide the baseline measurement of the zero-load transformation temperatures, *Differential scanning calorimetry* (DSC) is used. A DSC works by monitoring the heat flow needed to heat or cool a specimen at a predefined constant temperature rate. In SMAs, the forward and reverse transformations are exothermic and endothermic, respectively; investigation of the associated heat flow peaks and valleys allows one to determine the zero-load transformation temperatures. A typical DSC response for a NiTi SMA is shown in Figure 10.17.[1]

Once the critical temperatures required to form pure martensite and pure austenite are determined, standard isothermal mechanical loading can be applied to determine the apparent elastic response and plastic yield limit of each phase. It is important to characterize both phases, as each may exhibit different apparent elastic properties. Polycrystalline SMA materials are

---

[1] The SMA medical applications community has established ASTM Standard F-2004 for the DSC testing of SMA materials (ASTM 2005). However, the annealing step described in this standard is not applicable when characterizing materials intended for SMA actuation applications.

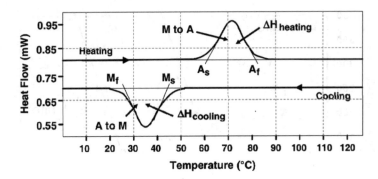

Figure 10.17 Example plot of differential scanning calorimetry (DSC) results for a conventional SMA showing all four stress-free transformation temperatures

elastically isotropic, thus standard tensile or compressive tests can be applied (e.g., see ASTM Standards E-8 and E-9, respectively (ASTM 2004, 2000)). Conventional thermal expansion characterization can also be performed on each of the pure phases.

Following thermoelastic characterization, the full transformation response of a given SMA must be carefully assessed. While DSC testing provides some information on stress-free transformation temperatures, further characterization is necessary to address the influence of stress on transformation temperatures and also to assess the magnitude of recoverable inelastic strain (transformation strain) generated. When the transformation temperatures are plotted in a stress-temperature space, the relationship is observed to be approximately linear (see the schematic illustration in Figure 10.3); the slope of these lines has been referred to as the *stress rate* (Duerig *et al.* 1990) and the *stress influence coefficient* (Qidwai and Lagoudas 2000; Lagoudas *et al.* 1996). This dependence of transformation temperatures on applied load can be seen in the experimental NiTi phase diagram shown in Figure 10.18. The recoverable transformation strain can also be dependent on the applied stress level. Thus, by monitoring transformations occurring under various stress and temperature loading conditions, the phase diagram can be constructed and the stress dependency of maximum transformation strain magnitude can be assessed. One of two experimental loading paths is commonly employed to assess transformation behaviors at non-zero stress levels:

(1) *Pseudoelastic Testing*: This response was discussed in Section 10.1.2. The mechanical test is performed at constant temperature, usually above A_f. Stress is applied to the specimen until transformation into martensite is induced and is increased until transformation is completed. The specimen is then unloaded and will begin transformation back into austenite, which is eventually completed as the unloading progresses. Similar stress-induced transformation cycles are imposed at different temperatures above A_f. For each cycle performed at a given temperature above A_f the critical transformation stresses σ^{M_s}, σ^{M_f}, σ^{A_s}, and σ^{A_f} are recorded and plotted in the stress-temperature space. The SMA medical device community has established ASTM Standard F-2516 for the pseudoelastic testing of SMA material (ASTM 2006).

(2) *Isobaric Testing*: This response was discussed in Section 10.1.2. In this test the applied stress is held constant while the specimen undergoes thermal cycling. For example, a

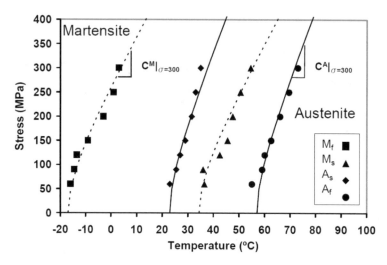

Figure 10.18 Experimental phase diagram determined using the *isobaric* transformation method (Hartl *et al.* 2010a). Reprinted from "Use of a Ni60Ti shape memory alloy for active jet engine chevron application, Part II: experimentally validated numerical analysis" by D. Hartl, J. Mooney, D. Lagoudas, F. Calkins, and J. Mabe, Figure 10.5. Copyright 2010. Reproduced by permission of IOP and D. Hartl

specimen is loaded to some stress while in the austenite phase. Forward transformation is induced as it is cooled; eventually the martensite phase completely develops. Then the specimen is reheated and reverse transformation is initiated, and then eventually completed. This test is carried out at multiple constant stress levels. At each applied stress (σ) the critical transformation temperatures of the cycle (M_s^σ, M_f^σ, A_s^σ, and A_f^σ) are recorded and plotted in the stress-temperature space. This is the more appropriate method for characterizing materials intended for morphing or other actuation applications.

Taken together, the methods described above represent a straightforward and focused process for characterizing an SMA material specimen. The resulting response curves provide important information on elastic and transformation behaviors. To generalize these behaviors as representing a "material response", and further to use a material response in the predictive analysis and design of application components, special considerations regarding specimen and component history must be addressed.

10.3.1.2 Special Experimental Considerations

In addition to knowing the alloy composition, it is imperative that one understand the complete history of an SMA that is proposed for use in any planned design. Specimens and components from the same raw (cast) material can behave differently depending on any subsequent processing they have undergone. Due to the complex mechanisms that underlie their behavior, SMAs are especially sensitive to thermal treatments (e.g., annealing, precipitation hardening, etc.) and large deformations (e.g., hot and cold working). Specimens with different histories should not be expected to exhibit common behavior. Likewise, characterization data obtained

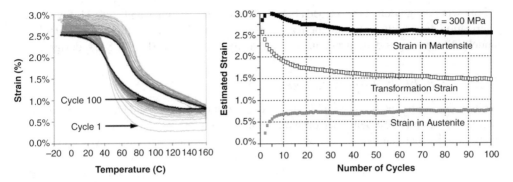

Figure 10.19 Training of a Ni60Ti40 (wt.%) SMA (Hartl *et al.* 2010b). Reprinted from "Use of a Ni60Ti shape memory alloy for active jet engine chevron application, Part I: thermomechanical characterization" by D. Hartl, D. Lagoudas, F. Calkins, and J. Mabe, Figure 10.6. Copyright 2010. Reproduced by permission of IOP and D. Hartl

from a given specimen may not be useful in predicting the behavior of an active structural component formed from the same raw material but having a different history. However, it has been shown that SMA specimens and components with the same material composition and the *same* processing history will perform similarly, though some stochastic variation may be observed (Mabe *et al.* 2004). Thus, when application design is the goal, characterization should be performed on specimens with the same composition and processing history as the intended SMA component.

Further, the topic of response repeatability and material stabilization must be addressed. As previously discussed (Section 10.1.2), most SMA compositions in the as-received state will exhibit the generation of some irrecoverable strain from cycle-to-cycle, the generation being most pronounced during initial cycling and then decreasing as the number of cycles increases. The process of thermomechanically cycling a specimen or component to reach a repeatable response free of irrecoverable strain is known as stabilization or *training*. This effect can be observed in the context of isobaric cycling as shown in Figure 10.19. For actuator design, isobaric training can be performed directly on the component/specimen by placing it under a high constant stress level (relative to the proposed application) and imposing 100–500 thermal actuation cycles.

However, it is not always necessary to stabilize the response of an SMA specimen or component. Both single use and multi-use SMA applications have been proposed and implemented. In the case of a single use device (see, for example, Figure 10.16), the active component will likely be derived from processed, but untrained, material. Considering the previous discussion, characterization of the SMA for use in such an application should be performed on likewise untrained specimens. Conversely, if the SMA application is to be used repeatedly and a predictable response is required (as is the case for morphing aerostructures such as that shown in Figure 10.14), the active SMA component must be stabilized prior to installation. Thus, characterization of the material chosen for such a multi-use application must be performed on stabilized specimens (Hartl *et al.* 2010b).

Following the guidelines described above will ensure the accuracy and applicability of characterization data, both for use in application development and in the calibration of predictive models. Now we consider current and popular analysis tools available for SMA design.

10.3.2 Established Analysis Tools

While work continues on developing the next generation of SMA-enabled aerospace applications, research is also being performed to enhance and implement constitutive models and analysis tools that can assist in the design process. Traditional design of SMA components and the systems that incorporate them has not taken advantage of such analytical tools; instead design-build-test cycles have comprised the brute-force effort underlying the development of smart structures. This can be attributed both to the lack of familiarity with SMA constitutive modeling among designers as well as the absence of model implementations from many of the legacy structural analysis codes. Each problem has been addressed in recent years.

As a method of making powerful constitutive models accessible to a wide range of engineers, some researchers have focused on developing essentially one-dimensional (1-D) formulations. These are especially useful for the consideration of SMA bodies in which the solution fields (stress, strain, etc.) do not vary significantly with location, and can be tuned for uniaxial tension/compression or shear applications (e.g. wires and thin torque tubes, respectively). The 1-D model of Brinson (Brinson 1993), based in part on earlier developments (Tanaka 1986; Liang and Rogers 1990), is the most cited in the SMA literature and is useful in its consideration of both martensitic transformation and reorientation while also being relatively straight forward in its implementation. This model successfully synthesizes and simplifies the body of literature preceding it and is entirely phenomenological and easily calibrated from the common SMA experiments previously described. Another 1-D model worth mentioning is more unique in its approach and implementation, while providing the capability of capturing the same effects. The model of Seelecke and coworkers (Seelecke and Muller 2004) uses statistical mechanics to consider the "energy landscape" of martensite transformation and reorientation and the associated probabilities that either of these will occur (and in what direction). The resulting mathematical relations can be written as a set of ordinary differential equations in time, and can be solved accordingly. While these two models are commonly used, there are many other notable 1-D SMA models. A more comprehensive list can be found elsewhere (Lagoudas 2008).

With SMA applications increasing in complexity and advancing in capability, the simplicity of 1-D models begins to preclude their usefulness. For complex SMA shapes and associated loading, fully three-dimensional (3-D) constitutive models are required, and these are only as capable as the frameworks in which they are implemented. The first published 3-D model, though rarely acknowledged, was that proposed by Bertram (Bertram 1982), and was based on finite strain plasticity modeling. One of the most commonly cited 3-D models that has also been efficiently implemented in a robust FEA environment is that of Boyd and Lagoudas (Boyd and Lagoudas 1996). This model is based on the concepts of thermodynamics, assumes an infinitesimal strain formulation (sufficient for almost all SMA applications, where local strains rarely exceed $\sim$5%), and is analogous to conventional plasticity models in its structure. For these latter two reasons, it can be implemented using the same methods popular in small strain plasticity analysis (Qidwai and Lagoudas 2000). It does not, however, consider the effects of martensitic reorientation, as this behavior is rarely utilized in repeated-use applications.

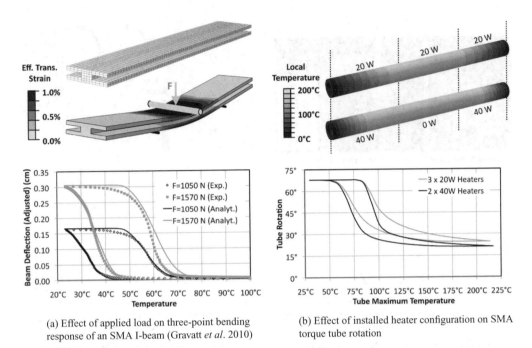

(a) Effect of applied load on three-point bending response of an SMA I-beam (Gravatt *et al.* 2010)

(b) Effect of installed heater configuration on SMA torque tube rotation

Figure 10.20 Numerical analyses of thermally actuated SMA components with aerospace application and exhibiting conventional transformation behaviors

The 3-D extension of the Brinson model (Panico and Brinson 2007) and an expanded form of the Boyd-Lagoudas model (Popov and Lagoudas 2007) are two examples of similar models that do account for the reorientation of martensite, though at the cost of simplicity. Several other 3-D models with interesting attributes are also worth mentioning. The model of Turner (Turner 2000) represents a class of fully empirical models, in which an "effective coefficient of thermal expansion" is used to capture the thermally-induced effects of the inelastic, yet recoverable, transformation strain. The models of Auricchio and coworkers (Auricchio and Taylor 1997; Petrini *et al.* 2003) assumed a finite strain formulation from the earliest versions, which were limited to capturing the pseudoelastic effect. In more recent years, these models have been extended to thermal transformation, and an implementation is included with all installations of the ABAQUS Unified FEA suite.

The capabilities of such conventional three-dimensional SMA constitutive models are demonstrated in Figure 10.20, where thermally induced actuation in bending and twisting are both shown. Figure 10.20(a) considers the analysis of an SMA I-beam subjected to two different bending loads and it is shown that the temperature-force-deflection predictions of the analysis tool are in close agreement with experimental data (Gravatt *et al.* 2010). The implemented model also provides information on the distribution of recoverable transformation strains during actuation. Figure 10.20(b) summarizes the thermomechanically coupled analysis of an SMA torque tube actuated by a distributed heating system. The selection of heater placement and wattages can be seen to have an impact on the actuation characteristics

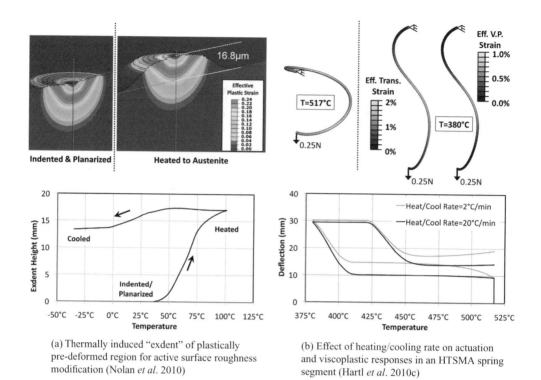

(a) Thermally induced "exdent" of plastically
pre-deformed region for active surface roughness
modification (Nolan *et al.* 2010)

(b) Effect of heating/cooling rate on actuation
and viscoplastic responses in an HTSMA spring
segment (Hartl *et al.* 2010c)

Figure 10.21   Advanced numerical analyses of thermally actuated SMA components exhibiting recoverable and irrecoverable deformations

of the tube, where higher wattages at the tube ends are essential in mitigating the "heat sink" effects of an assumed attached passive structure.

Finally, some of the more advanced models of recent years should be mentioned. With respect to conventional SMA behaviors, the model of Christ and Reese (Christ and Reese 2009) is perhaps the most advanced. The model captures both martensitic reorientation and transformation, is formulated using finite strains, and considers full thermomechanical coupling, including the effects of the latent heat of transformation on the thermal energy balance. Other effects in SMAs have been considered, including the generation and evolution of plastic (Hartl *et al.* 2008) and viscoplastic (Hartl *et al.* 2010c) deformations. These models will become essential as engineers seek to develop new materials, push SMA designs to new temperature and loading regimes, and consider the critical concepts of component behavior under extreme operating conditions. Example analyses of SMA components experiencing plastic and viscoplastic deformations are shown in Figure 10.21. Specifically, Figure 10.21(a) summarizes the advanced analysis of micro-scale surface roughness adaptation using SMAs, with potential applications for boundary layer modification (Mani *et al.* 2008). A surface exhibiting such three-dimensional behavior is formed by first indenting a martensitic SMA substrate to the point that local plastic strains are generated, resulting in irrecoverable deformations. The surface is then "planarized" by polishing, removing the residual indentation but leaving regions of plastic strain. Subsequent heating into austenite causes an "exdent" to be formed, which is

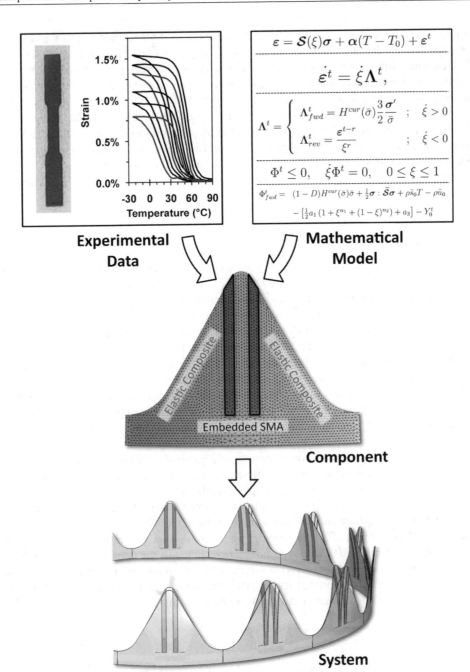

Figure 10.22 Methodology of SMA-based hybrid morphing aerostructure design: characterize, analyze, integrate (model taken after Hartl *et al.* 2010a).

partially recoverable (Nolan *et al.* 2010). The distribution of plastic strains and the response of the surface feature to thermal inputs are shown. Figure 10.21(b) summarizes the analysis of a *high temperature shape memory alloy* (HTSMA) spring actuator. Components fabricated from these materials are capable of exhibiting actuation at temperatures that may also induce irrecoverable viscoplastic strain generation (e.g., 400–500°C). Here a spring segment with a wire diameter of 0.5 mm (0.02 in.) is subjected to a small constant load and thermally cycled. At temperatures exceeding 475°C, substantial (rate-dependent) viscoplastic strains can be observed, especially at slower heating/cooling rates (Hartl *et al.* 2010c). The analysis captures both the distribution of viscoplastic strain in the spring at the end of cooling (contour plot) as well as the irrecoverable deflection observed at the end of heating (deflection-temperature plot).

10.4   Conclusion

SMAs are unique materials that exhibit important engineering behaviors. Since the first widely publicized work in the early 1960s, they have been continuously studied by a community of researchers seeking to better understand these behaviors. Initially, most focused on understanding and utilizing their superelastic response, but over the last two decades the number of thermally induced actuation applications has grown rapidly. Of primary use to engineers in the aerospace industry is the ability of this material to convert thermal energy to mechanical energy by means of a martensitic transformation that manifests itself through what is known as the shape memory effect. This makes SMAs particularly useful as solid-state actuators. With their high energy density, SMAs are appropriate for incorporation into aerospace morphing applications where space is limited and weight requirements are strict. Examples of such applications include SMA actuated flaps, rotor blades, wings, and deployment mechanisms for solar arrays. The continued research surrounding these materials and the response of components formed from them has allowed the derivation of increasingly accurate constitutive models. Once properly implemented, these models allow designers to avoid the experimental design-build-test cycles of the past, instead relying on computer analysis to support or even supplant early prototype development, reducing both development time and cost. Careful thermomechanical experimentation is essential for the calibration of these models and the validation of their predictions. The combined utility of careful experimentation and powerful models is schematically illustrated in Figure 10.22, which summarizes much of the current SMA research and development being performed worldwide. Given our increasing understanding of this material and our improved ability to predict its behavior, the number and scope of applications that incorporate SMAs will continue to expand well into the future.

References

ASTM International 2000 Standard Test Methods of Compression Testing of Metallic Materials at Room Temperature.

ASTM International 2004 Standard Test Method for Tension Testing of Metallic Materials.

ASTM International 2005 Standard Test Method for Transformation Temperature of Nickel-Titanium Alloys by Thermal Analysis.

ASTM International 2006 Standard Test Method for Tension Testing of Nickel-Titanium Superelastic Materials.

Auricchio F and Taylor R 1997 Shape-memory alloys: modelling and numerical simulations of the finite- strain superelastic behavior. *Computer Methods in Applied Mechanics and Engineering*, 143: 175–194.

Barbarino S, Ameduri S, Lecce L and Concilio A 2009 Wing shape control through an SMA-based device. *Journal of Intelligent Material Systems and Structures*, 20: 283–296.

Beidleman N, Freebury G, Francis W, Lake M, Barrett R, Keller P and Taylor R 2007 Large-Scale Deployable Solar Array. US Patent 0262204.

Bertacchini O, Lagoudas D and Patoor E 2003 Fatigue life characterization of shape memory alloys undergoing thermomechanical cyclic loading. *Proceedings of SPIE*, 5053: 612–624.

Bertram A 1982 Thermo-mechanical constitutive equations for the description of shape memory effects in alloys. *Nuclear Engineering and Design*, 74: 173–182.

Bo Z and Lagoudas D 1999 Thermomechanical modeling of polycrystalline SMAs under cyclic loading, part III: evolution of plastic strains and two-way shape memory effect. *International Journal of Engineering Science*, 37: 1175–1203.

Bombardelli C and Menon C 2008 Space power generation with a tether heat engine. *Acta Astronautica*, 63: 348–356.

Boyd J and Lagoudas D 1996 A thermodynamical constitutive model for shape memory materials. Part I: the monolithic shape memory alloy. *International Journal of Plasticity*, 12(6): 805–842.

Brinson L 1993 One-dimensional constitutive behavior of shape memory alloys: thermomechanical derivation with non-constant material functions and redefined martensite internal variable. *Journal of Intelligent Material Systems and Structures*, 4: 229–242.

Buehler W, Gilfrich J and Wiley R 1963 Effect of low-temperature phase changes on the mechanical properties of alloys near composition TiNi. *Journal of Applied Physics*, 34(5): 1475–1477.

Bushnell G, Arbogast D and Ruggeri R 2008 Shape control of a morphing structure (rotor blade) using a shape memory alloy actuator system. *Proceedings of SPIE*, 6928: 1–11.

Carpenter B and Lyons J 2001 *EO-1 Technology Validation Report: Lightweight Flexible Solar Array Experiment*, Technical report, NASA Godard Space Flight Center, Greenbelt, MD, pp. 1199–1204.

Chang L and Read T 1951 Plastic deformation and diffusionless phase change in metals. the gold- cadmium beta phase. *Trans. AIME*, 189: 47–52.

Christ D and Reese S 2009 A finite element model for shape memory alloys considering thermomechanical couplings at large strains. *International Journal of Solids and Structures*, 46: 3694–3709.

Cingolani E, Van Humbeech J and Ahlers M 1998 Stabilization and two-way shape memory effect in Cu-Al-Ni single crystals. *Metallurgical and Materials Transactions*, 30A: 493–499.

Contardo L and Guenin G 1990 Training and two way memory effect in Cu-Zn-Al alloy. *Acta Metallurgica Material*, 38(7): 1267–1272.

Dong Y, Boming Z and Jun L 2008 A changeable aerofoil actuated by shape memory alloy springs. *Materials Science and Engineering*, A485: 243–250.

Duerig T and Melton K 1989 Wide hysteresis NiTiNb alloys: In E Hornbogen and N Jost, eds. *The Martensitic Transformation in Science and Technology*, NDC, Fremont, CA, pp. 191–198.

Duerig T, Melton K, Stockel D and Waymen C 1990 *Engineering Aspects of Shape Memory Alloys*. Butterworth-Heinemann, Oxford.

Duerig T, Pelton A and Stockel D 1999 An overview of NiTinol medical applications. *Materials Science and Engineering*, A273-275: 149–160.

Dunne J, Hopkins M, Baumann E, Pitt D and White E 1999 Overview of the SAMPSON smart inlet. *Proceedings of SPIE*, 3674: 380–390.

Eckelmeyer K 1976 The effect of alloying on the shape memory phenomenon in NiTinol. *Scripta Metallurgica*, 10: 667–672.

Elzey D, Sofla A and Wadley H 2003 A bio-inspired, high-authority actuator for shape morphing structures. *Proceedings of SPIE*, 5052: 1–8.

Epps J and Chopra I 1999 In-flight tracking of helicopter rotor blades using shape memory alloy actuators. *Smart Materials Structures*, 10: 104–111.

Favier D and Liu Y 2000 Restoration by rapid overheating of thermally stabilized martensite of NiTi shape memory alloys. *Journal of Alloys and Compounds*, 297(1–2): 114–121.

Fernandez D, Cabas R and Moreno L 2007 Dust wiper mechanism for operation in Mars. *Proceedings of the European Space Mechanisms and Tribology Symposium*, 2007: 1–5.

Firstov G, Van Humbeeck J and Koval Y 2004 High-temperature shape memory alloys some recent developments. *Materials Science and Engineering*, A378: 2–10.

Funakubo H 1987 *Shape Memory Alloys*. Gordon and Breach Science Publishers, New York.

Georges T, Brailovski V, Morellon E, Coutu D and Terriault P 2009 Design of shape memory alloy actuators for morphing laminar wing with flexible extrados. *Journal of Mechanical Design*, 131: 1–9.

Godard O, Lagoudas M and Lagoudas D 2003 Design of space systems using shape memory alloys. *Proceedings of SPIE*, 5056: 545–558.

Golberg D, Xu Y, Murakami Y, Morito S, Otsuka K, Ueki T and Horikawa H 1995 Characteristics of Ti50Pd30Ni20 high-temperature shape memory alloy. *Intermetallics*, 3: 35–46.

Gore J, Bowles A, Maylin M, Chandrasekaran L, Forsyth D and Buyers M 2008 High temperature shape memory alloy actuators through mechanical treatments for an oil and gas down-hole valve. *Proceedings of SPIE*, 6930.

Gravatt L, Mabe J and Calkins F, and Hartl D 2010 Characterization of varied geometry shape memory alloys beams. *Proceedings of SPIE*, 7645: 1–12.

Guerioune M, Amiour Y, Bounour W, Guellati O, Benaldjia A, Amara A, Chakri N, Ali-Rachedi M and Vrel D 2007 SHS of shape memory CuZnAl alloys. *International Journal of Self-Propagating High-Temperature Synthesis*, 17(1): 41–48.

Hartl D, Chatzigeorgiou G and Lagoudas D 2010a Three-dimensional modeling and numerical analysis of rate-dependant irrecoverable deformation in shape memory alloys. *International Journal of Plasticity*, 26: 1485–1507.

Hartl D and Lagoudas D 2007a Aerospace applications of shape memory alloys. *Journal of Aerospace Engineering*, 221(4): 535–552.

Hartl D and Lagoudas D 2007b Characterization and 3-D modeling of Ni60Ti SMA for actuation of a variable geometry jet engine chevron. *Proceedings of SPIE*, 6529: 1–12.

Hartl D, Lagoudas D, Calkins F and Mabe J 2010b Use of a Ni60Ti shape memory alloy for active jet engine chevron application: I. thermomechanical characterization. *Smart Materials Structures*, 19: 1–14.

Hartl D, Mooney J and Lagoudas D 2008 Numerically implemented constitutive model for SMA applications experiencing general loads resulting in plastic deformation and large rotations. *Adaptive Structures and Intelligent Systems Conference Proceedings*, 1: 421–429.

Hartl D, Mooney J, Lagoudas D, Calkins F and Mabe J 2010c Use of a Ni60Ti shape memory alloy for active jet engine chevron application: II: experimentally validated numerical analysis. *Smart Materials and Structures*, 19: 1–18.

Hassan M, Scarpa F, Ruzzene M and Mohammed N 2008 Smart shape memory alloy chiral honeycomb. *Materials Science and Engineering A*: 481–482: 654–657.

Hutapea P, Kim J, Guion A, Hanna C and Heulitt N 2008 Development of a smart wing. *Aircraft Engineering and Aerospace Technology: An International Journal*, 80(4): 439–444.

Ikeda T, Masuda S and Ueda T 2007 Smart vortex generator transformed by change in ambient temperature and aerodynamic force. *Proceedings of SPIE*, 6525: 1–12.

Jackson C, Wagner H and Wasilewski R 1972 *55-Nitinol - The Alloy with a Memory: Its Physical Metallurgy, Properties, and Applications*. NASA Special Report NASA-SP-5110, pp. 1–86.

Jardine A, Bartley-Cho J and Flanagan J 1999 Improved design and performance of the SMA torque tube for the DARPA smart wing program. *Proceedings of SPIE*, 3674; 260–269.

Johnson A, Bokaie M and Martynov V 2008 Non-explosive releasable coupling device. US Patent 7422403.

Kudva J, Appa K, Jardine A and Martin C 1997 Overview of recent progress on the DARPA/USAF Wright Laboratory "smart materials and structures development – smart wing" program. *Proceedings of SPIE*, 3044: 24–32.

Kudva J, Martin C, Scherer L, Jardine A, McGowan A, Lake R, Sendeckyj G and Sanders B 1999 Overview of the DARPA/AFRL/NASA smart wing program. *Proceedings of SPIE*, 3674: 230–236.

Kumar P and Lagoudas D 2010 Experimental and microstructural characterization of simultaneous creep, plasticity and phase transformation of Ti50Pd40Ni10 high-temperature shape memory alloy. *Acta Materialia*, 58(5): 1618–1628.

Lagoudas D 2008 *Shape Memory Alloys*. Springer, New York.

Lagoudas D, Bo Z and Qidwai M 1996 A unified thermodynamic constitutive model for SMA and finite element analysis of active metal matrix composites. *Mechanics of Composite Materials and Structures*, 3: 153–179.

Lagoudas D and Entchev P 2004 Modeling of transformation-induced plasticity and its effect on the behavior of porous shape memory alloys. Part I: constitutive model for fully dense SMAs. *Mechanics of Materials*, 36: 865–892.

Lagoudas D, Miller D, Rong L and Kumar P 2009 Thermomechanical fatigue of shape memory alloys. *Smart Materials Structures*, 18; 1–12.

Lan X, Liu Y, Lv H, Wang X, Leng J and Du S 2009 Fiber reinforced shape-memory polymer composite and its application in a deployable hinge. *Smart Materials Structures*, 18: 1–6.

Lee I, Roh J, Yoo E, Han J and Yang S 2006 Configuration control of aerospace structures with smart materials. *Journal of Advanced Science*, 18: 1–5.

Liang C and Rogers C 1990 One-dimensional thermomechanical constitutive relations for shape memory materials. *Journal of Intelligent Material Systems and Structures*, 1: 207–234.

Mabe J 2008 Variable area jet nozzle for noise reduction using shape memory alloy actuators. *Acoustics 08* Paris: 5487–5492.

Mabe J and Ruggeri R 2006 Characterization of nickel-rich NiTinol alloys for actuator development. Paper presented at the International Conference of Shape Memory and Superelastic Technologies, May 7–11, Pacific Grove, CA.

Mabe J, Calkins F and Butler G 2006 Boeing's variable geometry chevron, morphing aerostructure for jet noise reduction. *American Institute of Aeronautics and Astronautics*, 2142: 1–19.

Mabe J, Ruggeri R, Rosenzweig E and Yu C 2004 NiTinol performance characterization and rotary actuator design. *Proceedings of SPIE*, 5386: 95–109.

Mani R, Lagoudas D and Rediniotis O 2008 Active skin for turbulent drag reduction. *Smart Material Structures*, 17.

Meng X, Cai W, Fu Y, Li Q, Zhang J and Zhao L 2008 Shape-memory behaviors in an aged Ni-rich TiNiHf high temperature shape-memory alloy. *Intermetallics*, 16: 698–705.

Meng X, Zheng Y, Wang Z and Zhao L 2000 Shape memory properties of the Ti36Ni49Hf15 high temperature shape memory alloy. *Material Letters*, 45: 128–132.

Mertmann M and Vergani G 2008 Design and application of shape memory actuators. *The European Physical Journal Special Topics*, 158: 221–230.

Miller D and Lagoudas D 2000 Thermomechanical characterization of NiTiCu and NiTi SMA actuators: influence of plastic strains. *Smart Materials Structures*, 9: 640–652.

Morgan N 2004 Medical shape memory alloy applications: the market and its products. *Materials Science and Engineering*, A378: 16–23.

Morin M and Trivero F 1995 Influence of thermal cycling on the reversible martensitic transformation in a Cu-Al-Ni shape memory alloy. *Materials Science and Engineering*, A196: 177–181.

Nolan J, Hartl D and Lagoudas D 2010 3D finite element analysis of indentation recovery due to the shape memory effect. *Proceedings of SPIE*, 7644: 1–10.

Otsuka K and Wayman C 1999 *Shape Memory Materials*. Cambridge University Press, Cambridge.

Panico M and Brinson L 2007 A three-dimensional phenomenological model for martensite reorientation in shape memory alloys. *Journal of Mechanics and Physics of Solids*, 55: 2491–2511.

Peng F, Jiang X, Hu Y and Ng A 2008 Actuation precision control of SMA actuators used for shape control of inflatable SAR antenna. *Acta Astronautica*, 63: 578–585.

Petrini L, Migliavacca F, Dubini G and Auricchio F 2003 Numerical analysis of vascular stents exploiting shape-memory-alloy behavior. Paper presented at 16th AIMETA Congress of Theoretical and Applied Mechanics 2003.

Pitt D, Dunne J and White E 2001 SAMPSON smart inlet SMA powered adaptive lip design and static test. *American Institute of Aeronautics and Astronautics*, 1359: 1–11.

Pitt D, Dunne J and White E 2002a SAMPSON smart inlet design overview and wind tunnel test part I: design overview. *Proceedings of SPIE*, 4698: 13–23.

Pitt D, Dunne J and White E 2002b SAMPSON smart inlet design overview and wind tunnel test part II: wind tunnel test. *Proceedings of SPIE*, 4698: 24–36.

Popov P and Lagoudas D 2007 A 3-D constitutive model for shape memory alloys incorporating pseudoelasticity and detwinning of self-accommodated martensite. *International Journal of Plasticity*, 23: 1679–1720.

Prahlad H and Chopra I 2007 Modeling and experimental characterization of SMA torsional actuators. *Journal of Intelligent Material Systems and Structures*, 18: 29–38.

Proft J, Melton K and Duerig T 1989 Transformational cycling of Ni-Ti and Ni-Ti-Cu shape memory alloys. *Materials Research Society*, 9: 159–164.

Qidwai M and Lagoudas D 2000 Numerical implementation of a shape memory alloy thermomechanical constitutive model using return mapping algorithms. *International Journal of Numerical Methods in Engineering*, 47: 1123–1168.

Ramrakhyani D, Lesieutre G, Frecker M and Bharti S 2005 Aircraft structural morphing using tendon- actuated compliant cellular trusses. *Journal of Aircraft*, 42(6): 1615–1621.

Rios O, Noebe R, Biles T, Garg A, Palczer A, Scheiman D, Seifert H and Kaufman M 2005 Characterization of ternary NiTiPt high-temperature shape memory alloys. *Proceedings of SPIE*, 5761: 376–387.

Roh J, Kim K and Lee I 2009 Shape adaptive airfoil actuated by a shape memory alloy and its aerodynamic characteristics. *Mechanics of Advanced Materials and Structures*, 16: 260–274.

Sanders B, Crowe R and Garcia E Defense advanced research projects agency: Smart materials and structures demonstration program overview. *Journal of Intelligent Material Systems and Structures*, 15: 227–233.

Schroeder T and Wayman C 1977 The two-way shape memory effect and other "training" phenomena in Cu-Zn single crystals. *Scripta Metallurgica*, 11: 225–230.

Seelecke S and Muller I 2004 Shape memory alloy actuators in smart structures: modeling and simulation. *Applied Mechanics Reviews*, 57(1): 23–46.

Singh K, Sirohi J and Chopra I 2003 An improved shape memory alloy actuator for rotor blade tracking. *Journal of Intelligent Material Systems and Structures*, 14: 767–786.

Sofla A, Elzey D and Wadley H 2009 Shape morphing hinged truss structures. *Smart Materials Structures*, 18: 1–8.

Song G and Ma N 2007 Robust control of a shape memory alloy wire actuated flap. *Smart Materials Structures*, 16: N51–N57.

Song G, Ma N, Lee H and Arnold S 2007 Design and control of a proof-of-concept variable area exhaust nozzle using shape-memory alloy actuators. *Smart Material Structures*, 16; 1342–1347.

Straub F, Kennedy D, Domzalski D, Hassan A, Ngo H, Anand V and Birchette T 2004 Smart material- actuated rotor technology - SMART. *Journal of Intelligent Material Systems and Structures*, 15: 249–260.

Sun H, Pathak A, Luntz J and Brei D 2008 Stabilizing shape memory alloy actuator performance through cyclic shakedown: an empirical study. *Proceedings of SPIE*, 6930: 1–11.

Sutou Y, Omori T, Wang J, Kainuma R and Ishida K 2003 Characteristics of Cu-Al-Mn-based shape memory alloys and their applications. *Materials Science and Engineering*, A378: 278–282.

Tanaka K 1986 A thermomechanical sketch of shape memory effect: One-dimensional tensile behavior. *Res Mechanica*, 18: 251–263.

Tian Q and Wu J 2003 Characterization of mechanical properties of Ti50.6Ni19.4Pd30 alloy showing different phase transformation behaviors. *Proceedings of SPIE*, 5116: 710–717.

Tian Z, Guo Z, Tan H and Wang C 2009 Wrinkling deformation control of inflatable boom by shape memory alloy. *Proceedings of SPIE*, 7493: 1–7.

Turner T 2000 A new thermoelastic model for analysis of shape memory alloy hybrid composites. *Journal of Intelligent Material Systems and Structures*, 11: 382–394.

Turner T, Buehrle R, Cano R and Fleming G 2004 Design, fabrication, and testing of SMA enabled adaptive chevrons for jet noise reduction. *Proceedings of SPIE*, 5390: 36–47.

Wang F, Buehler W and Pickart S 1965 Crystal structure and a unique "martensitic""transition of TiNi. *Journal of Applied Physics*, 36(10): 3232–3239.

Wollants P, Bonte M and Roos J 1979 A thermodynamic analysis of the stress induced martensitic transformation in a single crystal. *Z Metallkunde*, 70(2): 113–117.

Zhang X, Yan X and Yang Q 2010 Design of a quick response SMA actuated segmented nut for space release applications. *Proceedings of SPIE*, 7647: 1–9.

11

Hierarchical Control and Planning for Advanced Morphing Systems

Mrinal Kumar[1] and Suman Chakravorty[2]
[1]*University of Florida, USA*
[2]*Texas A&M University, USA*

11.1   Introduction

This chapter discusses an integrated hierarchical approach to simultaneous planning and control for morphing dynamics. Research in the field of morphing structures has seen recent surge in interest, especially with the advent of smart structures (e.g. shape memory alloys) that have made realization of shape changing structures feasible. In addition, the ever increasing demands on a single structure to accomplish a variety of mission objectives (e.g. an aircraft required to conduct both bombing and reconnaissance) has led researchers to explore the field of morphing structures in greater detail (Rodriguez 2007; Grant *et al.* 2006; Hurtado 2006; Wickenheiser and Garcia 2004). Study of morphing dynamics is in general different from the study of dynamics of the object itself, and the two may be coupled with each other. For example, flight dynamics of an aircraft is traditionally described using a twelve dimensional state-space (six translational and six rotational). On the other hand, morphing dynamics of the same aircraft is described by differential equations that govern reconfiguration of the aircraft from one shape (mode of operation) to another. These equations could include dynamics associated with smart structures used to build the wings of the reconfigurable aircraft. The objective of morphing control then is to find controllers that transform the structure from one shape to another along a best possible path based on a prescribed metric. In the majority of cases, true dynamics governing morphing is unknown because of underlying complexity. As a result, model free methods like reinforcement learning (Valasek *et al.* 2005; Lampton *et al.* 2007; Doebbler *et al.* 2005) (e.g. Q-learning) are popular for control of such systems. Reinforcement learning "learns" the best possible path to the desired goal shape by gathering information about rewards and penalties over numerous Monte Carlo episodes.

Morphing Aerospace Vehicles and Structures, First Edition. Edited by John Valasek.
© 2012 John Wiley & Sons, Ltd. Published 2012 by John Wiley & Sons, Ltd.

In this chapter, a model-based hierarchical approach for the integrated planning and control of morphing dynamics is described. All the potential target morphing states to be achieved are contained within the so-called morphing-performance envelope. The objective is to design control laws that transfer the system from one operating point in the envelope to another. The presented methodology is an integrated planning and control technique and as such, is closely related to the sequential composition methods (Burridge *et al.* 1999; Conner 2007; Conner *et al.* 2007) for deterministic systems and that of hierarchical reinforcement learning (RL) for stochastic systems (Sutton *et al.* 1999; Parr 1998; Kaebling 1993). In these methods a global control policy (for stabilization, tracking etc.), is designed by concatenating local policies that have smaller (local) domains of operation. The local policies constitute the lower level of the hierarchy and form the edges of a graph which is superimposed on the performance envelope and used as a "highway-system" to traverse inside the envelope. The best path on the graph is then found between the current and desired points, constituting the higher level of the hierarchical planning.

11.1.1 Hierarchical Control Philosophy

As briefly mentioned above, the methodology described in this chapter is hierarchical in nature, illustrated in Figure 11.1. The starting point is a performance map (shown in top right

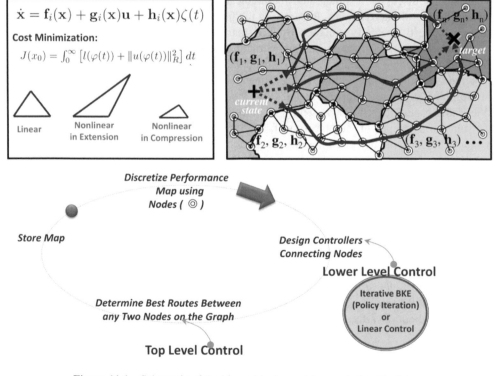

Figure 11.1 Schematic of the hierarchical morphing control methodology

section of Figure 11.1), inside which it is desired to move the system from one operating point to another. Each point inside the performance map depicts a morphing trim state where the structure is required to operate to fulfill particular mission objectives. Such a map could potentially contain a continuum or a discrete set of trim states. In either case, the objective of hierarchical control is to design controllers at multiple levels to reach a desired trim state from the current state. In general, the dynamics of morphing inside the performance map may be hybrid in nature, i.e. governed by different dynamical equations in different regions of the map (shown in Figure 11.1). In this chapter, we will consider the special case of uniform dynamics all across the performance map.

The problem as described above, is to transfer the system from its current operating trim state to a different morphing trim state on the map, possibly to accomplish a different set of mission objectives. In order to break this problem down, decision-making is divided into two levels (hence the hierarchy). The top-level of hierarchy comprises of a connected graph superimposed on the performance map. The graph acts like a highway network on which the system traverses to reach the vicinity of the target state (Figure 11.1). In other words, the presented approach ensures that the structure can morph from any state in the performance map to any other state in some sense of optimality by traversing along the nodes of a connected graph on the map. Finding the best route on this highway network to get to the desired destination constitutes the top level of the hierarchy. The nodes on the graph are connected to each other bi-directionally (i.e. if it is possible to go from node A to node B, it is also possible to go back from node B to A) by means of local controllers. These local controllers constitute the lower level of the hierarchy. In summary, the hierarchical control works in the following manner: first, a lower level local controller transfers the current morphing-state to the closest available node on the connected graph. At this point, the top level planner takes over and activates a sequence of lower level controllers to traverse the graph by following a path that minimizes a prescribed cost to arrive at the node closest to the desired trim state. The lower level control takes over again and delivers the morphing-state from the final node arrived at to the final, desired morphing trim state. The design of such hierarchical controllers must address the following three questions:

- How is the high level graph containing interconnections of local policies generated?
- How are these local policies/controllers designed?
- How are the edge costs of the higher level graph, which characterize the higher level planner, evaluated?

There exists no generic methodology to answer these three questions and most methods mentioned above provide solutions to particular applications. In this chapter, a method is provided for automating the solution of the integrated planning/control problem for the class of morphing dynamical systems. Answers to the key questions above are provided by: (1) designing the local policies by leveraging optimal linear controllers that are designed to robustly operate near certain nodes/landmark/trim states of the system; (2) automating the graph construction on the global domain using these nodes through a novel recursive algorithm such that every point in the morphing space is reachable; and (3) using the optimal costs obtained from the local linear designs to specify the edge costs of the graph resulting from step 2, to facilitate planning at the higher discrete level.

The end result of hierarchical planning/control design is a hybrid control system (Branicky 1995, 1998), or more accurately, a switched linear system in our case (Sun and Ge 2005; Bemporad and Morari 1999; Leonessa *et al.* 2001). Typically such systems can show very complicated behavior even when the component systems are essentially very simple and well understood. Thus, control of such systems is a difficult problem and substantial research in recent years has concentrated on solving the control problem (Sun and Ge 2005). This chapter presents a particular instance of such hybrid control systems in which, due to the switching strategy that is used between nodes encoded in the discrete higher level graph, the problems of stability do not arise as in more generic hybrid systems. Essentially, the stability of the local control systems assures the global stability because of the switching strategy that is enforced on the system. One must also note here the connection to linear parameter varying (LPV) (Leith and Leithead 2000; Rugh and Shamma 2000) and the state dependent Ricatti equation (SDRE) (Cloutier 1997; Hammett *et al.* 1998) based control of nonlinear systems. In these methods, the nonlinear plant is represented in a linear form dependent on an external parameter (as in the case of LPV) or the state of the system (as in SDREs). A stabilizing controller is then found by either solving a family of parameter dependent LMIs or a family of state dependent Riccati equations. However, there is no "planning" involved in these controllers, i.e., they do not tell us where to go next in the context of the morphing problem. Thus, the difference between the approach presented here and the above-mentioned methods is the hierarchical nature of the planner/controller and in particular, the discrete higher level decision-maker in the hierarchical controller while using standard LQ techniques for the design of the lower level controllers.

11.2 Morphing Dynamics and Performance Maps

In this section, mathematical definitions for the various concepts involved in this chapter are presented and the framework for building the hierarchical control strategy is set up. In view of simplicity, we will consider the following deterministic dynamical model for morphing dynamics:

$$\dot{\mathbf{x}} = \mathbf{f}(\mathbf{x}, \mathbf{u}); \quad \mathbf{x} \in \Re^N, \quad \mathbf{u} \in \Re^M \tag{11.1}$$

where, $\mathbf{x}$ depicts the morphing state of the structure. An example is shown in Figure 11.2(a), comprising a triangle with a fixed base. The other two sides change their lengths and are modeled with spring-damper assemblies. The lengths of the morphing sides along with their time derivatives $(x_1, x_2, \dot{x}_1, \dot{x}_2)$ constitute the morphing state in Equation 11.1 for this structure. The vertex is prescribed to move inside the rectangular region shown, which defines the performance map for this structure. Therefore, the performance map for this structure in defined on the subspace (x_1, x_2).

In general, the performance map, $\mathcal{M}$ of a morphing system is prescribed on a subspace of the morphing state in the following manner:

$$\mathcal{M} \triangleq \{(x_1, x_2, \ldots x_n) \subset \Re^n\}; \quad n \leq N$$
$$\text{e.g., } (x_1, x_2, \ldots x_n) \in [a_1, b_1] \times [a_2, b_2] \times \ldots [a_n, b_n] \tag{11.2}$$

The problem of optimal morphing control can then be posed in the following manner: For the system given by Equation 11.1, design an optimal controller that transfers the system from

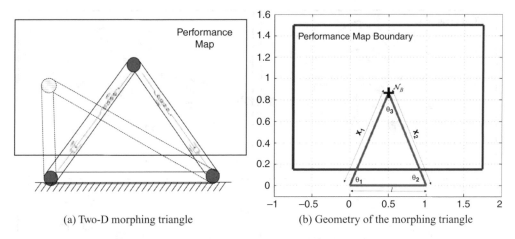

(a) Two-D morphing triangle

(b) Geometry of the morphing triangle

Figure 11.2 A simple morphing structure modeled with nonlinear oscillators

an initial morphing state of $\mathbf{x}_s$ to a target morphing state, $\mathbf{x}_t$, minimizing in the process the following cost function along the path:

$$J = \int_0^\infty (\mathbf{x}^T Q \mathbf{x} + \mathbf{u}^T R \mathbf{u}) dt \tag{11.3}$$

The above problem can be solved in a suboptimal manner by constructing a connected graph, $\mathcal{G}$ on the performance map $\mathcal{M}$, that provides bi-directional access between all points on the map.

11.2.1 Discretization of Performance Maps via Graphs

The hierarchical approach builds its foundation on a discrete graph that is laid upon the performance map of the morphing structure. All points on the performance map can be made accessible from every other point via this graph. In general, there can be many ways of constructing this graph. Here, two methods are described: first, a method in which considerable manual input from the user is required and another which can be completely automated and is amenable to discretization of high dimensional performance maps.

11.2.1.1 Graph Construction: Method 1

This section describes the first of two graph construction techniques described in this chapter. The basic idea is to initialize the graph with a base node and then expand outward by constructing a nested sequence of envelopes of accessible regions. These envelopes are denoted by Ω_i, $i = 1 \ldots Q$. The last constructed envelope is such that it engulfs the performance map, i.e. $\mathcal{M} \in \Omega_Q$, thus making almost all points accessible (Figure 11.3). Let us begin with the definition of the *region of influence* (ROI) of a node on the graph.

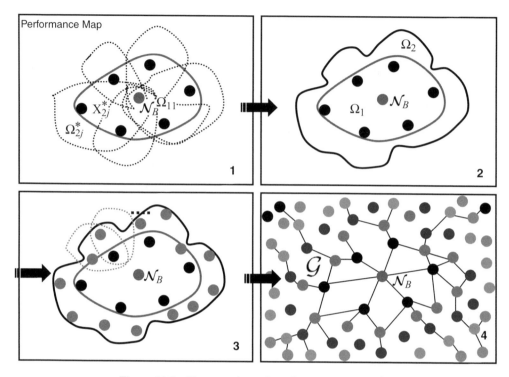

Figure 11.3   The procedure of graph construction on $\mathcal{M}$

Definition 11.1. ***Bi-reachable points:***   *Points* **x** *and* **y** *are said to be bi-reachable from each other if* **y** *can be reached from* **x** *and vice versa using (in general different) linear controllers. (e.g. LQR-based design)*

Definition 11.2. ***Region of Influence*** *of node* $\mathbf{x}_{ij}^*$:   *The region of influence of a node* $\mathbf{x}_{ij}^*$ *on the graph* $\mathcal{G}$ *is defined as the set* Ω_{ij}^* *such all pairs* $\{(\mathbf{x}_{ij}^*, \mathbf{y}), \mathbf{y} \in \Omega_{ij}^*\}$ *are bi-reachable.*

The nomenclature used above for nodes belonging to the graph, namely $\mathbf{x}_{ij}^*$, will become clearer in what follows. The double subscript "$_{ij}$" means the following: ode $\mathbf{x}_{ij}^*$ is the jth node of the ith envelope constructed on the map. Below, a step-by-step procedure for constructing the graph $\mathcal{G}$ on the map $\mathcal{M}$ is laid out. We must first, however, state the following assumptions about the morphing dynamical system:

$\mathcal{A}$ **11.1.** *There exists finite steady state control* $\mathbf{u}^{hold}(\mathbf{x})$ *for almost all* $\mathbf{x} \in \mathfrak{R}^N$ *such that* $\mathbf{f}(\mathbf{x}, \mathbf{u}^{hold}) = \mathbf{0}$. *The set for which the holding control does not exist (call it* Φ*) has measure zero.*

$\mathcal{A}$ **11.2.** *The gradient of the dynamics, i.e.* $\frac{\partial \mathbf{f}}{\partial \mathbf{x}}$ *exists so that the system 1 can be linearized to* $(\mathbf{A}(\mathbf{x}), \mathbf{B}(\mathbf{x}))$ *for almost all* $\mathbf{x} \in \mathcal{M}$.

$\mathcal{A}$ **11.3.** *The domain of reachability,* $\mathcal{R}(\mathbf{x})$, *of any point* $\mathbf{x} \in \mathfrak{R}^N|\Phi$ *is connected. Additionally, there exists an open set* $\vartheta \subset \mathfrak{R}^N$ *such that* $\vartheta \subset \mathcal{R}(\mathbf{x})$.

The set Φ represents points that are not reachable in the morphing system 1. This chapter is only concerned with systems for which this set has zero measure and thus excluded from analysis. Assumption 11.1 can be relaxed in practice to perform the analysis for only the reachable points inside $\mathcal{M}$. Assumption 11.2 restricts the realm of the described approach to those systems for which a linearized representation can be found for almost all points (excluding sets of zero measure) inside the performance map. Assumption 11.3 is essential for the present approach for determining regions of influence. Note that $\mathcal{R}(\mathbf{x})$ is different from ROI($\mathbf{x}$). From definition 11.2, it is clear that ROI($\mathbf{x}$) $\subset \mathcal{R}(\mathbf{x})$. A parametric-sweep approach will be utilized for determining ROI($\mathbf{x}$) which would formally work for systems satisfying assumption 11.3.

Given the validity of the above assumptions, the following result can be stated:

Theorem 11.1.   *For the morphing system 1 with a continuous performance map, $\mathcal{M}$, given assumptions 2.1, 2.2 and 2.3, a connected graph, $\mathcal{G}$, can be constructed on $\mathcal{M}$ with a finite number of nodes, $\{\mathbf{x}_{ij}^*\}$ ($\sum_{i,j} = P$) such that all points $\mathbf{y}_t \in \mathcal{M}$ can be reached from any other point $\mathbf{y}_s \in \mathcal{M}$ to within a specified tolerance, i.e., $\|\mathbf{x}(t = \infty, \mathbf{y}_s) - \mathbf{y}_t\| \le \epsilon$ by traversing $\mathcal{G}$.*

The following steps outline the procedure for graph construction and also serve as a constructive proof for the above theorem. As mentioned previously, the basic idea is to construct a sequence of expanding envelopes, Ω_i, $i = 1 \ldots Q$ that eventually engulfs the map $\mathcal{M}$, i.e. $\mathcal{M} \in \Omega_Q$. Figure 11.3 illustrates this process.

1. Graph construction begins with the base node. This node represents the most likely trim-state of the morphing dynamics, and is denoted by $\mathcal{N}_B$ in Figure 11.3. For the morphing triangle, this represents the equilateral-triangle configuration. (see Figure 11.2(b)) Denote this node by $\mathbf{x}_{ij}^* = \mathbf{x}_{11}^*$.
2. Estimate the region of influence of this node. This is done by performing a parametric sweep of the boundary of the performance map and determining the farthest point that is bi-reachable for each value of the parameter set. (see definition 11.1 of bi-reachability) A parametric representation is thus obtained for the boundary of the region of reachability by joining the farthest bi-reachable points. Figure 11.4(a) illustrates this process for a two-dimensional map. In this figure, a rough estimate of the region of influence of the shown node has been obtained by utilizing a single parameter (θ) sweep with 6 points. The farthest points bi-reachable from the node for each value of the sweeping parameter have been joined to obtain the region of influence. In general, an N dimensional performance map would require a parameter set of $(N - 1)$ independent parameters. The farthest point for any particular value of the parameter set is estimated by the process of successive LQR (Figure 11.4(b)). In this process, progressively closer points are chosen (in Figure 11.4(b) by bisection) until a bi-reachable point is obtained. Note that this approach requires the validity of assumption 11.3 for an accurate estimate of ROI($\mathbf{x}_{ij}^*$). The sweeping process results in the boundary of ROI($\mathbf{x}_{ij}^*$), namely, Γ_{ij}^*. Also note that ROI($\mathbf{x}_{ij}^*$) is referred to as Ω_{ij}^*. The first in the sequence of envelopes, Ω_1 is simply the ROI of the base node, i.e. $\Omega_1 = \Omega_{ij}^*$.
3. Discretize Γ_{ij}^* by placing nodes as shown in Figure 11.3. These nodes form the base for constructing the next envelope and we denote them by $\mathbf{x}_{2j}^*$, where $j = 1, 2, \ldots R$. (number of nodes used to discretize Γ_1)

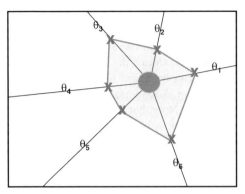

(a) Parametric sweep on a two dimensional performance map

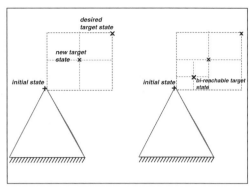

(b) Successive LQR approach to determine bi-reachable pairs

Figure 11.4 Determining the region of influence for a node on the graph

4. Determine the ROI's for $\mathbf{x}^*_{2j}$, i.e. Ω^*_{2j}.
5. Determine the new envelope as $\Omega_2 = \cup^R_{i=1} \Omega^*_{2j} \cup \Omega_1$. Denote boundary $(\Omega_2) = \Gamma_2$. Note from Figure 11.3 that the construction results in a sequence of nested envelopes $\Omega_2 \subset \Omega_1$. The process is repeated until Q envelopes are generated so that the final envelope engulfs the performance map: $\mathcal{M} \subset \Omega_Q$. The entire set of nodes used in this construction constitutes the graph and is seen in Figure 11.3.

Step 3 in the above algorithm can be manually intensive and require input from the user. This becomes increasingly difficult as the dimensionality of the performance map grows. For high dimensional scenarios, an alternate technique is therefore desired, one which may be fully automated. The section below describes one such method, based on the use of pseudo-random numbers.

11.2.1.2 Graph Construction Method 2: Pseudo Random Graphs

This section describes an alternate method of graph construction based on pseudo random numbers. Dimensionality of the performance map can become a serious issue in the graph construction method described in the previous section. In dimensions three and higher, it is very difficult to manually place nodes to discretize the envelopes in step 3. Instead, pseudo random sampling can be used to construct a connected graph to cover the entire performance map efficiently with no manual input. Pseudo random numbers have been widely used to sample real spaces for the purpose of numerical integration. They are generated using an algorithm, with the particular algorithm used determining the variety of psuedo random numbers obtained, e.g. Halton pseudo random numbers, Sobol numbers, Fauvre numbers, etc. A pseudo random sequence, even though algorithmically generated, gives the appearance of having a uniform random distribution over the sampled region (hence the qualification "pseudo"). The actual separation of the sample from a true uniform distribution is typically quantified using certain discrepancy parameters (Niederreiter 1992). In the present context, they can be utilized to

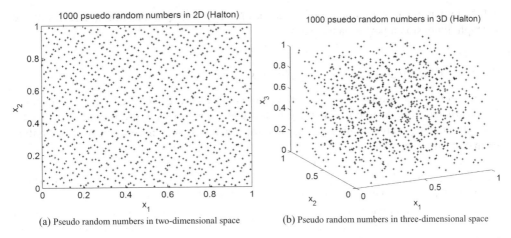

(a) Pseudo random numbers in two-dimensional space   (b) Pseudo random numbers in three-dimensional space

Figure 11.5   Examples of pseudo random numbers (halton sequence) in two- and three-dimensional spaces

uniformly distribute nodes on the performance map which can be connected to construct the graph of interest. Examples of pseudo random distributions (Halton sequence) in two and three dimensions are shown in Figure 11.5. It is also important to note that it is very easy to locally sample pseudo random points if the density in a certain area is low. Additionally, it is also easy to generate high dimensional pseudo random numbers, thus making them suitable to high dimensional performance maps. The following steps briefly outline the graph construction procedure:

1. Let the dimensionality of the performance map be n, i.e. $\mathcal{M} \subset \mathfrak{R}^n$. Generate a total of P_0 n dimensional pseudo random numbers $\mathbf{x}_i \in \mathcal{M}, i = 1, \dots P_0$. The number P_0 is the starting guess for the total number of nodes in the graph $\mathcal{G}$. The nodes $\mathbf{x}_i, i = 1, \dots P_0$ form the initial estimate of the graph (currently not connected).
2. For each $i = 1, 2, \dots, P$, do the following
   (a) Consider a n dimensional box $\mathcal{M}_o \subset \mathcal{M}$ whose volume is a small percentage (perhaps 5%) of the volume of $\mathcal{M}$. Translate the box such that the current node ($\mathbf{x}_i$) is its centroid. Find all the nodes lying inside $\mathbf{M}_o$, labeling them $\mathbf{x}_{ij}, j = 1, 2, \dots Q_i$, the potential neighbors of $\mathbf{x}_i$.
   (b) Attempt to design controllers (the type of controller is up to the user, e.g. LQR) to transfer the system from $\mathbf{x}_i$ to $\mathbf{x}_{ij}$ and back from $\mathbf{x}_{ij}$ to $\mathbf{x}_i$. In other words, determine which points out of $\mathbf{x}_{ij}$ are bi-directionally connected to $\mathbf{x}_i$. If this set is not empty, move to the next point, i.e. $i \to i + 1$ and go back to step 2, otherwise go to the next step.
   (c) (If node $\mathbf{x}_i$ does not have any bi-directional neighbors.) Resample the box $\mathcal{M}_o$ with a small number of pseudo random points to increase node density and re-do step 2(b). Record the bi-directional neighbors for node $\mathbf{x}_i$.

Given the validity of assumptions 11.1–11.3, the above steps guarantee the construction of a connected graph on $\mathcal{M}$ such that all points inside it are reachable from every other point in

$\mathcal{M}$. Note that the above sequence of steps does not require any manual input and is suitable for high dimensional performance maps.

11.2.2   Planning on Morphing Graphs

In this section, the top level of the hierarchical control strategy is described. Once is graph is constructed, it is desired to know the best routes on it from any given node to any other node. Depending on the number of nodes on the graph, this search may be performed online or may need to be offline and stored away for future access. There are numerous techniques in the literature that may be used to search for optimal paths on a graph. Here, we describe a two-level A^* algorithm for this purpose. Note that the objective here is not to find a path of shortest "distance," but one of least cost which is defined based on the design of the lower level controllers used to connect the nodes on the graph with each other. This cost may be related to a time parameter or fuel expense or something else. The problem therefore is to find a path connecting two nodes on the graph along which this particular cost of interest is minimized.

Standard A^* algorithms work well for path-planning applications where it is needed to find a minimum-distance path between any two points on the graph. The performance of the A^* algorithm hinges on a heuristic function that estimates the cost-to-go from the current node to the destination node. In order to guarantee convergence to the optimal path, it is required (though not always) that the heuristic function *under*-estimate the cost-to-go from the current node. Such a heuristic function is said to be admissible. For a problem that seeks to find the minimum distance path, it is easy to find an admissible heuristic function, simply as the Euclidean distance between the concerned points. In the current application however, it is required to find an optimal path based on the metric given in Equation 11.3 (or any other prescribed cost on the basis of which the local, low level controllers are based). We note that it is extremely difficult to find an admissible heuristic function for such an arbitrary cost function. The two-level A^* search described below takes care of this problem and generates a feasible heuristic function. Such a function ensures convergence, but not necessarily to the optimal path because it does not always provide an under-estimate of the cost-to-go. The two-level A^* is described in the next section.

11.2.2.1   Two-Level A^*

Problem statement: Given graph $\mathcal{G}$, find the optimal path from node $\mathbf{x}_o$ to $\mathbf{x}_f$. Two-level algorithm:

- **Let** $\mathcal{OL}$ be the current open-list of the search. Open-list is the collection of points that have already been visited but not expanded (explored) yet.
- **Define** auxiliary heuristic cost, $\tilde{h}(\mathbf{x}) = \|\mathbf{x}_f - \mathbf{x}\|$. This is simply the Euclidean distance cost for which the standard A^* algorithm works well.
- For each $\mathbf{x}_k \in \mathcal{OL}$, **run** the A^* algorithm to determine the optimal path from $\mathbf{x}_k$ to $\mathbf{x}_f$ using the auxiliary heuristic function, $\tilde{h}(\mathbf{x})$. Let the obtained path for $\mathbf{x}_k$ be $\mathcal{P}_k = \{\mathbf{x}_k, \mathbf{x}_{k1}, \mathbf{x}_{k2}, \ldots, \mathbf{x}_f\}$.
- **Determine** the heuristic cost for the node $\mathbf{x}_k$ as:

$$h(\mathbf{x}_k) = \int_{\mathcal{P}_k} (\mathbf{x}^{\mathrm{T}} Q \mathbf{x} + \mathbf{u}^{\mathrm{T}} R \mathbf{u}) dt \qquad (11.4)$$

- Using $h(\mathbf{x}_k)$ as the heuristic function, determine the lowest cost node to remove from the open-list and add to the closed-list, $\mathcal{CL}$.
- Continue until $\mathbf{x}_f \in \mathcal{CL}$.

The above algorithm results in a sequence of nodes connecting $\mathbf{x}_o$ to $\mathbf{x}_f$ which may be stored away for each such pair in the graph for future reference.

11.3   Application to Advanced Morphing Structures

In this section, example problems will be considered to illustrate the hierarchical control technique described above. The first example considered is a morphing triangle with a fixed base, shown in Figure 11.2(a). The geometry of the structure is further detailed in Figure 11.2(b). The base of the triangle is fixed while the other two sides change lengths by means of spring-damper assemblies. There are two controllers, exerting axial forces along the two morphing sides of the triangle. Both sides are assumed to be massless and the entire mass of the structure, m, is modeled to be concentrated at the vertex. The nonlinear morphing dynamics for this model essentially comprises of two coupled second-order oscillators. Consider the exploded view of the triangle shown in Figure 11.6. The inertial frame ($\mathcal{I}$) and two body frames ($\mathcal{B}_1$, $\mathcal{B}_2$) are used. We have the following kinematic equations for the position vector of the point mass, m:

$$\mathbf{r} = x_1 \hat{\mathbf{p}}_1,$$

$$\dot{\mathbf{r}} = \dot{x}_1 \hat{\mathbf{p}}_1 + x_1 \dot{\theta}_1 \hat{\mathbf{q}}_1, \quad \text{and}$$

$$\ddot{\mathbf{r}} = (\ddot{x}_1 - x_1 \dot{\theta}_1^2) \hat{\mathbf{p}}_1 + (2\dot{x}_1 \dot{\theta}_1 + x_1 \ddot{\theta}_1) \hat{\mathbf{q}}_1 \tag{11.5}$$

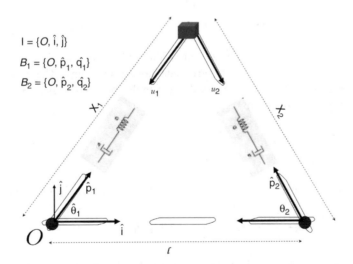

Figure 11.6   Exploded view of the morphing triangle

The spring/damper forces and the controls can be expressed as:

$$\mathbf{F} = \underbrace{[k_1(x_1) + c_1(x_1, \dot{x}_1) + u_1]}_{f_1}(-\hat{\mathbf{p}}_1) + \underbrace{[k_2(x_2) + c_2(x_2, \dot{x}_2) + u_2]}_{f_2}(-\cos\theta_3\hat{\mathbf{p}}_1 - \sin\theta_3\hat{\mathbf{q}}_1)$$

$$(11.6)$$

Consideration of geometrical constraints for the triangular structure leads to following the equations relating the angular rates, $\dot{\theta}_1$ and $\ddot{\theta}_1$ to the morphing states:

$$\dot{\theta}_1 = \frac{1}{lx_1 \sin\theta_1}(x_2\dot{x}_2 + l\dot{x}_1\cos\theta_1 - x_1\dot{x}_1)$$

$$\ddot{\theta}_1 = -\frac{1}{x_1}\left[x_1\dot{\theta}_1^2 - \frac{f_1 + u_1 + (f_2 + u_2)\cos\theta_3}{m}\right] \qquad (11.7)$$

We are thus lead to the equations for morphing-dynamics in state-space form:

$$\dot{x}_1 = x_3$$

$$\dot{x}_2 = x_4$$

$$\dot{x}_3 = x_1\dot{\theta}_1^2 + \frac{1}{m}[f_1 + u_1 + (f_2 + u_2)\cos\theta_3]$$

$$\dot{x}_4 = \frac{1}{x_2}[\dot{x}_1^2 - \dot{x}_2^2 + (x_1 - l\cos\theta_1)\dot{x}_3 + 2l\dot{x}_1\dot{\theta}_1\sin\theta_1 + lx_1\dot{\theta}_1^2\cos\theta_1 + lx_1\ddot{\theta}_1\sin\theta_1] \qquad (11.8)$$

The various trigonometric functions appearing in Equations 11.7 and 11.8 can be obtained easily in terms of the states, x_1 and x_2. Finally, the nonlinear spring-damper forces can be modeled with the following constitutive equations: (there can be numerous other constitutive laws)

$$f_1 = k_{1l}(x_1 - l) + k_{1nl}(x_1 - l)^3 + c_{1l}\dot{x}_1 + c_{1nl}x_1\dot{\theta}_1$$

$$f_2 = k_{2l}(x_2 - l) + k_{2nl}(x_2 - l)^3 + c_{2l}\dot{x}_2 + c_{2nl}x_2\dot{\theta}_2 \qquad (11.9)$$

In order to implement the successive LQR algorithm, it is required to linearize the dynamics (Equation 11.8) about the current steady state condition (trim). The following are the linearized equations of motion for the morphing triangle about a trim state, $\mathbf{x}_{ss}$: (all subscripts 'ss' denote steady state conditions)

$$\delta\dot{x}_1 = \delta x_3$$

$$\delta\dot{x}_2 = \delta x_4$$

$$\delta\dot{x}_3 = -\frac{1}{m}[\delta f_1 + \delta u_1 + \cos\theta_{3ss}(\delta f_2 + \delta u_2) - \sin\theta_{3ss}(f_{2ss} + u_{2ss})\delta\theta_3]$$

$$\delta\dot{x}_4 = \frac{x_{1ss} - l\cos\theta_{1ss}}{x_{2ss}}\delta\dot{x}_3 + l\frac{x_{1ss}}{x_{2ss}}\sin\theta_{1ss}\delta\ddot{\theta}_1 \qquad (11.10)$$

where, $\theta_3 = \pi - (\theta_1 + \theta_2)$. The linearized equations for the angles and their rates used above are given by:

$$\delta\theta_1 = \frac{-1}{lx_{1ss}\sin\theta_{1ss}}[(x_{1ss} - l\cos\theta_{1ss})\delta x_1 - x_{2ss}\delta x_2]$$

$$\delta\theta_2 = \frac{-1}{lx_{2ss}\sin\theta_{2ss}}[(x_{2ss} - l\cos\theta_{2ss})\delta x_2 - x_{1ss}\delta x_1], \quad \delta\theta_3 = -(\delta\theta_1 + \delta\theta_2)$$

$$\delta\dot{\theta}_1 = \frac{1}{lx_{1ss}\sin\theta_{1ss}}[x_{2ss}\delta x_2 + (l\cos\theta_{1ss} - x_{1ss})]\delta x_3$$

$$\delta\ddot{\theta}_1 = \frac{-1}{mx_{1ss}}[(f_{2ss} + u_{2ss})\cos\theta_{3ss}\delta\theta_3 + \sin\theta_{3ss}(\delta f_2 + \delta u_2)] \tag{11.11}$$

It is easy to obtain the departure values for the forces, i.e., δf_1 and δf_2 in terms of the morphing-states from Equation 11.9. Since it is required to transfer the morphing-state from one trim to another, the problem at hand is one of non-zero set point regulation; wherein, it is desired to obtain a non-zero steady-state value for the departure state. We will now look at that problem. The linearized equations above can be assembled into linear state-space form as $\delta\dot{\mathbf{x}} = \mathbf{A}\delta\mathbf{x} + \mathbf{B}\delta u$. Let the desired steady-state value of the departure motion be $\delta\mathbf{x}^*$. Then we perform the following transformation of coordinates:

$$\delta\tilde{\mathbf{x}} \triangleq \delta\mathbf{x} - \delta\mathbf{x}^*$$

$$\delta\tilde{u} \triangleq \delta u - \delta u^* \tag{11.12}$$

The steady-state condition requires that: $\mathbf{A}\delta\mathbf{x}^* + \mathbf{B}\delta u^* = \mathbf{0}$. The transformed equations then reduce to:

$$\delta\dot{\tilde{\mathbf{x}}} = \mathbf{A}\delta\mathbf{x} + \mathbf{B}\delta u - \mathbf{A}\delta\mathbf{x}^* - \mathbf{B}\delta u^* = \mathbf{A}\delta\tilde{\mathbf{x}} + \mathbf{B}\delta\tilde{u} \tag{11.13}$$

Note that the above transformation reduces the problem to the standard regulator problem, in which it is desired to obtain $\lim_{t\to\infty}\delta\tilde{\mathbf{x}} = \mathbf{0}$. The standard LQR solution to this problem is given by $\delta\tilde{u} = -\mathbf{K}\delta\tilde{\mathbf{x}}$. It remains to find δu^*. To this end, we exploit the steady-state condition and note that:

$$\delta\mathbf{x}^* = \begin{Bmatrix} \delta x_1^* \\ \delta x_2^* \\ 0 \\ 0 \end{Bmatrix}; \quad \delta u^* = \begin{Bmatrix} \delta u_1^* \\ \delta u_2^* \end{Bmatrix}; \quad \mathbf{A} = \begin{bmatrix} 0 & 0 & 1 & 0 \\ 0 & 0 & 0 & 1 \\ \times & \times & \times & \times \\ \times & \times & \times & \times \end{bmatrix}; \quad \mathbf{B} = \begin{bmatrix} 0 & 0 \\ 0 & 0 \\ \times & \times \\ \times & \times \end{bmatrix};$$

$$\therefore \mathbf{A}\delta\mathbf{x}^* + \mathbf{B}\delta u^* = \mathbf{0} \Rightarrow \begin{Bmatrix} 0 \\ 0 \\ c_1 \\ c_2 \end{Bmatrix} + \left\{ \begin{bmatrix} 0 \\ 0 \\ b_1 & b_2 \\ b_3 & b_4 \end{bmatrix} \begin{Bmatrix} \delta u_1^* \\ \delta u_2^* \end{Bmatrix} \right\} = \begin{Bmatrix} 0 \\ 0 \\ 0 \\ 0 \end{Bmatrix} \tag{11.14}$$

It is easy to obtain a solution for the steady-state control δu^* from the above equation.

11.3.1 Morphing Graph Construction

The graph construction for the morphing triangle begins with the base node shown in Figure 11.2(b) which represents the equilateral triangle configuration. As outlined in the algorithm

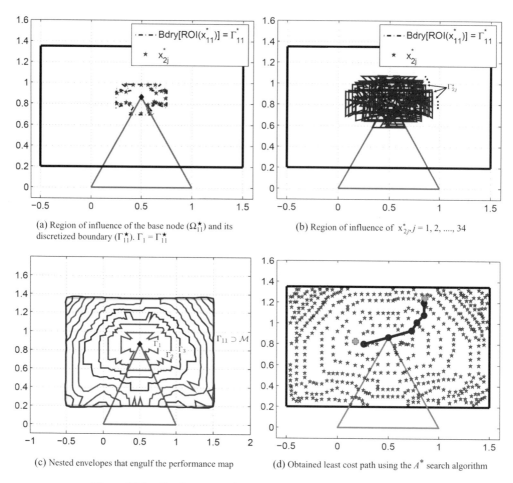

(a) Region of influence of the base node (Ω_{11}^*) and its discretized boundary (Γ_{11}^*). $\Gamma_1 = \Gamma_{11}^*$

(b) Region of influence of $x_{2j}^*, j = 1, 2, ..., 34$

(c) Nested envelopes that engulf the performance map

(d) Obtained least cost path using the A^* search algorithm

Figure 11.7 Graph construction and search for the morphing triangle

above, starting with the base node, we construct a graph that grows outward, eventually engulfing the performance map defined by the limits on the movement of the vertex. Figure 11.7 depicts this process. In Figure 11.7(a), the domain of the influence of the base node is shown. By construction, all points inside this region are accessible from the base node, and vice versa; i.e., the base node is bi-reachable with all points inside this region. Following the nomenclature in the algorithm, the depicted region is $\Omega_{11}^* = \Omega_1$. The shown boundary is $\Gamma_{11}^* = \Gamma_1$. Figure 11.7(a) shows the discretization of Γ_1 using 34 points ($= x_{2j}^*$). The domains of influence for these nodes ($= \Omega_{2j}^*$) are shown in Figure 11.7(b). Figure 11.7(c). shows that continuing with this process results in a set of expanding nested envelopes which eventually engulf $\mathcal{M}$. ($\mathcal{M} \subset \Omega_{11}$) Figure 11.7(d) shows all the nodes that comprise the graph $\mathcal{G}$ on $\mathcal{M}$. Also on this figure is shown the solved problem of finding an optimal path between two nodes. A two-level A^* algorithm was used to find this path.

A sample solution of the above algorithm is shown in Figure 11.7(d). Note that the heuristic cost evaluated for x_k in Equation 11.4 over the minimum distance path, $\mathcal{P}$, is not necessarily an

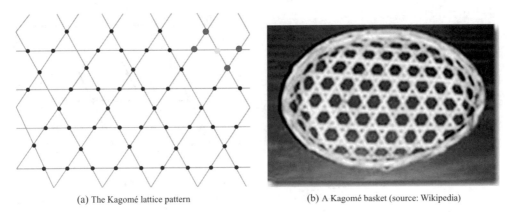

(a) The Kagomé lattice pattern   (b) A Kagomé basket (source: Wikipedia)

Figure 11.8   The Kagomé lattice

underestimate of the actual cost-to-go from x_k. Therefore, $h(x)$ is not admissible, only feasible. In the authors' experience, the results obtained from this approach have been extremely good, with no convergence issues.

11.3.2   Introduction to the Kagomé Truss

In this section, advanced morphing structural concepts using the Kagomé truss are briefly discussed. Kagomé, which literally means "a basket with eyes," ("kago" = basket, "me" = eyes) is a traditional Japanese weaving pattern, shown in Figure 11.8. Note from the highlighted nodes in Figure 11.8(a) that for any node on the lattice, there are four neighboring nodes.

The first paper on this subject was published in 1951 by Japanese physicist Itiro Syôzi. There have been numerous papers written on the Kagomé lattice, particularly in the structures community. The structure has emerged as being capable of bearing large passive loads at an extremely low weight (Hutchinson *et al.* 2003; dos Santos e Lucato *et al.* 2004). The use of the associated Kagomé truss has not been fully explored in the aerospace community. The authors believe that the superior load bearing capacity of the Kagomé truss can be utilized to great advantage for problems in aerospace engineering. In this section, a morphing structure based on the Kagomé truss from dos Santos e Lucato *et al.* (2004) is adapted and used to illustrate the the hierarchical control methodology. Figure 11.9(a) illustrates a morphing structure mounted on a Kagomé truss. The Kagomé truss (marked with broken lines) constitutes the base of the structure and comprises of morphing elements. A tetrahedral core (shown with solid lines) is mounted on top of the base and consists of non-morphing elements. In other words, the legs of the tetrahedral core are fixed in length. A face-plate (shown as a shaded surface atop the tetrahedral core) is attached to the core at the vertices of the tetrahedra, and it forms the outer surface of the morphing structure. This could be the outer surface of a wing. The desired shape of the face-plate is obtained by morphing the Kagomé truss (at the base) alone. Changing the lengths of the sides of the Kagomé truss causes the vertices of the various tetrahedra to move up or down, in turn moving the face-plate to the desired shape. Such a structure provides great flexibility and a wide range of attainable shapes. Figure 11.10 shows a possible wing morphing application using the Kagomé truss structure, wherein the top-surface of a symmetric wing is morphed into a wing with large camber.

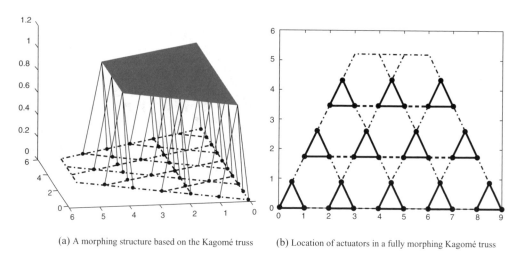

(a) A morphing structure based on the Kagomé truss   (b) Location of actuators in a fully morphing Kagomé truss

Figure 11.9   Details of the Kagomé truss

A great advantage of using the Kagomé truss to morph the face-plate is that the underlying morphing control problem is a two-dimensional structure (the Kagomé truss). All we need is a transformation describing the lengths of the Kagomé truss elements as a function of the heights of the various tetrahedral vertices. Figure 11.11 illustrates the details of such a transformation. Consider an isolated element of the Kagomé base shown in Figure 11.11(a). All the elements of the tetrahedral core are assumed to have the same length. It is desired that the vertex of the lower tetrahedron be at the position marked by the diamond. Top and side views are shown. The problem then is to determine what the new lengths of the triangle should be in order for the vertex to be located at the desired location. It turns out that this problem has a non-unique solution, shown in Figure 11.11(b). The locus of solutions is the circle drawn by the individual legs of the tetrahedron on the plane of the Kagomé truss. Since all three legs are assumed to have the same lengths, they all describe the same circle, centered at the projection of the desired vertex location on the base plane. The solution then is to simply move the vertices of the base triangle onto a point on the circle, as shown in Figure 11.11(b), leading to the new configuration on the base triangle (shown with broken lines). The non-uniqueness comes form the fact that the user the free to move the base triangle vertices to any point on this

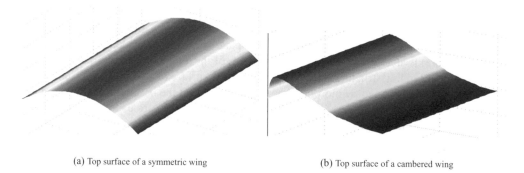

(a) Top surface of a symmetric wing   (b) Top surface of a cambered wing

Figure 11.10   Wing morphing using the face-plate atop a Kagomé truss assembly

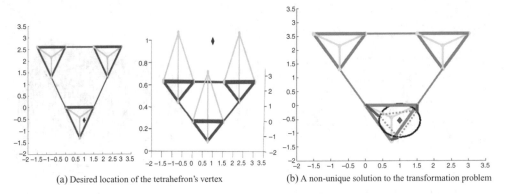

(a) Desired location of the tetrahefron's vertex　　　(b) A non-unique solution to the transformation problem

Figure 11.11　The problem of transformation of the tetrahedron-vertex location to the configuration of the base triangle

circle. A possible strategy could be to move the vertices to the closest respective points on the circle. This then becomes the equivalent morphing problem to obtain the desired position of the vertex. Note that in case the legs of the tetrahedron are of different lengths, there would be three concentric circles of different radii and it would be required to move the three vertices of the triangle to the appropriate circles.

11.3.3　Examples of Morphing with the Kagomé Truss

In this section, morphing examples are considered for the Kagomé truss structure. The first involves a constrained structure in which the morphing elements of the Kagomé base are the same as the morphing triangle shown in Figure 11.6 with fixed bases. A single Kagomé unit is extracted and the three triangular shapes shown in Figure 11.12 morph independently of each other. The desired shape of the face-plate is shown in Figure 11.12(b). Only the final result is shown here, including the final shape of the individual triangles. More complex morphing shapes can be achieved with the Kagomé truss if all three sides of the triangular units are allowed to morph. In this chapter, only an initial description of this problem is given and more detailed analysis is currently under investigation. Figure 11.9(b) illustrates the location

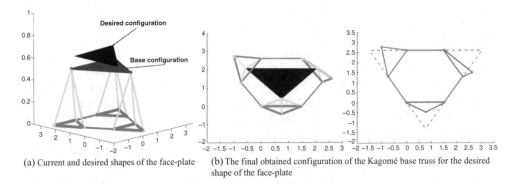

(a) Current and desired shapes of the face-plate　　(b) The final obtained configuration of the Kagomé base truss for the desired shape of the face-plate

Figure 11.12　An example morphing problem using the Kagomé truss

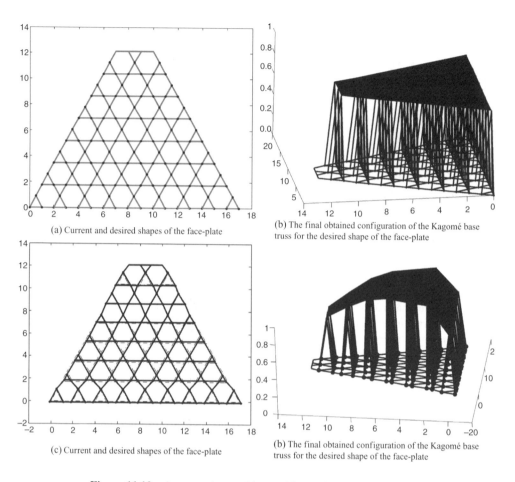

(a) Current and desired shapes of the face-plate

(b) The final obtained configuration of the Kagomé base truss for the desired shape of the face-plate

(c) Current and desired shapes of the face-plate

(b) The final obtained configuration of the Kagomé base truss for the desired shape of the face-plate

Figure 11.13   An example morphing problem using the Kagomé truss

of actuators in an assembly where all three sides of the triangular elements are allowed to move. This figure depicts a "three-channel" Kagomé truss with four hexagonal units in the lowest channel. In a more general structure, if the number of channels is c and the number of hexagonal units in the lowest channel is h, the total number of actuators is: $\frac{3}{2}c(2h - c + 3)$. Of course, the number of actuated triangles is one-third of this number, as is clearly visible from Figure 11.9(b).

The dynamic modeling of this scenario is more complex because it involves all hexagonal units of the Kagomé base moving together. The end result is a very high dimensional (possibly in the hundreds) morphing state space and equivalently high dimensional performance map. The problem can be greatly simplified if the structure is assumed to morph one hexagonal unit at a time, locking down the remaining Kagomé base until only the activated unit attains its target shape. Under this assumption, the dimensionality of the morphing state would be six, which despite being still a sizeable value can be easily handled using the pseudo random graph construction technique described in Section 11.2.1.

An example of a fully morphing Kagomé truss is shown in Figure 11.13. The base configuration is a flat face-plate, with the Kagomé base composed of 7 ($= c$) channels of hexagonal

Kagomé units and the lowest channel with 8 ($= h$) hexagonal units. This counts for a total of 126 actuators (a very large number!). The morphing problem is to convert the flat face-plate to the quadratic shape shown in Figure 11.13(d). The resulting morphed shape of the Kagomé base is shown in Figure 11.13(c). A comparison with the flat face-plate truss configuration is also shown in this figure, using dotted lines. Note that this figure only represents a geometrical solution to the described problem using the rules of inverse transform described in the above section and Figure 11.11. The development of dynamical equations and related control laws based on the hierarchical methodology for this type of structure is currently under investigation and will be the topic of a future article.

In summary, the authors believe that the above-described morphing structure based on the Kagomé truss holds great promise for building morphing structures for aircraft. There remains a lot of be studied yet and the current work exhibits initial promise. Some challenges include accurate modeling of the morphing elements of the Kagomé base, determination of the density of the tetrahedral core, dynamic structural analysis of the structure and aeroelastic behavior if used in a wing-application among several others.

11.4 Conclusion

In this chapter, a hierarchical, model-based approach for optimal control of morphing dynamics was presented. It was shown that a connected graph can be imposed on the performance map of a morphing structure, making all points on the map accessible from every other point via the graph. Two techniques for graph construction were presented, one requiring considerable manual input, and the other suitable for high dimensional applications using pseudo random sequences. The control laws for lower level control were designed using non-zero set point LQR. An example problem based on a morphing triangle with a fixed base was presented. A rudimentary description of morphing problems using the Kagomé truss was also given. It is proposed that a morphing structure based on the Kagomé turss can be used to great advantage in the aerospace community for morphing aircraft applications.

References

Bemporad A and Morari M 1999 Control of systems integrating logic, dynamics and constraints. *Automatica*, 35(3): 407–427.

Branicky MS 1995 Studies in hybrid systems: modeling, analysis and control, PhD thesis. Dept. of Electrical Engineering and Computer Science, MIT.

Branicky MS 1998 Multiple Lyapunov functions and other analysis tools for switched and hybrid systems. *IEEE Transactions on Automatic Control*, 43(4): 475–482.5

Burridge RR, Rizzi, AA and Koditschek D 1999 Sequential composition of dynamically dexterous robot behaviour. *International Journal of Robotic Research*, 18(6): 535–555.

Cloutier JR 1997 State dependent Riccati equation techniques. In *Proceedings of the American Control Conference*, Albuquerque, NM, June, pp. 932–936.

Conner DC 2007 Integrating planning and control for constrained dynamical systems, PhD thesis. Robotics Institute, Carnegie Mellon University, Pittsburgh, PA.

Conner DC, Kress-Gazit H, Choset H, Rizzi A, and Pappas GJ 2007 Valet parking without a valet. In *Proceedings of the 2007 IEEE/RSJ International Conference on Intelligent Robots and Systems*, San Diego, October.

Doebbler J, Tandale M, Valasek J, and Meade A 2005 Improved adaptive-reinforcement learning control for morphing unmanned air vehicles. AIAA Paper 2005–7159. Arlington, TX, USA, 26–29 Sept.

dos Santos e Lucato SL, Wang J, Maxwell P, McMeeking RM, and Evans AG 2004 Design and demonstration of a high authority shape morphing structure. *International Journal of Solids and Structures*, 41: 3521–3543.

Grant DT, Abdulrahim M, and Lind R 2006 Flight dynamics of a morphing aircraft utilizing independent multiple-joint wing sweep. AIAA Paper 20066505. Keystone, CO, USA, 21–24 Aug.

Hammett KD, Hall CD, and Ridgely DB 1998 Controllability issues in nonlinear state dependent Riccati equation control. *Journal of Guidance Control and Dynamics*, 21(5).

Hurtado JE 2006 Dynamic shape control of a morphing airfoil using spatially distributed actuators. *AIAA Journal of Guidance Control and Dynamics*, 29(3): 612–616.

Hutchinson RG, Wicks N, Evans AG, Fleck NA, and Hutchinson JW 2003 Kagome plate structure for actuation. *International Journal of Solids and Structures*, 40: 6969–6980.

Kaelbling LP 1993 Hierarchical reinforcement learning: preliminary results. In *Proceedings of the Tenth International Conference on Machine Learning*.

Lampton A, Niksch A, and Valasek J 2007 Reinforcement learning of morphing airfoils with aerodynamic and structural effects. AIAA Paper 2007–2805, Rohnert Part, CA, USA, 7 May.

Leith DJ and Leithead WE 2000 Survey of gain-scheduling analysis and design. *International Journal of Control*, 73(11): 1001–1025.

Leonessa A, Chellaboina V and Haddad W 2001 Nonlinear system stabilization via hierarchical switching control. *IEEE Transactions on Automatic Control*, 46, 2001.

Niederreiter H 1992 Random number generation and quasi-Monte Carlo methods. *Society for Industrial and Applied Mathematics*, Philadelphia, PA.

Parr R 1998 Hierarchical control and learning from Markov decision processes, PhD Thesis. Berkeley, CA: University of California.

Rodriguez AR 2007 Morphing aircraft technology survey. AIAA Paper 20071258. Reno, NV, USA, 8–11 Jan.

Rugh WJ and Shamma JS 2000 Research on gain scheduling. *Automatica*, 36: 1401–1425.

Sun Z and Ge SS 2005 Analysis and synthesis of switched linear systems. *Automatica*, 41.

Sutton RS, Precup D, and Singh S 1999 Between MDPS and semi-MDPS: a framework for temporal abstraction in reinforcement learning. *Artificial Intelligence*, 112: 181–211.

Valasek J, Tandale M, and Rong R 2005 A reinforcement learning-adaptive control architecture for morphing. *Journal of Aerospace Computing, Information and Communication*, 2(4): 1014–1020.

Wickenheiser A and Garcia E 2004 *Evaluation of Bio-Inspired Morphing Concepts with Regard to Aircraft Dynamics and Performance*. SSL, George Washington University, Washington, DC, pp. 202–211.

12

A Collective Assessment

John Valasek
Texas A&M University, USA

12.1 Looking Around: State-of-the-Art

12.1.1 Bio-Inspiration

Researchers have obtained impressive empirical results to date that have yielded much insight into the mechanisms of morphing. It has become clear that morphing in flying animals is far more complex than is generally appreciated, ranging from the rather subtle twist and camber changes used by insects for control, to the massive changes in span, aspect ratio, and wing area used by birds to adapt their flight morphology for different flight missions. The way forward will no doubt contain elements of the competing approaches of either bio-inspiration or bio-mimicry, or perhaps a combination of both. Neither approach has been taken advantage of to date, and while it is too early to tell which approach will ultimately prevail, it is certain that physics-based modeling that is validated with newer and more detailed empirical data holds much promise for advancing the state-of-the-art.

12.1.2 Aerodynamics

This is an area in which more work clearly needs to be done. The majority, if not all, of the morphing aerodynamics to date are modeled on the assumptions of steady, inviscid flow. This largely results from the tradeoff between physics-based analytical models (difficult to generate and validate accurately), Computational Fluid Dynamics (CFD) models (straightforward but computationally cumbersome), and empirical models generated from wind tunnel testing (expensive and time-consuming). Each of these modeling approaches is expected to see continued use and development since each is well suited to a particular analysis or application. Ultimately unsteady viscous flow will need to be modeled, too.

Morphing Aerospace Vehicles and Structures, First Edition. Edited by John Valasek.
© 2012 John Wiley & Sons, Ltd. Published 2012 by John Wiley & Sons, Ltd.

12.1.3   Structures

Perhaps no area holds more possibilities for creative morphing solutions than structures. Traditional monocoque and semi-monocoque structures do not hold any clear advantages, and in fact may be a poor approach. Various mechanical hinged approaches based on Origami principles are currently being used and offer some promise. As shown in this book, they are straightforward to design, analyze, and control. The Kagome lattice with its trihexagonal tiling is both a variation of and extension on the mechanically hinged approach. It offers the potential for multiple degrees-of-freedom in shape, and can be configured into a variety of non-planar geometries. Because of these features it poses challenges for automatic control, but the results presented in this book demonstrate that these challenges are not insurmountable. Finally, fluid-structure interaction or aeroelastic effects will be significant on a morphing air vehicle, and will need to be addressed. When this actually occurs will of course be dependent upon the quality and fidelity of aerodynamic and structural models.

12.1.4   Automatic Control

One of the last areas of morphing to be researched but one which appears to be progressing well and maturing rapidly is automatic control. All of the approaches that have produced good results to date possess some degree of adaptation, and some also feature learning. Regardless of the particular approach used, the control has always been centralized, rather than distributed. This is an abstraction that must be addressed in the future, since feasible large-scale shape changing will require distributed sensing and actuation. Current approaches to distributed sensing and actuation also incur significant weight penalties. Until the advent of lightweight, high strength actuators and robust and reliable sensors, the continuously smooth shape changing type of morphing will probably remain elusive. Another critical aspect is power requirements. Morphing air vehicles are expected to be unmanned, and therefore will not dissipate power for life support systems. Nevertheless the power required for shape changing actuation could be significant. It will also depend upon the power available, which varies depending upon the type of powerplant (reciprocating or gas turbine or solar). In any case, the control policy used will need to provide a minimum actuation energy solution.

12.2   Looking Ahead: The Way Forward

In spite of the progress that has been made, much needed insight remains to be discovered and new breakthroughs in materials and propulsion will be critical for success. The challenges and some potential ways forward are discussed below.

12.2.1   Materials

Applications incorporating active materials for aerospace actuation must satisfy three contradictory criteria: (1) they must be sufficiently rigid to carry flight loads; (2) they must provide sufficient deflection on demand to aircraft configurational changes; and (3) they must be sufficiently light to allow integration into a realistic aerostructure. For these reasons, decreasing the weight of Shape Memory Alloy-based designs or increasing the actuation deformation of piezo-electric systems each represent necessary improvements. Further, the properties of passive material regions coupled to active ones needs to be addressed. Specifically, for the flight speeds experienced by conventional commercial and military aircraft, Shape Memory Alloys are likely to be implemented as relatively strong rods or beams or torque tubes coupled to a transversely stiff skin that is pliable in-plane. The selection of the material and configurational design of such a skin is a major challenge, especially when one also considers the challenges of environment and fatigue. For small-scale deflections on a component level, Shape Memory Alloys have already shown promising results when directly and properly integrated with laminar composite panels, and such designs will likely see expanded use. Finally, while some active materials such as piezoelectrics exhibit sufficient deflection at high frequencies, the actuation frequency of other material systems such as Shape Memory Alloys will need to be increased if they are to be feasible for applications such as flutter control, gust and turbulence rejection, and vibration control.

12.2.2 Propulsion

A well-known and long-standing paradigm in aircraft design is that advances in propulsion drive advances in aircraft design. That has not necessarily been true in the case of recent morphing air vehicle concepts, where advances in smart structures have both inspired and driven the designs. Another paradigm in aircraft design is that a successful design can only be realized when the airframe-propulsion integration problem has been solved. The interdependency between propulsion and design that these paradigms address is even stronger for morphing air vehicles than conventional aircraft. Consider a morphing air vehicle powered with a reciprocating engine powerplant. The power-on effects, which are the effects on control surfaces and therefore control power due to the "prop-wash" or wake behind a propeller, are not only significant but also a function of airframe geometry downstream of the propeller. This geometry will be time-varying during flight, thereby producing time-varying power-on effects on dynamic response. Now consider a morphing air vehicle with a gas turbine powerplant. These powerplants pose an even bigger problem for morphing air vehicles than reciprocating engine powerplants, since inlet flow conditions affect thrust, and inlet flow conditions are a function of inlet geometry. Whether the inlet is of the flush, nacelle, or scoop type, changes in the local surface geometry due to morphing will affect flow in the inlet and therefore thrust characteristics. At present, very little research, if any, has been devoted to airframe-propulsion integration for morphing air vehicles, and this remains a major hurdle.

12.3 Conclusion

Morphing in the context of aeronautics is a rich research topic in a variety of individual and interdisciplinary technical fields. Much research remains to be done, and like morphing itself, can ultimately take many different shapes and forms. Yet this author is not just optimistic but certain that realization of the dream of aviation pioneers for a morphing air vehicle is almost within reach.

Index

Morphing Aerospace Vehicles and Structures, First Edition. Edited by John Valasek.
© 2012 John Wiley & Sons, Ltd. Published 2012 by John Wiley & Sons, Ltd.